The Structure of British Industry

The Structure of British Industry

Edited by P.S. Johnson

GRANADA
London Toronto Sydney New York

Granada Publishing Limited – Technical Books Division
Frogmore, St Albans, Herts AL2 2NF
and
3 Upper James Street, London W1R 4BP
Suite 405, 4th Floor 866 United Nations Plaza, New York, NY 10017, USA
117 York Street, Sydney, NSW 2000, Australia
100 Skyway Avenue, Rexdale, Ontario M9W 3A6, Canada
PO Box 84165, Greenside, 2034 Johannesburg, South Africa
61 Beach Road, Auckland, New Zealand

Copyright © 1980 by Granada Publishing Limited

ISBN 0 246 11211 5

British Library Cataloguing in Publication Data
The structure of British industry.
1. Great Britain – Industries
I. Johnson, Peter Stewart
338'.0941   HC256.6

ISBN 0-246-11211-5

First published in Great Britain 1980 by Granada Publishing
Limited – Technical Books Division

Distributed in the United States of America by Nichols Publishing Company
P.O. Box 96, New York, NY 10024.

Printed in Great Britain by
Richard Clay (The Chaucer Press) Ltd
Bungay, Suffolk

Contents

Preface   **xiii**

1 The changing structure of British industry   **1**

P. S. Johnson, Senior Lecturer, Department of Economics,
Durham University.

2 North Sea oil and gas   **28**

C. Robinson and C. Rowland, Professor and Research Fellow,
respectively, Department of Economics, Surrey University.

3 Coal   **57**

R. B. Thomas, Lecturer, Department of Economics,
Durham University.

4 Food manufacturing   **80**

P. Maunder, Senior Lecturer, Department of Economics,
Loughborough University.

5 Pharmaceuticals   **106**

W. D. Reekie, Lecturer, Department of Business Studies,
Edinburgh University.

6 Steel   **131**

A. Cockerill, Senior Lecturer, Department of Economics,
Salford University.

7 Computers 154

P. L. Stoneman, Lecturer, Department of Economics,
Warwick University.

8 Motor vehicles 179

D. G. Rhys, Lecturer, Department of Economics,
University College, Cardiff.

9 Synthetic fibres 207

R. W. and S. A. Shaw, Senior Lecturer and Lecturer, respectively,
Department of Economics, Stirling University.

10 Construction 231

M. C. Fleming, Senior Lecturer, Department of Economics,
Loughborough University.

11 Rail transport 254

K. M. Gwilliam, Professor of Transport Economics, Institute for
Transport Studies, Leeds University.

12 Retailing 280

F. Livesey, Professor and Head of School of Economics and
Business Studies, Preston Polytechnic.

13 Insurance 304

R. L. Carter, Professor of Insurance Studies, Department of
Industrial Economics, Nottingham University.

14 Medical care 330

I. Papps, Lecturer, Department of Economics, Durham University.

15 Tourism 357

A. J. Burkart, Senior Lecturer, Department of Hotel, Catering and
Tourism Management, Surrey University.

Index 383

List of tables

1.1 Changes in British industry, 1959–77   6
1.2 The public sector, 1967 and 1977   9
1.3 Plant sizes in manufacturing, 1948–68   10
1.4 Five-firm employment concentration ratios, 1972   11
1.5 Major economic indicators: some international comparisons
     for the post-war period   14
1.6 The UK's foreign trade in visibles, 1952–77   16

2.1 UK fuel production and consumption   32
2.2 Gross domestic fixed capital formation in the UK   34
2.3 The British proportion of licensed area by licence round   35
2.4 Licensed area by different types of companies   38
2.5 North Sea output by company, 1978   39
2.6 Recoverable oil reserves owned by company   40
2.7 Anticipated post-tax real net present values for North Sea
     oilfields onstream, end 1978   44
2.8 Government takes for the North Sea oilfields onstream by
     end 1978 – ranked by pre-tax real present value per tonne
     of output   53

3.1 Area statistics, 1978   60
3.2 NCB coal-mining profits, 1977/78   69

4.1 Major firms in some food markets, 1977   87
4.2 Rate of return on capital employed by large listed companies
     in manufacturing industry   93

5.1 Department of Trade and Industry output indices   109
5.2 Country of origin of discovery of single new chemical
     entities (1941–63), share of National Health Service
     market (1976) and world trade in pharmaceuticals (1975)   109

5.3	Analysis of companies by sales of ethical pharmaceuticals, 1965	110
5.4	Top twelve companies; number of products, main products' share of company sales and of sub-markets, 1969	112
5.5	Therapeutic sub-market competition: changes in market leadership between January 1962 and June 1965	114
5.6	(a) Position of 1976's leading ten products in 1965 and (b) Position of 1965's leading ten companies in 1976	115
5.7	Distribution of profit levels; large companies return on capital; home sales of NHS medicines	119
5.8	Grabowski and Vernon's estimates of concentration of innovational output in the US ethical drug industry	125
6.1	Net deliveries of finished steel to the UK market by source of supply, 1970 and 1977	135
6.2	Labour productivity and costs in the steel industries of the European Community, 1977, and rate of change 1973–7	144
7.1	Computer industry employment, 1966–76	155
7.2	Share in value of the stock of installed computers (31 December 1977)	159
7.3	Break-down of Western European computer market by manufacturer, 1972–3	159
7.4	Profit–turnover ratios, ICL, 1969–77	165
7.5	Market shares by notional value	166
7.6	Imports and exports of computer products, 1971–7	167
7.7	Imports and exports by commodity: first quarter 1978	167
7.8	Software industry: productivity 1971	167
7.9	Central government orders placed between 1 April 1971 and 31 January 1973 for computers	169
8.1	Share of car production	180
8.2	Trends in UK car production and exports, and total UK new car registrations per year	181
8.3	Estimated typical cost break-down for an average car	184
8.4	Import penetration into the UK car market	186
8.5	Shares of UK market, 1977	190
8.6	Share of European market, 1977	190
8.7	Car industry's largest firms world-wide, 1977	194
8.8	Rates of return on capital employed	198
8.9	Pre-tax profits (losses) for individual firms	199
8.10	Return on shareholders' funds, vehicle producers and component manufacturers (%): average 1970–3	200
8.11	Value added per man 1974 (£)	200
8.12	Vehicles produced per employee	201
9.1	UK synthetic fibre production, imports, exports and net available supply	209

9.2	Estimated market shares of total domestic consumption of synthetic fibres in the UK, 1969	212
9.3	Estimated UK production of synthetic fibres, 1969	212
9.4	Distribution of European synthetic fibre capacity, end 1974	213
9.5	Polyester staple costs per kilo of fibre	214
9.6	Production economies of scale in polyester staple fibre	214
9.7	Man-made fibre production and employment: selected countries, 1976	224
9.8	Number of synthetic fibre plants, total and average capacity, 1976	224
9.9	ICI synthetic fibres profitability, 1970–78	226
10.1	Number of firms, employment and output by size of firm in Great Britain, 1977	233
10.2	Sizes of firms in construction in Great Britain, 1948–77	234
10.3	Size distribution of orders for new work in Great Britain, 1977	235
11.1	Rail transport, 1948–76	255
11.2	Passenger transport: consumer cost indices (1970=100)	256
11.3	Summary of BR consolidated profit and loss account	261
11.4	International rail performance comparisons	271
11.5	Physical productivity in BR, 1967–77	271
12.1	Consumers' expenditure at current prices	281
12.2	Market shares for UK retailing by kinds of business	282
12.3	Retail trades in 1976: analysis by kind of business	283
12.4	Number of retail outlets by kind of business (%)	284
12.5	Share of retail sales by form of organisation (%)	284
12.6	Share of retail sales by kind of business and form of organisation, 1976 (%)	285
12.7	Leading multiples' estimated share of total grocery market, Great Britain	292
12.8	Own label and manufacturer brand prices for typical grocery product	294
13.1	World-wide net premium income of British insurers, including Lloyd's	306
13.2	World-wide premium income of British insurers as percentage of GNP (at factor cost)	307
13.3	Total investments of financial institutions at end of year at market values	307
13.4	Distribution of insurance companies' UK funds by class of asset at 31 December 1977	308
13.5	The contribution of insurance and other services to the UK balance of payments	309
13.6	Numbers of companies authorised to transact insurance business in Great Britain, end 1976	313

13.7	Concentration ratios in British insurance, 1976	314
13.8	Net acquisitions by life offices	323
14.1	National Health Service expenditures, selected years 1948–78	331
14.2	Manpower in the NHS, selected years 1951–76	332
14.3	Hospital beds, selected years 1951–76	333
14.4	Proportion of beds occupied in each speciality, 1959 and 1976	335
14.5	Waiting lists, average length of stay and throughput capacity, selected years 1955–71	341
14.6	Variations in hospital spending by area, 1971/72	346
14.7	Correlations between health and social status indicators and Health Service spending	347
14.8	Forecast requirements and outcomes: physician stock movements	348
14.9	Infant mortality rates (number of deaths of infants under 1 year of age per 1,000 live births), selected years 1930–75, for ten countries	349
15.1	Visitors to and from the UK, selected years 1946–69	358
15.2	Visitors to and from the UK, 1970–77	359
15.3	The diminishing cost of air travel	360
15.4	Contribution of tourism to the UK balance of payments: the leading six exports in 1977	361
15.5	Profitability of tour operators	373
15.6	Overseas tourism to and from the UK, 1968–77	374

List of figures

2.1   Possible North Sea oil output, 1975–2000   42
2.2   Government revenue and take for the twelve oilfields
        onstream by the end of 1978 under different rates of
        PRT   54
3.1   UK coal output and employment, 1947–78   58
3.2   'Cost' curve for coal   62
3.3   Productivity (output per manshift), 1947–78   71
3.4   Distribution of miners by productivity, 1967/68 and
        1976/77   72
5.1   Promotional expenditure per product promoted by age of
        product   117
6.1   World and UK crude steel production, 1970–78   131
12.1 Demand with alternative pricing strategies   290
12.2 Non-price competition and demand   297
14.1 Supply and demand curves for medical services   342
15.1 The effect of regulating fares   369

Preface N A

This book is designed to fulfil two purposes: first, to provide a number
of chapter-length studies on a wide range of industries that will give
the reader a good overview of the main structural, behavioural and
performance characteristics of the industry or industries in which he is
interested; and, second, to provide illustrative material for use in
courses whose contents relate to industrial activity. No such book has
been written in Britain since the two-volume work edited by Burn
appeared in 1958. In its day it was rightly regarded as an authoritative
source of reference; it is now however very much out of date. A
number of books dealing with a few industries have appeared – an
excellent recent example is that by Shaw and Sutton (1976) – but the
coverage has usually been rather limited. Unfortunately we also have
had to be more selective than we would have wished because of the
economics of publishing (as seen by the publisher!).

The coverage of this book was determined by two main factors.
First was the desire to cover as wide a spectrum of industrial characteristics as possible. Hence declining and expanding, private and
nationalised, capital and labour-intensive industries are covered. Both
goods and services are included. Second was the need to find someone
able and willing to write the chapters! It is perhaps a sad reflection on
the state of the economics profession that there are so few economists
who have detailed knowledge of, and who have recently written on, a
particular industry. Fortunately nearly all the contributors to this
book meet these criteria. Either or both of these considerations led to
the exclusion of certain industries, notably engineering. This
particular omission is regrettable given that much of the previous
Labour government's industrial strategy* was aimed at this sector.

---

*See footnote on page 1.

It had been intended originally to include a chapter on agriculture. Unfortunately only a few weeks before the final deadline, it became clear that this chapter was not going to materialise. I therefore faced the unenviable choice between either delaying the whole book or going ahead without agriculture. I chose the latter on the grounds that it would not be too difficult for the person interested in agriculture to find alternative sources.

Inevitably, the particular selection of industries given in this book will be subject to criticism. It is a very easy task to suggest other industries that might have been included. However, given the constraints to which I have already drawn attention, I feel that the industries chosen represent as reasonably balanced a view of industrial characteristics as is possible.

Most of the chapters are listed in the order in which the relevant industries appear in the Standard Industrial Classification (see pages 2–3). (The industries are not, however, always given precisely the same label as that provided in the SIC). The only industries which are not so ordered are the following. First, the chapter on North Sea oil and gas precedes the chapter on coal because the former also contains some information on the energy market as a whole. Second, tourism, which is not separately identified in the SIC, is covered in the last chapter of this book. It is given a separate chapter as it has a fairly distinct identity of its own.

To ensure a consistent level of exposition throughout the book, contributors were asked to assume that the reader's knowledge of economics did not extend beyond that contained in a first year university 'Elements' course. Contributors were free to express their own views on the industry about which they were writing. No editorial control was exercised in this respect. As a result a wide variety of views on topics such as nationalisation or government intervention in industrial affairs is expressed (compare, for example, the chapters on coal and pharmaceuticals). The views expressed by individual contributors (and myself in the first chapter) are not necessarily shared by anyone else.

As editor, my first acknowledgement must be to the contributors. Most delivered their scripts on time and it has been a pleasure to work with them. I am also grateful to various people who encouraged me in this venture. Barry Thomas kindly read the first chapter and Denis O'Brien was a constant source of advice. David Fulton of Granada Publishing was always most helpful from the publishing end. Ann Loadman and Tricia Wears typed various parts of the manuscript with great efficiency and Amy Kent was a great help in the preparation of the index. Finally I owe a special word of thanks to my wife who has always been an enthusiastic supporter of this book.

P. S. Johnson
May, 1979.
Durham.

REFERENCES

Burn, D. (ed.) (1958) *The Structure of British Industry*. 2 vols. Cambridge: Cambridge University Press.

Shaw, R. W. and Sutton, C. J. (1976) *Industry and Competition*. London: Macmillan.

1 The changing structure of British industry

P. S. Johnson

In this chapter we examine some of the terms used by economists when analysing industrial activity (section 1.1), and also provide an overview of the main structural changes that have occurred in British industry in recent years (section 1.2). We single out for special treatment here two important phenomena: the growth of the public sector and the increasing level of both aggregate and market concentration in manufacturing. The third section of the chapter is devoted to an assessment of Britain's relatively poor industrial performance. This is discussed in the context of the industrial strategy initiated by the previous Labour government (section 1.4).*

1.1 SOME CONCEPTS

1.1.1 The industry

Much of our analysis in the theory of the firm is dependent on a concept of 'the industry'. For example, perfect competition, monopolistic competition and indeed monopoly, all require such a concept before much can be said about the equilibrium levels of output and price.

In defining an industry, we are attempting to classify firms in a way which brings out the major economic interrelationships among them.

---

*At the time of writing (May 1979) it is not clear how far the new Conservative administration intends to retain the objectives and procedures of this strategy. However most of the discussion in section 1.4 is applicable in greater or lesser degree to *any* form of government involvement in industrial policy. It is most unlikely that the new Government will opt out completely from an interventionist role in the industrial arena.

For statistical purposes, too, we also need some way of grouping firms together, simply to make data more manageable. There are however several bases on which firms may be so classified. We may for example link together those firms that use similar skills, processes or raw materials. Yet although this grouping may bring out their inter-relationships in factor markets, it may also mean classifying together firms serving quite different product markets. For example, glass producing firms may have much in common in terms of their raw material requirements and their processes, but it would be foolish to argue that, say, the container manufacturers compete directly with Pilkington, the flat glass producer. Again, the motor and shipbuilding industries each produce a vast array of goods, many of which serve quite distinct markets.

If we grouped together firms that serve broadly similar product markets we would meet the converse problem: many of the firms concerned would operate in different factor markets or use very different processes. It has been suggested that we might attempt to meet these problems by looking at the degree to which products are substitutable on either the supply or demand side, and that by estimating cross-elasticities between goods we could group together those firms which, for example, are regarded by purchasers as being close substitutes. Unfortunately, this idea raises more problems than it solves. First, there is the immense difficulty of calculating the relevant cross-elasticities. Second, the problem of where to draw the dividing line would still remain. Even Mrs Robinson's suggestion (1933, page 17) that 'gaps' in the chain of substitutability would enable us to distinguish between different industries faces the same problem: how big must such a gap be before it can mark an industrial boundary? Third, it may be that, even if the necessary calculations could be made, there is no dividing line between the product(s) of the firm that is used as the starting point and the output of the whole economy. As Stigler has pointed out, (1949, page 15) if we take '. . . any one product as our point of departure, each substitute has in turn its substitutes, so that the adjacent cross-elasticities may not diminish, and even increase, as we move farther away from the "base" firm in some technological or geographical sense'.

The classification of firms into an industry, whatever basis is used, is therefore unlikely to be entirely satisfactory. In this country, the main emphasis in the classification of activities is on supply features: products with a fairly strong element of technical substitutability are therefore linked together. The present classification system is the 1968 Standard Industrial Classification which is divided into twenty-seven major industrial groupings or orders. These groupings are further subdivided into 181 small sectors called Minimum List Headings (MLHs). Some of these MLHs are broken down into product groupings.

The basic production unit for classification is the establishment, i.e. the smallest unit that can provide information required for economic censuses. The total output of an establishment is usually classified to a particular industry if the products of that industry account for a greater percentage of the establishment's total activity than the products of any other industry. This system of classification raises a number of issues which cannot be examined here. However, it is worth noting that establishments of the same firm – or 'enterprise', as the statisticians call it – may be allocated to different industries and that it is possible for an establishment's total output to be allocated to an industry even though only a minority of that output relates to the industry's products.

Most of the industries in this book are defined, for statistical purposes at least, at sub-order level, and involve one or more MLHs. The only industry defined at order level is construction where only one MLH is involved.

1.1.2 The firm

Micro-theorists use the firm as an abstract concept, the characteristics of which change with the particular market structure under consideration. Any attempt to find such firms in the real work would commit what has often been called the fallacy of 'misplaced concreteness': *by definition* the abstract firm does not actually exist. When it comes to empirical work, however, some practical definition is required. At the most basic level we may define the firm as an independent legal entity which may take the form of a sole proprietorship, partnership or company. However such 'independence' may be limited in several ways. First, government involvement is bound to restrict a firm's freedom to act. [Even where a government is committed to an extreme *laissez-faire* position, it will still be responsible for providing the basic rules within which such an economy will operate. For this reason Cairncross (1972) has suggested that we should talk about the degree of 'firmness' within an economy]. Secondly, a firm may be very heavily dependent on others in factor and/or product markets, sometimes to the extent that it could not survive without them.[1] In the financial sphere a business may be legally independent but totally dependent for its survival on money lent by an institution or person that has only a small shareholding. Finally, all kinds of links may exist between businesses that stop short of a parent–subsidiary relationship but which mean that they do not act independently of each other (Richardson, 1972). Perhaps the most overt form of such links is the interlocking directorate (Johnson and Apps, 1979). There is, however, plenty of scope for less formal (and less detectable) ties (Scherer, 1971, pages 45–47). These issues should be remembered whenever the firm is discussed.

1.1.3 Structure, conduct and performance

There is a well established tradition among industrial economists – which goes back to the 1930s – of distinguishing between the following three aspects of an industry:

(a) *its structure* (e.g. the extent of vertical integration, diversification, concentration, barriers to entry, economies of scale);

(b) *its conduct* [how the firms in the industry act e.g. in relation to pricing, advertising, research and development (R and D), legal tactics]; and

(c) *its performance* (how individual firms and the industry have performed in relation to certain criteria e.g. profitability, productivity, innovative record, employment, international competitiveness).

This approach has been used in the literature not only as a classificatory device for describing the principal characteristics of an industry but also – on the assumption that a given structure generates a particular type of behaviour which in turn affects performance in a predictable way – as a theoretical framework for analysing it. It is perhaps fair to say that much of the theory of the firm has been concerned essentially with forging such links. In recent years however the structure–conduct–performance paradigm has come under increasing attack on several grounds. (Phillips, 1976; Sawyer and Aaronovitch, 1975, chapter I; Cowling and Waterson, 1976). First, feedback effects exist. Firms' behaviour almost inevitably generates a changed structure (e.g. increased advertising may raise entry barriers). Similarly, firms' performance may change their behaviour (e.g. the highly profitable firm may undertake more advertising). However, if there is a sufficient 'lag' before the feedbacks occur, it may still be valid to keep the original theoretical structure. Second, the theoretical relationship between a particular aspect of structure and the expected consequent behaviour and performance has often been very poorly specified. For example, although a very large number of efforts have been made to examine the relationship between concentration and profitability (see the survey by Weiss, 1971), relatively little effort has been directed, until recently, to the precise nature of the mechanism by which (a particular measure of) concentration affects (a particular measure of) profitability. Finally, important factors have often been left out of the analysis. Shepherd (1975, pages 24–31), for example, has argued that industrial economists have often adopted a very narrow view of an industry, and have thereby ignored important factors – such as links between industrial firms and financial institutions – that influence the behaviour of such firms.

These points are valid criticisms of the way in which the structure–conduct–performance framework has been used in the past. However there is no reason why the necessary analytical improvements should not be made while maintaining the basic framework. In many of the following chapters, this framework is used principally as a system of classification although several contributors have also looked at the way in which structure affects conduct, and conduct affects performance.

1.2 CHANGES IN BRITISH INDUSTRY

Table 1.1 provides some indication of the changes in employment, output and contribution to Gross Domestic Product by industry order since 1959.[2] Care should be used when interpreting the table for several reasons. First, the output growth figures are based on a wide variety of different types of measure. For example, sales, volume and employment are all used as proxies for net output changes. The measure chosen for any given industry depends very much on data availability, and may not be directly comparable with that for any other industry. Second, the summary nature of the data may disguise important differences within orders. For example, in textiles, the man-made fibres sector has fared very differently from industries based on natural fibres: between 1966 and 1976 production in the former increased by 55% while single cotton, woollen and jute yarn production declined by 45, 25 and 57% respectively. Third, no indication is given of variations in growth *within* the period. This limitation is particularly acute in mining and quarrying where the positive growth rate is almost solely due to the massive expansion of North Sea oil and gas production in the last few years (see chapter 2). Coal mining has of course been in almost continuous decline over the period (chapter 3). Fourth, the output data do not in general capture quality changes which have been extensive in many industries. Fifth, the employment data do not allow for changes in the composition of the labour force or for the number of hours worked. Finally, it should be remembered that industries are often heavily interdependent. For example, the 'vehicles' industry buys inputs from numerous other industries – especially metal manufacture – which in turn buy from other industries, including the vehicles industry. These qualifications should be borne in mind in the following discussion.

The main changes in industrial structure may be described as follows. Employment growth has occurred principally in services, especially orders XXIV and XXV. Nearly all of the other industries have lost labour. However only two small industries – orders X and

TABLE 1.1: Changes in British industry 1959–77

Order (1968, SIC)		Average annual growth rates, 1959–77		% of total employees in employment		% of total gross domestic product	
		Employment	Output	1959	1977	1959	1977
I	Agriculture, fisheries and food	-3.36	2.25	3.5	1.7	3.5	3.4
II	Mining and quarrying	-4.67	1.29	3.9	1.5	3.2	3.4
III–XIX	Manufacturing	-0.51	2.36	37.6	32.4	33.7	28.5
III	Food, drink and tobacco	-0.36	2.14	3.5	3.1	3.8	3.1
IV	Coal and petroleum products	-2.27	2.96	0.2	0.1	0.3	0.1
V	Chemicals and allied industries	0.00	5.97	2.0	1.9	2.5	2.6
VI	Metal manufacture	-1.11	0.03	2.7	2.1	2.9	2.0
VII	Mechanical engineering	-0.07	2.65	4.4	4.1	3.9	3.2
VIII	Instrument engineering	0.50	6.09	0.6	0.6	0.5	0.6
IX	Electrical engineering	0.54	4.20	3.1	3.3	2.8	2.8
X	Shipbuilding and marine engineering	-2.19	-0.83	1.2	0.7	0.9	0.6
XI	Vehicles	-0.58	0.73	4.0	3.4	3.9	3.2
XII	Metal goods not elsewhere specified	0.29	1.29	2.4	2.4	2.1	1.8
XIII	Textiles	-2.64	1.12	3.7	2.1	2.7	1.7
XIV	Leather and fur	-1.81	-0.84	0.2	0.1	0.2	0.1
XV	Clothing and footwear	-1.67	1.38	2.4	1.6	1.3	1.0
XVI	Bricks, pottery, etc.	-0.91	2.79	1.4	1.1	1.2	1.1
XVII	Timber, furniture, etc.	-0.31	2.03	1.3	1.1	1.0	1.0
XVIII	Paper, printing, etc.	-0.11	1.96	2.6	2.4	2.6	2.3
XIX	Other manufacturing	1.25	5.04	1.2	1.4	1.0	1.4
XX	Construction	-0.52	1.09	6.4	5.5	6.5	7.1
XXI	Gas, electricity and water	-0.55	4.67	1.7	1.5	2.8	3.7
XXII	Transport	-0.74	2.78	7.7	6.4	8.7	9.6
XXIII	Distribution	0.17	1.78	12.3	12.0	11.9	9.4
XXIV	Insurance, banking and finance	3.18	4.32	3.0	5.0	} 29.67	} 34.7
XXV	Professional and scientific services	3.41	3.10	9.2	16.0		
XXVI	Miscellaneous services	1.62	1.91	8.2	10.4		
XXVII	Public administration and defence	1.29	1.13	5.9	7.1		
	Total	0.30	2.42	100	100	100	100

Source: *Department of Employment Gazette,* various years; *National Income and Expenditure,* various years.
Notes: The output data refer to the UK and the employment data to Great Britain. The data in the last two columns are estimates, based in part on the gross output indices of the Central Statistical Office. The basis on which the output index for each industry is calculated is given in *The Measurement of Changes in Industrial Production Studies in Official Statistics* No. 25, HMSO, 1976. The GDP base on which percentages in the last two columns are calculated excludes ownership of dwellings and adjustments for financial services. The average annual growth rates are calculated on a compound basis.

XIV – had an absolute decline in *output*.[3] If we take the employment and output data together, we can see that this clearly implies that increases in labour productivity do not necessarily ensure that employment is maintained. We shall return to this point later. The biggest expansions in output have been mainly in the science-based manufacturing industries (the most rapidly growing part of 'other manufacturing' is the production of plastic goods, also science-based). As a consequence of differential growth rates in employment and output across industrial sectors, manufacturing, considered as a unit, has become relatively less important in both of the measures used in the table (last two columns). Several other advanced economies have also experienced a decline in the share of both total employment and output accounted for by manufacturing, although the picture varies considerably across countries (Brown and Sheriff, 1979). Most services, apart from distribution, have gained in relative importance in terms of one or both measures. Labour productivity growth (as measured by the difference between output and employment growth) has been most rapid in the non-services sector and in particular, in the science-based industries. Of course much of this growth is due to the employment of more capital. However a fairly high correlation exists between the growth of labour productivity and that of 'total factor' productivity in which the contribution of capital is taken into account (Wragg and Robertson, 1978).

The change in the relative importance of different industries is due to a host of interacting factors. Conceptually, we may distinguish among those factors, especially changes in tastes and incomes, that primarily affect the demand side, and those factors, such as the introduction of new materials and processes and changes in costs that influence supply. However in practice these two sides are usually interwoven. Advertising, for example, raises the costs of producing a given output, i.e. it alters the conditions of supply, but its purpose is to shift the demand curve (see page 297). Supply and demand elements also overlap in the field of invention and innovation. (See, for example, Schmookler, 1966, and Rosenberg, 1974). There seems to be a fairly close relationship between an industry's growth and its R and D intensity, as measured, say, by R and D expenditure as a percentage of net output (Freeman, 1962). Other things being equal, a higher level of R and D expenditure will generate larger numbers of inventions and innovations and of improvements in processes. But it may be previous expansions in demand or 'latent' demand that stimulate this expenditure. This question is very closely related to the more general one of the relationship between productivity and output growth. There is little doubt that there is a fairly strong statistical association between these two indicators (Salter, 1969; Wragg and Robertson, 1978) but of itself this offers no clue to the direction of causality. On the one hand, Salter has argued that technical change (the source of which he does not identify – it appears to be autonomous) generates increases in productivity, which in turn affect prices. The industries that gain most in productivity, and hence experience the greatest relative price falls, also find that their output increases most rapidly because demand is responsive to such falls. Salter's theory is thus very much supply orientated. On the other hand Kaldor (1966, 1975) has argued that the output expansion generated by exogenous demand increases leads to increases in productivity by encouraging dynamic and static economies of scale. In all probability both forces are at work and reinforce each other. Whether productivity or output growth is the prime mover is uncertain although the recent study by Wragg and Robertson (page 76) gives rather more support to the latter.

1.2.1 The growth of the public sector

One of the most marked features of the post-war industrial scene, that is not immediately apparent from table 1.1, has been the growth of the public ownership of productive capacity and the increasing involvement of government in economic and social affairs. The measurement of this development is particularly difficult for the following reasons. First, the 'public sector' is not a clearly defined entity. (This problem of definition is illustrated by the treatment of the nationalised industries in the national accounts. Up to 1975, they were included in the public sector; they have been subsequently excluded.) Second, the government is involved in very diverse economic activities. It taxes, consumes, invests, lends, borrows and transfers resources. Consequently a wide range of possible definitions of public sector activities exists. Third, there is the problem of the choice of the aggregate yardstick against which public sector performance should be measured. Even where the extent and activities of the sector are clearly defined, the conclusions reached on its relative size may be greatly influenced by the particular denominator employed.

In table 1.2 a number of possible measures are given for the years 1967 and 1977. The nationalised industries are included here as part of the public sector. The first and second measures give some idea, respectively, of the numbers employed in, and of the incomes derived from, the sector. The third measure provides a rough indication of the overall extent of the sector. As can be seen its relative importance varies considerably, depending on the yardstick used. However, whichever measure is used it is clear that there has been a considerable increase in the importance of the public sector in the last decade.

International comparisons in this area are difficult to make. However the evidence we have suggests that the relative importance of public expenditure in the UK is not substantially out of line with that

TABLE 1.2: **The public sector, 1967 and 1977**

Measure	1967	1977
1. Employment (thousands)	6 173	7 386
As a % of total working population	24.7	29.7
2. Factor incomes (£m, current prices)	8 867	36 672
As a % of GDP (factor cost)	25.7	29.9
3. Total public expenditure* (£m, current prices)	19 386	68 533
As a % of GDP (market prices)	43.3	48.8
As a % of GDP (factor cost)	49.8	55.6
As a % of National Income	54.3	63.5

Source: *National Income and Expenditure 1967–1977,* HMSO, 1978.
*The published figures were adjusted to include the public corporations (see *Economic Trends*, March 1977 for the method of adjustment used).

in other advanced economies (Brown and Jackson, 1978).

We cannot here examine in detail the economic case for and against state involvement in different parts of the economy. However in the last part of the chapter we do raise some important issues connected with the growth of this sector, particularly as it affects industry. Most of the following chapters are also very much concerned with the role and effects of government policies. It is now virtually impossible to describe *any* British industry adequately, without a fairly extensive discussion of the influence of government.

1.2.2 The increasing level of concentration in manufacturing

We now have fairly firm evidence that, in the post-war period, the share of manufacturing net output accounted for by the 100 largest firms in that sector has steadily increased: from 22% in 1949 to over 40% in 1970 (Prais, 1976, table 1.1). The level of concentration in UK manufacturing is now higher than in the US or Germany (HMSO, 1978, page 9).

One possible explanation for this increase in concentration is that it is simply a consequence of increases in the size of plant that have occurred over the same period. Certainly it is true that the absolute size of plant has risen very considerably as shown by the measures given in table 1.3. The Florence Median[4] given in the table is obtained by ranking all employees in terms of the size of plant in which they work and then taking that plant size which contains the central worker. The 'central range' gives the plant sizes in which the central

TABLE 1.3: Plant sizes in manufacturing, 1948–68

Year	Florence Median	Central range
1948	340	100–1220
1958	440	120–1650
1968	480	130–1600

Source: Prais, 1976, table 3.2.

50% of employees work. However this increase in size does not appear to have caused the higher concentration, for the *share* of the 100 largest plants in total manufacturing output only rose from 9.0 per cent in 1948 to 10.8 per cent in 1968 (Prais, page 46). Thus the rise in concentration appears to have come mainly through a rise in the average number of plants owned by the largest firms. It is perhaps also worth noting that the absolute range of plant sizes in which the central 50% of workers are employed has increased, implying that a wider range of plant sizes than previously can now coexist.[5]

The dominance of the 100 largest firms is now felt in most manufacturing industries. In only five of the seventeen orders in this sector was the share of the 100 largest firms in 1972 less than 30% (HMSO, 1978, page 47). Utton (1974) has shown that they are often market leaders.

At the other end of the size spectrum, the relative importance of the small firm has also been declining. We do not have data on market shares of a given number of the smallest firms which would be comparable with the information on aggregate concentration, but we do know that in manufacturing, the share of net output of firms of 200 employees or fewer fell from 35% in 1935 to about 16% in 1968 (Bannock, 1976). The decline may have levelled off in the early 1970s (Johnson, 1978). Nevertheless, we appear to have a smaller small firm sector than many European countries. It should however be remembered that the experience of small firms has not been uniform across industries; in some sectors, e.g. scientific instruments, they have done very well. Unfortunately we do not know whether the overall relative decline has been due to birth or death-rate changes or to some combination of both.

An increasing level of aggregate concentration is of course compatible with declining or static concentration levels in individual markets if the former is derived principally from higher levels of diversification.

However, market concentration, as measured in terms of the percentage of an industry's sales accounted for by the five largest firms, appears to have increased between 1951 and 1958 and between 1958 and 1968.[6] The increase in market concentration was particularly rapid between 1963 and 1968 (George, 1975): of 340 product groups, 118 experienced a rise of 5 percentage points or more while only 27 had a 5% or more drop. The latest firm employment concentration ratios in each manufacturing order is given in table 1.4. If we use the data in table 1.1, it is apparent that about 65% of manufacturing's contribution to GDP is produced in industries in which the level of concentration is 40% or above.

International comparisons are particularly difficult in this area. Probably a fair conclusion from the studies undertaken so far[7] would be that in general, the level of market concentration is no lower in the UK than in Western Europe or the US but that in several industries it may well be higher.

TABLE 1.4:   **Five-firm employment concentration ratios, 1972**

Industrial order	Number of industries	Weighted average percentage of employment in five largest firms
Food, drink and tobacco	12	56
Coal and petroleum products	1	45
Chemical and allied industries	13	56
Metal manufacture	5	64
Mechanical engineering	18	34
Instrument engineering	3	38
Electrical engineering	9	62
Shipbuilding and marine engineering	1	51
Vehicles	5	68
Metal goods not elsewhere specified	7	41
Textiles	8	34
Leather and fur	2	19
Clothing and footwear	7	21
Bricks, pottery, etc.	6	44
Timber, furniture, etc.	4	15
Paper, printing, etc.	6	25
Other manufacturing	6	46
Total*	116	48

Source: HMSO (1978), table 2.
Note: *Includes 3 industries in mining and quarrying with a weighted average employment in the five largest firms of 40%.

The market concentration data given above must be interpreted carefully for several reasons. First, a wide range of market structures is possible for any given concentration ratio.[8] Second, and more fundamentally, international trade has as we shall see increased considerably over the post-war period. The concentration data based on UK production therefore overstate the extent to which a given number of firms dominates the relevant market. The prospect of *potential* imports may also curtail market power. On the other hand, the existence of isolated local markets may mean that the ratios understate the degree of such power held by the leading firms. Third, we do not know whether it is the same firms that are increasing their market share, or whether the increasing concentration is being accompanied by a continuous movement of firms up and down the size spectrum. A market structure which is volatile in this sense may give less cause for concern than one in which the same firms increase their market share. Fourth, the data ignore inter-firm links (see page 3). Finally they give no indication of the extent of buyer concentration. The latter will almost certainly influence the market power of producers.

Despite these limitations the increased level of concentration remains a source of concern on several grounds. First, there is now substantial evidence (see the study and survey of earlier research contained in Meeks, 1977) that suggests that the expected gains from merger activity – which has been an important factor in raising the level of concentration in many industries – have not in general materialised. Second – and linked to the first point – increased concentration does not seem to have arisen in order to take advantage of economies of scale at plant level. The data we have suggest that most of these economies are exhausted at a fairly low level of output; only sixteen of the forty-nine products for which we have estimates of minimum efficient plant scale require a market share of more than 30% to achieve all the economies (HMSO, 1978, pages 87–88). Moreover, it may be argued that the selection of the forty-nine products was itself biased towards those in which economies of scale are generally more important (O'Brien, 1978). This suggests that we may have to look beyond *technical* production economies to explain much of the increased concentration which has occurred. It may be, of course, that such economies, on which most empirical studies have been concentrated, are not in fact the most important area for potential savings from larger size; financial, marketing and managerial economies may be of much greater significance. However, we have little evidence on this score and there are indications that diseconomies may exist in at least some of these areas. For example, there are data to suggest that the incidence and length of strikes rises with the size of plant (*Department of Employment Gazette*, February

1976, page 116).

In the financial sphere, there are good grounds for supposing that the financial institutions prefer to invest in larger units: less risk is usually attached to the latter, their shares are more easily marketable, and the administrative costs involved are likely to be relatively lower. The greater role played by such institutions in recent years[9] may be one factor in the trend towards higher levels of concentration. It is not clear however that this trend has resulted in any 'real' improvement in productive efficiency.

The above discussion suggests that the increase in concentration cannot be explained by the search for increases in productive efficiency. Other possible explanations are not difficult to find. Most obviously, greater concentration may simply reflect the desire for more market power. This applies particularly to market concentration, but it will also be relevant to aggregate concentration in the cases in which market power is related to size *per se*. Another motivation has been suggested by Newbould (1970), who has argued that many recent mergers have resulted from the relevant managers' search for the greater security which is found in larger size. A much more fundamental reason for the increased concentration has however been suggested. If the probability distribution of growth rates facing each firm is the same, being independent of both the firm's size and its past growth, then concentration is bound to increase over time. The evidence on whether this 'law of proportionate effect' is in fact valid is rather mixed, (see the survey by Scherer, pages 125–130) although it may operate in a rather dilute form.

Although it is not possible to define precisely the relative importance of different factors causing the increased concentration at both aggregate and market levels, it is nevertheless clear that this trend, which may enable firms to abuse their market positions, does not appear to reflect any obvious move to increase efficiency. A case therefore exists for making the present anti-trust framework more hostile to increases in concentration.

We have not considered concentration in non-manufacturing orders, because the data in these industries are relatively sparse. Three of these orders are in any case almost wholly dominated by nationalised industries. A fourth relates to public administration. In the remaining six non-manufacturing orders, it is almost certain that the post-war period has seen a considerable rise in concentration (chapters 12–15 give some indication of trends in a few non-manufacturing industries).

1.3 ASSESSING BRITISH INDUSTRIAL PERFORMANCE

By most of the conventional economic indicators[10] the performance of

TABLE 1.5: Major economic indicators: some international comparisons for the post-war period

(Average annual growth rates)

Country	Industrial production			Output per man hour in manufacturing			Consumer prices			Wage costs per unit of manufacturing output		
	1951–8	1958–69	1969–77	1951–8	1958–69	1969–77	1954–8	1958–69	1969–77	1954–8	1958–69	1969–77
Canada	4.19	5.98	3.79	—	—	3.69	1.84	2.40	7.51	—	—	7.04
France	5.60	5.72	3.72	5.66	5.94	4.87	5.06	4.02	8.51	2.05	2.00	8.54
Germany	8.65	6.50	2.66	4.39	5.85	4.46	2.07	2.35	5.35	1.38	2.04	4.90
Italy	7.00	8.00	3.20	1.53[1]	7.37	4.26	2.46	3.25	12.05	1.90	—	14.99[4]
Japan	11.78	15.61	4.69	—	9.53	7.28	0.47	4.93	10.25	0.0	1.89	9.33
Netherlands	4.87	7.72	4.25	—	—	7.29[3]	3.05	—	7.44	—	—	—
United Kingdom	2.18	3.52	0.60	1.67	3.85[2]	2.66	3.53	3.24	12.74	2.60	2.28	13.71
United States	1.96	5.64	2.65	2.52	3.47	3.42	1.84	2.18	6.48	0.0	0.33	3.79

Sources: Calculated from data provided in National Institute *Economic Review* (statistical appendices).
Notes: (1) 1954–8 all industries.
  (2) 1959–69.
  (3) 1969–74.
  (4) 1969–76.
  A dash indicates the absence of suitable data.

the British economy has been poor in comparison with that of its major competitors in the post-war period. Table 1.5 provides data on some of these indicators for much of this period. These data must be treated very carefully. They are highly aggregated and do not by any means cover all the important aspects of an economy's operation: for example, the output per man hour figures cover only labour productivity; they also only relate to manufacturing, and make no allowance for differences in capital endowments. However it is likely that whatever performance measure was used for the post-war period, Britain's record would still be relatively poor. For example, a comparative study of a large number of manufacturing sectors in West Germany and Britain over the period 1952–74 showed that total factor productivity growth in the former country was very much better than in the latter (Panic *ed.*, 1976).

Even if we discount the period up to 1958 on the grounds that our European competitors were still 'catching up' after the war, the assessment of the UK's relative performance remains the same. Moreover our relative performance appears to have worsened over the past two decades.[11]

So far we have only considered growth rates of different performance indicators. *Levels* are more difficult to compare. However there is little doubt that GDP per head in Britain is lower than that in our major competitors,[12] and comparative studies on labour productivity in manufacturing come up with the same answer, even when allowance is made for differences in capital (e.g. Panic, *ed.*, 1976; Pratten, 1976). Our innovative ability also seems to be relatively poor across a fairly broad spectrum of industry (Pavitt *ed.*, 1980). Interestingly, however, our gross investment rate in manufacturing does not compare too badly with that of our major competitors although our incremental output–capital ratio does (Mueller, 1977). This suggests – although the evidence is very tentative – that it is not so much the relative amount of gross investment that is holding British manufacturing back, but the *efficiency* with which it uses that investment.

On the trade front, the UK's share of the exports of manufactured products by the major advanced economies fell from about 20% in 1954 to just under 10% in 1977.[13] Moreover, this decline was not the result of a substantial fall in one or two isolated industries; a broad spectrum of manufacturing experienced relative losses. By themselves these data may not be of major significance because they may simply reflect a fall in the UK's share of world production arising from the catching-up by other 'younger' economies. However as table 1.6 shows the UK's share declined in a period when world trade was growing quite rapidly. Apart from 1972–77 the UK's growth of exports was at a very much lower rate than the growth of world trade. We also have some evidence (NEDO, 1977) to suggest that British exports in several

TABLE 1.6:   The UK's foreign trade in visibles, 1952–77

	(Average annual growth rates)			
Period	UK import volume	UK export volume	World trade	UK GDP
1952–60	5.10	3.33	5.11	2.93
1960–67	4.07	3.04	6.81	3.08
1967–72	6.41	5.73	9.70	2.24
1972–77	3.98	6.48	5.41	1.50

Sources: The British Economy: Key Statistics, 1900–1970 (published for the London and Cambridge Economic Service by Times Newspapers); National Institute *Economic Review*; UN *Statistical Year Book 1977.*

areas, especially engineering, are less attractive in terms of their quality and design. For example, in 1974 the average value per ton of German and French exports in a substantial majority of the thirty-five industries for which data are available[14] exceeded, often by a considerable margin, the UK value. Such data do of course have to be treated extremely carefully. Some of the difference may be accounted for by greater price competitiveness of UK exports obtained from the decline in the value of sterling. However, considering that large differences in price for identical goods are unlikely in world markets, that in all but three of the industries the UK's export share *fell* between 1970 and 1974, whereas Germany's and France's *rose* in thirty-one and twenty-seven industries respectively, and that other supporting evidence is available (Pavitt *ed.*, 1980), it seems reasonable to suppose that Britain is tending to export products of lower quality and to avoid the more 'sophisticated' markets. If this is the case, then by 'trading down' Britain may be moving into world markets where demand is less income elastic. Thus as world income grows, our share of exports would be expected to decline.

There may have been some improvement in the last year or so. Our share of world manufacturing exports rose between 1976 and 1977, but it remains to be seen whether this is the start of long-run improvement.

It is also clear from table 1.6 that apart from the last few years when the economy has benefited from the depreciation of sterling the volume of visible exports has been unable to keep pace with the volume of visible imports; growth in the latter has been very much faster than that of real GDP throughout the period. While it is true that many advanced economies have also experienced a rise in import penetration, the UK seems to have been especially hard hit, partly as a result of an apparent higher income elasticity of demand for imports (Panic, 1975).[15] Furthermore it may be argued that the rise in UK exports relative to GDP, which is implied by the figures, is due in part at least to our sluggish growth in a time of increasing world trade rather than to increased competitiveness (Brown and Sheriff, pages 244–5).

Before looking at the possible causes of the remedies for this decline, it is worth noting the following. First, although the UK may have a comparative advantage in *services* – a sector which we have largely ignored in the present discussion – it remains true that even a major expansion in such activities would not do much to offset the decline in our manufacturing competitiveness. As Blackaby (1979, page 3) has pointed out, the UK's share in world exports in services would have to increase by one-third to compensate for a 1% point fall in its share of world exports in manufactures. Secondly, experience has differed among manufacturing industries. There are, of course, a number of measures of international competitiveness that could be used, but if we look, for example, at import penetration over the period 1968–76 we find that some manufacturing industries such as several of the food MLHs, have gone against the overall trend and have considerably reduced that penetration. The same variability also exists when the measure used is exports as a percentage of manufacturers' sales (Wells and Imber, 1977). Such variability is to be expected given the many diverse factors that influence relative competitiveness. Thirdly, our overall performance between 1948 and 1970 (as measured by growth of GDP) was *better* than that in the inter-war period.[16] (Much of this improvement was due to increased productivity in the services sector: see George, 1974b, pages 21–23). Fourthly, and notwithstanding the previous point, Britain's performance in relation to other countries has been poor over a very long period.[17] It is doubtful, therefore, whether the causes of our present problems can be found in the post-war period alone, let alone recent years in that period. Indeed, there is fairly substantial evidence to suggest that many of the seeds of our current decline were sown at the end of the nineteenth century (see, e.g. Aldcroft, 1964).

It is much easier to reach broad agreement on the general symptoms of the UK's overall relative weakness than it is on the causes and possible policy measures that may be adopted. All we can do is to indicate the main lines of thought on this issue. Many of these are closely interwoven and the classification of causes given below must be regarded as very schematic.

1.3.1 Policy mistakes

This category can be further subdivided into specific and more general policy errors. Under the first of these headings we may include the argument put forward by the Cambridge Economic Policy Group (CEPG), (Moore and Rhodes, 1976) and George (1974a) that rigid adherence to an overvalued exchange rate in the 1950s and 1960s started a cumulative process of decline in competitiveness with low profits causing a low rate of investment which in turn led to low productivity growth, and hence back to low competitiveness. The CEPG has advocated a number of fairly substantial policy measures aimed at lifting the British economy out of what they see as a vicious circle of decline. They suggest, *inter alia*, the introduction of import controls to reduce the balance of payments constraint and fairly extensive government intervention to raise the level of industrial investment.

Under the heading of 'general' policy mistakes, the following views may be classified. First, Bacon and Eltis (1976) have suggested that the very rapid growth of the sector producing non-marketed output, which includes most of the public sector and some of the private sector, has crowded out output and investment in the industries producing marketed output. Thus although the former does not produce goods and services for sale it nevertheless provides its employees with claims on such goods. Bacon and Eltis showed that between 1961 and 1974, the spending power before tax of the non-market sector as a percentage of total marketed output at factor cost rose from 41 to 60% (pages 187–188). They also showed that this process had gone further in the UK than in many other advanced economies. The only ways in which the increased claims of the non-market sector employees can be met are through increased imports, which obviously cannot be a long-term solution unless export capacity is increased, or through a reduction via taxation in the claims of those workers in the marketed goods sector. The second of these is likely in turn to lead to inflationary pressures as workers try to maintain their real incomes (unless of course these workers can be persuaded that the increased 'social wage' derived from the non-marketed output is sufficient compensation for their increased taxes). The main policy implication of this analysis is either a reduction in the non-marketed goods sector or extensive controls that contain the pressures in the marketed goods sector.

Second, is the view supported (predictably) by the CBI – (see their evidence to the Wilson Committee: HMSO, 1977) – that the absence of stability in the general economic climate, caused in part by government activities and high taxation, has reduced the effectiveness of the market mechanism which is capable of working well under the right conditions. The right investment is not forthcoming from private industry, not because of lack of finance but because of the absence of profitable opportunities. No new financial institutions are therefore required.

Third, it is argued that there has been undue concentration of public expenditure on 'high technology' R and D and too little regard for the support of R and D in less prestigious areas (Freeman, 1974, page 268). The policy implication of this view is clear.

1.3.2 Long-standing economic and social characteristics

Some of the factors discussed below may, on some grounds, be regarded as the result of policy errors; however they are given separate treatment here as they relate to more fundamental and long-term issues. First is the argument presented (predictably) by the TUC (and indeed implicitly by the CEPG) that the market mechanism has inherent deficiencies. In this view, rates of return are not necessarily the best guide for investment and even where they may be a useful indicator, they do not always lead to the right distribution of funds. On this basis it is argued that new financial organisations to direct funds to industrial investment are required. Both the CEPG and the TUC provide possible answers to the question: if the market opportunities exist, why does the private sector not respond? The sector may be in such a state of cumulative decline that it cannot invest even if it wanted to, and social benefits may exceed private benefits and may make projects that are not privately profitable socially worthwhile.

Second is the view – put forward originally by Kaldor in 1966 but since disowned by him (1975) – that UK manufacturing growth has been constrained by the supply of labour. To achieve more rapid growth in manufacturing therefore it would be necessary to shift labour from other sectors.

Finally it has often been suggested that, for numerous reasons including the way, historically, our education system and social structure have developed, the basic quality of British labour and management is poor (see e.g. Caves *ed.*, 1967, pages 300–306 and chapter VIII). It is contended that this has expressed itself in a variety of ways such as a poor innovative and marketing record, risk averseness, the low productivity discussed earlier and unsatisfactory industrial relations. Not all of these factors even if they were identified as being important would necessarily be very responsive to policy measures. For example, it may be argued that the industrial relations problems experienced in many industries stem from deep-seated social divisions which only fundamental social change would eliminate. If this were the case, the current policy instruments that basically accept the social status quo could be regarded as irrelevant.

Even where problems might be amenable to policy measures without such fundamental change, it is vitally important that, for the effectiveness of such measures, the problems are correctly assessed.

For example, if relatively low investment by private industry is caused principally by low after-tax profitability, then the provision of new financial institutions providing additional funds, or directing investment is unlikely to provide a long-term solution. Unfortunately it has not so far been possible to demonstrate conclusively that certain factors have been more important that others in causing the UK's relative decline. All of the above diagnoses are the subject of controversy. (See, for example, the diversity of views expressed in Blackaby *ed.*). It is hardly surprising therefore that the White Paper which set out the previous Labour government's proposals for an Industrial Strategy[18] implied that a wide range of interrelated factors – including most of those outlined above – had been responsible.

1.4 THE INDUSTRIAL STRATEGY*

This strategy was essentially based on the selection of certain industrial sectors that could be regarded as having potential in international markets. Management, trade unions and government departments engaged in tripartite discussions in each of these industries and attempted to identify areas in which action was needed. As such the strategy represented a major *supply* management exercise. Selective financial assistance through the provisions of the Industry Act, and including the activities of the National Enterprise Board were made available to promote the aims of the strategy. It is too early to assess the effects if any of this strategy on our industrial performance. However such an approach raises a number of important issues. First, it must be remembered that the managerial talent available in this country – at least in the short run – is relatively fixed. Thus any new institutions or initiative established to assist the 'regeneration' of British industry must draw on the same pool of talent from which industry itself obtains its supply. Government may use career civil servants to administer many policy measures. This however raises the question of whether such people have the requisite skills for the tasks involved and can spot 'winners' without at the same time spotting a large number of 'losers'. (A recent report – by a civil servant – of aircraft launching aid (Gardner, 1976) concluded that the financial returns to governments in this area had been extremely small.)

Second, and related to the first point, most policies are likely to have unwanted side effects. Given that a private market system exists and is politically acceptable, it is not enough, to justify intervention in that system, to show that it has certain deficiencies. The adverse effects of any intervention must also be assessed because these effects may

---

*See footnote on page 1.

outweigh the deficiencies the policies were designed to eradicate (Demsetz, 1969). There are at least four areas where this point may be of relevance to an industrial strategy of the kind adopted by the Labour Government.

a. Effects on employment

The Manpower Research group at Warwick University suggested in 1978 that the industrial strategy could actually lead to higher unemployment. Its argument was that although the strategy might promote higher productivity growth and thereby increase our international competitiveness, the resulting employment-creating effects would not be sufficient to offset the employment-*reducing* effects of that productivity growth.

b. Effects on small firms

Small firms are likely to be at a disadvantage relative to their larger counterparts in both the formulation and execution of this kind of strategy.[19] There are for example economies of scale in maintaining relationships with government. Large companies are able to release people to sit on relevant committees and to make contact with, and representations to civil servants, whereas the managing director of a small business is usually unable to devote much of his own or his employees' time to this kind of operation. Again, there are likely to be economies in the preparation of applications for selective assistance. The costs of submitting an application for £$2x$ are unlikely to be twice the costs of an application for £x if indeed they are greater at all. Moreover, the larger company because of its ability to spread overheads usually employs specialist accountants, lawyers and marketing and financial analysts who are better able to put its case in the best possible way. Government, for its part, is likely to prefer dealing with applications for larger firms because they are easier, and probably cheaper, to administer. Thus an industrial strategy based on selective aid may have an inbuilt bias against the small firm. This point is further emphasised by the long-run relative decline in small firms during this century and the evidence that we have on the important role they play in inventive and innovative activity (Johnson, 1975, chapter 3).

c. Effects on industry's own activities

Private companies may respond to the greater availability of investment funds from public sources by attempting to use these funds to finance projects that they would themselves have actually financed. In this way public money may act as a substitute for, rather than as a complement to, private money. Government departments may attempt to ensure that the principle of additionality (i.e. that public money is used as a complement) is adhered to, but there is no clear way in which it can be established. Evidence on this issue is difficult to find, but a study by Blank and Stigler (1957, page 28), provides a hint that it may have occurred in the US in relation to the government provision of R and D funds. There is also the possibility that government funds may lead to projects which are unprofitable in both private and social terms.

d. Effects on innovation

One unexpected side effect of the industrial strategy may have been to make industrial boundaries more rigid. Both the formulation and execution of industrial policies require some fairly explicit definitions of industries and the underlying assumption is often that the firms best able to analyse and make proposals on a particular industry are those currently in it. Yet there is some empirical evidence to suggest that important innovations often come from outside the traditional boundaries of an industry (Johnson, 1975, pages 64–66). Firms already well established in such an industry might therefore resist moves of this kind, because they are already 'locked in' to existing processes and products. The mechanism of the industrial strategy may have enabled them to do this more effectively than previously. This is a particularly important issue because of the crucial need for Britain, if it is to reduce its unemployment level without recourse to protectionist measures, to increase its competitiveness not so much in price terms but in relation to the technical attractiveness of the products it markets.[20] Thus we probably need a strong innovation policy, but it is by no means certain that a strategy of the kind we have had is the best way of providing it.

It should by now be clear that the whole question of Britain's comparative industrial performance is extremely complex, and that it is unlikely to be explicable in terms of one factor alone. The facts that we have are capable of sustaining several (sometimes related) interpretations and of providing the basis for a variety of policy recommendations. Given this kind of situation, and given the possible (and often unforeseen) side effects of policies outlined above, it is vitally important that current policies should be subject to stringent evaluation by people outside the policy formulation and execution process itself.

NOTES TO CHAPTER 1

1. Some examples from a recent study of new firms in the Northern Region (Johnson and Cathcart, 1979) may help to illustrate this point. One business was formed to mix detergent concentrate. All the inputs are brought in by a large company which also collects all the output. The large company does not hold any equity in the new business, but the latter would be unlikely to survive without the former's business. In another case, the normal supplier of a component required by a large company

decided to stop production of this line. The customer company then approached the foreman of the supplier and undertook that if he set up his own (legally independent) business to produce the component they would buy from him. Virtually all the new firm's output goes to the large company.

2. Consistent employment data only go back to this year.

3. It must be remembered, however, that the 'output' measurement is particularly difficult in the services sector, and frequently has to be based on employment data. It is at least arguable that increases in employment in the civil service (included in order XXVII) do not necessarily indicate increases in 'output'.

4. This term is used by Prais (1976) and is based on the work of P. Sargent Florence.

5. Nothing in the text necessarily implies that plants larger than those currently in existence would not be more efficient. There is for example clear evidence that in the motor industry, British plants are noticeable smaller than those in the US or Germany or France (Jones and Prais, 1978) and that this contributes to Britain's relatively lower productivity in this industry.

6. Changes in the SIC make worthwhile comparisons over the whole period 1951–68 impracticable. It is possible, although unlikely, therefore, that those industries that showed increases in concentration in the earlier period, experienced declining concentration in the later period. Data for later years can only be compared with those for 1968 with difficulty.

7. See the survey in HMSO (1978), annex A.

8. The concentration ratio implies nothing about the market shares of firms which are both inside and outside the ratio.

9. Between 1957 and 1973, the proportion of ordinary shares of UK quoted industrial companies held by financial institutions rose from 18 to 41%. See Prais (1976) page 119.

10. It can, of course, be argued that the 'conventional economic indicators' are not the criteria against which the economy's performance should be judged. Environmental, religious and political considerations may be seen as more important. The discussion of these issues must remain outside the scope of this book. However, it is worth noting in passing that it is not at all clear that conflict will always exist between 'economic' and 'non-economic' objectives.

11. If we express the UK's average annual growth rate as a percentage of the unweighted average of the average annual growth rates of the other countries given in table 1.5, we find the following results:

	1958–69	1969–77
Industrial production	44.6	16.8
Output per man hour in manufacturing	59.8	52.8
Consumer prices	122.7	154.9
Wage costs per unit of output	146.1	169.4

12. See the *UN Statistical Yearbook 1976*.

13. These figures are taken from the relevant issues of the National Institute's *Economic Review*.

14. These were all industries in which were set up Sector Working Parties under the industrial strategy.

15. In contrast with the UK's exports where, as shown on page 16 unit values tend to be lower than those of France or Germany, UK imports tend to have a *higher* unit value than those of her competitors (NEDO, 1977).

16. Between 1923 and 1938 the average annual growth rate of GDP was 2.26%, compared with 2.71% between 1948 and 1970. Growth in output per man year was about the same for the two periods overall although the 1960s saw much more rapid

growth than the inter-war period. These figures are based on data in *The British Economy: Key Statistics 1900–1970* published for the London and Cambridge Economic Service by Times Newspapers.

17. Between 1870–1913 and between 1913–50 the UK's average annual rate of growth of total output was lower than the average for twelve major industrialised nations in the West. The UK's average annual rate of growth of output per man hour was also worse than the average for 1870–1913. In the period 1913–50 it was equal to the average. However, it is below the average if Germany and France – both of whom suffered particularly badly from the effects of the two world wars in the period – are excluded (see Maddison, 1964).

18. *An Approach to Industrial Strategy*, Cmnd 6315.

19. For a detailed discussion of these issues see Johnson (1978).

20. For an excellent discussion of the issues involved here, see Freeman (1978).

REFERENCES

Aldcroft, D. H. (1964) 'The Entrepreneur and the British Economy'. *Economic History Review* **17**, 113–34.

Bacon, R. and Eltis, W. A. (1976) *Britain's Economic Problem: Too Few Producers*. London: Macmillan.

Bannock, G. (1976) *The Smaller Business in Britain and Germany*. London: Wilton House.

Blackaby, F. *ed.* (1979) *De-industrialisation*. London: Heinemann for the National Institute.

Blank, D. and Stigler, G. J. (1957) *The Demand and Supply of Scientific Personnel*. New York: National Bureau of Economic Research.

Brown, C. J. F. and Sheriff, T. D. (1979) 'De-industrialisation: a background paper' in Blackaby *ed.*

Brown, C. V. and Jackson, P. M. (1978) *Public Sector Economics*. London: Martin Robertson.

Cairncross, A. (1972) 'The Optimum Firm Reconsidered'. *Economic Journal* **82**, 312–320.

Caves, R. A. *ed.* (1967) *Britain's Economic Prospects*. London: Allen and Unwin.

Cowling, K. and Waterson, M. (1976) 'Price-Cost Margins and Market Structure'. *Economica* **43**, 267–274.

Demsetz, H. (1969) 'Information and Efficiency: Another Viewpoint'. *Journal of Law and Economics* **XII**, 1–22.

Freeman, C. (1962) 'Research and Development: A Comparison between British and American Industry'. National Institute *Economic Review* (20), 21–39.

Freeman, C. (1974) *The Economics of Industrial Innovation*. London: Penguin.

Freeman, C. (1978) *Government and Industrial Innovation*. J. D.

Bernal lecture, Birkbeck College (May).

Gardner, N. K. A. (1976) 'Economics of Launching Aid' in A. Whiting *ed. The Economics of Industrial Subsidies.* London: HMSO.

George, K. D. (1974a) *Big Business, Competition and the State.* An Inaugural Lecture, University College, Cardiff.

George, K. D. (1974b) *Industrial Organisation.* 2nd edn. London: Allen and Unwin.

George, K. D. (1975) 'A Note on Changes in Industrial Concentration in the United Kingdom'. *Economic Journal* **85**, 124–128.

HMSO (1977) *Evidence on the Financing of Industry and Trade* **2** (given to the Committee to Review the Functioning of Financial Institutions). London: HMSO.

HMSO (1978) *A Review of Monopolies and Mergers Policy*, Cmnd 7198. London: HMSO.

Johnson, P. S. (1975) *The Economics of Invention and Innovation.* London: Martin Robertson.

Johnson, P. S. and Cathcart, D. G. (1979) 'New Firms and Regional Development'. *Regional Studies* **13**, 269–80.

Johnson, P. S. and Apps, R. (1979) 'Interlocking Directorates among the UK's largest companies'. *Anti-Trust Bulletin,* xxiv, 359–369.

Johnson, P. S. (1978) 'Policies towards Small Firms: Time for Caution?'. *Lloyds Bank Review* (129), 1–11.

Jones, D. T. and Prais, S. (1978) 'Plant-size and Productivity in the Motor Industry.' *Oxford Bulletin of Economics and Statistics* **24**, 87–97.

Kaldor, N. (1966) *Causes of the Slow Rate of Growth in the United Kingdom: an Inaugural Lecture.* Cambridge: Cambridge University Press.

Kaldor, N. (1975) 'Economic Growth and the Verdoorn Law: A Comment on Mr Rowthorn's article'. *Economic Journal* **85**, 891–896.

Maddison, (1964) *Economic Growth in the West.* London: Allen and Unwin.

Meeks, G. (1977) *Disappointing Marriage: A Study of the Gains from Merger.* Department of Applied Economics, Cambridge University, Occasional Paper no. 51. Cambridge: Cambridge University Press.

Moore, B. and Rhodes, J. (March 1976) 'The Relative Decline of the UK Manufacturing Sector'. *Economic Policy Review.*

Mueller, A. (1977) 'Industrial Efficiency and UK Government Policy' in C. Bowe *ed. Industrial Efficiency and the Role of Government.* London: HMSO.

NEDO (1977) *International Price Competition, Non Price Factors and Export Performance.* London: NEDO.

Newbould, G. D. (1970) *Management and Merger Activity.* Liverpool: Guthstead.

O'Brien, D. P. (1978) 'Mergers – Time to Turn the Tide'. *Lloyds Bank Review* (130), 32–44.

Panic, M. (1975) 'Why the UK's Propensity to Import is High'. *Lloyds Bank Review* (115), 1–12.

Panic, M. *ed.* (1976) *The UK and W. German Manufacturing Industry 1954–1972.* London: NEDO.

Pavitt, K. *ed.* (1980) *Technical Innovation and British Economic Performance.*

Phillips, A. (1976) 'A Critique of Empirical Studies of Relations between Market Structure and Profitability'. *Journal of Industrial Economics* xxiv, 241–249.

Prais, S. (1976) *The Evolution of Giant Firms in Britain.* Cambridge: Cambridge University Press.

Pratten, C. F. (1976) *Labour Productivity Differentials within International Companies.* University of Cambridge, Department of Applied Economics Occasional Paper no. 50. Cambridge: Cambridge University Press.

Richardson, G. B. (1972) 'The Organisation of Industry'. *Economic Journal* **82**, 883–896.

Robinson, J. (1933) *The Economics of Imperfect Competition.* London: Macmillan.

Rosenberg, N. (1974) 'Science, Invention and Economic Growth'. *Economic Journal* **84**, 90–108.

Salter, W. E. G. (1969) *Productivity and Technical Change.* 2nd edn. Cambridge: Cambridge University Press.

Sawyer, M. C. and Aaronovitch, S. (1975) *Big Business.* London: Macmillan.

Scherer, F. M. (1971) *Industrial Market Structure and Economic Performance.* Chicago: Rand McNally.

Schmookler, J. (1966) *Invention and Economic Growth.* Cambridge, Mass.: Harvard University Press.

Shepherd, W. G. (1975) *The Treatment of Market Power: Anti Trust, Regulation and Public Enterprise.* New York: Columbia University Press.

Stigler, G. J. (1949). *Five Lectures on Economic Problems.* London: Longmans.

University of Warwick (1978) *Britain's Medium Term Employment Prospects.* Manpower Research Group, University of Warwick, Coventry.

Utton, M. (1974) 'Aggregate versus Market Concentration'. *Economic Journal* **84**, 150–155.

Weiss, L. (1971) 'Quantitative Studies of Industrial Organisation' in M. D. Intriligator *ed. Frontiers of Quantitative Economics* **1.**

Amsterdam: North–Holland.

Wells, J. D. and Imber, J. C. (1977) 'The Home and Export Performance of United Kingdom Industries'. *Economic Trends* (286), 78–89.

Wragg, R. and Robertson, J. (1978) *Post-War Trends in Employment, Productivity, Output, Labour Costs and Prices by Industry in the United Kingdom*. Research Paper no. 3. London: Department of Employment.

FURTHER READING

A more detailed treatment of topics covered in this chapter may be found in the following books which also contain extensive references.

Changes in industrial structure
Prest, A. R. *et al.* (1979) *A Manual of Applied Economics*. 7th edn. London: Weidenfeld and Nicolson. Especially chapter 4.
George, K. D. (1974) *Industrial Organisation*. 2nd edn. London: Allen and Unwin.
Brown, C. V. and Jackson, P. M. (1978) *Public Sector Economics*. London: Martin Robertson.
Prais, S. (1976) *The Evolution of Giant Firms in Britain*. Cambridge: Cambridge University Press.

Britain's industrial performance
Blackaby, F. *ed.* (1979) *De-industrialisation*. London: Heinemann for the National Institute. Especially chapter 10.

Industrial policy
Hartley, K. (1977) *Problems of Economic Policy*. London: Allen and Unwin. Especially Part III.
Morris, D. J. *ed.* (1977) *The Economic System in the UK*. Oxford: Oxford University Press. Especially chapter 9.

2. North Sea oil and gas

C. Robinson and C. Rowland

2.1 INTRODUCTION

This chapter is concerned with UK oil and gas *production*; that is, oil and gas are treated as primary industries, engaged in extracting non-renewable natural resources from the earth. However, we begin with some essential background on the world-wide development of oil and gas, and on the economic characteristics of the two fuels.

2.1.1 Oil and gas world-wide

The beginnings of the world oil industry are generally traced back to a well drilled in 1859 by 'Colonel' Drake in Pennsylvania. From then on, the industry expanded at remarkable speed, first in the United States and then in other areas, as the falling relative price of oil coupled with technological changes allowed oil to increase its share of fuel markets world-wide. Originally, oil was a lubricant and lamp fuel, but it became a source of energy for transport, for electricity generation and for industry; more recently it has provided the feedstock for a fast-growing petrochemical industry. From 1900 to 1970, the annual average compound rate of growth of world oil production was about 7%. Natural gas, which at one time had been regarded as a rather useless by-product of oil which could only be burned off (flared) at the wellhead, also came into increasing use, being extracted both from oil reservoirs as 'associated gas' and from gas fields.

During the post-Second World War period, oil and gas consumption expanded rapidly; as their prices fell relative to the price of coal (OECD, 1973), their shares of the world energy market rose sharply at the expense of coal. By the early 1970s the combined share of oil and natural gas in the world energy market was about 66%, compared with only 37% in 1950. After the oil 'crisis' of 1973–4, the rise in the relative prices of oil and gas brought about a change in trend: the shares of oil and gas in world energy fell slightly and coal's market share increased a little.

Except for North America and the Soviet Union, most industrialised countries had little oil or gas so that, as costs increased in the coal industries on which their early industrial growth had been founded and coal consumption fell substantially, there was a considerable expansion of world trade in relatively cheaper oil. In particular, in the 1950s and 1960s there was rapid economic growth in Western Europe and Japan, fuelled by oil imported from the Middle East and Africa. The share of oil in Western Europe's energy consumption rose from 12% in 1950 to 58% in the oil 'crisis' year of 1973. European coal output dropped over 20% and import dependence increased.

Natural gas is more costly to transport over long distances than oil; nevertheless, gas trade has increased considerably in recent years as techniques of liquefying gas for tanker transportation have been developed and long-distance pipelines have been laid.

2.1.2 Economic characteristics

Both crude oil and gas are characterised by relatively low price elasticities of demand. Although elasticities are difficult to estimate statistically, one study (Kouris and Robinson, 1977) suggests that for the Common Market area the price and income elasticities of demand for imported crude oil were of the following orders of magnitude in the period 1955–73:

	Short run	Long run
Price elasticity of demand	−0.15	−0.6
Income elasticity of demand	+0.5	+2.0

For all fuels, long-run price elasticities are likely to be significantly greater than short-run elasticities since the demand for a fuel is derived from the ownership of complementary fuel-using equipment such as a car, a central heating appliance or an industrial boiler. Short-run responses to price changes tend, therefore, to be relatively small. It is only over a period of years that the stock of fuel-using appliances adjusts to the effects of relative price changes (Tzanetis, 1978). Thus the impact of a sharp change in oil prices, such as the increases of 1973–4, may take many years to work through the system as consumers shift gradually away from oil-burning equipment, car manufacturers give fuel economy higher priority in engine design and other lagged adjustments take place.

Occasionally, crude oil is burned in power stations, but more generally it is refined into a variety of products which sell into submarkets with different characteristics. For example, motor gasoline (petrol) and jet fuel are products in highly inelastic demand because they have virtual monopolies of the motor car and aviation markets. The market demand for heavy fuel oil is, however, very elastic with respect to price because coal, natural gas and nuclear power (for electricity generation) are close substitutes. Natural gas requires relatively little treatment before sale to the final consumer. In many uses it can sell at a premium over oil because it is on tap and therefore requires no storage; moreover, it frequently has characteristics (such as comparatively low sulphur content) that are desirable environmentally and reduce equipment maintenance costs.

2.2 OIL AND GAS IN THE UK

The UK has no tradition as an oil and gas producer, as it does as a coal producer. In common with other European countries, the rising demand for energy was until very recently met principally by imported oil, although oil has a somewhat lower market share in the UK than in Europe as a whole. There was a radical change in the structure of energy consumption between 1950 and 1973 as coal prices rose relative to oil prices: in 1950 the energy market was still dominated by coal, but in the early 1970s oil overtook coal as the largest single fuel source and import-dependence consequently increased from about 10% in 1950 to nearly 50% in 1973. Import-dependence would have increased even more had it not been for the significant quantities of natural gas which by the early 1970s were being produced from the southern North Sea. By 1973 the share of natural gas in the energy market was over 12%.

Small quantities of oil have for many years been extracted from on-shore fields in the UK, but it was not until the early 1960s that hopes of substantial finds emerged. At that time, exploration began in the southern basin of the North Sea (off the east coast of England) stimulated by the very large Groningen natural gas find in Holland and some small gas discoveries in Yorkshire. There were two pre-conditions for exploration. First, international agreement was necessary on how rights to exploit the North Sea were to be apportioned among the countries bordering the North Sea. Particularly important was the division between Britain and Norway because they are the two countries with the longest North Sea coastlines. After this division was concluded by the median line principle for the area south of 62°N, UK law was extended to the North Sea by the Continental Shelf Act 1964 which was an enabling Act; this was subsequently amplified by successive Petroleum Production Regulations.

Success came quickly. In October 1965, British Petroleum made the first natural gas discovery in the West Sole field and a series of larger finds in 1966 and 1967 showed the North Sea southern basin to be a significant gas-bearing region. On the basis of these discoveries, the British gas distribution network was converted from manufactured gas to carry natural gas of about twice the calorific value per unit, and the nationalised gas industry became one of the fastest growing industries in Britain. Subsequent exploration has resulted in one major find of non-associated gas in the northern North Sea (the Frigg field which is about 60% in the Norwegian sector), discoveries of gas associated with oil in the Brent, Piper and several smaller fields, and one find to the west of Britain (the Morecambe field). At the end of 1977, remaining recoverable natural gas reserves offshore Britain were estimated at about 1550×10^9 cubic metres: that is, they were equivalent to around 2200 million tonnes of coal or 1300 million tonnes of oil.

North Sea oil finds turned out to be even more significant than the gas discoveries. By the late 1960s attention had switched to the deeper, northern areas of the North Sea offshore mainland Scotland, Orkney and Shetland. The oil companies were disappointed at the prices paid for natural gas by the Gas Council (now the British Gas Corporation), which the government had decided should be virtually sole buyer of offshore gas, and they also believed the larger gas reservoirs in the southern North Sea had already been found. Consequently they moved north to search for oil. Success again came rapidly. The first big North Sea oil discovery was Ekofisk in the Norwegian sector in 1969 and during the next six years there were numerous oil finds – mainly in the British sector, although one more large field (Statfjord) was found on the Norwegian side of the median line. UK recoverable oil reserves at the end of 1977 were estimated at about 3200 million tonnes, about two and one half times recoverable gas reserves (Department of Energy, 1978a).

In mid-1975 British North Sea oil production began and output has since increased rapidly. Table 2.1 illustrates UK fuel consumption and production trends since 1973, showing how since the oil 'crisis' total fuel consumption has declined somewhat while import-dependence has dropped sharply as production of offshore oil, and to a lesser extent offshore gas, have risen substantially. As the table indicates, if existing field development programmes are achieved, by 1980 British offshore oil output should be about equal to oil consumption (including non-energy uses such as petrochemical feed stock and international bunkers) and UK net imports of fuel should be very small. By that time the only significant net imports are likely to be natural gas from the Norwegian part of Frigg (all Frigg gas is piped to Britain), although there will still be a considerable two-way trade in oil. North Sea oil is of relatively high quality (light and low in sulphur) so that it commands a higher price than many other crude oils. Thus there is an

TABLE 2.1: **UK fuel production and consumption**

	million tonnes oil equivalent		
	1973	1978	1980 (forecast)
Fuel production			
Coal	78	73	68
Oil	—	53	100
Natural gas	25	34	38
Nuclear	6	8	11
Hydro	1	1	1
Total	110	169	218
Fuel consumption			
Coal	78	70	67
Oil (energy uses)	97	82	85
Natural gas	26	38	47
Nuclear	6	8	11
Hydro	1	1	1
Non-energy uses*	12	9	12
Bunkers*	5	3	4
Total	225	211	227
Production as % of consumption	49	80	96

Sources: 1973 and 1978: Department of Energy, *Digest of Energy Statistics*, 1978, Table 7; *Energy Trends*, January and February 1979.
Note: *Mainly oil.

advantage in exporting some North Sea oil provided transport costs do not exceed the quality premium. Moreover, there are technical advantages in refining some heavier imported crude oils as well as lighter North Sea oil in meeting the UK pattern of demand for oil products. In 1978, about 44 per cent of the oil produced from the North Sea was exported and the other 56 per cent refined at home (*Energy Trends*, February 1979).

2.3 OFFSHORE OIL AND GAS AND THE ECONOMY

The likely impact of North Sea oil and gas on the economy is a very complex issue (Robinson and Morgan, 1978). Clearly, the UK was fortunate in finding such large quantities of oil at just about the time when the oil producers of OPEC were raising prices so sharply. By 1980, Britain should be an oil producer comparable in size with some of the present middle-rank oil producers of the world such as Kuwait, Venezuela, Nigeria and Iraq. Moreover, it would not be surprising if Britain's offshore oil and gas reserves turn out eventually to be substantially higher than people now estimate: although it is believed that most of the best oil and gas prospects have already been drilled (UKOOA, 1978), there is plenty of exploration still to be done in the North Sea (provided costs do not rise too much in relation to oil prices and provided the tax system is not too onerous) and possibly in the areas to the west of Britain which have so far proved disappointing.

However, it is easy to exaggerate the effect of offshore oil and gas on the economy. Arithmetic self-sufficiency – that is, the condition that output equals home consumption – is not, in itself, particularly desirable. At a cost, any country can obtain self-sufficiency in almost any product. There may be some gain in terms of security of supply and lessened dependence on OPEC oil, but North Sea activities are, of course, vulnerable to industrial action and sabotage. It is also worth remembering that the real resource costs of North Sea oil (see 2.4.2 below) are substantially above the £9 per tonne which imported crude oil cost prior to the oil 'crisis' of 1973.

Any gain which accrues from North Sea oil will arise essentially because of a favourable price–cost margin. The costs of most fields, excluding taxes, are well below North Sea oil prices (which are related to world oil prices as explained in 2.4.4); consequently investments made in the North Sea are likely to yield relatively high returns, as compared with other investments that could have been made in Britain. The gap between price and cost, which will partly be taken by the British government in the form of extra taxation (see 2.6 below) and partly by the companies in profits, is the source of potential gain, but it is by no means certain that all or even most of the potential gain will be realised.

Without speculating on the extent of future gains from the North Sea, one can roughly assess the size of the oil and gas sector relative to the economy as a whole. According to official estimates (*Economic Progress Report*, October 1978), GNP at market prices arising from oil and gas production was about £1700m in 1977 (about 1.25% of market price GNP), and may increase to £6000–7000m at 1977 prices by the mid-1980s. The favourable net effect of North Sea oil and gas on the balance of payments (current and long-term capital account) in 1977 is officially estimated to be about £4000m and may rise to £8000m at 1977 prices by 1985. It must be emphasised that there are numerous conceptual and statistical problems in estimating the effects of North Sea oil and gas on GNP, the balance of payments and tax revenues; not everyone agrees with the official estimates (Robinson and Morgan, 1978; Robinson and Rowland, 1978a and b).

Other ways of demonstrating the size of North Sea oil and gas relative to the British economy are to make comparisons with industrial production and with investment expenditure. There is no published industrial production index component for the North Sea sector alone. However, the index for 'other mining and quarrying' shows extremely rapid growth from 1975 onwards: at the end of 1978 the index (1975 = 100) was well over 1000.

The size of North Sea investment relative to total UK investment is shown in table 2.2. By the end of the 1970s oil and gas investment was about 8% of gross domestic fixed capital formation. About two-thirds of the investment appears to have been carried out by foreign companies (*Bank of England Quarterly Bulletin*, March 1979).

TABLE 2.2:   Gross domestic fixed capital formation in the UK

	(£ million, current prices)		
	Total	Petroleum and natural gas	
	(1)	(2)	(2) as % of (1)
1972	11 604	120	1.0
1973	14 149	183	1.3
1974	16 924	608	3.6
1975	20 536	1 334	6.5
1976	23 597	2 092	8.9
1977	25 808	2 135	8.3
1978	29 121	2 218	7.6

Source: Monthly Digest of Statistics, June 1979.

2.4 THE NORTH SEA INDUSTRY

There are two features of the North Sea environment particularly relevant to an analysis of industrial structure. Since the early days of activity on the Continental Shelf successive Governments have shown a keen interest in offshore matters. They not only allocate rights to explore for and extract any hydrocarbon deposits found in British waters, but are also eager to be involved in and legislate for most areas of the industry. The market structure that has emerged in the 1960s and 1970s has evolved alongside an array of public policies (see 2.5 below).

Second, British oil and gas production is only a small segment of an internationally well-developed industry; oil reserves in the North Sea as a whole may be only 2 or 3% of total world resources (Moody,

1975). Although the international industry comprises many thousands of organisations exploring for and developing oil and gas, it is dominated by some of the largest multinational companies in the world. These vertically-integrated petroleum producers are headed by seven majors (the 'seven sisters'), whose sales and profits are by any standard massive: for example, Exxon, the largest oil company, had a net income in 1978 of $2760m.

2.4.1 Involvement of UK firms

Because of the international nature of the oil industry, one can hardly expect the majority of North Sea extraction rights to be held by British firms. Currently about one-eighth of the UK Continental Shelf is covered by production licences (issued as explained in 2.5.1 below), which give the licensees exclusive rights to exploit any underground oil or gas deposits. Of this licensed area around two-fifths is held by British companies, although as table 2.3 shows, the British proportion has increased substantially over the five licence rounds completed by 1978.

TABLE 2.3: The British proportion of licensed area by licence round

Licence round	Year	Number of blocks allocated	Per cent of area licensed to British companies
First	1964	348	30
Second	1965	127	37
Third	1970	106	36
Fourth	1971/72	282	43
Fifth	1976/77	44	70*
Sixth	1978/79	42†	na

Source: Department of Energy 1978b, page 9.
Notes: *Provisional.
†Conditional allocation in 1979.

Similarly the offshore supplies industry providing the exploration rigs, the production platforms, the supply boats and the pipelines and tankers to transport the oil and gas has international roots. Although companies engaged on the Continental Shelf at first imported many of these items, the establishment of a British offshore supplies industry has increased the UK share of the North Sea supplies market from under 30% in the early seventies to around two-thirds in 1977 (Department of Industry, 1978). Refining and marketing North Sea output also involves the international oil companies long established in the UK.

2.4.2 Economic characteristics of North Sea production

North Sea oil and gas projects are far from homogeneous (Robinson and Morgan, 1978; Robinson, 1979). There are, however, some common characteristics of producing oil and gas from the North Sea which make this industry conducive to certain types of enterprises. The geographical environment is a serious deterrent to companies not already involved in offshore oil and gas exploration, with water depths of around 200 metres in the northern North Sea, local winds of up to 100 miles per hour, waves as high as a five-storey building and reserves typically located a couple of miles under the seabed. More important, certain economic features of North Sea production restrict entry into the industry. For example, the return on investment in the North Sea is highly uncertain, and project costs are massive. The importance of these factors varies according to the stage of the exploration and production cycle: the greatest unknowns must be faced during 'wildcat' drilling in the exploration phase, but costs are highest and the potential for cost variation greatest during the subsequent development of any discovery.

Although a company has access to seismic information about the geology of the Continental Shelf, it can only be sure of the presence of oil or gas if it sinks a well through the seabed. The costs of this drilling activity have risen sharply in recent years and in 1978 each well cost £2–5m, depending on geographical and geological circumstances: companies must be able to withstand losses if no economically-exploitable find is made. In the period until the end of 1977 fewer than one in fifteen of the wells drilled in the British sector of the North Sea encountered oil reserves of at least twenty million tonnes, which is approximately the minimum size that would be considered for commercial exploitation (depending on location and other characteristics). Moreover, the success rate appears to have been falling since 1973–4.

Once a field has been located, its geology is appraised and if prospects seem worthwhile the company embarks on field development, normally installing a steel or concrete platform from which wells are drilled to extract oil or gas. There are then further risks on the cost side to be faced (in addition to uncertainty about oil prices and government policies). Offshore production in hostile waters has to rely on a little-tested technology where no one knows how production and transportation equipment will behave over the long lives of the fields (up to thirty years), there are significant risks of accidents and there are considerable uncertainties about the size of recoverable reserves and the rates at which oil or gas will flow. Unlike exploration risks, some of the development risks can be offset by insurance, but the size of development expenditure generally dwarfs exploration spending. The total cost estimates of the North Sea oilfields currently in production range from £110m for a very small find to over £3500m for a large discovery, so that all North Sea fields are very large investment projects – some of them 'giant projects' such as major hydroelectric schemes or very long pipelines. In the past initial cost estimates have had to be revised upwards very sharply as material prices soared and unforeseen technical and managerial problems arose (Department of Energy, 1976). While North Sea cost increases in the late 'seventies are well below the rates reached in the early 'seventies, there are uncertainties over operating costs in the long term and the higher costs of developing less attractive reserves (for example, in deeper water) are likely to increase North Sea costs further.

Another important characteristic of North Sea projects is the long pre-production period. From discovery to first output for a typical offshore project involves five years, during which time investment costs accumulate with no offsetting revenues. Thus the time profile of costs is heavily 'front end loaded', especially when costs are expressed in discounted terms. Once the field is on stream there may be another three to five years to wait before peak production is achieved, which may be maintained for a couple of years before output steadily declines. A North Sea investor must therefore be able to commit large-scale funds for a period of several years without suffering short-term financial strains.

There are other barriers to and incentives for entry into this industry – notably the government's licensing règime discussed in 2.5 below – but the economic characteristics discussed above tend to determine the types of companies which will undertake the great part of North Sea activities. Larger companies, with diversified and integrated operations, appear better suited to deal with the risks and high costs which are involved. Exploration risks can be spread and the companies can cope with the high and uncertain costs of development. Although there is a fringe of smaller firms (see 2.4.3 below), these economic considerations tend to restrict their activities in the North Sea.

2.4.3 Concentration

Consequently, the major multinational oil companies are prominent in the British North Sea. As is often the case in oil exploration and production, both the oil majors and the smaller companies have formed partnerships and consortia so that risks and costs to any one firm are scaled down to a manageable level. Even the two largest oil companies (Exxon and Shell) conduct most of their North Sea activities in partnership. Licences are issued to groups of anything up to fifteen companies with each member committed to a specified proportion of the costs incurred on the licensed area and in return entitled to the same proportion of any discovery, although there are a few cases of sole licensees.

These joint licensee opportunities have opened up the North Sea to a wide variety of companies, including a number of non-oil organisations which wished to use the North Sea to diversify their activities although they lacked the experience to operate an oil or gas project efficiently. Consequently firms involved in the North Sea range from the world's largest oil company (Exxon), through the medium-sized oil companies such as Phillips and Amoco, to the publishers Thomson and the institutional investors such as LASMO or SCOT. However, in terms of the areas licensed to the different types of companies shown

TABLE 2.4:   Licensed area by different types of companies

	Number of organisations	Per cent of area licensed
Majors*	7	37
Independents†	26	31
British Nationalised Corporations‡	2	17
Others	157	15

Source: Authors' estimates.
Notes: *BP, Exxon, Gulf, Mobil, Royal Dutch Shell, Standard Oil of California (Socal) and Texaco.
†The inclusion of companies in the 'independent' category is to some extent rather arbitrary. Here this group comprises AGIP, Amerada Hess, Amoco, Atlantic Richfield, Aquitaine Oil, Cities Service, Conoco, Deminex, Elf Oil, Getty, Hamilton, Kerr McGee, Marathon, Mesa, Occidental, Petrofina, Phillips, Placid, Ranger, Sun Oil, Superior Oil, Tenneco, Texas Eastern, Total, Unocal and Zapata.
‡British National Oil Corporation (BNOC) and British Gas Council (BGC).
The percentages are based on a count of the number of blocks and the proportion of blocks awarded to various companies. This approximates to percentages of area since most blocks are 250 square kilometres. Original awards of blocks by the government are used: any subsequent relinquishment of blocks by companies is not taken into account. 'Participation oil' taken by BNOC under participation agreements for pre-Fifth Round licences is allocated to the companies which were originally granted the licences and not to BNOC, since under these agreements the latter is primarily a marketer of crude oil (see section 2.5 below). The same procedure for participation oil is adopted in tables 2.5 and 2.6.

in table 2.4 the seven majors are most important, having been awarded over one-third of the licensed area.

There have been numerous discoveries, only a small proportion of which have been brought on-stream by the end of 1978. In early 1979 oil is flowing from twelve fields discovered offshore Scotland, Orkney and Shetland (listed in table 2.7) while gas production is mainly from seven accumulations located in the southern waters neighbouring the Lincolnshire and Norfolk coastlines and from the northerly Frigg field. Although, as table 2.4 shows, almost two hundred organisations hold licences, output in early 1979 was concentrated in fifty-one companies, twenty-six with oil interests, ten with gas as well as oil discoveries and fifteen with only gas production. This greater concentration of current output than of licences can be traced to the uneven geological dispersion of the hydrocarbon deposits, to the licence allocation methods of the Department of Energy (see 2.5.1 below), to the relative exploration skills (or good fortune) of the companies concerned and to the varying rates at which companies have developed their finds.

Concentration within the group of successful companies is notable in the production of both gas and oil. The largest four North Sea gas supplying companies accounted for over 40% of the thirty-four million tonnes of oil equivalent of natural gas produced from the North Sea in 1978 (table 2.5). The degree of concentration in oil supplies is even

TABLE 2.5:   **North Sea output by company, 1978**

Oil and gas combined (% of total output)		Gas (% of total output)		Oil (% of total output)	
BP	27	Exxon	12	BP	43
Exxon	9	R.D. Shell	12	Occidental	11
R.D. Shell	9	Amoco	9	Getty Oil	7
Occidental	6	BGC	9	Exxon	6
BGC	5	BNOC	8	R.D. Shell	6
		Conoco	8	Allied Chemical	6
		Amerada Hess	7	Thomson	6
Output million tonnes oil equivalent					
87		34		53	

Source: Authors' estimates.
Note: See table 2.4 for the treatment of BNOC's 'participation oil'.

more marked. Over half the 1978 oil production was provided by two companies, BP and Occidental, with BP alone producing twenty-three million tonnes of oil – two-fifths of North Sea oil production and one-quarter of UK domestic oil consumption. However, this apparent domination of oil supplies is rather misleading. The North Sea oil industry is in its formative years with most projects either in their pre-production phase or in their production build-up period. In 1978 oil output of fifty-three million tonnes included twenty-four million tonnes from the Forties field (mainly owned by BP) and thirteen million tonnes from Piper (operated by Occidental). Over the next few years the output from another ten oilfields already producing will increase rapidly, and these supplies will almost certainly be supplemented as development plans are pursued for another ten to fifteen projects involving various consortia. As table 2.6 demonstrates, the degree of concentration of established commercial reserves is significantly less than the degree of concentration of output shown in table 2.5. Nevertheless, of the fifty-nine firms with a share in established commercial reserves, the three companies with the largest shares are world majors and they have about half the reserves. Six of the seven majors operating in the North Sea are among the top ten privately-owned organisations shown in the left-hand column of table 2.6.

TABLE 2.6:   Recoverable oil reserves owned by company

Established commercial reserves (% of total)		Established commercial and potentially commercial reserves (% of total)	
BP	22	BP	18
Exxon	14	Exxon	12
R.D. Shell	14	R.D. Shell	12
BNOC	6	BNOC	7
Occidental	3	Texaco	5
Getty	3	Socal	3
Texaco	3	Conoco	3
Mobil	2	Gulf	3
Marathon	2	Mobil	3
Conoco	2	Occidental	2
Gulf	2		

Source: Authors' estimates.
Note: 'Established commercial' fields are those already producing or for which there are firm development plans. 'Potentially commercial' fields are finds already made for which there were no firm development plans early in 1979. See also note to table 2.4 for the treatment of BNOC's 'participation oil'.

By including a further nineteen oilfields that have been discovered but which do not as yet have any firm development plans ('potentially commercial' fields), one can obtain a still broader, albeit more speculative, picture of who owns North Sea reserves; it is worth remembering that actual North Sea reserves will only be known with certainty after the area has been totally exploited sometime in the twenty-first century. Inclusion of these additional fields raises estimated recoverable oil reserves from less than 1500 million tonnes to over 2000 million tonnes (compared with total estimated proved, probable and possible reserves of 3200 million tonnes – see page 31). Although an additional twelve companies now have a stake in North Sea oil, the pattern of ownership in table 2.6 does not change dramatically.

2.4.4 Market behaviour and conduct

Industries with concentration ratios as high as in the North Sea might normally be expected to display oligopolistic pricing strategies and marketing policies. However, conditions are different in the North Sea. In the gas market the producers face a monopsonist with considerable power to set prices in the form of the British Gas Corporation (see 2.5.2 below). In the oil market, as the North Sea is only a small segment of world oil trade and as production from other countries can be substituted for British crude with little difficulty, the North Sea producers are effectively price-takers faced by a very elastic demand curve. North Sea prices tend to be 5–10% above the world market price but these differences can be traced to the higher than average quality of North Sea crude (relatively low gravity and sulphur content) and the transport cost saving (compared with OPEC oil) of moving oil from the North Sea to European consumers.

So, despite the highly concentrated structure, North Sea companies tend to act competitively, extracting oil until the costs (including taxes and royalty) of the marginal unit of output are equal to the externally-set price of that output. Similarly the companies will adjust planned annual output until the discounted marginal profit from a barrel produced in one year is the same as the discounted marginal profit of producing that barrel in any other year. The analysis of market behaviour of North Sea companies, *qua* North Sea companies, is thus relatively straightforward and of less economic interest than is the case with many of the other industries discussed in this volume – although there is a great deal of interest in the behaviour of companies in the world oil market as a whole.

There is some 'merger' activity within the industry in the form of 'farm-out' deals, in which a company that has discovered an oil or gas reservoir 'farms out' all or part of its interest to another company in exchange for the other company meeting all or part of the development costs. Although large corporations tend to take over parts of discoveries made by smaller companies, the prospect of farm-out deals reduces perceived risks for smaller enterprises and gives them an incentive to explore the North Sea. From April 1978 to July 1979, the government required that either BNOC or BGC must be given the opportunity to participate in all assignments of licences.

2.4.5 Performance

We have already described the rapid expansion of offshore oil and gas to date and in the near future. However, while the 1980 forecast for gas production may be close to the peak for gas supplies, oil output should still be expanding until at least the late 1980s. Fig. 2.1 shows a possible profile for oil production from the British sector of the North Sea up to the end of the century. This aggregation of uncertain individual field depletion profiles is a speculative process resting on a number of assumptions concerning the unknown future: the diagram illustrates only a 'surprise-free' projection in which the future oil-producing environment (including the cost-price margin, the tax structure, government depletion policies and exploration success rates) is assumed to turn out roughly as the oil companies now expect.

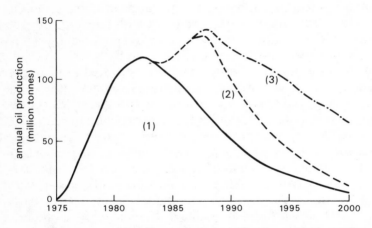

(1) = Output from established commercial oilfields
(2) = Additional output from potentially commercial reserves
(3) = Additional output from assumed new discoveries

FIG. 2.1:   Possible North Sea oil output, 1975–2000

Source: Authors' estimates.
Note: Further comments on the construction of 'surprise-free scenarios' are in Robinson and Morgan (1978) and Robinson and Rowland (1978a).

The lowest line in the figure, peaking at 115 million tonnes in the early 1980s, represents a pessimistic scenario comprising only twenty-three established commercial fields which are already producing or likely to begin production in the near future. Virtually regardless of foreseeable events, the plans for these fields are likely to go ahead, and North Sea oil supplies should reach this level at least (Robinson and Rowland, 1978a; Robinson, 1979). The middle curve includes another nineteen potentially commercial discoveries already made which appear to be economically exploitable, although considerable appraisal work needs to be carried out before the companies can declare firm plans to develop these reserves. If the likely production from these fields is included, supplies are projected to peak at 135 million tonnes in the late 1980s, but this will be followed by a fairly rapid decline in the 1990s. Lastly, the highest curve assumes that future exploration activity reveals further fields – although of a smaller average size and in remoter waters than discoveries to date. Our estimates of likely drilling activity, success rates and the unexplored area's geology suggest that on a surprise-free scenario North Sea oil supplies may be supplemented by the output from over thirty new discoveries. Development of these prospects would not increase peak supplies markedly but the decline towards the end of the century would be less rapid, as the highest line in fig. 2.1 indicates.

If UK oil consumption rises from less than 100 million tonnes a year in the late 1970s into the range 100 to 120 million tonnes a year in the 1980s, the surprise-free projection implies self-sufficiency in oil for Britain throughout the 1980s with modest export surpluses. However, these supplies are far from guaranteed. There might be big changes in the cost–price ratio, in taxes or in other government policy instruments; similarly, geological surprises (pleasant or unpleasant) might occur and significantly affect North Sea output prospects (Robinson and Rowland, 1978a).

The standard labour productivity measures are not particularly helpful when comparing North Sea oil with other energy industries because of sharply differing capital intensities. For example in 1977 only a little over one thousand men were directly employed in producing oil from the Continental Shelf; this yielded an output per person of almost forty thousand tonnes of oil compared with some 260 tonnes of oil equivalent produced by each British coal miner. Performance of the industry may to some extent be gauged by after-tax returns on individual projects. As yet there is insufficient history of oil developments to be able to assess profitability *ex post*, so instead the anticipated real net present values must be examined. Clearly such calculations are subject to wide margins of error. Remaining expenditures and future oil outputs are only known very approximately, and the price of oil will be dictated by events in the oil industry at large which is subject to political, social and economic shocks. It follows that a range of possible returns, based on the most reliable cost information available but varying with the trend of future oil prices, should be examined.

Table 2.7 shows some sensitivity calculations which indicate how estimated returns vary with assumptions about oil prices. The returns in this table are computed on a common 15% rate of discount in real terms so as to give a broad order-of-magnitude indication of net present values. Discount rates will differ among companies and over time – because each rate is based on the specific company's opportunity cost of capital – so there is no way of determining the 'correct' discount rate for the North Sea. The Crude Price Indexation (CPI) columns show post-tax real net present values, in total and per unit of production, if world oil prices rise in line with general inflation (that is, stay roughly constant in real terms). Limited Price Decline (LPD) indicates a scenario of an immediate drop in the oil price, slowly picking up to remain constant in real terms after the mid-1980s. The Use of Monopoly Power (UMP) scenario assumes significant increases in the oil price will occur over the next few years.

TABLE 2.7: **Anticipated post-tax real net present values* for North Sea oilfields onstream, end 1978**

| | Price scenario | | | | | |
| | CPI† | | LPD† | | UMP† | |
	(£ million)	(£/tonne)	(£ million)	(£/tonne)	(£ million)	(£/tonne)
Argyll	15	3	10	3	15	4
Auk	85	12	80	11	95	13
Beryl	40	1	–40	–1	135	2
Brent	–220	–1	–440	–2	150	1
Claymore	215	4	165	3	290	6
Dunlin	175	4	110	2	285	6
Forties	1140	5	995	4	1395	6
Heather	–65	–4	–105	–6	–15	–1
Montrose	–110	–7	–135	–9	–80	–5
Ninian	–15	0	–195	–1	260	2
Piper	620	8	555	7	725	9
Thistle	40	1	–50	–1	165	2

Source: Authors' estimates.
Notes: *At a 15% discount rate.
          †Assumed North Sea oil prices are

| | CPI | | LPD | | UMP | |
	($/barrel)	(£/tonne)	($/barrel)	(£/tonne)	($/barrel)	(£/tonne)
1980	17	63	15	57	19	72
1985	22	82	17	64	34	126
1990	31	115	24	89	47	177

A striking feature of table 2.7 is that on any given price scenario there are great differences in estimated profitability (deriving largely from cost differences) among fields currently on stream. One project

(Auk) is a very high earner per tonne, but its total net present value is relatively low since it is a small, short-life field. The rather lower values per unit on the larger reserve bases (Claymore, Dunlin, Forties and Piper) indicate the fields which appear to offer the highest total returns for their exploiters. Some of the other fields – particularly Heather and Montrose – must look rather marginal prospects to the producing companies.

In comparing North Sea profitability with that available in other sectors of the UK (*Bank of England Quarterly Bulletin*, December 1978), one must remember the economic features of offshore production. Companies operating in the North Sea face substantial risks and long lead times for their investments, and consequently tend to look for returns that would seem high in other industries. Second, the figures in table 2.7 are anticipated rather than achieved returns: experience so far suggests that North Sea costs turn out higher than expected so there may be some upward bias in the calculations. Third, the project costs only include expenditures specifically attributable to each discovery: abortive exploration costs and company overheads that must be accounted for somewhere are not incorporated in these returns.

Nevertheless, the North Sea does seem to contain some highly rewarding developments. Whilst the twelve fields in table 2.7 may well include the best North Sea investments, the next batch of fields to come onstream may still exhibit real returns of the same order-of-magnitude. Thus North Sea activities appear relatively profitable when compared with other investment opportunities in the UK.

2.5 GOVERNMENT POLICY TOWARDS THE NORTH SEA

Almost everywhere political forces have a significant impact on the activities of the oil industry. In most countries with oil and gas reserves there is either direct state involvement in the exploitation of those reserves or government 'regulation' of the oil industry; furthermore, there has in recent years been a clear trend towards increasing government control of oil and gas, particularly since the oil 'crisis' of 1973 drew attention to the uncertainty of energy prospects. How much government intervention there *should* be is a controversial matter which is discussed elsewhere (Robinson and Morgan, 1978; Robinson, 1978). Here our concern is to describe what has happened in Britain rather than to pass judgement on it.

There are many ways in which government exerts influence on company activities in the North Sea. The tax system is one of the principal means. In Britain, as in other countries, special taxes on oil have been devised: the tax regime and its effects are discussed in section 2.6 below. First, however, we shall look at the ways in which the Department of Energy regulates North Sea operations and at the roles played by two nationalised corporations – the British National Oil Corporation (BNOC) and the British Gas Corporation (BGC).

2.5.1 Licence allocation

Because petroleum resources are the property of the state, once the Continental Shelf Act 1964 had been passed (see page 30), the government had then to determine how licences to exploit oil and gas resources were to be allocated to private sector companies. Essentially there are two possible methods of licence allocation (Dam, 1976; Robinson, 1978). One is to hold an auction in which potential licensees bid in competition with each other. Competitive bidding is used in the US and a small number of licences was auctioned as part of the UK's Fourth Round of Licensing in 1971. However, in Britain, as in Norway and most other countries, licences have generally been issued by 'administrative discretion' with the only payments being relatively small rentals. Briefly, the system is that politicians lay down certain guidelines for licence issue and civil servants in the Department of Energy are supposed to decide, within those guidelines, which companies shall be allocated which areas. The British sector of the North Sea is divided into blocks, mostly of about 250 square kilometres, and production licences cover one or more blocks.

The initial guidelines for operating the discretionary allocation system, laid down by a Conservative government for the First Licensing Round in 1964, set the pattern for subsequent rounds. The criteria were rather vague. Rapid exploitation was to be encouraged and applicants should be making some 'contribution towards the development of resources of our Continental Shelf and . . . of our fuel economy generally.' Undoubtedly a considerable amount of discretion was left to civil servants. Further licensing rounds retained essentially the same system of awards (apart from the limited licence auction of 1971, already mentioned), but increasingly preference was given to British interests in general and to nationalised industries in particular. For example, in the 1965 Second Round, preference was given to groups of applicants in which there was a nationalised corporation; in the 1969 Third Round there was further preference for such groups and the Government insisted that the (then) Gas Council or the National Coal Board (NCB) must have shares in Irish Sea licences. By the 1977 Fifth Round 51% participation by BNOC or BGC was required and applicants were expected to agree participation terms for finds made under previously-issued licences. The 1978 Sixth Round, which is discussed under 2.5.4 below, was intended to strengthen further the positions of BNOC and BGC.

The decision to issue licences by civil service discretion, rather than by auctioning, had certain consequences. An auction, provided there is competition among the bidders, is in theory capable of extracting the rent associated with natural resources as well as allocating licences. Companies will bid what they believe the areas on offer to be worth (in a competitive situation they will not under-bid because of fear of not gaining licences) and in this way the state will collect much of the surplus which arises from resource exploitation. A discretionary award regime, however, only allocates licences – it does not collect rent – so some other means of revenue collection becomes necessary.

2.5.2 A monopsony for North Sea gas

In the case of oil a special rent collection mechanism was eventually established in the Oil Taxation Act 1975 (see 2.6 below). For gas, which was discovered much earlier than oil, a different method was used. Because production licences had been awarded almost free of charge, oil companies which were successful in finding gas might have made substantial profits had they been able to sell gas at market prices. However, a countervailing power had been established by the state's granting to the nationalised gas industry – which already had a monopoly of piped gas distribution in Britain – virtual monopsony rights over North Sea gas. Under section 9 of the 1964 Continental Shelf Act companies which had natural gas to sell had, with minor exceptions, to offer it to the Gas Council (acting on behalf of itself and the Area Gas Boards) which was constrained only to pay a 'reasonable price'. Clearly companies which found gas were in an inherently weak bargaining position since they had little alternative to selling to the Gas Council. Partly as a result of the Council's strong negotiating position and partly because of government pressure, the price fixed for natural gas from the large offshore fields in negotiations between 1966 and 1969 was low relative to then existing energy prices. How low cannot precisely be established, but one measure is to compare the gas price with the price of imported crude oil (both as sold to a buyer at the UK coast). One would normally expect gas to be priced higher than crude oil because the former is generally regarded as a superior product and it needs little processing in comparison with crude oil; in fact the gas price (1.2p/therm) was only about two-thirds of the imported crude price (1.8p/therm) in this period. Subsequently, the oil price rose sharply whilst the natural gas price increased only gradually under partial cost escalation clauses in the gas contracts, and the relative price of gas at the UK coast declined to only about 15% of the crude price in 1977. The economic rent from gas production was therefore extracted by rather unusual means – via a corporation granted sole buying rights by the state. Whether such a method can be regarded as satisfactory depends on what happened to the economic rent which was initially transferred to the Gas Council and Area Boards (which later became the British Gas Corporation – BGC). If the rent remained in the BGC–in the form of organisational slack for example – the initial method of removal would be difficult to justify, for the surplus would simply have been transferred from large private corporations to a large nationalised corporation rather than being used for the public benefit (Robinson, 1978).

2.5.3 Output and export controls

The first oil finds in the British North Sea occurred around 1970 (see 2.2 above) and the magnitude of Britain's offshore oil reserves began to emerge in the early 1970s at a time when there were radical changes and increasing uncertainty in the world oil market. Until that time there had been no explicit controls on production from North Sea fields except to the extent that output was governed by the BGC's ability to absorb gas. Generally speaking, governments had wanted rapid exploitation of gas in order to reduce oil imports. By the early 1970s, however, as first oil production neared, the two major political parties agreed that regulation of oil depletion rates might be necessary by the 1980s, although they differed on the way this control should be exercised (Robinson and Morgan, 1978). The Scottish Nationalists were in favour of much more drastic output controls than were either Labour or the Conservatives.

The Labour government elected in 1974 passed the Petroleum and Submarine Pipelines Act 1975 which, *inter alia*, contained powers to control output from North Sea fields. These powers were intended to regulate depletion rates from the early 1980s onwards – either by delaying the development of oil which had been discovered or by reducing output rates for fields already in production. Under the legislation, amplified by a Commons statement by Mr Eric Varley – then Secretary of State for Energy – in December 1974 (the 'Varley Guidelines'), companies with North Sea finds had to seek Department of Energy approval for their investment programmes and production rates. Plans initially approved could be subsequently modified within specified limits and with given periods of notice. The general intention was clearly to give scope for *reduction* of company output programmes, although a limited power to make companies increase production is also contained in the 1975 Act. The Energy Department has changed its method of approval of company programmes since depletion control was first instituted: instead of approval being given for the full life of a field, it is now only given in stages, the first stage being the period during which production builds up to its maximum.

There are other ways in which production can be controlled. For instance, the Energy Act of 1976 allows the Secretary of State for Energy to control oil output if he deems it necessary in the interests of energy conservation. Since then some official statements have suggested that the North Sea interests of BNOC and BGC might be used to influence production rates (Department of Energy, 1978b). Another obvious means of slowing North Sea development and reducing production is to issue a smaller number of production licences than in the past. This last policy is already in operation. As table 2.3 shows, the last large licensing round was the Fourth, in 1971; there was then a long gap until the 1977 Fifth Round and the 1978 Sixth Round, in both of which only a small number of blocks were on offer. Government policy in early 1979 is to issue relatively few licences at frequent intervals (Department of Energy, 1978b).

In addition to production control, there is also some restriction on exports of North Sea oil. All oil produced from the North Sea has to be landed in the UK unless the government gives specific exemption, but there is no legislation to prevent subsequent re-export. However, the government has operated loose export control in the form of a statement that 'up to two-thirds' of North Sea oil should be refined in the UK (that is, for subsequent sale either at home or abroad as refined products). Obviously the 'up to two-thirds' provision is so vague as to be almost meaningless in itself and in recent times much more than one-third of British North Sea crude oil output has been exported (about 45% in 1978). The government seemed by 1978 to be moving to informal export control on a company-by-company basis, although both the landing requirement and other forms of export control may be inconsistent with the rules of the EEC.

2.5.4 Participation

The other major change in government policy which has occurred in the last few years is the introduction to the North Sea of 'participation' by a state oil company – a procedure well-known in many oil-producing countries. As explained in 2.5.1 above, under the discretionary licence allocation system, the preference given to British nationalised industries (NCB and BGC) increased over the years. However, the Labour government decided that there should be a State oil company which would participate in North Sea licences. The British National Oil Corporation was set up in January 1976, under the Petroleum and Submarine Pipelines Act 1975, and now appears to be an established feature of the North Sea. BNOC's numerous functions (Select Committee on Nationalised Industries, 1977–8) can only be described briefly here: in effect they fall under two headings.

First, BNOC has access to substantial quantities of crude oil. Some comes from fields inherited in 1976 from the Burmah Oil Company and from the National Coal Board (which had to hand over its North Sea interest to BNOC). Some is from participation agreements with companies which found oil in pre-Fifth Round licensed areas. For such finds the companies came under strong Government pressure between 1975 and 1978 to give BNOC a 51% share (otherwise they would probably not have been given Fifth Round licences); participation in these existing finds is supposed to leave the companies no better and no worse off financially than they would otherwise have been. BNOC buys up to 51% of the oil at market price ('participation oil'), has voting rights and access to information about the fields. Under the terms of the Fifth and Sixth Licensing Rounds, BNOC has a 51% share in all licences awarded (except where BGC is involved); indeed the Sixth Round provides for companies to bid to give BNOC a share greater than 51% and to 'carry' some proportion of its exploration and appraisal costs until BNOC decides whether or not to participate in developing a find. It is also possible for BNOC, like BGC, to be given licences outside the main licensing rounds, and it has been awarded eleven blocks in this way. Finally, the government may decide to take in kind some of the $12\frac{1}{2}$% royalty payable by the oil companies on each barrel they produce: it will then most likely allow BNOC to handle such 'royalty oil'. In total, by the early 1980s BNOC is likely to have access to some 35 million tonnes of crude oil, making it a major operator in the world market (Department of Energy, 1978b).

Second, BNOC – by virtue of its membership of the operating committees which plan the development of North Sea fields and from its marketing of crude oil – gains experience in oil industry affairs and from this position advises the government on North Sea policy.

The activities of BNOC have become a matter of controversy – especially the extent of its preferential treatment compared with private sector oil companies (for example, its exemption from Petroleum Revenue Tax and its ability to receive licences outside the normal Rounds) and the possible conflict between its rôle as an oil company and its position as an adviser to government. This is one area of North Sea development where the attitudes of the two major political parties differ significantly. In mid-1979, the incoming Conservative government announced plans to curtail the functions of BNOC, although the Corporation will still remain in being.

2.6 OIL TAXATION

Tax regimes exert significant influences on oil company activities in all countries. The rather complex North Sea taxation system, which has gradually assumed a more important place in government North Sea policy, is explained very briefly below.

2.6.1 Objectives and means

In the early years of exploratory drilling activity, from the early sixties to the early seventies, the government sought a rapid expansion in UK oil and gas production, to establish the size of North Sea oil reserves quickly. As this expansion relied on attracting the multinational oil companies into British waters, the UK offshore fiscal environment was relatively favourable to the companies. Royalties (which are a common form of tax in oil-producing areas) were to be levied at a fixed $12\frac{1}{2}\%$ of the gross revenue derived from oil production, as valued at the wellhead, and corporation tax was to be charged on profits as defined by standard UK corporate taxation rules.

By the early 1970s, however, the considerable size of Britain's oil and gas reserves was apparent and the government's objectives began to change. Exploration activity was no longer the prime concern, proposals for controlling depletion began to appear (see 2.5.3 above) and there was a consensus in favour of changing the tax laws. It was argued that corporation tax rules would allow the multinationals to deduct from North Sea profits large onshore and overseas losses so that they would pay little tax on their North Sea activities. To raise its tax yield the Government proposed a 'ring fence' for corporation tax purposes, effectively isolating company North Sea profits from relief for losses or other allowances incurred in other areas of a company's business.

By 1975 the escalation in world oil prices pushed prospective North Sea returns higher, despite a considerable inflation of costs. Claims that companies operating offshore would make massive 'windfall' profits were made and the Government clearly felt it should increase its income from the North Sea. But whilst receipts from both corporation tax and royalties would rise automatically with higher oil prices, the additional receipts were thought to be insufficient given the anticipated sharp rise in company profitability. The competitive bidding system for licences (see 2.5.1) was ruled out by the politicians and civil servants, so to collect this oil rent – magnified by the OPEC price increases – the Government chose to re-structure the fiscal environment by introducing Petroleum Revenue Tax (PRT) in the Oil Taxation Act 1975.

Although the rent collection objective for PRT was clear, operationally it posed many problems. What are 'excess' profits? How can they be defined *ex ante* when their magnitude can be known only after field completion? How can one ensure that after-tax returns on less profitable projects are not pushed to sub-commercial levels endangering investments and the proper exploitation of UK reserves?

These difficulties were compounded by the great differences among North Sea fields which were explained in 2.4.2 and 2.4.5 above, and by the unpredictable dramatic changes which have characterised the oil industry in the 1970s. It is extremely hard to design a fiscal regime which will discriminate between the highly profitable and the less profitable oilfields, whilst also being sensitive to unanticipated changes in oil affairs.

PRT is a unique tax. It is the only British tax specific to an industry; it is levied on each field, not on the customary corporate basis, and it involves various concessions and allowances that make it extraordinarily cumbersome. Originally PRT was a 45% charge on net annual profits after allowing for three items – carried-forward losses, an 'uplift' depreciation provision amounting to 175% of capital expenditure (in effect an investment subsidy) and the value equivalent of one million tonnes of oil per year up to a total of ten million tonnes per field – but restricted by a 'tapering' limit. PRT payments in any year can neither reduce returns to less than 30% of accumulated capital costs nor collect more than four-fifths of the net revenue above this 30% figure. In the 1979 Finance Act the Government claimed that the yield from North Sea taxation was not coming up to expectations (although very little tax had by then been collected) and increased the rate of tax to 60%, decreased the capital cost uplift from 175 to 135% and halved the value equivalent oil allowance to half a million tonnes per year and five million tonnes per field.

2.6.2 Implications and problems

The government take – the total of royalties, corporation tax and PRT expressed as a percentage of net revenue – from all North Sea ventures is likely to be around 70%. Among individual projects, however, there will be considerable differences in take. Even among the twelve fields producing at the end of 1978 the probable take ranges from 62 to 76% and the range will almost certainly widen as new fields begin to produce. This variation is, however, only loosely related to expected oilfield profitability. The twelve fields are ranked in order of expected pre-tax net present value per tonne in table 2.8, which clearly demonstrates the lack of correlation between the expected government take and expected profitability.

Instead of a progressive tax regime, the Government appears to have introduced a complex tax structure with effects which are not at all clear. Superficially PRT appears to be a progressive tax on profits, but in practice the allowances and concessions – particularly the tapering limit – result in a rather arbitrary incidence of the royalty, PRT and corporation tax package. The PRT allowances provide little protection for high unit cost discoveries which are penalised by regressive royalty payments (levied on revenue, not on profits); thus only the more profitable fields can take full advantage of the capital uplift and the value equivalent oil allowance. It seems probable that government take will not be greatest from the most profitable fields but that the main burden will fall on the oilfields in the middle range of profitability (table 2.8).

TABLE 2.8:   Government takes for the North Sea oilfields onstream by end 1978 – ranked by pre-tax real present value* per tonne of output

	Pre-tax real present value (£/tonne)	Government take (%)
Auk	38	62
Piper	32	76
Forties	30	75
Argyll	22	65
Dunlin	21	75
Claymore	20	70
Thistle	14	68
Ninian	11	70
Brent	11	71
Beryl	9	63
Heather	5	66
Montrose	4	74

Source: Authors' estimates.
Note: CPI price scenario (see note to table 2.7) assumed.
   *Discounted at a 15% rate per annum.

Not only is the PRT burden oddly distributed but PRT is also a particularly poor control instrument. If a government sought an increase in its take from the North Sea, altering the rate of PRT would achieve a negligible change: the complex PRT allowances greatly restrict the ability to vary North Sea revenues by adjusting the tax rate. Fig. 2.2 demonstrates this insensitivity of government revenues to different rates of PRT. Whilst a PRT rate of 35% is estimated to collect total lifetime tax receipts of £27 000m from the twelve fields onstream by 1978, a rate of eighty per cent would increase real tax income from these projects by under £3000m. Thus a government has to tamper with the PRT allowances if any significant change in its tax revenue is to be achieved (Kemp and Crichton, 1978; Rowland, 1979).

   In spite of the curious characteristics of PRT, it is clear that the North Sea is going to be a substantial source of government revenue in

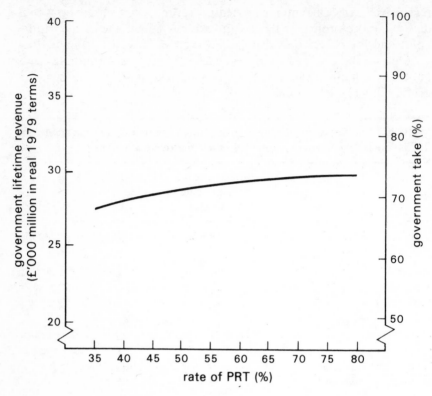

FIG. 2.2:   Government revenue and take for the twelve oilfields onstream by the end of 1978* under different rates of PRT

Source: Authors' estimates.
Note: *As in table 2.7.
          CPI price scenario (see note to table 2.7) assumed.

the next two decades. The size of tax receipts from offshore oil operations will depend on the future course of world oil prices and on the extent of North Sea oil reserves that will be brought into production. At one extreme oil prices might follow a depressed course (the LPD scenario – see page 44) with a limited number of economically exploitable discoveries yielding the lowest depletion curve in fig. 2.1. Under these assumptions real government income (in 1979 terms) would peak by the mid-1980s at just over £2000m, becoming much less significant in the 1990s. At the other extreme, oil prices might rise throughout the period (as described by the UMP senario), stimulating exploration and resulting in the highest output line of fig. 2.1. Real government revenues in 1979 terms would then rise until the early 1990s, providing substantial Treasury income of about £5000m to £6000m to the end of this century and well into the next.

2.7 CONCLUSION

North Sea oil and gas, together with their associated industries, are now well established as a principal growth sector of the British economy. During the next five years rapid growth will almost certainly continue, leading first to British self-sufficiency in fuel and then to a modest export surplus. Whether there will be further expansion beyond the mid-1980s is more problematical, depending as it does not only on the geology of the Continental Shelf but on such imponderables as the future course of world oil prices and the energy and fiscal policies adopted by British governments.

REFERENCES

Dam, K. W. (1976) *Oil Resources: Who Gets What How?* London: University of Chicago Press.

Department of Energy (1976) *North Sea Costs Escalation Study.* London: Energy Paper no. 7, HMSO.

Department of Energy (1978a) *Development of the Oil and Gas Resources of the UK.* London: HMSO.

Department of Energy (1978b) *Offshore Oil Policy.* Energy Commission Paper no. 19. London: HMSO.

Department of Industry (1978) *Offshore 1977.* London: HMSO.

Kemp, A. G. and Crichton, D. (1978) *A Review of the Proposed Changes in North Sea Oil Taxation.* University of Aberdeen Department of Political Economy Occasion Paper no. 13.

Kouris, G. and Robinson, C. (1977) 'EEC Demand for Imported Crude Oil, 1956 to 1985'. *Energy Policy* (June).

Moody, J. D. (1975) 'An Estimate of the World's Recoverable Crude Oil Resource'. *Proceedings of the Ninth World Petroleum Congress*, Tokyo (May).

OECD (1973) *Oil – The Present Situation and Future Prospects.* Paris.

Robinson, C. (1978) 'A Review of North Sea Oil Policy'. *Zeitschrift für Energie Wirtschaft (4/1978).*

Robinson, C. (1979) 'North Sea Investment and Profitability'. *Oil Now,* Den Norske Creditbank.

Robinson, C. and Morgan, J. (1978) *North Sea Oil in the Future: Economic Analysis and Government Policy.* London: Macmillan for the Trade Policy Research Centre.

Robinson, C. and Rowland, C. (1978a) 'An Economic Analysis of British North Sea Oil Supplies'. *OECD Workshops on Energy Supply and Demand,* Paris.

Robinson, C. and Rowland, C. (1978b) 'Marginal Effect of PRT Changes'. *Petroleum Economist* (December).

Rowland, C. (1979) 'Some Economic Aspects of North Sea Oil Taxation'. *Conference Papers,* Institute of Fiscal Studies, London.

Select Committee on Nationalised Industries (1977–8) *Reports and Accounts of the Energy Industries*. London: HMSO.

Tzanetis, E. (1978) *The Demand for Petrol in the UK: An Empirical Investigation*, unpublished Ph.D. thesis, University of Surrey, Guildford.

UKOOA (1978) *Exploration and Development of UK Continental Shelf Oil*. Energy Commission Paper no. 17 (by UK Offshore Operators Association). London: HMSO.

FURTHER READING

There are a great number of texts on the history of the world oil and gas industry: a useful introduction to this material may be found in *Our Industry*, British Petroleum (London: 1970). The growing literature relating to UK offshore affairs is primarily in various energy related journals (*Energy Economics, Noroil* and the *Petroleum Economist*) although several interesting books have emerged. C. Robinson and J. Morgan (1978) *North Sea Oil in the Future: Economic Analysis and Government Policy*, Macmillan for the Trade Policy Research Centre, provides a comprehensive discussion of the economics of North Sea oil whilst K. W. Dam (1976) *Oil Resources: Who Gets What How?* University of Chicago Press, focusses on the political dimension. More specialist topics are analysed in the series of occasional papers from the University of Aberdeen Department of Political Economy, which are of detail similar to the energy commission papers published by the Department of Energy. The Department of Energy also publish an annual record (*Development of the Oil and Gas Resources of the UK*, HMSO) describing the current stage of development of UK oil and gas resources and providing useful statistics on various North Sea matters.

3 Coal

R. B. Thomas

3.1 INTRODUCTION

The coal industry has a prominent place in the economic and social history of Britain. Its dominance of the energy sector during the last two hundred years of industrialisation, its unmistakable imprint on the landscape, and the distinctive characteristics of mining communities and organisations have been the hallmarks of a great industry. But times change. In post-war years there has been a spectacular decline in the size of the industry and it now accounts for only 1.5% of total output and employs only 1.2% of the labour force.

Since nationalisation in 1947 the National Coal Board (NCB) has been responsible for over 99% of UK production, so the firm and the industry are treated synonymously. The UK industry is the largest in Europe. In 1978, 232 collieries produced 105 million tons of coal and employed 240 000 workers. A further thirteen million tons were produced from about fifty opencast sites.

World output of coal is expanding, though most of the older industrial nations reached their production peak in the early years of this century. In the UK the most rapid period of contraction in post-war years was in the 1960s, as fig. 3.1 shows. Since then the industry's prospects have improved, and the NCB is at present undertaking a major investment programme.

Coal is a sedimentary rock, of vegetable origin. It varies greatly in its physical and chemical properties. Access to the coal seams is normally by the sinking of a shaft, though sometimes a drift mine, with direct tunnelling, is possible. The present general method of extraction in UK mines is longwall face mining in which a machine is moved back and forth along a coal face. As it moves it cuts a web of coal and loads it onto a conveyor. In some cases instead of advancing the face, complete access roads may be driven before cutting, which then begins at the most distant point and the face retreats.

Production in this extractive industry is quite different from that in manufacturing industry. It is as if 'a large part of the factory has to be uprooted and moved on every working day' (Berkovitch, 1977, page 96). Because working faces may be as much as five miles from the shaft, supervision is often difficult. Geological conditions are such that the raw material sometimes disappears or becomes so difficult to work that part or all of the 'factory' has to close. These risks can more easily be pooled in large-scale multi-plant organisations which are thus the appropriate industrial form for coal. Each year substantial replacement investment is required to make good the loss in capacity, which can be up to 3% of output per annum. Pit closures are usually irreversible because of flooding and choking-up with underground waste.

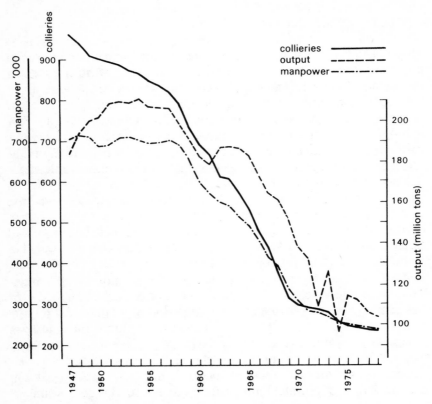

FIG. 3.1:   UK coal output and employment, 1947–78

Source: NCB *Statistical Tables*

Opencast, or surface mining, is making an increasingly important contribution to UK output. In 1970 95% of output was from NCB deep-mines, 4% from opencast, and 1% from licensed mines. By 1977, however, opencast output had risen to 11% and deep-mined fallen to

88%. Davison (1977) has shown that it is now possible to undertake opencast working at considerable depths so that for the first time a choice of technique, between surface and underground mining, is sometimes feasible. The quality of some deep-mined coal has deteriorated, because machines smash the coal and may mix dirt and coal. However, opencast coal is of sufficient quality to offset this deterioration and it has helped to preserve a mix of coals, without which some markets might have been lost. A major external diseconomy of opencast working is environmental despoliation, but there is at present no adequate machinery for weighing social costs and benefits.

The main coalfields in the UK are in South Wales, Scotland, the North-East, the central regions of Yorkshire, Derbyshire and Nottinghamshire, and the South and West Midlands. The present distribution of output and employment is shown in table 3.1. The geographical concentration of mining means that it has been a dominant activity in certain localities, some of which owe their development entirely to coal. When the coal was exhausted many mining communities proved to be very vulnerable and regional economic policy has therefore been closely associated with the coal industry. The pit closure programme has been most intense in regions with poor alternative employment prospects and this has meant that regional employment considerations have had a major impact on decision-making in the industry.

The NCB's business is divided into three profit centres: coal mining which accounts for 80% of turnover and 96% of employees, coal products (smokeless fuels, coke, etc.) and ancillary activities (including interests in distribution, engineering and property management). There is then relatively little forward or backward integration or diversification. Deep-mining and opencast are organised separately. The former has a structure which has become more streamlined over the years. This is to be expected in an industry where production levels have fallen drastically. At present there are three tiers: the NCB, the twelve Areas, and the collieries.

The coal industry has a wider range of duties and obligations than private industry but it is less subject to financial discipline in that the ultimate sanction of liquidation is absent and the government underwrites its finance. The NCB is subject to continuous political pressures arising from social, regional and other issues but the NCB–government relationship, which should be characterised by trust, continuity, and accountability, is ill-defined. A framework of institutions and criteria for agreements on long-term objectives is still lacking. This is a serious obstacle to sensible decision-making, though the government (Cmnd 7131, 1978) has now acknowledged the importance of specifying objectives.

TABLE 3.1: Area statistics, 1978

	Output deep-mined and opencast		Colliery average manpower		Colliery output per manshift		Costs		Profits
	(million tons)	(% of total)	(thousands)	(% of total)	(cwts)	(% of mean)	(£ per ton)	(% of mean)	(£ per ton)
Scottish	10.5	(8.9)	22.1	(9.2)	37.7	(87.5)	21.67	(99.6)	−0.31
North-East	15.3	(13.0)	34.9	(14.5)	36.0	(83.5)	23.07	(106.1)	0.66
North Yorkshire	8.7	(7.4)	15.5	(6.4)	50.5	(117.2)	19.39	(89.2)	0.09
Doncaster	7.4	(6.3)	17.2	(7.2)	45.2	(104.8)	21.11	(97.1)	−0.60
Barnsley	8.5	(7.2)	16.6	(6.9)	45.5	(105.6)	20.90	(96.1)	0.69
South Yorkshire	7.5	(6.4)	17.8	(7.4)	42.6	(98.8)	21.90	(100.7)	2.64
North Derbyshire	8.8	(7.5)	12.5	(5.2)	55.8	(129.5)	17.96	(82.6)	2.11
North Nottinghamshire	10.9	(9.3)	17.8	(7.4)	58.3	(135.3)	17.65	(81.1)	4.14
South Nottinghamshire	8.9	(7.6)	16.1	(6.7)	52.5	(121.8)	18.97	(87.2)	0.05
South Midlands	9.9	(8.4)	16.2	(6.7)	48.7	(113.0)	18.41	(84.6)	2.22
Western	11.7	(9.9)	24.3	(10.1)	42.1	(97.6)	24.53	(112.8)	−1.13
South Wales	9.8	(8.3)	29.5	(12.3)	25.4	(58.9)	33.43	(153.7)	−2.76
Total	117.9		240.5		43.1		21.75		0.63

Source: NCB *Report and Accounts 1977/78.*

3.2 THE STRUCTURE OF PRODUCTION, AND DEMAND

3.2.1 The structure of production

The production of coal is characterised by inflexibility. Output responses to changes in demand are slow because there is little 'spare capacity' and lead times are long. The industry has become more concentrated with the fall in the number of pits but the most significant feature of the industry's structure is that there is still great variation in pit size and productivity. In 1977/78 each of the 232 pits employed, on average, about one thousand men, produced about 450 000 tons and had a productivity level, measured in terms of output per manshift (OMS), of 42.4 cwts. The enormity of the dispersion across pits in these variables can be seen from the following coefficients of variation calculated from 1978 data: 0.56 for employment, 0.73 for output and 0.43 for OMS.[1]

There is a distinct and persistent geographical pattern to these differences. Some regions perform much better than others as table 3.1 shows. The general reliance on industry-wide collective bargaining means that the variation across Areas in earnings is less than that in productivity. This causes substantial variations in costs per ton. Inter-Area differences in prices are less than those in costs so profits vary considerably.[2] In Wales, for example, OMS is less than 60% of the industry average, costs per ton are more than 50% higher than the average and in 1977/78 there was a loss of £2.76 on each ton produced, whereas in North Nottinghamshire OMS is 35% higher than average, costs are only 81% of average, and there was a profit of £4.14 per ton. On short-term efficiency grounds the case for more concentration of production in profitable Areas is obvious but regional employment considerations limit this.

At pit level there are economies of scale. Bigger pits have lower costs although it is difficult to be exact about this because we have to rely on cross-sectional data which implicitly assume that all observations lie on the same cost function. This is unlikely because pits have unique geological and other operating conditions, employ different levels and types of technology, and do not therefore have the same production function. There is, however, a highly significant positive correlation between pit size (in tons) and OMS ($r = 0.7743$) and a highly significant negative one between OMS and costs per ton ($r = -0.9025$), so it seems reasonable to suppose that economies of scale do exist.

Some idea of the cost structure of the industry as a whole can be obtained from fig. 3.2 which shows a cumulative ranking of pits according to their productivity.[3] The inverted scale can be regarded as a proxy for costs per ton, and the curve is akin to a system marginal cost curve because it shows the 'cost' at which any increment in output (below the total output level *OC*) can be obtained. If all pits had equal 'costs' the curve would be *AB*, *OA* being the industry 'average costs', but fig. 3.2 clearly shows that a substantial proportion of total output is produced at a 'cost' (shown by the inverted OMS scale) much higher than the industry average.

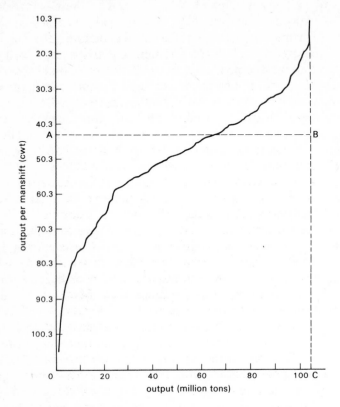

FIG. 3.2: 'Cost' curve for coal

Source: See note 3 on page 78.

Fig. 3.2 is drawn on the assumption that the NCB operates a merit-order of pits and, that like any cost-minimising multi-plant operator, runs the lowest-cost pits first. However, some writers, such as Bates and Fraser (1974), have noted that if the social constraint means that the high-cost pits have to be run at some minimum output level then some of the low-cost pits would run at less than full capacity until the constraint is met. Thereafter low-cost pits would provide the additional output and the system marginal cost curve may therefore fall.

The NCB is attempting to improve its competitive position. It is using a long-term strategy of further concentration on low-cost pits.

This will flatten the curve shown in fig. 3.2. It is also using a short-term strategy of increasing the productivity of all pits by an incentive payments scheme. This will shift the curve downwards.

3.2.2 Demand

There has been a long-term decline in the demand for coal. The demand for energy has a low positive income elasticity so although the energy market has been growing, coal's share has fallen. In the primary fuel sector it fell from 56% in 1967 to 36% in 1972, at which level it has remained. Among final users of energy solid fuel's market share fell from 74% in 1950 to 47% by 1963, and to a mere 15% by 1976.

In absolute terms the sales of coal fell from 210 million tons in 1948 to 122 million tons in 1978 whilst gas, electricity and petroleum consumption all increased. The fall in consumption has been accompanied by a marked change in the structure of coal markets. Electricity generating stations have steadily increased in importance; in 1978 they took seventy-eight million tons (64% of output) compared with twenty-nine million tons (14%) in 1948. All other markets have contracted. In the 1950s and 1960s two major markets, railways and gas production, were entirely eliminated with the change from steam locomotives and from coal-based gas making. More recently there have been falls in domestic and industrial consumption.

The demand for coal depends on price, non-price attributes, government policy, and, in the case of industrial consumers, their product demand. These are discussed seriatim. Cheshire and Buckley (1976) have shown that relative prices are the main explanation of the current pattern of fuel use. Higher prices reduce demand not only because other fuels are substituted for coal but also because coal itself is used more efficiently.

The price elasticity of demand is determined by the existence of substitutes, but where coal is a derived demand as in industry, product market elasticities and the ratio of fuel costs to total costs are also relevant. The short-run elasticity is low because equipment cannot easily be adapted to using different fuels. However, in the long run substitution is possible in the markets for large-scale industrial steam-raising, domestic central heating and power stations, though for some groups of consumers – such as coke ovens – the elasticity remains low because gas and oil are not realistic substitutes for coal.

Estimates of own-price elasticity of domestic coal have been put at −0.32 by Deaton (1975), and rather higher by Wigley (1968) at −0.83 in 1955 and −1.24 in 1965. This shows that the demand curve may not only have shifted left, but may also have flattened out because improved technology has made conversion to other fuel easier. Wigley found that various cross-price elasticities were all positive (though less than one). This confirms the suggestion that other fuels are coal substitutes.

The increased efficiency of fuel burning has reduced the demand for coal. In the case of non-nuclear power stations, for example, thermal efficiency increased by 30% between 1955 and 1977. There have also been significant improvements in the design of industrial and domestic equipment (for which much of the R and D has been an NCB response to falling market shares).

Non-price attributes of coal such as handling costs, cleanliness, and variability in quality, compare unfavourably with other fuels – a fact which gas and electricity advertising has emphasised. If tastes have changed such that consumers attach more importance to these product characteristics, or if the costs associated with them have increased then these will have contributed to the fall in demand, but evidence on this is weak.

The government has undoubtedly had a significant effect on coal demand, but it is difficult to quantify the size of this. Legislation was chosen as the method of combating the external diseconomies of coal burning and the Clean Air Acts of 1957 and 1968 (and subsequent regulations) caused a decline in demand, especially in the house coal market, which has not been fully offset by the consequent development and production of smokeless fuel. On the other hand, the government has, at various times, boosted the demand for coal. It has used a mixture of direct controls (e.g. a ban on imports in the 1960s), taxes (on fuel oil), subsidies (to induce the electricity generating and steel industries to stock more coal), exhortation (to the electricity industry and to government establishments – the latter were in fact obliged to burn coal even though it was up to 5% dearer than other fuels) and financial aid to make coal more competitive. These influences almost certainly moderated the long-run fall in demand.

The final determinant of coal demand is the demand for the products of industrial users. This is well illustrated by the recent recession in the steel industry which caused a 19% drop in the sales of coking coal between 1976/77 and 1977/78. The Central Electricity Generating Board (CEGB) is of especial importance. We have noted coal's increasing dependence on the CEGB as a consumer. But the dependence of the CEGB on coal is lessening. In 1960 82% of the fuel input of power stations was coal compared with 67% in 1975. The CEGB's current consumption of coal is largely fixed by existing coal-fired installations, though there can be some switching in the merit-order of power stations depending on relative prices. Future demand for coal depends on fuel choice for new power stations, so expected relative fuel prices become relevant. This in turn requires estimates of costs in the supplying industries. The CEGB's view of expected productivity in coal has usually been more pessimistic than that of the NCB. The disputes between the NCB and CEGB on this issue could perhaps be avoided by internalising the problem by merging the two industries. Such an organisational form would be fitting if, on welfare grounds, the appropriate objective function were some joint maximand for the two industries.

3.3 PRICING AND INVESTMENT

3.3.1 Pricing

We consider first the structure then the level of prices. Different consumers value differently the various physical and chemical properties of coal, e.g. the demand for carbonisation coals is mainly from coke ovens which require coal for processing rather than heat generation. The structure of pithead prices is based not only on costs in each Area but also on different demand conditions so there are separate pricing arrangements for domestic, industrial and carbonisation coals.

The fact that Area rather than pit costs are used implies some cross-subsidising among pits. There is also inter-Area cross-subsidising; costs per ton vary more than prices per ton, but it is difficult to pinpoint by how much. Uniform prices would usually indicate that low-cost Areas and consumers of low-quality coal were subsidising high-cost Areas and users of high-quality coal. Prices are certainly not completely uniform but there has recently been an interesting tendency for price dispersion to narrow. The cross-Area coefficient of variation in prices fell from 0.195 in 1974 to 0.137 in 1978. This trend away from pricing according to local costs, which has significant implications for the CEGB in its choice of type and location of power stations, means that the weaker peripheral regions are being increasingly subsidised by the stronger central regions.

Delivered prices are much higher than pithead prices. In the domestic sector, for example, the Price Commission (1976) showed that the average selling price is about 70% more than the pithead price, and it can be as much as 130% more. The size of this mark-up depends partly on the structure of the distributive sector. The wholesale trade is highly concentrated with the NCB accounting for over half, and twelve firms for a further 35–40%. The retail trade, however, is highly fragmented though this does not lead to a single competitive price prevailing for house coal. Substantial price dispersion occurs which is partly due to the existence of informal local price agreements. The Price Commission (1978) found evidence of such agreements which the NCB aids by operating a quota system in the allocation of domestic coal. This leads to market imperfections which are difficult to justify.

The price level is set to cover average costs although the prices of substitutes are also taken into account. In the 1960s, for example, when oil prices were relatively low, coal prices were mainly determined by coal's cost, but after the oil price rises of 1973 the price of coal could be raised.

In this current era of anti-inflation programmes involving price restraint it is perhaps surprising that coal prices – unlike those in gas, electricity, rail, postal services, steel and other nationalised industries – have not been restrained. This is in marked contrast to earlier periods. And despite the recent interest in the possibilities of using public utility prices as an anti-poverty policy coal prices have not been used as a device for redistributing income.

The absence of government price restraints and the desire to cover costs indicate that the NCB's deficits have been due to competitive pressures from other fuels and/or inefficiency.

3.3.2 Investment

The major determinant of the level of investment in the coal industry is long-run expected demand. This produced a pattern of moderate fixed investment in the 1950s, followed by a period of disinvestment in the 1960s. More recently there has been a heavy investment programme. These last two phases are reviewed here.

The substantial disinvestment of the 1960s raises the question of the optimality of the size and speed of the contraction. Posner (1973) has argued that the optimal rate of contraction of the coal industry requires the production in each year of that quantity of coal which minimises total resource costs of fuel subject to social and distributional constraints,[4] but it is clearly difficult to assess how nearly such a rate was achieved. In an industry where there is uncertainty about future demand, where fixed investment has long lead times and where pit closures are often irreversible, we should expect slow output responses to changes in demand. But even in a world of certain demand and zero gestation lags it would not be optimal to adjust output instantaneously if there were increasing marginal costs of adjustment. The more steeply these costs rise, the slower the optimal adjustment should be.

Labour is the main cost of production so it is labour adjustment costs which are the most relevant. The first of such costs are those borne directly by the coal industry, such as the financial costs of redundancy and early retirement, but these will be linearly related to the size of layoffs and so far as adjustment costs are concerned the optimal rate of contraction would thus be instantaneous. Other costs however, such as 'morale effects' and the costs of internal transfer, probably increase with the size of adjustment. 'Morale effects' show up in recruitment difficulties, in increased absenteeism, and in increased wastage of the younger and more skilled workers which the industry wishes to retain. This last effect reduces the average quality of employees. The impact of these 'morale effects' is to reduce OMS and raise average costs. The possibility of redeployment within the industry also becomes increasingly difficult as the more obvious possibilities of transfer and early retirement are used up. Thus the cost of closure rises as the rate of closure increases. It is difficult to quantify these adjustment costs but they do appear to be significant in the coal industry. Social costs of unemployed miners and equity factors relating to regional distribution of employment also have to be considered.

The scale of contraction in the 1960s was massive compared with other reallocations of resources in the economy. Between 1958 and 1970 the NCB's workforce fell by 388 000, an average of 32 000 men each year. Some critics have argued that the rate of run-down should have been faster, but, as we have shown, the various efficiency and social criteria suggest that the optimal rate of run-down was much less than instantaneous and there is therefore little reason to suppose that any serious misallocation occurred through sub-optimal rates of contraction.

We now turn to the expansion in investment in the 1970s. In 1974 the NCB began a major ten-year investment programme designed to provide forty-two million tons extra capacity by 1985 (about half from new mines and the rest by improvements and life extensions to existing collieries) and an increase in opencast output to fifteen million tons. This investment represents not so much an expansion of output beyond the 1974 level but rather a halting of the long-term downward trend in output. Much of the increase in capacity in the programme was required to cover capacity losses through exhaustion.

There is emphasis on efficiency in the choice of location of the new investment, which is heavily concentrated in the high-productivity pits which have low marginal costs. All the projects have internal rates of return of 30% or more, which compares favourably with the current 10% test rate of discount.

The estimated cost of the programme, in 1974 prices, was £1400m. In 1976, however, this estimate was raised by 29% in real terms – partly because of the inclusion of many projects aimed at keeping production costs down rather than providing additional capacity, and partly because, after the 1960s, the NCB lacked recent experience in costing major investments. An intensified programme of exploration has accompanied this investment programme. Workable reserves are now being proved at the rate of about 500 million tons per annum and the total operating reserves are sufficient for forty years at present extraction rates.

The present investment programme, which will determine capacity levels in the later years of this century and beyond, rests on the assumption that the long-term demand for coal is assured.

Long-term demand forecasting is, however, full of hazards. First, guesses are required about political factors that affect coal. It is difficult to exaggerate their significance, and it is interesting to note (Sheriff, 1978) that the NCB has found political factors to be so important in some cases that econometric techniques are counter-productive as an aid to planning decisions. Second, the relative price of fuels can – and does – change dramatically. In 1974 the ratio of coal to oil prices halved, and this gave a massive boost to coal, though there has already been some narrowing of the coal–oil price differential with the fall in the value of the dollar. Further erosion of coal's price advantage could destroy the economic justification of the investment programme.

Third, long-term developments in the oil, gas, electricity, steel and cement and other industries have to be forecast. Assumptions are thus required about the future scarcity of supplies of indigenous oil and natural gas, about the role of nuclear power stations and about technological developments – especially in steel-making. There is widespread agreement that by the year 2000 coal will have important markets in the production of substitute natural gas (SNG) and as a chemical feedstock, but in the intervening twenty years coal-burning power stations will provide a crucial source of demand. The CEGB has not ordered any new coal-fired stations apart from the Drax B station in Yorkshire, to which it was committed by the government.

It is hardly surprising, therefore, that the record of forecasting long-term demand in the industry is poor. In the 1950s the downturn in demand that came in the 1960s was not foreseen and, with the benefit of hindsight, it can be argued that investment was at too high a level in the 1950s. On the whole, explicit financial criteria do not appear to have been a major determinant of investment levels. The government, by capital rationing and *ad hoc* intervention such as deferring closure of particular pits or pressing the CEGB to order coal-fired stations, has been much more significant. Political decision-making may, however, be no worse than market tests in a world of great uncertainty where social factors are important.

3.4 PERFORMANCE EVALUATION

It is truly remarkable that in an industry so crucial to the economy that its stoppage can severely curtail the output of the entire economy, which raises vital social and environmental considerations and which has a £4bn investment programme (at 1978 prices), there is no effective framework for measuring performance and assessing managerial competence. This stems from a failure of governments, until now, to specify an objective function in operational terms and to assign weights to the equity and efficiency arguments. The principal indicator of performance which we shall consider is productivity. This is reasonable in a labour-intensive industry (where wages and wage charges account for 48 per cent of costs) but as the measure is subject to some limitations we also examine other indicators, beginning with finance.

3.4.1 Finance

Financial criteria for assessing performance are only possible if financial objectives are clear, but the strength of government commitment to the commercial criterion has varied. Throughout the 1960s and 1970s various financial criteria were set and subsequently waived or abandoned. At present the government is devising required rates of return (RRR) on new investment. These rates reflect the opportunity cost of capital. This indicates a central concern with allocative efficiency, although other performance criteria are still relevant because high rates of return do not necessarily reflect efficiency. The RRR is also intended to take account of social factors and will therefore be specific to each nationalised industry.

The financial record is not readily interpretable as a performance criterion because of the unclear objectives. Deficits have been made in almost all years since the mid-1960s though there were small surpluses (after interest payments and after taking account of government grants) of £27m in 1976/77 and £20m in 1977/78. The source of profits is given in table 3.2. The data, which are typical of recent years, show that opencast mining is highly profitable whereas losses are

TABLE 3.2: **NCB coal-mining profits,**[a] **1977/78**

	Output (million tons)	Total profit (£m)	Profit per ton (£)
Deep-mined coal	104.6	−13.4[b]	−0.13[b]
Opencast coal	13.3	88.1	6.63[b]
Total	117.9	74.7	0.63

Source: *NCB Statistical Tables: Report and Accounts* 1977/78.
Notes: [a]After government grants but before interest payments.
   [b]These figures have to be inferred from other information in the accounts.

made on deep-mined coal. There are, however, substantial variations among Areas in deep-mined coal profits, as table 3.1 showed, so it would be wrong to conclude that on efficiency grounds there should be a massive switch to opencast working. If, however, efficiency were the sole criterion and if profit figures reflected undistorted market signals, then some move in that direction would be appropriate.

The financial results shown are calculated after taking account of substantial government aid; this aid is small, however, when judged by the standards of other members of the European Coal and Steel Community (ECSC). A series of Coal Industry Acts has given several forms of assistance. First, there has been aid with the social costs of rundown, such as redundancy payments, aid with pension funds, payments to transferees and housing provision. Second, capital reconstructions have permitted the writing-off of substantial portions of debt. Third, as we have noted, direct subsidies have been given to coal buyers, especially the CEGB. Fourth, the government paid £100m in 1971/72 and £130.7m in 1973/74 to offset the deficits arising largely from national strikes in those years.

This aid is piecemeal and is not obviously based on some criteria for optimal subsidies. In effect there is an *ex post* subsidy and financing arrangement which has little to commend it. Clearly it is difficult to reach agreement in advance on the level and form of subsidies because of the fuzzy objectives and the change in operating and political circumstances. There has therefore been resort to *ex post* compensation, capital write-offs and capital restructuring as a means of rectifying deficits.

Some of the financial difficulties over the years have resulted from the obligatory dependence on debt finance. The NCB has to rely on fixed-interest, fifteen-year loans though it is now pressing for access to normal markets, for more freedom on the duration of government loans and for public dividend capital. The government does make public dividend capital, which is akin to equity finance, available to some nationalised industries, such as airways, steel, aerospace and shipbuilders, all of which operate in highly competitive international markets. It is, however, firmly resisting this for the coal industry, which has difficulty breaking-even, because it would become little more than an interest-free, non-repayable advance – in effect a grant. The government correctly argues that the present fixed interest loan and grant system does impose some financial discipline on the industry.

3.4.2 Productivity

There has been substantial growth in OMS in post-war years, although comparisons with other industries and other countries indicate that the performance has been relatively modest. Data provided by the Commission of the European Communities (1977) show that other ECSC members have enjoyed faster growth in productivity and consequently smaller rises in costs, especially in the 1970s. Fig. 3.3 shows that the main growth in the UK was between 1958 and 1971 and that the recent record has been poor.

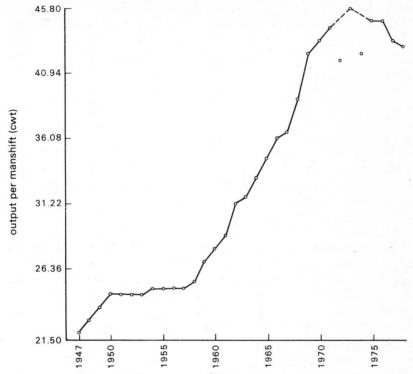

FIG. 3.3: **Productivity (output per manshift), 1947–78**

Source: NCB *Statistical Tables*
(1972 and 1974 observations affected by the national stoppages)

The first cause of productivity growth is concentration of pits and of faces. The concentration of faces has been at a faster rate than that of pits, and it has been accompanied by more emphasis on the higher-productivity retreat faces at the expense of the lower-productivity advancing faces. The move to fewer but larger pits and faces has brought economies of scale by spreading overheads (some labour is a quasi-fixed factor) and allowing greater use of machinery. Before 1957 closures were all due to 'exhaustion' but in the 1960s many pits were closed simply because they were 'uneconomic'. This is shown by fig. 3.4 which indicates that the reduced frequencies in the distribution of miners was in the low-OMS pits (the shaded area). In the 1970s 'exhaustion' has again been the sole reason for closure.

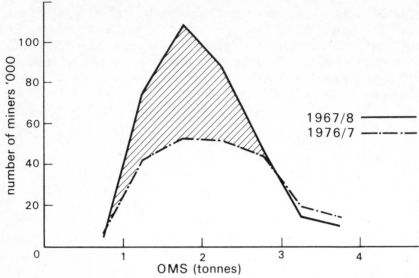

FIG. 3.4:   Distribution of miners by productivity, 1967/68 and 1976/77

Source: UK Digest of Energy Statistics

The second cause of increased productivity is mechanisation. The percentage of total output from faces with power-loaders jumped from 5% in 1953 to 92% in 1969. This virtually exhausted the scope for further mechanisation of this kind though some advances in other directions have been possible – for example, in the use of self-advancing roof supports. Most of the increases in mechanisation have been at the face. Between 1958 and 1978 face productivity increased by 125%, compared with 45% elsewhere underground and 67% for surface workers. However, further face mechanisation may yield diminishing returns unless complementary inputs such as road space and shaft capacity are increased.

Not all technological progress has been embodied in new equipment. Advances in pit-layout and roof-control techniques, for instance, have raised productivity. Mines differ greatly in their operating conditions and there is now more awareness that the best-practice technique of production is often pit-specific. It is as if each plant in an industry adopts a unique technology comprising a specific combination of general machines.

The forces of productivity growth, concentration and mechanisation, have been constrained in various ways. In the first place there are several constraints associated with the labour force. The substantial outflow of workers which persisted for many years had two effects. First, the average age of miners rose and this allegedly hampered OMS growth, but stronger recruitment in recent years and the introduction of an early retirement scheme in 1977 have now caused the average age to fall. The proportion of workers under 40 years of age rose from 36% to 45% between 1971 and 1978 so this constraint no longer applies. Second, the image of the industry was, for many years, one of decline rather than opportunity. This occasionally made it difficult to recruit young men for training and led to shortages of labour at some high productivity pits. Absenteeism, which has always been high may have affected the growth in OMS. The absence rate grew steadily to about 18% in 1966 and has remained thereabouts ever since. It is widely agreed that a marked reduction in absenteeism could make a major contribution to higher efficiency though this would be a once-and-for-all gain rather than a continuing source of productivity growth.

The mechanisation brought productivity growth but adversely affected industrial relations. In former times one shift would cut the coal, the next would load it and the next would advance the props and prepare the face for the next cycle of operations. Continuous coal-winning became possible with mechanisation, but a double or treble-shifted face is not always a happy one and it is not surprising that whereas the average number of face shifts per day rose from 1.42 to 2.11 between 1957 and 1967, it fell back to 2.03 by 1977. In general, however, poor industrial relations were not a constraint during the main period of productivity growth of the 1960s. Indeed, NUM co-operation on the closure programme was quite exceptional. But this position changed dramatically in the 1970s and productivity suffered. These arguments about the relevance of industrial relations suggest that team production and morale effects are important aspects of the production function.

A quite different constraint on productivity growth is that which arises from the peculiar nature of the production function in mining. For a given mine, or system of mines, there are two reasons why productivity may fall. The first is the usual short-run diminishing returns to labour, assuming that the level of technical knowledge and quantity of capital are fixed. The second is that each further ton of coal produced is won from more remote or difficult faces. (In a seven and one-quarter hour shift men may spend as few as five hours at the face). This means that productivity in terms of coal at the pit-head must fall. Even if the rate of output were to fall this would be so, which means that some part of the increase in mechanisation is merely offsetting the inevitable fall in productivity.

Productivity growth is also constrained by the putty-clay nature of the production function. In an industry experiencing severe contraction there is little scope for building new 'factories' embodying current best-practice with respect to mine layouts. The industry is committed to previous layouts which often involve excessive distances or complex patterns of underground workings. These require greater manning and more maintenance and reduce productivity. This is why the present increase in capacity and the opening of new mines offer such hope for raising productivity.

The state of the product market may determine the vigour with which higher productivity is pursued, though this should not be relevant if there were wholehearted commitment to cost-minimisation. From 1947–57, when the demand for coal exceeded supply, there was little serious drive for concentration or mechanisation. This only came with the unfavourable change in the product market in the late 1950s. Productivity growth in that early period may also have been hampered, as Harlow (1977, pages 177 and 195) has argued, by the lack of a decision-making machinery capable of formulating and implementing the relevant concentration and mechanisation decisions.

It is difficult to assess the relative importance of concentration and mechanisation as sources of past productivity growth. (Some crude regression analysis was undertaken which suggested that concentration was the more important force). The fall in OMS in recent years indicates that the principal gains from concentration and mechanisation have been reaped and that the industrial relations constraint has become more binding. The prospects for further growth are therefore uncertain though the industry's future performance crucially depends upon it. The NCB's strategy is to rely on an incentive wage scheme to reverse the short-term decline in OMS, and to rely on the investment programme for longer-term gains in OMS.

3.4.3 Innovation

The NCB has an impressive innovation record. It has been a leader in the development of new machines and techniques to a surprisingly large degree given its size in the world coal industry. It has generally been quick to adopt best-practice techniques from abroad, where these are appropriate to the difficult UK conditions, and many machines, such as the early cutter-loaders and powered roof supports, have been developed by the NCB at its Mining Research and Development Establishment (MRDE) and its forerunners. There have been substantial sales of equipment to the USA and other countries where the longwall face system of mining is being increasingly used. The MRDE has also developed hydraulic transport of coal in pipes and pneumatic transport, where fine coal is pumped to the surface to increase the throughput of the main shaft. Computerised control systems for underground coal transport are also being developed successfully though more comprehensive automation, where there is remote control of a completely integrated system of underground operations, is still at the experimental stage.

Product innovations, which have largely been responses to

deteriorating market conditions, have been of two sorts. First, there has been fuel processing to provide smokeless fuels, and improved blending techniques to allow the use of poorer quality coals. Second, the NCB has been involved in the development of more efficient combustion systems and techniques for handling coal and ash. These innovations reduce both the price per therm and the unfavourable non-price attributes such as dirt and inconvenience.

In some longer-term developments such as the conversion of coal into SNG, liquid transport fuels, and chemical feedstocks, the NCB is a world leader. An interesting feature of these developments is the high degree of collaboration in R and D with other EEC countries (for which the ECSC gives grants) and with other industries such as equipment manufacturers, the British Gas Corporation and Shell Chemicals.

At present the conversion of coal to petrol or SNG is not economic. It will only become so if the production of North Sea oil and gas eventually declines and alters relative prices in favour of coal-based stocks. This is not likely to happen until the 1990s so coal conversion will probably first become economic in countries such as Australia, USA and South Africa where coal can be mined cheaply. These countries are therefore likely to have fully developed technologies before UK needs arise. Whether it will be better for the UK to pursue its own R and D or buy in technology from abroad will depend on the expected relative costs of each. The NCB has chosen the former because the estimated cost is small in relation to potential licence fees. It also enables the NCB to keep its options open. Many of the processes will be specific to UK conditions, so the lengthy induction period necessary if the NCB were to become an informed buyer and a successful adaptor of foreign technology, would be shortened by involvement in pilot plant work.

3.4.4 Labour

The accelerated closure of high-cost pits in order to improve productivity is limited by regional employment considerations. Direct incentives to labour are therefore currently being used. In December 1977 a pit-based incentive payment scheme was eventually agreed. In its first year this brought major increases in pay which outstripped the resulting gains in productivity. The NCB claims to be well satisfied but the long-term labour cost position is uncertain because there are considerable pressures for further major increases in miners' pay. The move to an incentive scheme was not surprising because the prevailing flat-rate payments system, which was introduced in 1966 as a replacement for the earlier piecework scheme, had had a lengthy life. Pay systems seldom have a life of more than about ten years; it is often a change in the pay system rather than the type of system *per se*, which affects productivity.

Coalmining in the UK, as in other countries, is a strike-prone industry. Miners have always played a notable part in the history of labour conflict in the UK and in the first two decades of nationalisation over half of all recorded stoppages were in the coal industry. After 1958 the number of disputes fell dramatically because of the fall in employment (workers in a declining industry are more prone to be on the defensive) and the abolition of piecework in the 1960s (which had been a major source of dispute). This quiet period was shattered by the national strikes of 1972 and 1974 in which the tonnage lost was as great as that in all other post-war years together. The significance of these disputes lies not only in their immediate economic and political consequences (the three-day week and the change of government) but also in the fact that they marked the end of the period of union acquiescence. These two strikes were caused primarily by the deterioration in miners' relative pay and meant that labour costs were under pressure at a critical time in the industry. The CEGB's confidence in the ability of coal to remain competitive was jeopardised. More recently industrial relations have improved but the traumata of 1972 and 1974 have not been entirely eradicated and resurgence of disputes has accompanied the new incentive scheme.

The substantial improvement in safety in mines has been greater than in other countries such as the USA where the industry is privately owned. But the industry still has to cope with past failure. There are 39 000 registered pneumoconiosis sufferers. An aid scheme has now been devised, but if the present industry has to bear the costs of cases which arose in a previous period when the industry was much larger, then present consumers are in effect subsidising those of the past. The government recognises that this should not be so and is likely to bear some of the financial cost.

3.5 GOVERNMENT POLICY

In that world much-loved by welfare theorists, where perfectly competitive conditions prevail and ignorance, uncertainty and externalities are absent, the price mechanism may be relied upon for an efficient allocation of resources and the government may concentrate on producing an equitable distribution of real income. In all essentials, however, this world fails to approximate reality and the case for government intervention is clear. The long lead times, substantial externalities, great uncertainty and risk, high degree of interdependence between the fuel industries and the importance of the energy sector for the rest of the economy make an energy policy essential.

The Department of Energy (1977, page 8) recently stated that 'the object of energy policy is to secure that the nation's needs for energy are met at the lowest cost in real resources, consistently with security and with environmental, social and other objectives'. As a long-run basis for determining the size and structure of the coal industry such a view, that the social opportunity costs of energy provision should be minimised, is entirely appropriate. Unfortunately, it has proved difficult to translate this broad aim into operational proposals with associated performance criteria. The chairman of the NCB, for example, still asks publicly 'How much "profit" are nationalised industries supposed to make?' (letter to *The Times*, 28 July 1978). The real problem is that of devising a means of handling both efficiency and distributional considerations. We cannot bypass the question of what is the appropriate institutional framework simply by assuming, as some economic analysis does, that decision-makers with the relevant knowledge, responsibility, and authority, do exist. Should the government take direct responsibility for social factors or should it operate via taxes and subsidies? This question is too large to be tackled here but it does require an answer. The government is now paying increasing attention to such matters.

At present the role of the government has been to try and co-ordinate the plans of different sectors of the fuel industry to ensure compatibility. It has recognised the essential role of coal in future energy supplies by declaring its support for the current investment programme. Without such a commitment by the government it is unlikely that such a major programme would have been undertaken so swiftly. The uncertainty associated with long-range demand and technology forecasts, the inflexibility of production and the likelihood that the industry will become a high-wage one, all suggest that moderation is required in the rate of expansion. Such a strategy of caution would be unlikely to result in under-capacity if it were allied with a policy of more emphasis on opencast mining as a means of meeting peaks in demand. The faster return on investment in opencast coal, because of the shorter lead times, would overcome some of the inflexibility of the deep-mined production. In effect, as Charlesworth and Gravelle (1978) have argued, the opencast coal could act as a buffer stock being stored underground.

3.6 CONCLUSION

The coal industry suffered a severe contraction in the 1960s but its prospects are now buoyant. There is a wide dispersion in pit productivities but the current investment is being directed mainly at the high productivity pits which have considerable potential to achieve even higher levels. In the investment programme there is then, a clear emphasis on efficiency and the projects have high expected rates of return. This is desirable because there are unmistakable signs that coal will soon become – and will then remain – a high-wage industry. Because labour costs are a high proportion of total costs this will reduce its competitiveness. We know, however, that the National Union of Mineworkers (which is strongly district-based) and the government both constrain the closure of low-productivity pits in depressed regions. Social obligations are important and the NCB itself has begun to move towards more subsidising of weaker pits by stronger ones by raising prices in low-cost Areas at a faster rate than those in high-cost Areas.

How exactly are these social and economic considerations to be handled? The issues are large and politically sensitive, but some clarification of the NCB–government relationship is necessary. Should it be 'arm's length' or close involvement? If the NCB's expenditures and receipts truly represented social costs and benefits, then it could be left free to make its own decisions and pursue commercial objectives. Through the market mechanism the industry would achieve its socially optimal size and structure. Perhaps the government could ensure this by appropriate taxes and subsidies. It has partially attempted this. Alternatively it could take direct responsibility for the social obligation and then compensate the industry. This commendable view is gaining wider acceptance.

NOTES TO CHAPTER 3

1. The coefficient of variation is the standard deviation divided by the mean. It allows us to compare the *relative* variability of distributions with different means.

2. The 1978 cross-Area coefficients of variation were earnings per manshift 0.02, OMS 0.20, costs per ton 0.19 and value of production (i.e. prices) 0.13. It should be emphasised that there are large variations *within* Areas.

3. I am grateful to the NCB for providing data and to Adrian Darnell for writing a computer programme which enabled me to draw fig. 3.2.

4. The National Board for Prices and Incomes (1970) calculated that in 1969–70 marginal resource costs were between 5 and 10% less than marginal accounting costs, depending on the assumptions made about re-employment rates of miners. The resource costs take account of the low social opportunity costs of employing miners in high-unemployment areas.

REFERENCES

Bates, R. and Fraser, N. (1974) *Investment Decisions in the Nationalised Fuel Industries*. London: Cambridge University Press.

Berkovitch, I. (1977) *Coal on the Switchback.* London: Allen and Unwin.
Charlesworth, G. and Gravelle, G. (1978) *The UK Coal Industry: Its Position in the Light of an Expected Energy Surplus in the 1980s.* Open University Energy Research Group. Mimeo.
Cheshire, J. H. and Buckley, C. M. (1976) 'Energy Use in UK Industry'. *Energy Policy* (September).
Cmnd 7131 (1978) *The Nationalised Industries.* London: HMSO.
Commission of the European Communities (1977) *25 Years of The Common Market in Coal. 1953–78.* Brussels: ECSC/EEC/EAEC.
Davison, D. J. (1977) 'Opencast Coal Mining in the UK and its Role in the Mining Industry'. *The Mining Engineer* 215–221 (November).
Deaton, A. S. (1975) 'The Measurement of Income and Price Elasticities'. *European Economic Review* (6), 261–273.
Department of Energy (1977) *Energy Policy Review.* Energy Paper no. 22. London: HMSO.
Harlow, C. (1977) *Innovation and Productivity under Nationalisation.* Political and Economic Planning. London: Allen and Unwin.
National Board for Prices and Incomes (1970) *Coal Prices.* Cmnd 4455. London: HMSO.
Posner, M. (1973) *Fuel Policy.* London: Macmillan.
Price Commission (1976) *The Distribution of Domestic Coal and Solid Smokeless Fuel.* Report no. 12. London: HMSO.
Price Commission (1978) *Margins of Coal Merchants in West Wales.* London: HMSO.
Sheriff, T. D. (1978) 'Medium Term Planning in UK Nationalised Industries'. *National Institute Economic Review* (84), 57–64.
Wigley, K. (1968) *The Demand for Fuel 1948–75.* Chapman and Hall for the Department of Applied Economics, University of Cambridge.

FURTHER READING

The most accessible sources of data are the NCB's annual *Report and Accounts* and *Statistical Tables*, the Department of Energy's *UK Digest of Energy Statistics* and *Energy Trends* and the *Monthly Digest of Statistics*. Useful additional references are

Cook, P. L. and Surrey, A. J. (1977) *Energy Policy.* London: Martin Robertson.
Kelly, D. M. and Forsyth, D. V. C. *eds.* (1969) *Studies in the British Coal Industry.* Oxford: Pergamon Press.
Ezra, D. (1978) *Coal and Energy.* London: Ernest Benn.
Jackson, M. P. (1974) *The Price of Coal.* London: Croom Helm.

4 Food manufacturing

P. Maunder

4.1 INTRODUCTION

Compared with many of the other industries examined in this book food manufacturing is a sector of the UK economy whose characteristics and problems have received very little academic study. The inevitable political interest in the availability and price of processed foods makes the dearth of published material on both food manufacturing companies and products all the more striking. Yet the value added to domestically produced and imported foods by food manufacturers and distributors has exceeded the value of food output from British farmers and overseas suppliers for much of the last twenty years. The disinclination by agricultural economists in the UK to interest themselves in the economics of food beyond the farm gate contrasts with the impressive collection of research studies made in the United States of the 'agri-business' sector of the economy.

There is not one food manufacturing industry but several, and they differ widely in terms of their capital intensity of production, variety of production and the nature of their markets. Any definition of the food manufacturing *sector* is therefore necessarily arbitrary. It is defined here in terms of eleven of the Minimum List Headings contained in Order III (Food, drink and tobacco) of the Standard Industrial Classification: 211–219 (grain milling; bread and flour confectionery; biscuits; bacon curing, meat and fish products; milk and milk products; sugar; cocoa, chocolate and sugar confectionery; fruit and vegetable products; animal and poultry foods), 221 (vegetable and animal oils and fats) and 229 (margarine and miscellaneous foods). These eleven industries contribute about 2% to the UK's gross domestic product and employ a similar proportion of the working population. They account for about one tenth of the gross output of all manufacturing industries.

Firms engaged in food processing are of course helping to satisfy one of man's basic needs. Because food is essential to life, household spending on most foods is relatively insensitive to price changes. Individual food product markets are large. Butter, tea, coffee and biscuits were all markets whose retail sales in 1977 exceeded £200m. Markets in which sales exceeded £100m included sugar, margarine and breakfast cereals.[1] But while these markets are big their annual real growth is small. Although household spending on food in the UK at current prices rose from £5485m in 1967 to £16 268m in 1977 (an increase of 196%) the volume of sales rose only marginally. Measured at 1975 constant prices the growth in total sales was less than 2% over this same period.[2] The cause of slowly rising food sales is 'the narrow capacity of the human stomach' (Smith, 1776, page 269). The data available from the annual reports of the National Food Survey (NFS) show that nearly half of all processed foodstuffs have a negative income elasticity of quantity purchased. Neither the country's population growth nor rising real incomes can promise buoyant market conditions. Consumers must replace fresh foods by those food-stuffs that have undergone some form of processing – for example, fresh fish by fish fingers or frozen cod steaks – if the sector is to expand. Food processors therefore are keen to develop new products which have a high added-value and in particular are appreciated by women who have jobs and who need to get meals quickly – in other words the so-called convenience foods. What constitutes convenience in a foodstuff is inevitably open to argument, but in 1978 two-thirds of total household spending on food involved some measure of pre-purchase processing by food manufacturers.

Demand for convenience foods, defined by the NFS as 'those processed foods for which the degree of preparation has been carried to an advanced stage by the manufacturer and which may be used as labour-saving alternatives to less highly processed products',[3] increased much faster than that for food as a whole until 1974. For example, NFS data indicate that while the volume of household spending per head on all foods in Great Britain rose little between 1963 and 1972, that on convenience foods jumped by one-fifth over the same period. Frozen foods provided the most dramatic rise in the volume of sales of all convenience foods, more than doubling over this same period. Between 1974 and 1976 only frozen foods maintained their rapid sales growth while, in real terms, sales of other conven-ience foods remained static, in common with all other household food spending. The 'trading-down' by consumers in response to the squeeze on real incomes in 1974 has thus further heightened the problems for manufacturers in expanding sales of processed foods.

The food manufacturing sector has become more closely tied to British agriculture in the last two decades. In 1972 the sector purchased nearly half of the total output of British agriculture compared with one-fifth in 1963 (Ashby, 1978, page 213). The competitive threat from imports is necessarily very weak in the case of fresh foods such as milk and eggs. But the markets for processed foods are not protected on grounds of perishability and thus this sector does have to face some international competition. Imports of manufactured foods still well exceed exports but there was a reduction in the absolute size of the trade deficit between 1968 and 1976. The size of the trade deficit as a proportion of the market for processed food fell from 21 to 14% between these two years (Ashby, page 215).

Britain's high level of apparent self-sufficiency in processed food, however, should be cautiously interpreted, because manufacturers are heavily dependent on imported raw materials. For example, a tin of baked beans includes cornflour and beans from North America and tomatoes from Italy as well as imported sugar and spices. As major buyers on world markets for their inputs, food manufacturers are inevitably affected by changes in commodity prices. For example, a rise in the price of imported wheat will in due course mean dearer flour for bread and cake manufacturers. Increased costs of animal feeding-stuffs will indirectly affect these same industries as the prices of eggs, milk and butter are adjusted upwards.

4.2 MARKET STRUCTURE

Firms engaged in food processing at the start of the present century were, relative to those in other manufacturing industries, typically very small concerns. For example, in 1905 there were only two food firms – Bovril and Huntley & Palmers – among the country's fifty largest industrial concerns (size is measured here by capital invested) (Lawrence, 1976, page 200). The food manufacturer at this time generally supplied a product to the specification of a wholesaler who held the balance of power over both this supplier and his own customers who were mainly one-shop independent grocers. The balance of power however began to swing towards the food processors in the inter-war period following the development of pre-packaged branded products supported by national advertising. The concentration of production was, however, still generally low in the inter-war years. The 1935 Census of Production indicated few instances in the food trades where the three largest firms accounted for 70% or more of employment (Leak and Maizels, 1945). The 1951 Census of Production showed that there had been few marked changes in the concentration of production between 1935 and 1951. Indeed there was only one food industry – ice-cream – which had become more concentrated.

There was not much change in the market structure of the industries in the early 1950s while trading in food products remained subject to wartime-imposed government controls. It was not until 1953 that government purchasing of cereals and animal feedstuffs ended. In the following year private trading in oils and meat products was resumed. Consumer rationing and price controls on both chocolate and sweet confectionery and sugar ended in 1953. A year later rationing of butter, margarine, cheese and cooking fats ceased, although in the case of meat and bacon, a free market did not emerge until mid-1955.

4.2.1 Increasing concentration and diversification

The lifting of wartime controls intensified further the competitive pressures in the food industry which had already been generated by the growth in supermarkets, the development of private brands and demise of resale price maintenance. The 1956 Restrictive Trade Practices Act also stimulated competition, particularly in grain milling, baking, sugar, butter and cheese. The growing bargaining power of the multiple food retailers from the mid-1950s onwards further increased the pressures on food manufacturers. Whereas in 1960, 500 multiple buying points (head offices) accounted for 27.9% of grocery turnover, ten years later just 202 buying points accounted for 42% of turnover.[4] Smaller manufacturers lacking a strong brand name were taken over by others or ceased to trade.

In view of the increase in competition, it is hardly surprising to find that in the 1960s there was a notably large fall in the number of food manufacturing firms compared with all manufacturing industry. Census of Production data show that between 1958 and 1972 the number of food enterprises fell by 40%.

In the case of the bread industry the relaxation of government controls on the importation of grain in 1953 quickly precipitated a profound change in the industry's market structure. Allied Bakeries, the largest bakery concern, began importing flour from Canada and this prompted Spillers and Ranks, the leading milling firms, to integrate vertically into baking so as to ensure continued outlets for their flour. Competition among these three concerns to buy up bakeries was very keen after 1953 and the number of bakery enterprises fell rapidly during the next decade: by 1963 their total number was only half that in 1958. Allied Bakeries also acquired milling concerns in the UK so that it no longer needed to buy flour supplies from Spillers and Ranks. The rapid creation of three integrated milling–baking concerns after 1953 thus transformed the structure of both these industries. In 1962 Ranks extended its flour milling interests by acquiring Hovis McDougall, which was itself a recent merger of two formerly independent concerns, each of which had a long tradition for milling particular types of flour.

In the case of biscuits and packaged cakes we find that membership of the relevant trade association, the Cake and Biscuit Alliance, fell from 286 members in 1954/55 to just 86 by 1971/72. Facing increasingly competitive trading conditions many firms that had only a very small interest in cakes and biscuits ceased manufacturing for this market. The 1960s also saw the membership of the Cocoa, Chocolate and Confectionery Alliance fall from 500 to 225 companies. Competitive pressures also affected many of the long-established traditional parts of the industry. For example, the thirty or so small privately-owned pickling businesses located in and around Newcastle-upon-Tyne and Hull in the mid-1950s found that their quality and brand image were inadequate to withstand the growing competitiveness in their market. By 1978 all except three of these firms had ceased production.[5]

Faced with the growing concentration of buying power from retail chains such as Sainsbury and Tesco, the voluntary buying groups such as VG and Spar and the wholesale cash-and-carry warehouses, a number of leading food manufacturers tried in the late 1960s to extend their product range. The aim of diversification was mainly achieved by takeovers. For example, Cerebos diversified by acquiring A & R Scott (porridge oats), pet foods (Stamina Foods), meat pastes (Brand & Co. and J & A Sharwood) and suet (Hugon & Co.) as well as into the animal feeds industry. The Bibby Group, which had large interests in this last named industry, diversified into foods for human consumption – for example, canned fish and fruit – by acquiring Princes Foods in 1968. In the same year Liebig's Extract of Meat merged with Brooke Bond. Spillers extended their product range into meat processing with the takeovers of Tyne Brand Products in 1967 and of Meade Lonsdale two years later. Schweppes acquired Moorhouses, Hartleys and Chivers – all of which produced jams, jellies and preserves – and also Typhoo Tea. In 1969 it merged with Cadbury. HP Sauce, National Canning (better known for their brand name of Smedleys) and the Ross Group were all acquired between 1967 and 1969 by Imperial Tobacco which already had a stake in the food industry through Golden Wonder potato crisps. All the firms just cited that were taken over had leading brands in their particular sections of the food industry. The value placed by the bidders on these brands was capitalised in the prices paid for them – e.g. Schweppes's purchase of Typhoo Tea in 1968 cost £45m, of which £31m represented the 'goodwill' the name bore.

The rapid pace of takeover activity led one investment analyst to suggest that food processors bought whichever firms were available for sale, irrespective of the products they manufactured, rather than only those that really fitted in with their true company interests (Capel, 1970). This does not in retrospect seem too extreme a judgement. Indeed, it is supported by the evidence of companies disposing of recently acquired firms. In 1969 Allied Suppliers sold Richmond Sausage to Unilever. In the same year Ranks Hovis McDougall (RHM) and the newly-merged Brooke Bond Liebig sold their joint crisps subsidiary, Chipmunk Ltd, to Golden Wonder, and British–American Tobacco sold Tonibell Manufacturing, an ice-cream supplier, to J. Lyons, having owned the company for just five years. Then, in early 1970 Associated British Foods (ABF) sold Allied Farm Foods ('Buxted' chicken) to Imperial Tobacco; they had purchased this company only fifteen months previously.

The proposition that previous acquisitions and attempts at diversification now required a 'sorting-out' strategy by the major food firms also draws support from the consolidations among the leading firms themselves. Cadbury–Schweppes and United Biscuits merged their packaged cake interests to form McVitie and Cadbury Cakes in 1971. Neither firm had found their recent investment in cakes very profitable because of slower growth of this market than had seemed likely in the mid-1960s. In the same year the flour milling and baking interests of Spillers, J. Lyons and the CWS were amalgamated to give the new group, Spillers–French, one-fifth of the bread market. A year later Spillers acquired the pet food interests of RHM and in the biscuit industry United Biscuits consolidated its position as market leader by purchasing the biscuit interests of Cavenham Foods.

These mergers contributed to an increase in the concentration of production in many individual food product markets. In most markets, the level of concentration was already high. In 1970 a government list of markets in which an individual firm accounted for more than half of output involved seven food markets.[6] In 1973 a further list of markets in which a single firm was thought to account for between a quarter and a third of production was prepared. This included no less than fifteen food items.[7] Table 4.1 shows the level of concentration (in 1977) in several of these markets.

At the aggregate level, food manufacturing firms are now strongly represented in the list of Britain's biggest firms. There are eleven companies with substantial food manufacturing interests among the fifty largest firms as measured by sales. One-fifth of the largest 100 are firms with important food manufacturing interests.[8]

The development of large diversified food companies cannot be disassociated from the continued growth in the past decade of multiples – led by Sainsbury and Tesco – in the retail grocery trade at the expense of small independent grocers. Whereas in 1970 some 650 buying points dealt with 80% of retail sales, by 1977 nearly the same proportion of sales (77%) was accounted for by only 308 buying points (the 6 largest multiples' head offices, 52 smaller multiples, 44 symbol buying groups and 206 co-operative societies).[9]

The many mergers amongst food processing firms during the past two decades have been accompanied by a growth in plant size. Whilst average numbers employed per establishment in manufacturing as a whole remained static between 1958 and 1972 at around eighty-six persons, in food manufacturing there was a marked jump of 63% during this period. This was initially due to the merger activity in the bread industry, but the figure continued to rise until 1972 when it reached a level of some 124 employees (Ashby, pages 216–217). By 1972 average sales per establishment in food manufacturing was £1.29m, twice that in manufacturing generally. Unfortunately, Census of Production data after 1972 concerning both sales and average numbers employed per establishment are not readily comparable with those just cited. However it would appear that in 1975 the average sales per establishment in food manufacturing was still double that for all manufacturing industry. For both the food manufacturing sector and all manufacturing industry average numbers per establishment showed a fall between 1973 and 1975, but the mean size of plant in food processing in 1975 remained about 40% larger than that for all manufacturing industry.

As table 4.1 shows, foreign-owned firms, especially American ones, are strongly represented amongst Britain's leading food manufacturers. Some have been long-established in certain markets. For example, Heinz quickly became the market leader in soups after introducing its first range in 1930 (Walshe, 1974, page 45). Quaker Oats Company Ltd began production in the UK in 1920, Shredded Wheat (now Nabisco Ltd) in 1925 and Kellogg in 1938. General Foods Corporation first produced 'Maxwell House' coffee in the UK in 1956, but the company had owned a British subsidiary, Alfred Bird & Sons, to market imported foods since 1947.

4.2.2 Economies of scale and barriers to entry

Data on the nature of scale economies in food production are very sparse. What are available suggest that in most product markets the minimum efficient plant size usually accounts for a low proportion of industry sales. In the case of plant bread the proportion was estimated by the Monopolies Commission at 0.5% of the market: the same source suggested a rather higher figure – 2% – in the case of flour (Monopolies Commission, 1977a). Scale economies seem to be somewhat more important in potato crisp manufacture where a minimum efficient sized plant accounts for about 10% of industry sales (Bevan, 1974). But even if this latter figure is indicative of the extent of scale economies in other food processing industries it does seem doubtful whether high concentration of food processing is really required in order to realise scale economies, at least in respect of production.

Scale economies in production are therefore unlikely to represent a

TABLE 4.1: **Major firms in some food markets, 1977**

Market	Size of retail market (£m)	Leading companies	% Market share
Bread	750	Ranks Hovis McDougall	27
		Associated British Foods	26
		Spillers–French	23
Frozen food	533	Unilever (Birds Eye)	32
		Findus	11
		Ross	11
Biscuits	470	United Biscuits	40
		Associated Biscuits	20
Packaged cakes	280	Lyons–Hales	20
	(1976)	United Biscuits–Cadbury	17
		Spillers	9
		Own label	25
Potato crisps	200	Imperial Tobacco (Golden Wonder)	29
		General Mills* (Smiths)	23
		Walkers	20
Tea	200	Brooke Bond	37
	(1976)	Lyons Tetley	18
		Cadbury–Schweppes (Typhoo)	16
Canned fruit	150	Del Monte Foods*	39
	(1976)	Libby, McNeill & Libby*	20
Breakfast cereals (ready-to-eat)	125	Kellogg*	51
		Weetabix	21
		National Biscuit (Nabisco)*	10
		Quaker Oats*	4
Baked beans	100 (1976)	Heinz*	64
Canned soup	85	Heinz*	64
	(1976)	Crosse & Blackwell (Nestlé)†	17
		Campbells*	17
Condensed milk	40	Carnation Foods*	54
	(1976)	Nestlé†	17

Source: R. A. Critchley *ed. MGN Marketing Manual of the UK 1978.* Mirror Group Newspapers Ltd, 1978.
The precise levels of market shares given in the table must be treated with caution as they are based on the proportion of housewives using the named manufacturer's products 'only or most often' as determined by the British Market Research Bureau's self-completion Target Group Index Survey, rather than on a volume or value share of the market.
Notes: *An American-owned subsidiary.
†Parent company is Nestlé Alimentana, S.A. Switzerland.

significant barrier to entry. Problems in winning shelf space in supermarkets and the level of marketing expenses incurred in support of
new brands however present more formidable problems for entrants to
many food markets. There is, moreover, the need for a new entrant to
find a novel product so as to challenge existing brands. The high
failure of new product development makes this issue itself a strong
deterrent for potential competitors. Thus the Monopolies Commission regarded the risks of product development and cost of marketing
new brands to be 'substantial' barriers to entry into breakfast cereals
(Monopolies Commission, 1973, page 26).

Where entry involving nationally branded goods does occur it is, as
the earlier discussion has indicated, usually by established rather than
new firms. Only the former can finance the often high costs of new
plant and of the promotion and marketing of a new brand. For
example, the expansion of Golden Wonder crisps from being a small
Scottish-based firm to the second largest national concern has been
estimated to have cost Imperial Tobacco £10m between 1961 and 1965
(Bevan, page 292). Bovril reportedly spent £3m in marketing expenses
in addition to some £2.5m in plant and machinery in developing a
granulated meat cube to challenge Oxo's domination of the meat and
vegetable extract market in 1977.[10] Entry into food manufacturing is
indeed virtually synonymous with diversification by existing firms.
Two recent examples further illustrate this point. Both Green Giant,
well-established in the canned vegetable market, and Kellogg decided
in 1978 to enter the retail frozen food market: the first by internal
expansion, the second through acquisition. Kellogg's extension of its
product range by takeover was more typical of how other food
manufacturers have tried to achieve the goal of diversification. It is
surely significant that one is hard placed to name even one new food
manufacturer dependent on a national selling leading brand that has
emerged in the 1970s in any of the major food markets. The growth of
Don Miller's Hot Bread Kitchens[11] since 1973 hardly qualifies in view
of its link with a flour supplier, its limited national coverage and the
restricted availability of the firm's product through its own shops: even
here what is pertinent is the relatively low entry barrier. Entry into the
bread industry in the form of in-store bakeries involves capital costs of
less than £20 000[12] and promotional costs are minimal.

The difficulties of entry are much eased when firms supply products
for sale by a retail chain under the latter's own name or for the institutional (catering) market. In either case, they can avoid the extensive
advertising and marketing costs associated with brand names. Thus
Northray Farm Products Ltd was formed in the 1950s by two
Lincolnshire farmers to freeze their own products, and it quickly
developed a significant market share in own label frozen peas. Romix
Foods began supplying a retail chain with own label pastry mixes

using two machines together costing less than £20 in 1969.[13] The frozen food industry is an example of how entry is not at all difficult for firms keen to supply the catering and own label market. Birds Eye's extensive retail sales have rather hidden the fact that many small specialist companies have entered this market and have successfully exploited the potential in serving the rapidly growing number of freezer centres.

Exit may also occur. Even large food firms may find that despite heavy promotional expenditure they have developed an inadequate brand image and have only a low market share. Thus to take just two examples, Walls pulled out of the yogurt market in 1970 and Unigate from canned puddings in 1978. Both did so having incurred heavy losses in unsuccessful attempts to compete with market leaders in these products.

We now turn to a fuller discussion of the character of competition in the food processing industries.

4.3 MARKET BEHAVIOUR

Reference has already been made above to the changing balance of power between food manufacturers and food retailers in the post-war period. It has been shown that both these stages in the food marketing chains have become more concentrated in character so that situations of bilateral oligopoly have developed in most individual food markets. The expansion of the multiple food retailers at the expense of independent and co-operative food stores – an expansion which was based on the self-service and supermarket style of selling – provided the basis for these food chains to negotiate and secure more advantageous terms from food processors. These terms include not only higher trade discounts off published prices but also cash payments in support of in-store promotional activity. This bargaining between food processors and retailers or 'vertical conflict' provides the essence of competitive pressures facing food manufacturers (Palamountain, 1955). The magnitude of the trading deals secured by the multiple retail chains is rarely made known but in recent times it has caused small independent retailers to call for trading terms offered by food processors to be strictly based on size of orders and not on the bargaining power of buyers. The level of discounts conceded by plant bread manufacturers in recent years have been of particular importance concerning the industry's structure. Excess capacity in the bread industry, due to falling consumption per head, has greatly increased the bargaining power of the leading food retailers and contributed to exit from the industry. The third biggest plant bread producer, Spillers–French, was particularly vulnerable because unlike RHM or ABF, both of which owned some shops, it owned very few retail outlets. Moreover, for historical reasons, it also had a relatively higher cost structure compared with its two rivals. It was therefore unable to survive a period of keen discount competition and was forced, after making heavy losses, to cease baking in 1978.

Food manufacturers have also had to face another consequence of the movement of power in favour of large food distributors: the development of own label brands of the multiple food retailers. The enthusiasm for private brands shown, in particular, by the fast expanding Sainsbury, Tesco and Fine Fare chains, is readily understandable because overall, private brands have a price differential of 10% or more over the leading national brands. This price advantage reflects the economies obtained by the retailers in marketing and distribution costs in respect of private brands.

The attitude of food processors towards own label products during the past two decades has in general been unenthusiastic. It is true that the supply of own label foodstuffs offers the opportunity to use spare capacity and to obtain the benefit of longer production runs. However, food manufacturers have also felt own label production discourages new product development. They have claimed that low profit margins necessarily limit research effort and that even in cases where manufacturers introduce a superior branded product, they are unable to recoup heavy development costs and to enjoy ultimately an acceptable return on investment incurred.

This argument against own labels is in fact rarely substantiated by food manufacturers, and the alleged highly superior quality of their national brands is debatable. The so-called 'parasitic' effect of own brands on innovation is indeed suspect. For one thing, some of the takeovers in the late 1960s were clearly made to give the large acquiring firms a stake in own label production, e.g. United Biscuits' purchase of Meredith and Drew which specialised in own label potato crisps and biscuits. The same motive explained Schweppes's acquisition of Moorhouse who produced own label jam. Indeed some manufacturers have subsidiaries specialising in this trade. These latter include Sol Café and SFK (owned by J. Lyons) and Goldhanger (owned by Express Dairy).

Many food manufacturers, however seem reluctant to devote more than about one-fifth of capacity to own label products. Some firms such as Cadbury and Birds Eye (Unilever), resisted the trend towards own label production for many years, but gradually the number of leading manufacturers opposed to it has dwindled. Own label products now have a significant share (about one-third) of some food markets such as butter, fruit squashes, instant coffee, tea bags, jam and evaporated milk. However, fears expressed by food manufacturers in the early 1970s that the continuing growth in own labels (made by themselves!) would threaten the market position of all their national brands seem to have been premature. Overall, own label products have not risen much above one-quarter of total grocery sales, which is a share similar to that in the United States market. Nevertheless, own label products clearly represent an important aspect of the competitive pressures in this sector of the economy.

'Horizontal conflict' among food processors, to use Palamountain's terminology, manifests itself in a struggle for shelf space in retail outlets. Competition among the leading manufacturers has resulted over time in the minor, seemingly less popular, brands being displaced. For example, the total number of biscuit and packaged cake lines has fallen substantially. The cake range of Huntley & Palmers included eleven varieties in 1963: by 1970 it only produced three types of cake. The total number of biscuit brands fell from some 900 in 1967 to 800 in 1974.[14]

Competition among food manufacturers, and the limited possibilities for expanding the market overall, emphasise the crucial role of new product development. Coffee creamers, soya meals, snack soups, cheesecake, muesli and frozen bakery goods are but a small selection of recent new food products. However, the returns to such development are very uncertain because new products have a high failure rate: up to 60% of new products are withdrawn from sale within five years. One-third of new brands have a life of less than two years (Kraushar, Andrews & Eassie, 1976).

Sums expended by food manufacturers on advertising have risen steadily. In 1977 media expenditure on all food (fresh and processed) was £143m (Media Expenditure Analysis Ltd, 1977), of which about £137m involved the promotion of manufactured foodstuffs. Total advertising expenditure on all food products appears to exceed the sums expended on other individual household goods such as toiletries and cosmetics or drink.

Expenditure in absolute terms has been greatest in the case of chocolate confectionery, breakfast cereals, margarine and biscuit manufacturers. These food manufacturers resort to advertising to promote their new products which are introduced to try and increase sales above the generally static level of sales in these industries. Meanwhile, sales of long-established brand names are believed to be sensitive to the degree of advertising support and require continued promotion. (See, for example, Wright, 1969).

The enthusiasm with which chocolate and sugar confectionery firms, to take just one example, spend sums equivalent to about 10% of consumer sales is not hard to appreciate. The UK already has the highest per capita consumption in the world. The falling birth-rate and growing public concern over dental health and child obesity are likely to reduce still further the industry's present slow rate of growth in sales. Intense marketing support is thus seen as the only way of maintaining sales volume. Given the importance of impulse purchasing of sweets, claimed to account for two-thirds of sales, manufacturers are willing to commit large sums on television commercials, consumer and trade promotions.

But, with all this said, the oligopolistic character of the confectionery (and other food industries) itself favours non-price competition. As the Monopolies Commission declared in its report on breakfast cereals, 'the reluctance to compete in price ... is largely attributed to the structure of the industry' (Monopolies Commission, 1973, page 25).

The foregoing discussion indicates that the growing concentration of production in particular sections of food processing has not necessarily implied that competitive pressures are weak in this sector of the economy. Potato crisps illustrate this point. There were some 800 crisp manufacturers shortly after the war. But by 1960, Smiths accounted for 65% of industry sales. However, it paid the price for a complacent attitude to the market's development and innovation. Its market share was halved in three years as a result of very keen competition not only from Golden Wonder and Walkers in the crisp market but also from other suppliers of packeted snacks (Bevan, 1974).

The oligopolistic character of most food markets has led to some firms becoming price leaders. ABF in bread, Kellogg in breakfast cereals, Brooke Bond in tea and Van den Berghs & Jurgens (a subsidiary of Unilever) in margarine seem to exert a significant influence on pricing policy in their respective industries (Mitchell, 1972). Brooke Bond's rise to price leadership in the tea market is particularly interesting. Its market share rose from 23 to 43% between 1954 and 1970 and was achieved by 'an overall combination of skilful marketing techniques' (National Board for Prices and Incomes (NBPI), 1970c, page 16). The NBPI showed that the company was not the lowest cost supplier among the four leading tea firms but its rivals claimed that they could not undercut Brooke Bond's prices because consumers would then regard their tea as inferior.

4.4 MARKET PERFORMANCE

The source material available for appraising the market performance of the food processing sector of the UK economy is extremely limited, especially if we ignore the assessments by the Monopolies Commission (which has reported on flour milling and bread, tea, baby foods and breakfast cereals) and the NBPI (which has reported on bread and flour, sweet confectionery, edible fats, tea and ice-cream). The next section on public policy reviews the conclusions reached by both these two bodies from their study of particular food industries. The focus of attention here now is rather more at the macro level and considers the sector's profitability, productivity in factor use and technical progress.

Since 1960 the rate of return on capital, measured at replacement cost, in food manufacturing has almost invariably been above the average for all manufacturing industry as table 4.2 shows. However,

TABLE 4.2: Rate of return on capital employed by large listed companies in manufacturing industry

Year	Food manufacturing At replacement cost including/excluding stock appreciation		All manufacturing industry At replacement cost including/excluding stock appreciation	
1960	15.8	16.0	14.2	13.7
1961	14.8	14.3	11.9	11.4
1962	14.9	14.7	10.5	10.3
1963	15.9	14.3	11.8	11.1
1964	14.7	15.2	12.9	12.0
1965	14.7	15.1	12.0	11.0
1966	12.0	11.4	10.1	9.2
1967	12.6	11.6	10.2	9.6
1968	12.5	10.5	11.4	9.9
1969	10.6	9.2	10.5	8.7
1970	9.3	6.5	9.0	6.8
1971	9.3	6.6	9.3	7.2
1972	12.2	9.8	11.1	8.9
1973	11.9	1.3	12.9	7.1
1974	11.6	3.5	12.0	3.5
1975	10.7	5.5	8.5	2.6
1976	12.7	5.7	10.8	4.6

Source: Monopolies and Mergers Commission Accountancy Staff (private communication); 'Companies' rate of return on capital employed, 1960–1976'. *Trade and Industry*, 16 September 1977, page 520.

both series have exhibited a downward trend. The falling level of profitability has caused great concern in the food manufacturing sector. This concern was particularly acute in 1973 when profits, after allowing for stock appreciation, fell to a very low level. Moreover, the sector's cash flow situation deteriorated sharply. For a sample of thirty large manufacturers, which between them accounted for one-third of total industry sales, a positive cash flow of £50m in 1971 became a negative one of £70m in 1973.[15] The liquidity problems of food manufacturers became so serious that dire warnings were offered by many major companies about long-term prospects concerning investment and new product development. The source of the problem was the operation of government price_policies. There was a real difficulty for the major firms in achieving a speedy adjustment in product prices during a period of rising world commodity prices when price rises had to be approved by the Price Commission.

The alleged harm to the industry's future market performance stemming from its reduced profitability is not easy to assess. In particular, the argument that lower profits have resulted in an inadequate rate of capital investment seems less persuasive in the light of the results of a recent study of the matter. But before discussing this study the basic issue of low profitability warrants special attention in two food industries.

Profitability has been very low for many years in both bacon curing and bread manufacture. In the case of bacon keen competition from Danish curers, who have built up a reputation for quality for a low value-added product and who have benefited from government subsidies, has been at the heart of the problem for British bacon curers. In bread, the leading firms have endlessly pleaded the problem of government interference which they see as arising from the politically sensitive nature of their activities. However, for the integrated concerns low profits on bread-making have invariably been offset by high profits on flour milling. In fact excess capacity exists in both of these industries, and there has been an insufficient depletion of resources in response to market pressures.

Compared with all manufacturing industry the food industries have become relatively more capital-intensive during the past two decades. By 1976 capital expenditure as a percentage of gross output had risen 31% above its 1958 level compared with a rise of 28% over the same period for all manufacturing industry (Ashby, page 218). However, studies of the productivity of capital suggest that it has fallen rather sharply. One estimate is a fall in output per unit of capital of nearly 30% between 1960 and 1976 compared with a fall of 18% for all manufacturing industry (Ashby, page 219). A separate calculation of the change in total factor productivity between 1960 and 1975 has also indicated that productivity growth in this sector was below that for manufacturing as a whole (Food and Drink Manufacturing EDC, 1978). Output of food manufacturing grew less rapidly than all manufacturing over this fifteen-year period but was not accompanied by a lower rate of growth of capital stock or a larger reduction in labour inputs. It is difficult to resist the conclusion that, overall, there has been over-investment in the food manufacturing sector.

International comparisons are of course difficult in this area, but it is worth noting that in both the US and West Germany labour productivity between 1970 and 1975 rose not only faster but with much less extra investment than in the UK. The growth of output per head in food manufacturing in the US and West Germany between 1968 and 1975 was, respectively, 25 and 37%, compared with 12% in the UK. Yet in both these two countries investment as a per cent of value added was markedly lower (Food and Drink Manufacturing EDC, 1978). These figures emphasise the need for a more productive use of labour and capital inputs by food manufacturers if they are to improve their international competitiveness.

While the food manufacturing sector may not be as science-based as the electronics or chemical industries, new product development increasingly involves the application of advances in food chemistry and microbiology. Two examples are the development of textured vegetable proteins based on soyabeans and the use of enzymes to produce high-fructose corn syrup. Processed foods contain additives which control the texture, colour and flavour of products and extend their shelf-life. The increasing use of artificial sweeteners, anti-oxidants, emulsifiers and stabilisers is reinforcing the importance of technical issues.

The innovative character of this sector has been previously indicated. Mergers among leading food firms in the late 1960s were frequently justified on the grounds that only big firms could survive in increasingly competitive world markets. As the size of Britain's leading food firms appear easily large enough to exhaust the benefits of plant economies of scale, it is apposite to consider whether large firms have a faster rate of innovation than small firms.

It is clear that most of the innovations have come from the large firms. The Bolton Committee's research on this sector indicated that firms with more than one thousand employees accounted for three-quarters of the thirty-eight important innovations introduced in this sector in the period 1945–70 (Freeman, 1971, page 12). The share of innovations accounted for by firms employing fewer than 200 employees was much less than their share of net output. Their three innovations, which included the important advance of frozen broilers, represented just 8% of the total number of significant innovations in the industry, compared with their 16% share of the industry's net output.

Food research is carried out not only by individual companies but in co-operative industrial research associations, government research institutes and universities.[16] In fact the size of the industry's R and D effort is difficult to establish. There is a real lack of information available but recently the industry's Economic Development Committee (EDC) considered the level of spending to be low relative to other UK industries and also to food industries in other countries.[17]

The British Baking Industries Research Association has developed one of the industry's more significant technical advances: the Chorleywood Bread Process. This process was quickly adopted in the bread industry: within six years of its publication, it was used to produce three-quarters of the bread made in plant bakeries. As we have seen innovative activity is inevitably risky. Consequently, some new processing techniques have so far failed to realise expectations. For example, accelerated freeze-drying has not had the general applicability that at first seemed likely, and has only been extensively used for coffee.

As regards the industry's technical progressiveness, the Director of the British Food Manufacturing Industries Research Association stated in 1968 that 'food processing is one of the few industries in the UK where there is no technological gap *vis-à-vis* the US'.[18] Whether this bold assessment was indeed correct is, of course, difficult to say but on one recent, albeit crude, test the food processing sector's present competitiveness in a dynamic sense has seemed suspect. It was strongly expected in the early 1970s that the food manufacturing sector would benefit greatly from British entry into the EEC. This was because of the widely-held belief in the greater efficiency and technical 'know-how' of British firms compared with their European counterparts. In fact, with some notable exceptions such as biscuits, the rise in exports of processed foods has been below expectations. Moreover foreign direct investment by food manufacturers – an alternative to exporting – has not increased substantially since entry into the EEC. A recent study of the impact of the EEC on this sector prompted the comment that 'We can no longer pretend that the UK food industry is more expert at marketing than the continental EEC food industry' (Nicholls, 1978, page 330). Its conclusion was that 'the UK food industry has largely or in some cases completely lost its competitive edge, as against the EEC food companies during the last five years. Just prior to accession there appeared to be an enormous number of opportunities for the UK food industry to seize; many of those opportunities have now evaporated' (*ibid.*).

4.5 PUBLIC POLICY

Producing goods essential to life has ensured that the food manufacturing industries have always been subject to close scrutiny in political quarters. Thus legislation to protect the interests of consumers when buying food has a long history. The first Weights and Measures Act was passed in 1878.) The 1955 Food and Drugs Act still provides the basis for government regulations concerning the composition and nutritional quality of food as well as its description. While the aims sought by such Acts do not involve political controversy it is important that such regulations should not be so detailed and slow to adapt that they preclude advantageous substitution of ingredients by food manufacturers. During the 1970s the growing demand for consumer legislation and British entry into the EEC have emphasised the importance of these technical matters. This can be briefly indicated by reference to the Food Standards Committee.

Established in 1947 to advise the government in drawing up regulations on the composition of food, this body was probably not well-known until the publication of its reports on date marking in 1971 and 1972 and on novel proteins in 1975. The FSC recommended that manufacturers of 'short-life' foods should show a 'sell-by' date on their products and that long-life foods should exhibit a date of manufacture. The merits of open dating had of course been much discussed throughout the food industry and the practice was the subject of favourable prompting by the press. Harmonisation of food legislation within the EEC has been a subject of concern for processing firms and the government. Thus in 1977 the Government supported the sector's concern over proposals by the EEC Commission that only products containing dairy fats should be called 'cream'. One only has to consider British ice-cream and cream cracker biscuits to realise that national traditions sometimes need protection!

We now turn to the impact of government policies since 1945 on the behaviour of food processing firms. As we have seen, wartime controls on the supply of ingredients and packaging materials, and on production were generally not lifted until 1952/53. Political concern over the rise in food prices that would result from the expected post-war shortages and the outbreak of the Korean war explains the delay in dismantling these regulations. This concern was particularly well illustrated in the bread industry where removal of price control was delayed until September 1956. The operation of competition policies and prices and incomes policies since 1956 have continued to manifest the sensitivity of successive governments to rising food prices. These policies are now briefly summarised.

4.5.1 Competition policy

In many of the food processing industries firms agreed after 1945 to strong restraints on competitive behaviour. Analysis of the registered agreements following the passing of the 1956 Restrictive Trade Practices Act shows that in the grain milling, baking and flour confectionery, biscuits, sugar, butter and cheese sections of the industry price competition was effectively minimal (Cuthbert and Black, 1959).

Those firms which were parties to price agreements and which have tried to justify them have not found support in the Restrictive Practices Court. For example, plant bakers in both England and Wales and Scotland – whose agreements were among the first heard in the Restrictive Practices Court – were unsuccessful in defending their agreements.

The Restrictive Practices Court has also had responsibility for hearing applications for exemption from the ban on resale price maintenance under the 1964 Resale Prices Act. For many food grocery products resale price maintenance had in fact largely collapsed by 1960, partly as a result of the ending of the collective enforcement of the practice under section 24 of the 1956 Restrictive Trade Practices Act. A further important factor in its demise was the growth in competitive pressures both among food manufacturing firms themselves and between the latter as a group and the rapidly growing food retailing chains as discussed previously. Even so at the time of the passing of the Act profit margins for retailers continued to be fixed by manufacturers of bread, breakfast cereals, confectionery and certain preserves. The first case heard in the Court related to chocolate and sugar confectionery. After a lengthy hearing the Court ruled in 1967 that the manufacturers had failed to prove their case for exemption from the Act. This decision undoubtedly led many other industries to abandon their plans for justifying resale price maintenance in the Court.

The concentration of production in certain individual food markets has been sufficiently high to make several food manufacturing firms potential references to the Monopolies Commission under the terms of the 1948 Monopolies and Restrictive Practices Act. The fact that hardly any firms were passed to the Commission for study until 1970 lends support for the view that successive governments believed that competitive conditions were reasonably adequate to maintain acceptable levels of market performance by the constituent units of those industries (Maunder, 1970, page 458).

Since 1970, however, the Monopolies Commission has had to devote much more time to particular food processing industries and the greater willingness of governments to make such references raises the question whether the above proposition remains true. If the more frequent reference of food processing industries to the Commission is not to be taken as an indication of doubts on the part of the government about competitive behaviour, then one has to look to the political dimension as prompting the references. This does, therefore, make the timing of references to the Commission worthy of close attention. For example, it may be significant that at a time of rising world tea prices in 1956 the government was prompted to refer the tea trade to the Commission. The reference was described as 'a most dubious sop to vociferous housewives'.[19] Tea was the first food trade to be investigated by the Commission and it was the organisation of the tea auctions and other arrangements for regulating sales that brought the trade within the terms of the Act. The Commission in its report in

1956 considered that neither the phasing of supplies of tea to auctions nor the practice whereby the major firms selling packaged teas maintained individual resale prices, were contrary to the public interest. However, it is of interest to note that all but one of the agreements between tea firms were later abandoned following the 1956 Restrictive Trade Practices Act.

The Monopolies Commission has since 1956 reported on the supply of infant milk foods (1967), starch and glucose (1971), ready-cooked breakfast cereals (1973), frozen foods (1976), bread and flour (1977) and pet foods (1977). At the time of writing (May 1979) the Commission was still continuing work on the supply of ice-cream which had been referred to it in October 1976.

The investigation into the manufacture of infant milk foods was noteworthy in being the first undertaken in response to allegations of specific abuses of trading arrangements, such issues falling within the remit of the Commission under the terms of the Monopolies and Mergers Act of 1965. In its report the Commission, with one dissension, recommended that the three leading firms should lift their restrictions on supplies to the general retail trade in places where there were no retail chemists. The reference in 1969 of starch and glucose excluded these goods when made up for sale by retail firms. The Commission made few criticisms of Brown and Polson which was the leading supplier.

The reference of ready-to-eat breakfast cereals in 1971 confined the Commission to the issue of prices, and the timing of this reference also suggested the relevance of political pressures. It is surely significant that Kellogg had twice raised its prices within the space of nine months prior to the announcement of the reference! The Commission reported that Kellogg's profits had been excessive until 1970 and although they were no longer unreasonable, it recommended that the company's prices be kept under scrutiny. The Government accepted the report and thus required Kellogg to seek its approval before making any future price increases. The basis of the Commission's view was that competitive forces in the industry were not themselves sufficient to restrain prices. Both the concentration of production and the emphasis on advertising expenditures in support of branded goods by all five major competitors meant that price competition was limited. The Commission was convinced that product differentiation had rendered the market insensitive to price competition: it accepted the view that Viota's sale of own label cornflakes was not restraining Kellogg's pricing policy.

The Heath government's concern with rising food prices provided the setting for its references in 1973 to the Commission of flour and bread and frozen foods (other than whole frozen poultry). Neither industry was subject to keen criticism from the Monopolies Commission and this fact was taken by leading firms in both industries as confirmation of the political nature of their original reference.

During the study of the bread industry it was revealed that seventy-seven unregistered price agreements, mainly in respect of discounts offered to retailers, had been in operation between 1968 and 1974. These were later formally registered with the Office of Fair Trading and in May 1977 the parties gave undertakings to the Restrictive Practices Court as to their compliance with the requests of the 1956 Restrictive Trade Practices Act. But notwithstanding these agreements, the Commission considered that keen competition existed in the industry at the retail level, and that the identical prices of the three national companies was not evidence of restricted competition. It recognised that statutory controls had exaggerated the relative returns from flour milling as against bread making. The Commission's lack of strong criticisms appear to contrast with those made previously by the NBPI in the period 1965–70 (see below). In fact the heightening of government intervention in the bread industry and the creation of the Price Commission met the principal concern of the NBPI – the need to keep the price of bread under close scrutiny.

The supply of pet foods was one of the first references (July 1975) to the Commission by the newly-appointed Director-General of Fair Trading. The Monopolies Commission concluded that the monopoly positions of both Pedigree Petfoods and Spillers were not against the public interest. It is particularly worth noting that the Commission offered no substantive criticism of the industry's advertising expenditures as a barrier to entry that had apparently prompted the reference. Moreover, the only recommendation made by the Commission in its 1976 report on the supply of frozen foods concerned the practice of Birds Eye Foods whereby those retailers willing to reserve space in their freezer cabinets were given discounts. After nearly a year's discussion with the Director-General of Fair Trading the company undertook to drop this restriction of competition, an offer not matched by the other two major suppliers.

In October 1976 the supply of ice-cream was referred to the Commission by the Director-General of Fair Trading. Given that the NBPI had stated that 'there is a degree of competition sufficient to allow the consumer a good measure of protection' (NBPI, 1970d, page 13), the reasons for this reference are unclear. Moreover competition in this industry appears to have become keener since 1970 partly because of the development of United States-style franchise outlets.

Apart from the threat of a reference, which led to a bid for Smith's Crisps being dropped by Imperial Tobacco, none of the horizontal mergers that took place among food firms has as yet been referred to the Commission. It is true that the proposed Unilever–Allied Breweries conglomerate merger was reported on by the Commission in 1969 but the reference stemmed essentially from the then general concern with sheer size rather than with any enhancement of monopoly power in either the food or drink industries. The decision not to refer to the Commission either the Tate & Lyle bid for Manbré and Garton in 1976 or Imperial Tobacco's proposed acquisition of J. B. Eastwood in 1978 was clearly contrary to the views of both the Office of Fair Trading and the Secretary of State for prices and Consumer Protection. Sugar-using food processors, such as confectionery firms, and multiple retail chains were also critical of the Government's decision not to subject the Tate & Lyle bid to scrutiny by the Monopolies Commission. In both cases fears concerning employment were uppermost in the mind of the Government and the Minister of Agriculture in favouring the mergers.

4.5.2 Prices and incomes policies

The bread industry was the subject of no fewer than six reports during the Labour government's prices and incomes policies between 1965 and 1970. In its first enquiry into baking the NBPI (1965) was concerned with the industry's use of labour. It recognised that profit margins were narrow but felt the major firms were too prone to regard rising wage costs as a trigger for price rises. Market pressures in the industry were regarded as being insufficiently strong to restrain costs and prices. The Board's attempts to get an improvement in labour productivity by more flexible shift working met with only a little success for in its final report (1970) it found the industry was still suffering from the labour problem arising from high turnover and long hours that it had found four years previously. However, plant bakers viewed the NBPI's investigation as being based not on government concern with economic problems of the industry but on the political importance of bread prices. Certainly no other food processing industry was subject to such extensive NBPI study.

The reports on the sweet confectionery industry (1968), margarine and cooking fats (1970), tea (1970) and ice-cream (1970) devoted considerable attention to the related issues of heavy advertising expenditure and limited direct competition among a few major firms who were producing goods having a low price sensitivity. The Board was generally satisfied with the quality of management and the technical efficiency of the various major firms but was nevertheless perturbed that production economies were being increasingly offset by defensive marketing expenditures.

The foregoing has indicated the effect of prices and incomes policies between 1964 and 1970 on food processing firms. Since 1970 such policies have become even more a matter of concern for a sector of the economy which was crucially affected by an escalation in world commodity prices in 1973–74. The concern with declining profitability at a time of price controls, as implemented by the Price Commission, has already been indicated. The policy of providing selective subsidies for certain essential foods which was begun in 1974 was a short-term attempt to help reduce the problem of rising product prices and generally to lower expectations of a further escalation in wage and price inflation. Maximum prices for the subsidised foods (bread, cheese, household flour, tea and milk) were fixed to ensure that the benefits of the food subsidies were passed on to the consumer. In the case of the baking industry, the Government also controlled discounts to retailers in an attempt to ensure that bread consumers, rather than the multiple chains, benefited.

Of the studies made by the Price Commission of particular food processing firms or trades, that on the tea trade has involved most public attention. Like the NBPI the Commission felt competitive pressures were too muted – 'Our study suggests that the consumer would be better protected if what one blender described as a gentlemanly trade were to become rather less gentlemanly and rather more competitive' (Price Commission, 1978, page 19). Partly because of intervention by the Secretary of State for Prices and Consumer Protection reductions were made in tea prices. The Price Commission has also criticised parallel pricing by suppliers of animal feedstuffs. Following its report the six major firms revealed that they had been parties to a price-fixing agreement for some eight years.

The effects of government planning, another important area of public intervention, on this sector are difficult to assess. The Food Processing Economic Development Committee (EDC) and the Chocolate and Sugar Confectionery EDC merged in 1967 to form the Food Manufacturing EDC but this then disbanded in 1971. There had been little enthusiasm in the industry for the work of this body. Management of leading firms apparently felt that the high level of efficiency in this sector left minimal scope for co-operative activity on problems such as those facing other EDCs. In retrospect this viewpoint indeed seems to have been too self-congratulatory. A new EDC for the food and drink industries was created in 1976 as part of the 'industrial strategy' and its merit as judged by the published study of the sector's profitability and productivity record is arguably already less open to doubt than its predecessor.

4.6 ASSESSMENT

The above review of government policies has shown how many and varied have been the political pressures affecting food processing firms. The various food industry trade associations have come to feel the need for a body to express matters of concern facing all food manufacturers. They formed the Food and Drink Industries Council (FDIC) in 1973 to point to the sector's low level of profitability and the need for reform of the Common Agricultural Policy. It has been suggested that government intervention in this sector is unlikely to improve its performance (Allen, 1974, page 18). Indeed one critic has argued that while Common Market entry has had some adverse effects on UK food processors (due to raw material cost increases and some harmonisation costs), 'it is difficult to resist the conclusion that the recession and repeated UK government intervention in the food industry have done more to reduce the competitive efficiency of the industry than has the EEC' (Nicholls, page 330). As yet the sector is not, like many parts of British manufacturing industry that are seriously depressed, technically backward and over-manned but its future health seems much less assured than for many years.

NOTES TO CHAPTER 4

1. Data taken from *Grocers' Markets, 1977* published by A. C. Nielsen, Oxford.

2. These figures are derived from *National Income and Expenditure 1967–77*, 1978, 38–40.

3. National Food Survey Committee (1977) *Annual Report on Household Food Consumption and Expenditure.* London: HMSO. 173.

4. These figures are derived from 'The Annual Review of Grocery Trading' in the *Nielsen Researcher*, 1961 and 1971. Oxford: Nielsen.

5. R. Ross, letter to *The Grocer.* 16 December 1978.

6. *Hansard* **799.** 6 April 1970. columns 25–6.

7. *Hansard* **852.** 5 March 1973, columns 13–14.

8. *The Times 1000*, 1978–9. 30–32. Size is measured here in terms of sales.

9. 'The Annual Review of Grocery Trading', in the *Nielsen Researcher*, 1978. Oxford: Nielsen.

10. G. Nuttall, 'All beefed up for battle of the cubes'. *Sunday Times*, 26 February 1978.

11. D. A. Miller, 'The hot bread shops'. *British Baker*, 15 August 1975. 9–10.

12. R. Milner, 'The hottest thing in baking'. *Sunday Times*, 8 February 1976.

13. '£250,000 factory expansion by Romix'. *The Grocer*, 20 April 1974. 85.

14. *Action for Profit: Biscuit Study* no. 6. United Biscuits, 1974. 5.

15. Data from a survey by the Food Manufacturers' Federation reported in *Financial Times*, 25 September 1974.

16. A report, published in 1975, by the European Commission on Industrial Food Research indicated that 24% of all research expenditures in the food industry came from public sources whereas 56% of all expenditure on research in all industries came from public sources.

17. Food and Drink EDC, *Progress report 1978.* NEDO. 10.

18. A. W. Holmes, 'Food Processing'. *Financial Times*, 8 July 1968.

19. 'Tea, windows and the public'. *The Economist*, 12 January 1957. 142.

REFERENCES

Allen, G. R. (1974) *Government Intervention in Agribusiness*. Paper presented at Oxford Agricultural Economics Symposium.

Ashby, A. W. (1978) 'Britain's Food Manufacturing Industry and its Recent Economic Development'. *Journal of Agricultural Economics* **XXIX** (3).

Bevan, A. (June 1974) 'The UK potato crisp industry, 1960–72; a study of new entry competition'. *Journal of Industrial Economics* **XXII** (4), 281–297.

Capel, James & Co. (1970) *Food Majors in the Seventies*. London: Capel.

Cuthbert, N. and Black, W. (1959) 'Restrictive Practices in the Food Trades'. *Journal of Industrial Economics* **VIII** (1), 33–57.

Food and Drink Manufacturing EDC (1978) *Productivity growth in the UK food and drink manufacturing industry*. London: NEDO.

Freeman, C. (1971) *The Role of Small Firms in Innovation in the UK since 1945*. Research Report no. 6 for Committee of Inquiry on Small Firms. London: HMSO.

Kraushar, Andrews and Eassie Ltd (1976) *New Products in the Grocery Trades: A UK Study*. London: Kraushar, Andrews and Eassie.

Leak, H. and Maizels, A. (1945) 'The Structure of British Industry'. *Journal of Royal Statistical Society* **108,** parts 1–2, 142–207.

Lawrence, G. K. (1976) '100 years of progress in the food processing industry'. Ministry of Agriculture, Fisheries and Food in *Food Quality and Safety: a century of progress*. London: HMSO.

Maunder, W. P. J. (1970) 'The UK food processing and distributive trades: an appraisal of public policies'. *Journal of Agricultural Economics* **XXI** (3), 455–464.

Media Expenditure Analysis Ltd (1977) *Monthly Digest of Advertising Expenditure*. London.

Mitchell, Joan (1972) *The National Board for Prices and Incomes*. London: Secker & Warburg.

Monopolies Commission (1956) *Tea*. HCP 15. London: HMSO.

Monopolies Commission (1967) *Baby milk foods*. HCP 315. London: HMSO.

Monopolies Commission (1971) *Starch, glucoses and modified starches*. HC 615. London: HMSO.

Monopolies Commission (1973) *Ready cooked breakfast cereal foods*. HC 2. London: HMSO.

Monopolies Commission (1976) *Frozen foodstuffs for human consumption*. HC 674. London: HMSO.

Monopolies Commission (1977a) *Wheat, flour and bread*. HC 412. London: HMSO.

Monopolies Commission (1977b) *Pet foods*. HC 477. London:

HMSO.

NBPI (1965) no. 3, *Prices of Bread and Flour.* Cmnd 2760. London: HMSO.

NBPI (1968) no. 75, *Costs and Prices of the Chocolate and Sugar Confectionery Industry.* Cmnd 3694. London: HMSO.

NBPI (1970a) no. 147, *Margarine and Compound Cooking Fats.* Cmnd 4368. London: HMSO.

NBPI (1970b) no. 151, *Bread Prices and Pay in the Baking Industry.* Cmnd 4428. London: HMSO.

NBPI (1970c) no. 154, *Tea Prices.* Cmnd 4456. London: HMSO.

NBPI (1970d) no. 160, *Costs, prices and profitability in the ice-cream manufacturing industry.* Cmnd 4548. London: HMSO.

Nicholls, J. R. (1978) *The impact of the EEC on the UK Food Industry.* London: Wilton Publications.

Palamountain, J. C. (1955) *The Politics of Distribution.* Cambridge, Mass.: Harvard University Press.

Price Commission (1978) *Tea Prices.* Report no. 32.

Smith, A. (1776) *The Wealth of Nations* Book 1. Reprinted in A. Skinner *ed.* London: Pelican, 1970.

Walshe, G. (1974) *Recent Trends in Monopoly in Great Britain.* Cambridge: Cambridge University Press.

Wright, A. T. (1969) 'Quaker Puffed Wheat, the rebirth of a brand' in J. S. Bingham *ed., British Cases in Marketing.* London: Business Books. 1–29.

FURTHER READING

Development Analysts Ltd (1975) *A Study of the Evolution of Concentration in the Food Industry for the UK* (3 volumes). Commission of the European Communities, Luxembourg. These volumes document the changes in concentration in food markets between 1969 and 1972.

Food and Drink Manufacturing EDC (1979) *Progress Report 1979.* London: NEDO.

Reekie, W. D. (1978) *Give Us This Day . . ..: an economic critique of political intervention between men and women and their daily bread* Hobart Paper 79. London: Institute of Economic Affairs.

Wardle, C. (1977) *Changing Food Habits in the UK.* London: Earth Resources Research.

5. Pharmaceuticals *106−30*

W. D. Reekie

5.1 INTRODUCTION

5.1.1 The nature of the industry

No two firms in the pharmaceutical industry are alike. Their products range from fertilisers to antibiotics, from emulsion paints to tranquillisers. Many are subsidiaries of overseas parents, principally American, but also German, Swiss, Italian, Dutch and French. Only a few are quoted on the London Stock Exchange and one of these, ICI, has only a small part of its turnover in pharmaceuticals. A precise definition of the 'pharmaceutical industry' is obviously necessary in order to isolate it conceptually from the wide variety of company types which participate in it.

The industry, as seen by the consumer, is the group of firms that manufacture and distribute medicines in finished forms such as ointments, capsules, tablets and syrups. As seen by the producer, it performs the following manufacturing and processing activities:

(a) bulk manufacture of synthetic organic chemicals such as vitamins, antihistamines, diuretics and sulphonamides;

(b) bulk manufacture by fermentation, synthesis, or both, of antibiotics;

(c) preparation of sera and vaccines by micro-organism culture;

(d) production from naturally occurring animal or vegetable sources of drugs such as insulin and hormones; and

(e) processing of bulk drugs into finished forms.

Both definitions are necessary and are complementary. In addition, the industry manufactures products for veterinary use and also proprietary medicines. Proprietary products are sold 'over the counter' to the general public and may be publicly advertised. The remaining products, known as ethical or prescription drugs, are advertised primarily to the medical profession. They are generally available only if supplied by a pharmacist authorised by a doctor's prescription. A further distinction between ethical and proprietary medicines is that the latter tend to have a low research content and a long product life. Ethical drugs tend to be relatively short-lived and usually stem from a comparatively high degree of research.

5.1.2 History

The beginnings of chemotherapy are associated with Paul Ehrlich (1854–1915) who built on Robert Koch's observations that certain aniline dyes could kill bacteria. Ehrlich realised that if these dyes could attach themselves to diseased bacteria without harming whole body tissues then he would have made a tremendous contribution to medical science. His search for the 'Magic Bullet', a drug that would seek out its own target, was not short.

Eventually in 1904 his researches produced salvarsan, a Magic Bullet that kills cellular organisms connected with syphilis. Despite this promising start it was not until 1935 that what is now called the therapeutic revolution was launched. Gerhard Domagk discovered the antimicrobial qualities of Prontosil, a red dye. Later it was established that it was an active constituent of the dye, sulphonilamide, which was active therapeutically. Attempts to improve the efficacy of Prontosil resulted in the production of May & Baker Ltd's M & B 693 in 1938.

Penicillin, although discovered by Alexander Fleming in 1928, only became available for practical purposes after 1940. Streptomycin, a drug effective against tuberculosis, was discovered in 1943, and the first of the broad spectrum antibiotics (chloramphenicol) was introduced in 1949. Tetracycline (1953) was the first antibiotic to be produced whose chemical formula was known prior to the drug itself.

By 1950 the therapeutic revolution was well under way. Corticosteroids, antihistamines, antidepressants, diuretics and many other preparations helping to alleviate human ailments were discovered, developed and are now being produced by the industry. Retailers who had begun to manufacture in the nineteenth century had to adopt many new techniques. Knowledge associated with chemical processing, dyestuffs and fermentation was essential. Simultaneously, entry into pharmaceuticals by firms engaged in industries that already used these techniques – for example ICI Dyestuffs Division and Distillers Co. Ltd – was occurring.

The process of industrial expansion and technological advance was replicated overseas. This is mirrored in the record of entry by overseas companies into the UK. The Association of the British Pharmaceutical Industry (ABPI) has around fifty foreign-owned member companies. Six of these are companies long-established in the UK with dates of entry of 1920 or earlier. A further nine entered between

1920 and 1935. The remainder all entered the British market as subsidiaries subsequent to the discovery of Prontosil in 1935. These companies did not gain a foothold here because they were attempting to produce existing drugs at a lower price; they succeeded because they were offering newly discovered, unique products. This process is still going on. Around twenty companies have set up subsidiaries here since 1960, half of them in the 1970s. Similarly, Beecham, a UK firm with a number of major discoveries to its credit, has set up five overseas manufacturing subsidiaries since 1963.

A more comprehensive picture of the impact of the post-1935 wave of discoveries can be obtained from Cooper (1977). Ninety-five per cent of today's products were unknown in 1950. In the 1920s, six drugs, singly or in combination, accounted for over 60% of prescriptions. Most of these innovations have been made in industrial laboratories (Schwartzman, 1975). The contribution of the industry's innovations to the treatment of ill health is reflected in the growth of its output, investment, research expenditure and employment. It is a science-based industry dependent on new discoveries for continued growth.

5.1.3 Current supply and demand patterns

Although very small in absolute terms the industry is among the faster growing sectors of British manufacturing. The industry's 1977 output of just over £1650m amounted to only around 1% of all manufacturing gross output. Of this total output, about 35% was supplied to the National Health Service and an almost equal proportion was exported; the remainder was accounted for by privately purchased medicines, veterinary medicines and miscellaneous items. The level of activity as measured by the index of industrial production, however, increased by 66% between 1970 and 1977, compared with a rise of 31% for the general chemical industry and only 4% for manufacturing as a whole (table 5.1). The innovations on which this growth is based are international in origin. As a consequence it is no accident that the leading innovating countries are also the leading exporting countries and that in turn only a minority share of the British market is supplied by domestic firms (see table 5.2).

One final introductory point is the peculiar nature of demand facing the industry. Since its products are essential to health it is generally considered that demand is inelastic. It can also be argued that this inelasticity is reinforced in the ethical market in that the patient (or consumer) does not select the product. The doctor chooses but does not pay and as a consequence he will be relatively price indifferent. Moreover, in the UK domestic market the patient pays only a zero or nominal, non-cost related prescription charge. This too will decrease demand elasticity.

TABLE 5.1: Department of Trade and Industry output indices

Pharmaceutical chemicals and preparations		All chemical industry	All manufacturing industry
1963	48	63	79
1970	100	100	100
1974	146	128	108
1977	166	131	104

Source: Association of the British Pharmaceutical Industry (1978).
Note: (1970=100).

TABLE 5.2: Country of origin of discovery of single new chemical entities (1941–63), share of National Health Service Market (1976) and world trade in pharmaceuticals (1975)

Country	No. of Drugs	% of Total	No. of Firms	Share of NHS Sales (%)	Exports ($m)	Imports ($m)	Surplus ($m)
USA	355	61.1	32	39.7	876.4	170.7	668.6
Switzerland	44	7.9	—	—	839.3	237.2	639.2
West Germany	32	5.7	—	—	1060.4	215.3	610.4
UK	27	4.8	15	28.2	825.9	532.0	528.4
France	21	3.5	—	—	635.1	341.7	293.4
Holland	8	1.3	—	—	332.0	246.2	85.8
Denmark	6	1.0	—	—	141.0	94.9	46.3
Others (a)	94	14.7	—	—	—	—	—
Others (b)	—	—	27	31.1	—	—	—
Total	587	100.0	74	99.0	—	—	—

Sources: Paul de Haen Inc; Intercontinental Medical Statistics Ltd; *UN Yearbook of International Trade Statistics.*
Note: The twenty-seven firms in the 'Others' (b) category are European-owned and most are incorporated in the countries already listed in the table.

The converse of these arguments is that consumers rarely choose intermediate goods in any industry. Thus the separation of consumer choice from consumption in health care delivery will have no more unique an effect on elasticity than for any good whose demand is derived. In addition the domestic industry faces a monopsonistic buyer (the NHS) which exerts downward pressures on prices. In export markets either similar monopsonistic situations exist or patients pay direct, cost-related prices to dispensing pharmacists. Thus the separation of consumption, choice and payment may not have such a unique effect on demand in this industry as is suggested.

5.2 MARKET STRUCTURE

5.2.1 Concentration

Although some 120 firms manufacture and distribute ethical drugs in Britain, it was estimated by the Sainsbury Committee that fifty-three account for approximately 90% of all sales to the NHS. Table 5.3 gives the size distribution of firms by sales to both home and export markets for these companies. Twenty-three companies supply 7.9% of the sales of the top fifty-three, but at the upper concentration levels 61% is supplied by only eleven companies.

Table 5.3 reveals that a large number of small producers exist side by side with large or medium-scale firms. This is at least partly explained by the absence of any obvious benefits deriving from economies of scale. Only a small minimum size is required for efficient operation of manufacturing processes. Moreover, the wide variety of products turned out by the industry permits a small plant concentrating on only a few products to compete effectively with a larger factory turning out a wider range.

TABLE 5.3:   Analysis of companies by sales of ethical pharmaceuticals, 1965

Sales (£m)	No. of companies	(% of total sales made by leading firms)
Less than 1	23	7.9
1–2.5	10	10.5
2.5–5	9	20.6
5–7.5	5	17.0
7.5–10	3	16.8
Over 10	3	27.2
Total	53	100.0

Source: Sainsbury Report (1967) pages 100–1.

Within the ethical market itself there are a number of sub-markets, the medicines produced to satisfy the demand in any one being of little or no value to satisfy the demand in the others. Between the sub-markets there is generally a very low cross-elasticity of demand although cross-elasticity of supply may well be quite high if the same producers can supply a variety of sub-markets. This is not a contra-dictory concept because the same manufacturing techniques can frequently be used to produce drugs with entirely different pharma-cological functions. There is consequently much scope for com-petition within the various sub-markets but for very little between them. Within the sub-markets the picture of market structure is somewhat altered. The number of companies operating in any one of over forty sub-markets ranges from one to thirty-six, with a mean value of thirteen. The proportion of any one sub-market held by its leading company ranges from 18.9 to 100% with a mode of around 36%. Companies in the industry are not therefore faced with a highly fragmented market but a series of markets with varying degrees of oligopolistic concentration (Reekie, 1975).

Table 5.4 summarises the pattern of market structure in the industry.* No firm controls more than 9.2% of the total market (Company B is the largest company). All but the top three firms hold a smaller than 5% market share. Nevertheless, at the level of the sub-market, industrial structure is not atomistic but highly concentrated. Most firms, moreover, are heavily dependent on a few leading products. The three large US antibiotics firms who dominated the industry in the late 1950s and early 1960s for example, are nowhere to be seen in table 5.4. This, as will be shown later, has important implications for competitive behaviour.

5.2.2 Barriers to entry

Entry is common and continuing albeit mainly from cross-entry from other nations or industries. An analysis of the industry's age structure indicates a continuous and fairly even flow of firms into it since 1950. Over 30% of industry sales in 1966 was made by post-1949 entrants. Further, there is no relationship between age and company size. Unlike more traditional industries both rapid relative and absolute growth can occur soon after entry (Reekie, 1975).

What are the barriers to entry in the drug industry? The principal absolute cost advantage of existing firms is the ability to preclude competition with identical products unless royalties are paid to the patentee. In 1965 some 72% by value of all prescription sales was of patented products. Nevertheless, there would seem to be little to prevent a firm entering the remaining 28% non-patented market.

*The table is based on confidential market research information; thus the identities of the companies cannot be divulged.

TABLE 5.4: Top twelve companies; number of products, main products' share of company sales and of sub-markets, 1969

Company	No. of products	Main products	% of total company sales	% of sub-market
A	49	1	39	37
		2	31	29
		3	10	33
		All others	20	
B	56	1	42	75
		2	28	51
		3	13	30
		All others	17	
C	75.	1	49	49
		2	11	16
		All others	40	
D	36	1	76	45
		2	7	15
		All others	17	
E	37	1	36	29
		2	24	9
		3	19	43
		4	10	95
		All others	11	
F	56	1	17	48
		2	16	25
		3	10	29
		All others	57	
G	11	1	85	56
		All others	15	
H	28	1	30	25
		2	30	20
		3	13	8
		All others	27	
I	71	1	25	7
		All others	75	
J	62	1	18	43
		2	17	7
		3	10	40
		All others	55	
K	45	1	21	8
		2	18	34
		3	13	19
		All others	48	

Source: Intercontinental Medical Statistics.

Economies of scale appear to be largely unimportant as an inhibitor of entry. In promotion there are no evident economies of large-scale advertising. The most effective method of pharmaceutical promotion is the medical representative. At a local level there is no case to assert that the small firm's representative force need have less impact on a doctor's prescribing habits than a large firm with a detail force covering the country. Similarly direct mail advertising can be carried out on a restricted scale geographically. Journal advertising, however, may require to be carried out nationally. Even so this form of promotion is not very important, accounting for only around 10% of all pharmaceutical promotional expenditure and the absolute cost is not prohibitive. (A full black and white page in the *Lancet* in 1974 cost only £158).

Product differentiation advantages of existing firms are the most obvious entry barriers. With over 2400 branded drugs available and an average duplication of only 1.1 brands per formulation the extent of product differentiation is vast. The entry deterrent provided by product differentiation is measured by the extent of the financial sacrifice an entrant firm must incur to sway prescribers bound by loyalty away from existing brands towards the entrant's products. Existing firms will, of course, attempt to strengthen this loyalty. They can do this by emphasising product differences through advertising and/or by creating new ones to produce new or improved therapies through conducting research and development (R and D).

Entrant firms can only hope to revoke this loyalty if they incur some financial sacrifice not currently incurred by existing firms. This implies, for example, selling at a cheaper price, promoting more effectively, producing products which are different from those already on the market – for example by initiating successful R and D – or some combination of these or other sacrifices. If existing firms are attempting meanwhile to strengthen the loyalty of prescribers to their own brands, then a spiral commences. Entrants must cut prices still further, shout still louder through the promotional media or make even greater technical advances through R and D if their products are going to have the marginal attractiveness to cause customers to shed existing loyalties. What form this 'spiral' takes, and what its net effects are, is the most contentious issue in the economic debate over the industry's behaviour and performance.

5.3 MARKET BEHAVIOUR

5.3.1 Innovation

The R and D efforts of drug firms produce streams of new products which enable them to engage in innovatory competition. In the seven years 1960–6, 1189 new drugs were introduced to the market by the industry. Not only is the rate of introduction very high but the importance of these new drugs to the competitive position of the manufacturer is also great. Of the leading 150 drugs by sales value in 1972, 96% were developed after 1947, and over half after 1963.

Because of this high rate of new product introduction a static sub-market analysis is inadequate. It fails to illustrate the high degree of product competition which exists and which in turn ensures only a very short-lived period of control in any one sub-market. Demand for ethical pharmaceuticals is highly sensitive to quality differences resulting from R and D.

Cooper (1966) provides evidence of the brevity of sub-market domination by any one product. He illustrates the necessity of product innovation if company domination of the sub-market is to continue. Such innovation must have clear advantages over the new products almost certain to appear from rivals' R and D laboratories. Table 5.5 indicates that this does not always occur, and if it does, it is frequently too belated to prevent a loss of market position. Of the sub-markets 37% had product leadership (as determined by sales value) changes in the three and one-half year period covered by table 5.5. In 32% of the sub-markets leadership was lost by the original leading firms, while in 11% of the markets studied, more than one change in class leadership occurred. Thus while the sub-markets are oligopolistic in structure there is little chance, from a dynamic point of view, for long or even medium-term oligopolistic domination to occur.

TABLE 5.5:   **Therapeutic sub-market competition: changes in market leadership between January 1962 and June 1965**

Sub-markets		Number	%
Firms:		90	100
	Change in leadership	29	32
	More than one change	10	11
Products:	Change in leadership	33	37
	More than one change	8	9

Source: Cooper (1966) page 60.

The great attention thus paid by the industry to R and D, as a normal business strategy intended to raise or maintain market shares and/or profits, becomes understandable. This form of competition may well be beneficial to the community. Assuming other things are equal, new and better medicines are evolved and the rigid pricing patterns of oligopoly are unlikely. In a traditional oligopolistic situation firms can be expected to assess the likelihood of new competition arising and will set a price just below the level at which such entry might be expected to be attractive. Where entry to an industry is easy – as its frequency indicates it is in the drug industry's sub-markets – one would expect a nearly competitive price level to emerge.

Even at the level of the total market the vigour of this 'competition in creativity' can be seen. Table 5.6 shows that only two of the leading ten products in 1976 had been in the top ten in 1965. A further two were either out of the top 150 or not available in 1965. Of the leading ten firms in 1965, only six remained in that group in 1976. The second-ranked company in 1965 had fallen to nineteenth position by 1976; the third placed to thirty-third and so on.

TABLE 5.6: **(a) Position of 1976's leading ten products in 1965 and (b) Position of 1965's leading ten companies in 1976**

| (a) Products | | (b) Companies | |
1965	1976	1965	1976
4	1	1	1
—	2	2	19
13	3	3	33
—	4	4	9
22	5	5	8
—	6	6	3
—	7	7	10
3	8	8	24
—	9	9	22
—	10	10	6

Source: Intercontinental Medical Statistics.
Note: Ranking by total value of sales.

The reason for this high degree of company volatility is, of course, R and D. Successful research is essential for maintaining corporate market position and, by association, national market position in world markets. According to trade estimates, in 1975 total expenditure on R and D conducted and financed by the industry in the UK was almost double the amount spent in 1972 and reached an estimated £150m in 1977. Basic and applied research, which concerns the search for new chemical entities or biologicals absorbed about 52% of the industry's research effort in 1975. Such research is highly speculative, and, out of every 10 000 or so new compounds discovered and investigated, on average only one reaches the market. Of the industry's research expenditure 31% was on development research, which covers the development of methods of manufacture and formulation of new and existing drugs for therapeutic use and the development of more economical methods of production. The remainder was capital investment. The industry has a higher proportion of qualified staff engaged in research than any other British industry (Association of the British Pharmaceutical Industry, 1978).

5.3.2 Price

The emphasis on competition by innovation has traditionally been assumed to have arisen from two sources: the supply of new technology arising from the therapeutic revolution and the rising demand for ever improving levels of health care. The latter has been encouraged by the growth of health care insurance schemes throughout the world (either private or, as in Britain, state sponsored). These factors, coupled with the nature of the product (a 'necessity') and the structures of the therapeutic sub-markets if observed at any one point in time (highly concentrated) have led most observers to believe that the level of consumption will be determined by disease incidence and not by price. Moreover, the relative levels of these factors implies that the low price and high quality elasticities of demand will be further exaggerated by the fact that the market is 'over-insured'. Insurance is generally a service provided to guard against situations which are likely to involve an individual in exceptionally high expense relative to his total income or wealth and/or one whose occurrence is improbable. (The average cost of a prescription to the NHS in 1977, including the retailer's margin, was £1.90). Except for the chronically sick and the indigent it is difficult to see why insurance (private or state initiated) is required in the pharmaceutical market. Nevertheless, as a consequence of this 'over insurance' neither doctor nor patient will be price sensitive and price competition, it is argued, has little if any role to play in the drug industry. Recent studies (see Reekie and Weber, 1978 and section 5.5 below), however, have cast considerable doubts on the view that price competition is absent in pharmaceuticals or that demand is wholly inelastic.

5.3.3 Promotion

As a percentage of turnover, promotional expenditure by the industry has remained constant for the decade since publication of the Sainsbury Report in 1967 at just under 14%. The break-down by media type has also remained similar. Nearly half is spent on journal advertising, direct mail, samples, meetings and other forms. Medical representatives who account for the other half provide a means of two-way communication between firms and doctors. It is now well established that promotion is significantly associated with innovation in the industry. Fig. 5.1 shows that while relatively new medicines are by no means the only ones promoted, recent innovations are regarded as the products requiring the greatest intensity of marketing back-up. Once a product has gained acceptance, there is still a need for some advertising of the reminder type. Doctors, like any other human 'buyers', 'do not have perfect memories; nor are they a static body: there are continually new potential recruits to be drawn from the newly employed . . . familiar products are from time to time improved or adapted to different purposes, and the manufacturer must make known their new look' (Harris and Seldon, 1958, page 75). Fig. 5.1 indicates the comparative steadiness of reminder advertising on a product after it is accepted by the market. The average expenditure in the first two months of 1965 on products introduced between 1953 and 1962 varied from £1100 to £1500 in the period of examination.

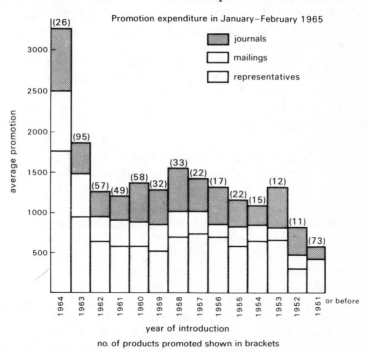

FIG. 5.1:   Promotional expenditure per product promoted by age of product

Source: Teeling-Smith (1968).

5.4 PERFORMANCE

Measuring the benefits produced by the industry raises a number of complications beyond the scope of this discussion. Benefits can be social, economic or a mixture of the two. They may well be the results of costs other than those required to purchase the manufacture of existing drugs or to discover new ones.

Identification of that part of improved health due to the industry's operations is almost impossible. Improved health is also a consequence of higher standards of hygiene, of nutrition, of increased knowledge in fields such as physiology and of improved surgical techniques. Improved health is usually measured by comparative mortality and/or morbidity statistics. Unfortunately such statistics are not easily convertible into meaningful economic measures. In a few disease areas, however, it is possible to obtain a picture of the welfare contribution of the industry to society. This occurs where the incidence or killing power of the disease has abruptly declined after a relevant pharmaceutical breakthrough. The decline in mortality from tuberculosis (TB) since the introduction of streptomycin, para-aminosalicylic acid and isoniazid has been one of the most dramatic medical advances of the century. In 1975 there were only 563 deaths from TB compared with 11 420 in 1951.

The discovery of the first of the tranquillisers in 1952 and of the anti-depressants in 1960 signalled the beginning of psycho-pharmacology. The use of psychotherapeutic drugs was a major cause, in 1956, of the first-ever annual decrease in the number of hospital beds occupied due to mental illness. From 151 000 in-patients in 1956, the mental-illness hospital population fell to 125 000 in 1966 and 92 000 in 1975. Decreased use of mental-hospital beds has also been paralleled in other diseases. Despite these dramatic benefits which the advent of chemotherapy has provided, the proportion of total NHS expenditure on pharmaceutical services has remained virtually static over the years. Since 1973 the steady proportion of 10–11% has begun to fall, and is now down to 8–9%.

Yet despite these achievements, which are impressive in both absolute and in cost effective terms, there are still many categories of illness where pharmaceutical R and D may still have a large potential contribution to make. For example, no drug yet known can do other than treat the symptoms of rheumatism and arthritis. The Sainsbury Committee found little to criticise in the industry's R and D record. They considered that the figures for research expenditure did not suggest any major defect in the industry's involvement in fundamental research. Nor did they find any avoidable waste of resources. The NEDO report, *Focus on Pharmaceuticals* (1972) concluded that expenditure on pharmaceutical research in the UK was about two and one-half times as productive as the corresponding expenditure in the US. This assertion must be qualified, however, by the comments which follow on international legislative differences.

Figures for profitability in the pharmaceutical industry must be treated with caution because many companies are subsidiaries of larger, often international groups. For various reasons, this type of company will normally show a higher return on capital than the average for British industry in general. Also, higher than average return on capital might be a consequence of substantial assets such as research know-how, patents and trade marks being excluded from pharmaceutical companies' capital value. It is also worth directing attention to the distribution of rates of return among leading companies, for this provides an indicator of underlying market factors. Table 5.7 indicates the widely differing profit-levels of companies selling more than £1m of medicines to the NHS. The first lesson is that whatever the industry's average profits may be, they are not equally shared by all companies. In 1972 14.5% of firms showed a loss, while 9.5% showed a return on capital of over 30%.

TABLE 5.7: **Distribution of profit levels; large companies return on capital; home sales of NHS medicines**

	Per cent of total companies in each profit range			
	Rate of return (%)	1963–5 (%)	1969 (%)	1972 (%)
Losses:			6	14.5
Profit:	0–5	6	10 } 19	7 } 28.5
	5–10		3	7
	10–15	13	10	19
	15–20	6	26	19
	20–25	38	13	14
	25–30	6	13	10
	Over 30	31	19	9.5
		100	100	100

Sources: Sainsbury Report (1967) page 110; DHSS returns. Reprinted in *Competition, Risk and Profit in the Pharmaceutical Industry* (Runnymede Research) page 10.

In the USA, Conrad and Plotkin (1967), and in the UK, Merrett–Cyriax Associates (1968), have shown that this type of variation is much more marked in pharmaceuticals than in industry generally. Their studies suggest that drugs are characterised by extreme riskiness in the form of a substantial probability of either a negative return on investment or a very high reward for success. Moreover, table 5.7 shows how, since 1963–5, the risk of a loss or low return has substantially risen, whilst the prospect of exceptional success has sharply diminished. The 6% of firms making a loss or a return below

10% on capital had increased to 28.5% by 1972. Conversely, the 31% of extremely successful firms making over 30% return on capital in 1963–5 had fallen to 9.5% by 1972. In addition the most common rate of return in 1963–5, 20–25%, fell to 15–20% in 1969 and to 10–20% in 1972.

Two main questions are raised by profitability figures. First, are they fair and reasonable? Second, to what extent does the continued performance of R and D depend on profitability? The two are closely related. These issues are central to public policy and it is to this we now turn.

5.5 PUBLIC POLICY

5.5.1 Prices and profits

Firms are subject to the Pharmaceutical Price Regulation Scheme (PPRS) which, despite its name, aims to control profits rather than prices. Firms negotiate prices with the DHSS and are obliged to supply the Department with annual financial returns. However, the DHSS 'think that it is unrealistic to allocate all of a company's costs . . . between the different medicines it supplies'. Instead it prefers to look at a firm's overall return on capital 'on the assumption that if that is reasonable, what the NHS pays for the totality of supplies . . . will also be reasonable'.

'Reasonableness' is a concept with no generally accepted meaning. The DHSS accept this and regard a level of profitability which would be common to all firms at all times as 'quite impracticable and certainly undesirable'. Nevertheless, it must work within the general guidelines laid down to all Departmental purchasers, namely that *'suppliers of goods to Government must earn the same sort of profits as British industry in general'* (emphasis added).[1]

The rationale for a price control scheme is the belief that unregulated market forces are failing to bring about price-levels that would result in reasonable profits in drugs. This belief may exist because on the demand side of the market doctors and patients do not pay directly for the medicines they prescribe and consume and are therefore indifferent to the prices paid by the NHS; or it may be because on the supply side firms are believed to have the ability persistently to price their products above reasonable levels because competitive market rivalry is absent, for whatever reason. Firms can also be referred to the Monopolies Commission. In particular, in 1973 the Commission in its Report (The Monopolies Commission, 1973) on Roche Products, the British end of the Swiss multinational Hoffman–La Roche, revealed that in 1970 the Swiss parent was charging its British subsidiary £370 and £922 per kilo for the ingredients of Librium and Valium respectively. These same ingredients were simultaneously available from other manufacturers at £9 and £20 in Italy. The Commission notionally adjusted the firm's accounts and pronounced that the profits made by Roche were 'quite unjustified' and were the direct result of 'excessive prices charged'. The company was ordered to cut the 1970 prices of its two main products, Librium and Valium, by 60 and 75% respectively. Roche was condemned for charging prices for the two drugs which were 'manifestly too high'. The Commission did report that their daily dosage costs were 'amongst the lowest when compared with competitive products', but then went on to claim that there was a *virtual absence of price competition'* (emphasis added).

The difficulty for policy-makers in innovative industries is, of course, the confusion caused by the words 'perfect competition'. These suggest that the phenomenon (and its associated condition of price equal to marginal cost) is an *ideal*. In fact, the concept is a *predictor*. And in an innovative industry, where unit variable costs are near to zero (as in drugs) but fixed costs such as R and D expenditure are relatively very high, the problem of correctly defining marginal cost is well nigh insuperable. Unless this is understood, we are in the hypothetical area of homogeneous products, where no improvement or innovation can bring extra profits exclusively to the supplier. If he cannot reap the rewards there is no incentive to make improvements. Hence the observation by Schumpeter (1948) that 'perfect' price competition (or price equal to short run marginal cost) is a prescription for the non-existence of innovation.

It is worth noting that many new drugs are priced at levels lower than leading substitutes (Reekie, 1978). Those priced at high levels relative to competitors tend to be innovations providing important therapeutic gains. This complies with the behaviour pattern one would expect from simple price theory. Firms *can* charge a higher price in those cases where consumers are willing to pay that price. Consumers *will* pay if the innovation is relatively more productive than alternative products. Minor variants, conversely, can only penetrate a market if their price is below that of existing rivals. Given the Sylos postulate, their demand curve is that part of the market demand curve to the right of ruling price.

Moreover, the evidence suggests that new drug prices tend to fall over time; that existing products tend to be cut in price in the face of innovation as firms attempt to gain a price advantage where a quality advantage has been lost; and that price elasticity of demand either increases as products mature (and so are subject to competition from later drugs) and/or is lower initially the more important is the therapeutic gain represented by the innovation.

Price should not be interpreted as cash price. The real price of a pharmaceutical must be modified by the quality of the product. Like any other good or service, a pharmaceutical's selling price is measured by the amount of other goods and services the customer must forgo in order to purchase the characteristics of the drug. For example, if an existing drug requires four pills per day to be consumed for one week at 10p per pill, with the additional requirement of confinement to bed then the real price of that drug to the consumer is £2.80 (7 × 4 × 10p) *plus* the week's wages he has forgone by being confined to bed. (Alternatively, if the total cost is borne by society through socialised medicine and health insurance, the social cost is the same, namely £2.80 plus the value of goods and services the patient could have produced had he been at work). On the other hand, if an alternative drug becomes available at £2.00 per pill, to be consumed at a rate of one pill per day for three days with only a three-day home confinement, then the real cost to the consumer is £6 plus only the proportion of one week's wages represented by three days' loss of work.

The new drug costs £6 for a full treatment, the first £2.80. But the second drug is by far the more competitive in terms of real price. For a five-day week for a patient normally earning £20 per day the second drug's real price is £6 plus three days' wages – £66; the first drug's price is £102.80. The second drug has lowered the price of treatment by £36.80. That is price competition in the real meaning of the phrase.

In the simple example just described, the new drug lowered the real price of treatment. If competition works we would expect the price of the existing drug to fall to combat the price of advantage of the innovation. Because the quality of the existing product cannot be changed, the alteration must occur in its cash price. The evidence suggests that this is precisely what happens (Reekie, 1978). As new products are introduced into the market, the cash prices of existing products are pushed down by competitive forces, and the elasticity of demand for existing products increases. Doctors continue prescribing older products only if they are reduced in cash price and their real price disadvantage relative to better quality products is minimised.

Similarly, the empirical evidence (Reekie, 1978) indicates that new drugs that do not reduce the real price of treatment via improved therapeutic quality must, in order to enter the market, reduce the real price of treatment by offering a lower cash price. There is little or no evidence on the demand side of the drug market to suggest that doctors are unaware of real price differentials. Little support is provided for the apparently obvious Sainsbury view that drug prices need to be regulated by government because demand is highly inelastic.

Sainsbury (1967, page 16) explicitly concluded that they 'did not gain the impression that there was any significant degree of price competition in medical speciality products'. This conclusion was arrived at after the Committee had surveyed firms and asked how prices were determined. Some said they considered the prices of alternatives, others that they aimed to obtain a required rate of return on investment and others that they tried to recover cost in a given period. These objectives, of course, need not be incompatible, but the latter two in particular could appear to depart from perfect competition as an *ideal* (although not necessarily as a *predictor*; that is an empirical question). It is on just this point that the qualitative evidence of Sainsbury seems to depart from the actual behaviour patterns of drug industry prices both over time and among products. Price competition is present and *works* as predicted. Perfect competition is, however, absent.

5.5.2 Advertising

Sainsbury suggested two advantages to be expected if brand names were prohibited: more effective price competition would result and a source of confusion arising from a multiplicity of names for the same drug would be removed.

Confusion due to a proliferation of different brand names for the same product is more illusory than real, however. In 1965 a total of 2403 brands involved 2177 different chemical formulations, an average of only 1.1 brand names per formulation. The emergence, *ceteris paribus*, of a greater degree of price-competition if branding were to disappear is, of course, indisputable. Other things are not equal, however. Innovation occurs and entry barriers to the industry may be increased. Currently the promotional emphasis is on the brand advertised.[2] Because the average life of a drug is short, the average length of brand-name-induced monopoly is also relatively short. When the drug disappears from the market, so too does any monopoly position it may have provided. If, however, doctors prescribed by manufacturer, then promotional stress might well shift from product to company names. In such a situation, any monopoly position or market preference created by unique name advertising would not wither away with the demise of a product but would last for as long as the firm. An innovating company previously unknown in the market would be at a marked disadvantage. There are other dangers existing from regulation of promotion. Qualitative control may be misleading. And quantitative control, as exercised under the present PPRS, may either hamper entry or slow down the diffusion of innovation. An example of the faulty guidance which may be given to British prescribers when they have to listen to a single (government) source of information as opposed to making decisions – given their own peculiar circumstances – based on data from competitive advertising emanating from multiple sources, has been given by Teeling-Smith (1978).

Quantitative control of promotion may in turn hamper both entry and the rapid spread of the benefits of innovation. Even if expenditure is high, it may be better in an innovative industry to bear some waste than to suffer the costs of low diffusion. In the Soviet Union, promotion of new drugs is undertaken by the Health Ministry, not by the industry. Information about new drugs is usually restricted to mailed literature or journal articles. It is frequently overlooked, forgotten or ignored. It is neither prompt enough, voluminous enough, nor sufficiently persuasive to encourage the doctor to use new advances. The result is a substantial lag between the introduction of a new medicine and receipt of incremental benefits by the patient.

Professor Sam Peltzman (1975) attempted to measure the benefits that might have accrued to society (in the USA) had diffusion been more rapid in the case of two major drug innovations, TB drugs and tranquillisers. He suggests that if one considers only the added earnings of potential TB victims in present value terms of, say, $50 000 per life, then the present value, in the year of innovation, of more rapid diffusion of TB drugs would have been $3bn. For the tranquillisers Peltzman obtains estimated savings of $9bn by calculating savings in hospitalisation costs alone (ignoring productivity increases from shorter patient confinements). He concludes: 'By way of comparison, gains of this order once per decade could easily pay for a doubling of current drug promotion expenses, if that is what it takes to realise them.'

5.5.3 Research and development

The debate surrounding the topic of market structure is intimately connected with the relationship between R and D and size of firm. The proposed merger between Beecham and Glaxo was turned down by the Monopolies Commission (1972) primarily because of the adverse effects it might have had on pharmaceutical R and D in the UK. The controversy has two main aspects. First, whether or not larger firms perform proportionately more R and D than smaller ones. Second, whether or not larger R and D efforts produce proportionately more innovations.

R and D is absolutely expensive. It is presumed that firms must be of some minimum size in order to undertake a meaningful effort. Those who argue that larger firms conduct proportionately more R and D do so on the basis that larger firms (i) have greater resources and (ii) have a greater degree of market power than can be used to generate an absolutely higher level of profits from any resulting innovation. Disagreement arises not over the need to have some degree of size and market power to encourage R and D activity, but over whether or not an increase in market power and size above such a threshold would result in a relatively complacent large firm whose urge to engage in the risks of innovative activity would be relatively less.

The second facet of the controversy, whether larger R and D efforts are more productive, is, of course, merely a restatement, in the R and D context of the question as to when, if at all, scale economies are exhausted. No definitive case for or against a higher level of concentration in the industry can be made. Economic theory is too imprecise to predict with certainty the strength of any relationship between market structure and innovation. Indeed it is too imprecise to predict even the direction of the relationship.

A number of empirical studies about pharmaceutical R and D have been published in recent years (e.g. Comanor, 1965). The investigations all arrive at broadly the same conclusion: the largest pharmaceutical firms, while possibly the biggest absolute performers of R and D, are not the most research-intensive firms. A large number of studies have provided evidence that diseconomies of scale exist in R and D irrespective of which index of input or output is used. Only in recently reported investigations has this picture been challenged (e.g. Schwartzman). This may be significant and may indicate changing circumstances in pharmaceutical R and D. The real costs of R and D are rising. This is attributable to two factors. First, the areas of unconquered disease remaining provide relatively difficult technological problems. Second, the costs of meeting the requirements for new drug registration, both in the UK and overseas, are rising dramatically. Both phenomena originally appeared in the 1960s and may be responsible for the apparent contradictions. Confirmation for the view that the relationship between firm size and innovative output has altered in recent years is provided in table 5.8. Grabowski and

TABLE 5.8: Grabowski and Vernon's estimates of concentration of innovational output in the US ethical drug industry

	1957–61	1962–6	1967–71
Four largest firms' share of innovational output	24.0	25.0	48.7
Four largest firms' share of total sales	26.5	24.0	26.1

Source: Grabowski and Vernon (1977).
Note: Innovational output is measured by new drug sales during the first three full years after product introduction.

Vernon (1977) explicitly compared different time periods. The findings indicate that the four largest firms in the industry accounted for a share of innovational output from 1957 to 1966 not dissimilar to their share of sales. By 1967–71, however, their share of innovational output was much greater (at 48.7%) than their share of total sales.

In an attempt to ascertain why the change depicted has occurred the US results were compared with those from another country (UK) where the regulatory climate was much less stringent. The authors suggested that the depletion of R and D opportunities would affect the productivity of R and D in all countries in a similar manner. However, any negative effects of regulation would show up as an additional influence in a country with a stiffer regulatory framework. They found, in a comparison between the UK and USA, that in the USA, R and D productivity declined about sixfold between 1960–1 and 1966–70. The corresponding decrease in the UK was only half as great. They argue as a consequence that the 1962 Amendments to the Food, Drug and Cosmetic Act, by themselves, roughly doubled the cost of producing and introducing a new drug in the USA.

Wardell and Lasagna (1975, page 122) found that from 1962 to 1971 nearly four times as many new drugs became available in the UK as in the USA; for those drugs marketed in both countries twice as many were introduced first in Britain as in the USA; that specialist physicians in the USA were often unaware of the drug lag but when informed of the existence of new, effective drugs abroad wished they were available in America; that Britain exercised a more permissive policy towards new drugs but a stricter post-marketing surveillance of innovations. Wardell and Lasagna thus recommended that surveillance of new drugs after marketing be intensified in the USA.

Such studies have changed official American attitudes to stringent regulation and the US may now be beginning to move away from strict controls. It is not clear, however, that those responsible for the structure of controls in Britain have learned from the American experience; it is possible that the British industry will move into a period of stultifying regulation just as its American counterpart emerges from a costly legislative straitjacket.

Finally, there is the issue of state support of R and D. Government subvention of R and D in an industry (by subsidy or actual performance) is generally justified on one or more of the following grounds:

(a) the size of project requires more resources than the industrial unit has available;

(b) project risks are too great for the industry to assume them; and/or

(c) the market mechanism fails to reflect adequately the social benefits.

State aid to R and D, or its actual performance by a nationalised unit, cannot be justified on the first two grounds. There is no evidence that R and D projects are of a size beyond the resource pool of firms. Most, in fact, conduct several projects simultaneously. Equally there is no information to indicate that firms are risk averters to the extent that R and D is not being conducted. With a one in 10 000 success rate, the evidence rather points in the reverse direction.

The third category, however, is more likely to provide grounds for government support of industrial R and D in commercially unattractive disease areas in which the benefits recoupable through the market are less than the cost incurred, and both, in turn, are less than the social benefits. Clearly, in such circumstances a profit-maximising businessman will allocate his R and D effort towards the more common disease areas where the surplus of commercial benefits over costs is greatest.

This is an attractive argument. The opportunity cost of such interference would, however, be far greater than any benefits. Because of a fixity in resources for pharmaceutial R and D, any increase in the research effort directed towards finding cures for less common diseases implies, of necessity, a reduction of R and D activity in the areas of high disease incidence. (This is not an unrealistic assumption; the main R and D resource is trained manpower which is a fixed pool. An increase in the number of chemists, pharmacologists and the like cannot be obtained at a stroke). Consequently government interference of this type might help the few, but it would harm the many.

5.6 CONCLUSIONS

These can be set down in a series of findings.

(a) The drug industry is a young, research intensive industry.

(b) It has made immense contributions to the health and well-being of people in all countries.

(c) Large areas of disease remain which probably can be conquered with further pharmacological advances.

(d) Because drugs do not fall within the category of expenditures on unforeseen and large catastrophes (they are absolutely inexpensive and are also cheap in relation to personal incomes: illness is *not* a rare occurrence), it is at least arguable that drugs should not be paid for on the insurance principle (private or state). This would encourage a more responsible attitude to their consumption, and conceivably also towards the consumption of other health-care provisions.

(e) The industry is 'competitive' by almost all yardsticks used by economists:

    (i)   entry is frequent and easy;

    (ii) prices tend to be forced towards marginal cost;

(iii) promotion facilitates entry and innovation;

(iv) profitability is not dissimilar to that experienced by comparable industries; and

(v) scale economies are unimportant.

(f) Government regulatory activity, however, has been founded on the belief that the industry is not competitive and has

(i)   imposed price restraints;

(ii) effected profit controls;

(iii) laid down promotional constraints; and

(iv) increased or introduced safety and efficacy guidelines.

(g) These regulatory activities have

(i)   raised entry barriers to the innovative sector of the industry by restricting the promotion which facilitates entry and imposing regulations that have made R and D susceptible to scale economies and an activity that only large firms can perform;

(ii) reduced the attractiveness of entry by imposing downward pressure on prices and profits and exerting upward pressure on costs; and

(iii) removed pharmacological benefits from consumers, either in the future as a consequence of reducing the attractiveness of current R and D or in the present (as in the USA) by over-zealously protecting the public from drug hazards but not from disease.

Until politicians are judged by the yardstick of forgone alternatives a continuance of such myopic behaviour is likely.

NOTES TO CHAPTER 5

1. Information and quotations were abstracted from a speech by Alan Beard, Controller of Supply, DHSS to the Pharmaceutical Manufacturers Association of the USA (*ABPI News*, September 1977).

2. For example note that Roche Products often advertise their products 'Bactrim Roche', 'Valium Roche', etc. to project their corporate image. This is a recent development.

REFERENCES

Association of the British Pharmaceutical Industry (ABPI) (1978) *The Pharmaceutical Industry and the Nation's Health*. London.

Comanor, W. S. (1965) 'Research and Technical Change in the Pharmaceutical Industry'. *Review of Economics and Statistics* **47**, 182–190.

Conrad, G. R. and Plotkin, I. H. (1967) *Risk and Return in US Industry*. New York: Arthur D. Little, Inc.

Cooper, M. H. (1966) *Prices and profits in the Pharmaceutical Industry.* Oxford: Pergamon.

Grabowski, H. G. and Vernon, J. M. (1977) 'Consumer Protection Regulation in Ethical Drugs'. *American Economic Review* **67** (Papers and Proceedings), 359–369.

Harris, R. and Seldon, A. (1962) *Advertising and the Public.* London: Deutsch.

Merrett-Cyriax Associates (1968) *Profitability in the Pharmaceutical Industry.* London.

The Monopolies Commission (1972) *Beecham Group Ltd, Glaxo Group Ltd: The Boots Co. Ltd and Glaxo Group Ltd: A Report on the Proposed Mergers.* HC 341 Session 1971–72. London: HMSO.

The Monopolies Commission (1973) *Chlordiazepoxide and Diazepam.* HC 197 Session 1972–73. London: HMSO.

National Economic Development Office (NEDO) (1972) *Focus on Pharmaceuticals.* London: HMSO.

Peltzman, S. (1975) 'The Diffusion of Pharmaceutical Innovation' in Helms, *Drug Development and Marketing.* Washington, D.C.: American Enterprise Institute.

Reekie, W. D. (1975) *The Economics of the Pharmaceutical Industry.* London: Macmillan.

Reekie, W. D. (1978) 'Price and Quality Competition in the US Drug Industry'. *Journal of Industrial Economics* **26**, 223–237.

Reekie, W. D. and Weber, M. H. (1978) *Profits, Politics and Drugs.* London: Macmillan.

Sainsbury Report (1967) *Report of the Committee of Enquiry into the Relationship of the Pharmaceutical Industry with the National Health Service.* Cmnd 3410. London: HMSO.

Schumpeter, J. A. (1948) *Capitalism, Socialism and Democracy.* New York: Harrap.

Schwartzman, D. (1975) *The Expected Return from Pharmaceutical Research.* Washington D.C.: American Enterprise Institute.

Teeling-Smith, G. (1968) *Economics and Innovation in the Pharmaceutical Industry.* London: Office of Health Economics.

Teeling-Smith, G. (1978) *Brand Names in Prescribing.* London: Office of Health Economics.

Wardell, W. M. and Lasagna, L. (1975) *Regulation and Drug Development.* Washington, D.C.: American Enterprise Institute.

FURTHER READING

Association of the British Pharmaceutical Industry (ABPI) (1978) *The Pharmaceutical Industry and the Nation's Health.* London.

Cooper, M. H. (1966) *Prices and Profits in the Pharmaceutical Industry.* Oxford: Pergamon.

National Economic Development Office (NEDO) (1972) *Focus on Pharmaceuticals*. London: HMSO.
Reekie, W. D. and Weber, M. H. (1979) *Profits, Politics and Drugs*. London: Macmillan.
Sainsbury Report (1967) *Report of the Committee of Enquiry into the Relationship of the Pharmaceutical Industry with the National Health Service*. Cmnd 3410. London: HMSO.
Schwartzman, D. (1975) *The Expected Return from Pharmaceutical Research*. Washington, D.C.: American Enterprise Institute.

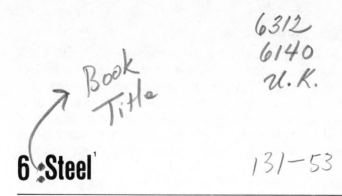

6 Steel[1]

A. Cockerill

6.1 THE ECONOMIC BACKGROUND

World steel production in 1978 was an estimated 663 million tonnes, only slightly below 1974's record output of 677 million tonnes (fig. 6.1). The recession which followed the 1973 oil crisis and the cyclical

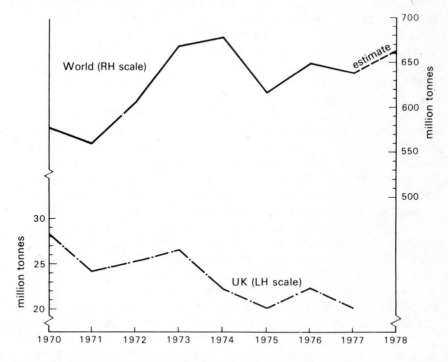

FIG. 6.1:   World and UK Crude Steel Production, 1970–78

Source: Department of International Economic and Social Affairs (November 1978) *Monthly Bulletin of Statistics* **32,** (11). New York: United Nations; and Iron and Steel Statistics Bureau *Annual Statistics 1978.* Croydon: ISSB.

downturn in demand, combined to depress output sharply in 1975, but two out of the following three years saw rising output. UK steel production traced a similar pattern of fluctuations, but since the record output of 28.3 million tonnes in 1970 (4.7% of world production), the trend has been clearly downward. By 1977, the UK's share of world output had fallen to 3%. Most advanced industrialised nations experienced similar falls in both relative and absolute terms as production in the developing countries and centrally-planned economies increased, but the contraction has been particularly severe in the UK.

Steel is an important basic material for a number of industries including motor vehicles, domestic appliances, shipbuilding, construction and engineering. Its demand is very sensitive to the rate of growth of the Gross Domestic Product (GDP) and because of sharp changes in the level of stocks when final consumption is expected to increase, steel production exhibits the strong cyclical fluctuations characteristic of capital goods subject to an accelerator effect.

Although the link between GDP growth and steel demand is well-established, the *share* of steel in total output – the steel 'intensity' – tends to fall as nations develop and their income levels rise. Consumers' expenditure becomes increasingly devoted to higher-value goods with little or no steel content, and to services. Moreover, technical progress, itself associated with economic growth, has enabled lighter steels to be used for many products, thereby reducing the tonnage required, and has led to the substitution of other materials (for example plastics and aluminium). Finally, the export markets of many of the traditional large-scale steel-producing nations have been eroded as developing nations have established their own steel-making facilities, which have allowed them to supply much of their own indigenous demand and to provide a substantial margin of capacity for export. These factors have led both to excess capacity in the major steel-producing nations and to severe competition in export markets.

The effects of these factors have been heavy financial losses among many firms in the major steel-producing nations. Steel manufacture is capital-intensive and a large part of costs are fixed. As a result, break-even volumes are a high proportion of available capacity, and losses escalate as output falls. Three additional factors make the problem worse. First, the industry is a major employer, and its production is usually concentrated in depressed areas. There are therefore strong political pressures to avoid lay-offs and redundancies when demand falls, making labour costs more of a fixed charge. Second, steel prices tend to rise during the upswing of the economic cycle as demand runs ahead of output and stocks fall. Governments may then impose various forms of price control as they try to check inflation. These reduce profits in the boom but do not alleviate falling prices and associated losses during recessions. Finally, technical advances and the need to replace ageing equipment have required substantial investment, much of which has been financed externally through borrowing, partly because of the sheer size of the investments involved, and partly because of low profits. A heavy burden of interest charges has been placed on many firms.

The rate of technical change in the industry has been dramatic. The principal stages of production for bulk steels are iron production in a blast furnace; its conversion, together with scrap, to steel in a furnace; followed by casting and rolling. Until the mid-1950s, most major manufacturers produced bulk steels in the Siemens' open hearth furnace, which had been developed in the latter half of the nineteenth century. Its main advantage was the flexibility possible in the composition of the metal charge: hot or cold metal could be used and the proportions of iron to scrap could be varied easily. The largest furnaces took up to three hundred tonnes of metal, but the conversion time was lengthy, lasting four hours or more.

With the introduction of basic oxygen steelmaking (BOS), in which oxygen is blown into molten metal contained in a vessel lined with basic refractories, the cycle time fell dramatically to around forty minutes. The rate at which the technique was introduced by the main steel-making nations differed (Meyer and Herregat, 1974; Aylen, 1977, 1980), but by 1977 it accounted for more than one-half of output in all, with the exception of Italy and Sweden. The BOS process raised the potential production of steelworks considerably: a complex of three converters can produce seven million tonnes of crude steel a year. The converters need a large supply of molten iron, which normally forms at least 70% of their total metal charge, and so steel production on integrated sites became indispensable and improvements were made in blast furnace efficiency. In the main this was achieved by increasing the internal dimensions of furnaces, reducing the cycle time and improving the quality of the ore charged (Gold, 1974). The largest furnaces now produce as much as 10 000 tonnes of iron a day (or about three and a half million tonnes a year). Improvements were also made at the rolling and finishing stages to cope with the increased volume of production and to raise the quality of the final product. This was done chiefly by increasing speeds, improving tolerances and reducing labour requirements – mainly through automation. Considerable economies of scale are available: production costs per tonne fall as the output of flat products from integrated works is increased to at least ten million tonnes a year (Cockerill, 1974). In several countries large new works were built at coastal sites so that raw materials (chiefly iron-rich ore and coking coal) could be imported and finished steel products exported cheaply and easily.

But in most countries a parallel force was also at work. The post-war growth of manufacturing industry created not only a primary demand for steel but also for a secondary supply of scrap metal. The development of continuous casting methods avoided the need for heavy and expensive rolling mills with large fixed capacities. With the real price of electricity beginning to decline in many countries during the 1960s, it became feasible to produce common grades of long products (rods, bar, wire, etc.) from scrap melted in electric arc furnaces and cast continuously into billets.[2] Previously, electric arc furnaces had been used mainly in the production of special steels, but by avoiding manufacture of both hot iron and flat steel products (sheet and strip), small scale operations could be established. The first of these 'mini-mills' appeared in the USA.

The steel industries of the industrial nations have thus been faced with stationary or falling demand, mounting losses, severe competition from imports and rapid technical change. Rationalisation, modernisation and substantial reductions in workforces have been necessary. Each nation has had severe problems, but, for a combination of reasons, these have been particularly acute in Britain.

6.2 THE STRUCTURE OF THE INDUSTRY

6.2.1 Its size

The iron and steel industry[3] is a major component of the UK economy. It accounts for about 5% of output and employment in manufacturing and almost 12% of investment. In 1973 there were 1414 enterprises in the industry as defined in the Standard Industrial Classification. These operated 1682 establishments. However the number of actual steelmaking units is very small. In 1977 only fifty-six produced crude steel, of which thirteen were fully integrated from the iron making to the finishing stages. Operations are typically on a large scale: the average employment sizes of establishments and enterprises are more than two and one-half times those for all manufacturing. Over 70% of sales, net output and employment are concentrated in the five largest enterprises and establishments.

A wide range of steel products is supplied, the bulk (more than 80%) being divided equally between long products (rods, bars, sections, etc.) and flat products (plate, strip, sheet and tinplate). The remainder consists of semi-manufactured products for further processing, tubes and pipes, railway tyres, wheels, axles etc. and forgings and castings. More than one-quarter of deliveries pass through stockholders, the rest being shipped directly to the user, of which motor vehicle manufacturing (9% of total deliveries in 1977); wire and wire manufactures (7%) and cans and metal boxes (6%) are the most important.

The industry is dominated by the British Steel Corporation (BSC), formed in 1967 by the nationalisation of the fourteen largest steel producers. BSC produces virtually all the nation's iron (99%) and an overwhelming proportion of crude steel (86%). There are about 130 companies in the independent steelmaking and processing sector of the industry of which about thirty produce and process crude steel; the remainder are re-rollers and finishers. Independent producers account for about 14% of crude steel output; about three-quarters of this is non-alloy grades, the rest being alloy steels. Through their rolling and finishing operations, the independents account for about one-third of finished steel deliveries from UK mills and are important purchasers of semi-manufactured steels, both from BSC and from abroad.

During the period 1967 to 1977, total supplies to the UK market passed through two distinct cycles, with peaks occurring in 1970 and 1973. In 1975 in the depth of the recession, supplies to the home market were at their lowest for twelve years. Domestic producers' sales were more volatile still as a result of the rising penetration of imports and the contraction of export markets. Between 1970 and 1977, the share of imports in the home market rose from one-twentieth to more than one-fifth (see table 6.1). Rather more than one-half of these supplies comes from elsewhere in the European Community. Of the remainder, the majority comes from other Western European nations, particularly Sweden and Spain. In 1977 Japanese producers accounted for less than 5% of imports.

TABLE 6.1:   Net [a] deliveries of finished steel to the UK market by source of supply, 1970 and 1977

Source	1970		1977	
	(million tonnes)	(% of total)	(million tonnes)	(% of total)
British Steel Corporation	13.4	70.4	8.3	54.6
Independents	4.6	24.1	3.8	25.1
Imports	1.0	5.5	3.1	20.3
Net deliveries to UK market	19.1	100.0	15.2	100.0

Sources: ISSB (annually); BSC (annually).
Note: [a]excluding semi-manufactures for further processing.

Foreign competition has been particularly severe in the markets for sheet steel (where imports accounted for 40% of supplies in 1976); plate (30%); tubes and pipes (29%) and reinforcing rods and bars (21%). In the last two markets, import penetration has been assoc-iated with the growth in demand as North Sea oil and gas exploration and production have proceeded and with the inability of the UK industry to produce certain types of steel. In the construction reinforcement market competition has been especially strong from low-cost mini-works.

Although imports have risen sharply, their market share in the UK is low by comparison with most of the other nations of the European Community. Imports account for more than one-quarter of the market in France and West Germany, and more than two-thirds in the Netherlands, Denmark, the Irish Republic and Belgium–Luxembourg. The UK's problem, it may be argued, is not so much that imports have increased as that exports have failed to grow correspondingly. Export volume has exceeded six million tons only twice in the last decade. Western Europe is the most important market, taking almost one-half. The North American market absorbs a further 15%. The UK maintained a trade surplus in steel products until 1974, the first of three years of deficits. In 1977, the trade surplus was 320 000 tonnes, valued at $38.4m.

BSC has been the principal victim of the growth in imports, as table 6.1 shows. Its share of the finished steel market fell from over 70% in 1970 to 54% in 1976. Helped by the mini-mills the independent producers have maintained a fairly constant market share.

6.2.2 The British Steel Corporation

The intentions of the 1964–70 Labour government to re-nationalise the iron and steel industry were set out in a White Paper published in April 1965 (Cmnd 2651, 1965). This proposed the transfer of the relevant assets of the companies that produced more than 475 000 gross tons (=483 000 metric tonnes) of crude steel in the period July 1963–June 1964 to a National Steel Corporation. Compensation was to be paid at a rate determined by the average value of shares over the five-year period before 1964. The ensuing Act of 1967 provided for the establishment of the British Steel Corporation, which was to absorb the fourteen largest companies.[4] At its formation, BSC's crude steel-making capacity was about twenty-four million tonnes a year, making it then second only to the United States Steel Corporation.

The Act provides for the Corporation to have a Board consisting of a Chairman and up to twenty members appointed by the Secretary of State. The Minister is also given powers to approve the capital invest- ment programme and the Corporation's borrowings. He may set a financial target and can give directions to the Board relating to certain matters specified in the Act, and also to any general matter affecting the public interest.

At vesting day, BSC acquired the assets of fifty-eight iron and steel producing and re-rolling works. These included thirty-nine crude steel producing works of which twenty-one were fully integrated pig iron to finished steel units. [5] The capital employed in the companies absorbed by BSC amounted in 1966 to £1409m; their turnover was estimated at over £1000m and their employment at 270 000 persons. By any standards, therefore, the formation of the Corporation represented the consolidation of a massive amount of assets. Had it taken place in the private sector it would have been the largest industrial merger ever in the UK manufacturing sector. It posed equally large problems of management co-ordination and rationalisation.

In addition to the day-to-day problems of co-ordinating these facilities, a substantial proportion of total capacity was in plant which was small scale, obsolescent or had been inadequately maintained. The average annual capacity of the larger works was only slightly above one and a half million tonnes of crude steel, the lowest of all the principal steel-producing nations, at a time when the economies of scale were known to extend to six or seven times this level (Cockerill, 1974). The Labour government of 1964–70 had recognised explicitly that rationalisation and modernisation was necessary – indeed the White Paper of 1965 made plain that this was a major, if not the principal, reason for public ownership. Nationalisation, in its post-1945 form, was to be used as an arm of interventionist industrial policy for restructuring, for modernisation and for increasing productivity.

The Corporation's initial steps towards rationalisation consisted of concentrating investment on those works whose efficiency could be improved by modernisation and expansion. Steelworks embrace a number of large-scale sequential processes with different optimal output rates. Thus it is possible to release considerable economies of scale and to raise overall capacity by bringing each section into balance through selective investment at particular stages in the process. The principal schemes which went ahead shortly after vesting day under this heading were the construction of basic oxygen steel-making, continuous casting and rolling facilities at the Appleby–Frodingham works in Scunthorpe (the 'Anchor' project) and the enhancement of steelmaking and rolling at Llanwern and Ravenscraig.

However, after rising steadily between 1967/68 and 1971/72, annual investment expenditure in real terms dropped substantially in 1972/73. As a result, much of the initial impetus of BSC's restructuring was lost, projects were delayed and costs escalated. There were two main causes behind this fall in investment expenditure. The first was the initial hostility of the Conservative government elected in June 1970. Tory policy at that time was undecided between denationalisation, splitting the Corporation up into smaller units (perhaps with the introduction of some private capital and the encouragement of joint ventures) or maintaining the status quo with a commitment to raising efficiency. Eventually, a Joint Steering Group (JSG) was established in March 1971 to review the Corporation's prospects over the long term and to define its strategy. The Corporation, the Department of Trade and Industry and the Treasury were represented on the JSG. There were no representatives from the relevant trade unions; with hindsight it may be argued that this omission was fatal to the chances of success of the JSG's eventual proposals. In their final report of August 1972 the JSG accepted BSC's case that a substantial increase in investment in steel producing and finishing capacity should be undertaken up to the middle of the 1980s. In fact the Corporation's success proved to be a Pyrrhic victory: the JSG's deliberations had delayed the investment programme by two years, and UK steel demand was rising to the pre-recession peak of 1973. The parade had already gone by.

The JSG's report provided the basis for BSC's Ten-Year Development Programme, published as a White Paper in February 1973 (Cmnd 5226, 1973). The Government took the view that home demand was likely to grow at about 2.55% per annum during the 1970s and that there would be substantial export opportunities resulting from the UK's accession to the European Community together with the expected fast rate of growth of world trade in steel. The Corporation would need a capacity of between twenty-eight and thirty-seven million tonnes by 1980/81. The Government accepted the Corporation's proposals for a development programme that would raise its liquid steel capacity from twenty-seven million tonnes in 1973 to thirty-six to thirty-eight million tonnes during the first half of the 1980s, but that would, at the same time, maintain the necessary flexibility in planning and timing of investments for meeting changes in the market forecasts. The increase in the share of steelmaking capacity contributed by large-scale basic oxygen converters would require rich foreign ores to be imported. This could be done most cheaply by developing large-scale integrated works at coastal sites. The intention was to concentrate bulk steelmaking at five existing major steelmaking plants, each of which would be considerably expanded, and to begin the construction of a new large-scale works on South Teesside.

The total cost of the development programme was estimated at over £3000m (at March 1972 prices). Annual expenditure would rise until around 1976/77 and then be determined by conditions in the market for steel. There would be a net reduction of 50 000 job opportunities over the period of the strategy. Although these proposals were widely welcomed by the industry and by the plant suppliers, they brought a storm of protest from the trade unions, both at national level and in the plants scheduled for closure. This reaction was all the more intense because they had not been party to the discussions which had led to the

White Paper.

Progress during the initial stages of the development strategy was slower than expected and more costly. Preliminary planning and design work was time consuming, and in some cases changes in the specification of equipment was necessary. There were also industrial relations problems, particularly on large construction sites. But the most severe check to progress came with the General Election of February 1974 and the return of a minority Labour government. It was apparent that another election would be necessary within a short time: because of this the new Secretary of State for Industry (Mr Benn) was unable to make firm proposals for the Corporation's development. However, following strong representations from the trade unions it was announced in May 1974 that the Corporation's closure plans would be reviewed by Lord Beswick, Minister of State in the Department of Industry. He reported in February 1975 on the proposed closures for England and Wales and on those in Scotland in the following August.

Of nineteen proposed closures, the Beswick review confirmed the Corporation's proposals in seven plants (covering 7470 jobs, or 26% of the total) and deferred closure in the remainder. No steps were taken to compensate the Corporation for the additional financial burden resulting from keeping the outdated units in operation: by July 1978 the additional direct operating costs were at least £100m a year (BSC, 1978, page 6). Nor did the Government make any firm statement on its attitude to the development strategy. The Government and the Corporation continued to pay lip-service to a programme of investment which, it became increasingly plain, would never be implemented. However, during the early stages of the development strategy the fears of those who thought the plans too ambitious were assuaged somewhat as world steel demand increased sharply. In the UK, net deliveries (including imports) were 23.3 million tonnes in 1973, a record high and 10% above the previous year's level. BSC's profits after tax and extraordinary items rose from £3m in the financial year 1972/73 to £50m in 1973/74. Nevertheless, because of delays in commissioning new plant, the lack of appropriate equipment, technical and industrial relations problems, and shortages of raw materials (especially pig iron and scrap), the Corporation was unable to meet the whole of its potential demand and imports took an increasing share of the market.

The boom was short-lived. The Yom Kippur War and the oil crisis of the autumn of 1973 reversed the advance of steel demand. In the UK the miners' strike and the three-day week of January 1974 dealt an additional blow to the industry by denying it key raw materials and energy. BSC's crude steel production fell progressively in the two years to 1975 when at 17.2 million tonnes it was the lowest level since its formation. There was a modest recovery in 1976, but output fell back in 1977. All this was a grave set-back because the fall in demand removed the need for additional capacity. Much of the Corporation's capital expenditure was in projects which would take some time to complete, and in the meantime the heavy financing costs had to be met. To make matters worse, BSC was prevented from closing much of its obsolete capacity. Steel prices rose less quickly than raw material, energy or capital costs. Industrial relations, both with site contractors and within the Corporation, were a major problem, with manning levels for new plants proving particularly difficult issues. The pressure on cash-flow – and hence on profits – was too great. BSC lost £225m after interest and tax in 1975/76, £95m the following year, and a record £437.7m in 1977/78.

By October 1977 it was apparent that urgent steps were necessary in respect of both plant closures and the development programme. The Select Committee on Nationalised Industries, which was completing a lengthy enquiry into the organisation and performance of the Corporation, extended its enquiries to take account of the worsening situation. In its reports, it called, *inter alia*, for closure of the 'Beswick' plants and a scaling-down of the investment programme. In March the Government published a White Paper on the Corporation's position (Cmnd 7149, 1978). The major expansion proposed for Port Talbot and the construction of electric arc plants at Shelton, Hunterston and Ravenscraig were to be deferred, but the Government were prepared to approve an investment programme in which schemes substantially underway (chiefly at Ravenscraig and Redcar) would be completed; essential replacements and schemes to balance primary and finishing facilities would be undertaken; product quality and customer service would be improved; and proposals for cost reduction, projects with rapid pay-back periods and schemes of under £2m, would be brought forward. BSC's management were to be allowed 'at their discretion' to proceed with further closure proposals subject to prior discussion with the trade unions.

In the period since its formation, BSC has made considerable progress in reducing the number of plants operated, increasing their average capacity, and introducing modern technology. The developments have proceeded at the fastest rate for iron and steelmaking, rather less quickly for rolling and finishing. The technical specifications of much of the new equipment are good by international standards. Unfortunately, the ambitious reconstruction programme has coincided with a period of intense political pressure and the collapse of the market for steel.

6.2.3 The independent sector

The output threshold laid down in the nationalisation Act of 1967 was designed to capture the principal producers: enterprises with small outputs or which were ironmakers or steel re-rollers and finishers only were excluded from public ownership. The independent sector was thus formed as a residual virtually by legislative accident, and its composition is diverse as a consequence.

Most of the thirty or so independent steelmakers manufacture special steels, chiefly in Sheffield, and supply about 44% of the output of these grades. The remaining producers manufacture common grades of steel for rolling, forging or casting, and include divisions of large engineering companies as well as independent firms. The independent sector is the sole supplier of high speed and tool steels, as well as the bulk of wire and wire products, bright steel bars and alloy forgings.

Whilst the total number of independent companies has increased in the period since nationalisation and the share of home-market deliveries has remained fairly steady, considerable rationalisation has taken place, chiefly among the Sheffield producers. Although there are more than a dozen independent special steel producers, and many more re-rollers and finishers, this part of the industry has come to be dominated by four large companies which together account for more than two-thirds of production. There are four main types of special steels: stainless, tool (for cutting and boring tools), high speed (for aerospace and high technology uses) and low-alloy general purpose steels. Johnson Firth Brown Ltd (JFB), the largest company, produces a wide range of special steel products. The next largest is Dunford and Elliott Ltd which together with JFB produces the bulk of low alloy general purpose steels. The major tool and stainless steel producers are Edgar Allen Balfour and Samuel Osborn respectively. Cross-share holdings between the Sheffield companies increase the consolidation of the sector still more.

The objects of rationalisation have been to achieve economies of scale and to concentrate production on fewer sites. This has involved a number of mergers and acquisitions, including the transfer of assets between the public and independent sectors.[6] Government assistance and encouragement with rationalisation has been important. The former Industrial Reorganisation Corporation (IRC) supported Dunford and Elliott's bid for Hadfields, another Sheffield steel producer, in October 1967. In January 1969 IRC acquired Brown Bayley Ltd at a cost of 5.8m, subsequently selling it to Dunford and Elliott. The following year, IRC made a loan of £1.75m to Samuel Osborn to help finance its move to a new site and the building of a new works. In spite of these developments and by contrast with some other European countries (for example Austria, Sweden and West Germany) in which special steel production is controlled by a single company, the Sheffield sector is still very fragmented and is currently suffering severely from foreign competition, particularly in the market for low alloy steels. It is unlikely, therefore, that the consolidation process has yet ended.

Although special steels account for the overwhelming proportion of the independent sector's output by value, the bulk of production in tonnage terms is of non-alloy steel (2.3 million tonnes in 1977, or 78% of output). Production has increased considerably in recent years, both because of transfers of capacity from the public to the private sector[7] and because of a net growth of output. Much of the latter has been met by the construction of mini-works. Canadian, Scandinavian and Greek interests are represented among the new producers. The growth of non-alloy steelmaking in the independent sector may be attributed to three main factors. One is the availability of scrap as a result of the recession. Another is low hourly wage costs, offering low unit production costs when allied to high productivity. New entrants have found increased productivity easier to achieve in small, new steelworks than has BSC, with its large complexes and entrenched workforce attitudes. Third, there has been periodic dissatisfaction on the part of many steel users with BSC's supply.

6.3 PERFORMANCE

Until the onset of the recession towards the end of 1973, the post-war trend in the British steel industry had been one of expansion. Despite marked cyclical variations, output at the top of each of the regular four or five-year cycles steadily exceeded the previous peak until in 1970 the industry achieved its record output. Growth was steady but unremarkable, output in the peak year of 1973 being only 8% higher than in 1960 (another peak). The benefits of this modest growth were more than wiped out by the recession: by 1977 crude steel production was more than 17% below its 1960 level. By comparison with its major competitors, the British industry had grown more slowly during the years of expansion, and suffered more severely in the recessions. In considerable measure this was a result of the general and well-known structural difficulties of the British economy but in recent years it has been made worse by the collapse of some major markets (motor vehicles and shipbuilding in particular) and by steel's inability either to hold on to its home market share or to penetrate export markets. The greater part of the increase in import penetration has taken place since 1967, the year of BSC's formation and, as has been shown, has largely been at the Corporation's expense. In contrast, there has been no trend increase in exports, and from 1974 to 1976 the UK was a net importer of steel.

The fall in the steel industry's share of its home and export markets has reflected its declining international competitiveness. This has been caused by both price and non-price factors. Whilst during the 1970s UK steel prices rose more slowly than those of manufactured goods as a whole, they increased more rapidly than the prices of other major steel-producers, even when account is taken of the fall in the sterling exchange rate. Before the UK entered the European Community in 1973, steel prices were subject to Government control and were frequently held below the market level. Although this damaged profitability, it afforded effective protection against imports, and the domestic producers' share of the home market remained high. Upon entry to the Community, there was a staged reduction in tariffs, and prices rose to European levels, a process accelerated by the need to adopt the basing-point pricing system. Under this, producers' prices are set in relation to a particular geographical location (usually the point of production or close by) to which additional charges are added for transportation. The system is designed to ensure 'transparency' in pricing, so that competition is not distorted by secret discounts or the absorption of freight costs by the producer. In practice, it is deficient in this, but nevertheless its introduction raised effective prices in the UK. By the end of 1977, UK producers' prices were in general at parity with those elsewhere in the Community, and for some products for which domestic producers had a market advantage, they were higher.

With the opening of the UK market to international competition prices are now determined chiefly by market conditions. The rate at which prices can be increased is largely governed by the stage of the steel cycle, overall demand being sensitive to the growth of real income rather than to price. However, given the largely homogeneous nature of specific products, price elasticities are high for *unilateral* price cuts by producers. With a high ratio of fixed to variable costs, there is a clear incentive for producers to try to undercut the prevailing price level when demand is weak. But such action induces matching cuts on the part of rivals, the effect of which is to bring all prices down. For this reason, since 1977 the European Commission has sought to stabilise prices through voluntary and statutory measures.

As might have been expected, within these constraints BSC has emerged as the price leader for most products in the UK market. The independent producers enjoy more leverage over the prices of those products for which they are the sole domestic suppliers. But BSC has considerable potential influence over the independent sector's profitability because of its importance both as a competitor and as the main supplier of semi-finished steel. By holding its final product prices steady whilst increasing the prices of its semi-manufactures, BSC could severely damage the independents' margins. While there was some evidence of this occurring soon after the Corporation was formed, such action is now effectively prevented by imports, by competition legislation and by the strength of public opinion.

Although prices have increased, profitability has not in general improved because costs have increased much more – particularly those of energy, employment, overheads and finance. But despite the industry's poor productivity record, direct labour costs per tonne of output have not been a principal problem in recent years. Table 6.2

TABLE 6.2:   Labour productivity and costs in the steel industries of the European Community, 1977, and rate of change, 1973–7

	Hours worked[a] per tonne of crude steel produced	Index of change (1973= 100)	Hourly labour costs EUA[b]	Index of change (1973= 100)	Labour cost per tonne EUA[b]	Index of change (1973= 100)
Belgium	6.19	102	9.44	204	58.43	207
France	7.17	91	6.69	204	47.97	186
West Germany	6.46	104	8.43	182	54.46	189
Italy	5.42	105	5.55	159	30.08	151
Luxembourg	6.09	104	na	170[c]	na	184
Netherlands	5.81	na	na	na	na	na
UK	11.75	112	4.05	169	47.59	190

Source: Eurostat (annually).
Notes: [a]Manual workers. [b]The average rate of exchange in 1977 was 1 European Unit of Account (EUA) = £0.425931. [c]1973–6.

shows that in 1977 although the UK had the highest hourly labour requirement per tonne of crude steel produced of each of the main European nations – and thus the lowest labour productivity – this was offset by low hourly labour costs so that of the five countries for which a comparison can be made, labour costs per tonne were lower than in all except Italy. Nevertheless the UK has the worst labour productivity growth record and, when measured in terms of domestic currencies, has had the fastest rate of increase of labour costs per tonne.[8] Neither is low labour productivity compensated by higher capital productivity: in BSC between 1968 and 1975 the rate of growth of total factor productivity (labour plus capital) was below that for output per head (NEDO, 1976). As the exchange rate stabilises with the development of North Sea oil production, the low level and growth rate of productivity will become an increasing problem for the steel industry, pushing up its costs of production in relation to those of other countries. A major cause of low productivity is the chronic degree of over-manning. In large part, this results from the importance placed by the trade unions on maintaining the level of employment, and from the concern of the several unions represented in each workplace with the relative status of their members. The consequence is an excess of labour and intense rigidity in its deployment.

It is frequently claimed that new investment is required to raise labour productivity to international standards. This was a cornerstone of the 1973 White Paper and it is undeniably the case that an increase in the investment rate was urgently needed. Subsequent capital expenditure has modernised the industry's equipment but at a slower rate than elsewhere (Aylen, 1979). By 1977 slightly more than one-half of total crude steel output was produced in basic oxygen furnaces – still less than in the other major steel-producing nations with the exception of Sweden and Italy, but a marked improvement on the late 1960s when only a quarter was made by this process. In addition new large blast furnaces, continuous casting machines and rolling mills have been installed. But in cases where major investments have been attempted, the results have often not been encouraging. Some new facilities have been late coming into operation because of construction delays, commissioning problems and disputes over manning levels. These problems have been felt both in BSC and in the private sector. They have been part of the wider inability of the industry to get the best out of its investments. Once commissioned it has proved difficult, sometimes impossible, to run plant up to its rated capacity.

Technical problems have contributed to this and have been made worse by the lack of experience of building and commissioning large units of plant in the British industry because of the low level of investment in the years immediately prior to 1969. But workforces have also failed to co-operate in running the industry's stock of capital in the most efficient manner. This has been most evident in BSC's attempts to concentrate declining overall production levels on the most efficient plants by closing the small, high-cost units. Workforce opposition has resulted in too much production being carried out in the less efficient plants, which in turn reduces the performance of the more efficient units.

The productivity difficulties have been made worse, especially within BSC, by recurrent failures to meet demand, not only when orders were plentiful, but also during recessions. During the 1973 boom BSC ran short of hot iron – necessary for supplying the basic oxygen steel furnaces – at Scunthorpe. Part of the deficiency was made up by the use of scrap, so far as the technical constraints would allow. But this in turn reduced the supply of scrap to the independent electric arc producers and raised its price. Construction delays and commissioning problems with new plant have reduced effective capacity, especially when steps have been taken to close old plant in the expectation that its replacement would be in operation. As noted earlier, there have also been complaints about the quality of some finished steel products. In part this has been due to the continued operation of outdated rolling facilities. In 1976 the top quality of hot rolled coil in the UK was well below the premier qualities produced in West Germany.[9]

It has been claimed that BSC has lost some of its market share as a result of the reorganisation in 1974 of its production and marketing functions. Centralisation of orders and their allocation to mills meant that many customers were supplied from works with which they had not previously dealt, as orders were allocated on the basis of plant suitability and availability. It is hard to judge whether this affected overall product quality, but many customers, reacting unfavourably to their inability to make direct contact with the mill processing their orders, certainly felt that it did. That the fear had some justification is confirmed by the fact that certain major customers (automobile manufacturers among them) have been able to specify the mills at which their orders are produced. Missed delivery dates, due to plant breakdowns, and production disruptions have been a further problem. These have severe consequences for customers engaged in large-scale process or assembly operations. For example, in the year to September 1976, only one-third of BSC's supplies to British Leyland was delivered on time, and less than two-thirds within two weeks of the promised date.[10] In some cases, the Corporation has been unable to supply particular types of product, despite excess overall capacity. This has been most marked in the case of submarine pipe for oil and gas operations on the UK Continental Shelf, where the Corporation has not had the appropriate equipment to make either the required diameter or quality of pipe. As a result, virtually all requirements have been imported.

In these circumstances, it has not been difficult for foreign suppliers to increase their share of the UK market, especially when faced with declining demand in their traditional markets. As we have seen, most of the challenge has come from producers elsewhere in the European Community. The key advantages possessed by imported steel have been its availability, quality and price. The inability of domestic sources to supply the home market has given foreign suppliers the opportunity to negotiate long-term contracts and, provided satisfactory service is given, it is often difficult for them to be dislodged when the contract is due for renewal. Foreign suppliers also probably encounter a more elastic demand curve for their products because they account for only a small proportion of the UK market. In such circumstances slight reductions in their prices below the going level are likely to induce a more than proportionate increase in demand as customers switch their marginal demand from home suppliers. Import penetration has also been helped by the UK's steel distribution system in which more than a quarter of total deliveries moves through stockholders, who draw their supplies from a number of domestic and foreign sources. Foreign suppliers have steadily increased their share of this part of the market, despite efforts by BSC to expand its own stockholding operations.

The collapse of the steel market has seriously damaged the profitability of the industry in both the public and the private sectors. The independent producers have been the most resilient, owing to their greater flexibility, lower overheads, more specialised product ranges and (in many cases) their ability to draw on the financial resources of the diversified groups of which they are part. But by any standards, BSC's financial performance has been disastrous. The combination of falling sales and prices, rising unit costs and a heavy investment programme has led to escalating losses and burgeoning borrowings. By November 1977 the Corporation was bankrupt by the standards of private sector companies. Profits after interest, taxation and other items were made in only four of the eleven accounting periods to the end of March 1978. By that time accumulated losses totalled £913m, against profits of £138m. There is no clear relationship between profits and the volume of steel production as movements in prices and costs are also important. Prices have been held back as part of the counter-inflation programmes of successive Governments, both by statutory and voluntary limitations. By 1976 it was claimed that price restraint had cost the Corporation £783m in lost revenue, exceeding its accumulated deficit to that date and for which there had been no compensation. Overt price control ceased with Britain's entry into the European Community, but BSC remained highly conscious of the sensitivity of the inflation rate to movements in steel prices. On the cost side, in addition to (and indeed exacerbating) the underlying productivity problem, delays have occurred in the introduction of new plant, both through construction and commissioning set-backs, and also through difficulties in obtaining approval for projects from the Department of Industry. Moreover, the Beswick review of 1974–75 imposed on BSC the obligation to keep open a number of high-cost plants, in order to maintain employment.

Interest charges have been an increasing burden, rising from £44m in 1972–73 to £197m in 1977–78, as the development programme was implemented and as costs rose faster than revenue. As recently as April 1976, it was hoped to finance at least one-half of the development programme from retained profits, depreciation and investment grants, but by December of that year, this was realised to be impossible. Total capital expenditure between 1972/73 and 1977/78 totalled £3bn, but little more than 2% of this was met from internal sources, the remainder coming either from domestic or foreign borrowing, or from issues of public dividend capital (PDC). Without PDC, which was first made available in 1969, and which is remunerated by variable dividend payments according to the level of profits, rather than by fixed interest charges, the Corporation's interest burden, and hence its losses, would have been much greater. By late 1977, it was clear that the expansion of sales which formed the basis of the 1973 White Paper would not be realised and that the Corporation, under the policies then current, faced an indeterminate future of low output and rising losses. In the White Paper of 1978, the Government accepted the need for works closures and a reduction in capital expenditure. It also proposed a financial reconstruction to take place at some future date in which, presumably, substantial amounts of debt would be written off. In the meantime all fresh injections of capital into BSC were to be in the form of non-interest bearing state equity, which would be fully remunerated after the reconstruction. In March 1978 BSC set itself the target of breaking-even by the last quarter of 1980, without taking account of a financial reconstruction.

6.4 PUBLIC POLICY

There is no doubt that the net effect of public policy in the post-war steel industry has been harmful. To chronicle the problems is an easy, if melancholy, task: to propose alternatives which give hope for the future is much more difficult. The root cause has been continuous political interference for reasons of dogma and short-term expediency.

The dogma was starkly illustrated in the opening years of the 1950s. The first post-war Labour government had been pledged to the public ownership of major industries, and it was clear from 1945 that iron and steel would be a principal candidate. There was considerable uncertainty in the industry as it tackled its reconstruction, and an unwillingness to invest for fear of sequestration of its assets. The return of the second administration in 1950, albeit with a small overall majority, confirmed these expectations, and an Act nationalising the entire industry was passed soon after. However, little was done in the industry by way of restructuring or the preparation of cohesive plans, because the defeat of the Government the following year, and its replacement by a Conservative administration, again made the future of the industry uncertain. A de-nationalisation Act was passed in 1951, and the process of returning the industry to private hands began. This was largely accomplished by 1955, with the exception of the loss-making concern of Richard Thomas and Baldwins in which the Government remained the major shareholder. The consequence was that no effective strategy was evolved for the industry in the first post-war decade.

Even after the majority of the industry had been returned to the private sector, Government interference continued, because the Iron and Steel Board had powers of control over prices and investment. Prices were held down in the boom, and cash-flow, profitability and investment suffered. Pressure was also brought to bear on the timing, size and location of new investment. Moreover, political uncertainty continued, because the Labour Opposition were committed to re-nationalisation on their return to office. Another wasted decade of little investment or rationalisation ensued.

The situation was not eased with the return of a Labour government with a very small overall majority in 1964, and it was not until the election of June 1966, in which Labour obtained a substantial overall majority that it became certain that the major part of the industry would pass once again to the public sector. After the 1967 Act the private sector remained in considerable uncertainty about both its future and its freedom of action. The Secretary of State for Industry was given powers over its investment, and there was the likelihood that capacity expansions by firms above the 483 000 tonnes threshold of the Act might result in their too being taken into public ownership.

The terms of nationalisation and the initial valuation of BSC's assets had left it under-capitalised and without a reserve, a condition which was rectified in part by the financial reconstruction of 1969. Investment began to increase, but in conditions of immense uncertainty, because the Conservative Opposition were actively considering dismemberment of the Corporation. As has been seen, after the 1970 election investment proposals were delayed and when the development programme was at last approved, the change of government in 1974 halted rationalisation. No effective action was then taken until the financial crisis in 1977.

It is plain that the effects of public policy could not have been much worse but it is by no means certain that alternative policies would have been much better. Would things have been better if nationalisation had not taken place? In that event, it is probable that a measure of concentration would have occurred in the industry through mergers and acquisitions, as the more profitable firms sought to increase their assets, and as others combined for defensive reasons. Although this would have led to some strengthening of the industry, several producers would have found themselves in financial difficulties, and the strategic and political position of the industry in the economy would have brought Government involvement, if not through outright ownership, certainly through the provision of funds. Constraints on investment and redundancies would still have applied. The development of the more successful enterprises may have been held back as a consequence of the support for the less profitable producers. There would have been a larger number of smaller-sized producers, and this might have inhibited the acquisition of the economies of scale and the rate of introduction of new technical processes, especially basic oxygen steel-making. But, on the other hand, there would have been greater flexibility in production, which would have helped in the adjustment to the recession. The financial position of some producers could have been stablised by increased diversification into more profitable areas. The end result might have been a more fragmented industry, with marked variations in performance among its members, but still with a substantial public sector involvement. It is impossible to say whether, on balance, the industry would have been any stronger. The key element is not the form of ownership but rather the nature of the political environment. As the 1965 White Paper recognised, there were strong economic reasons why public sector involvement in the industry was necessary – chiefly to increase and co-ordinate investment. But it has been the subsequent frustration of those objects which has been at the root of many of the industry's problems.

Granted the inevitability of nationalisation, was the formation of a monolithic producer the best structure for the public sector of the industry? It is hard to sustain the argument that BSC is too big in terms of output or capacity, for it produces less than half the output of the world's two largest producers, Nippon Steel and United States Steel. There is more strength in the argument when it is related to employment, for with a workforce of almost 200 000, BSC is the world's largest steel company. The co-ordination and administration problems which this entails are obvious. Yet these could be dealt with in large part if productivity could be increased to international levels, an objective frustrated so far by excessive government interference and the constraints of industrial relations.

The problem lies not so much in the absolute size of BSC as in its method of formation. Vesting the assets of the largest steel-makers unselectively in a single enterprise amounted to the largest corporate merger to have occurred in the UK. Any group of that size would have had enormous managerial problems. It might have been better to have established three or four separate companies in the public sector, perhaps with a view to allowing them to combine at a later date, if economies of scale and conditions in the market made that desirable. But the additional benefits would have been small, and would certainly have been overwhelmed by the tide of political and economic events.

Finally, is it sensible for UK governments to continue to support the steel industry? The decline in the industry's world market share may reflect a comparative disadvantage in relation to other countries, in which case economic welfare would be increased by moving the resources to other occupations. Yet the UK has abundant human and capital resources and easy access to the European market, so that there are no structural constraints to the development of a strong, internationally competitive industry. What is needed is a dramatic improvement in operating efficiency and product quality, and public policy must be directed unswervingly to this end, as it has been in most other Western European countries and in Japan.

The difficulties must not be underestimated. There is still no sign of a sustained upturn in the demand for steel in the UK. The European industry will have a chronic excess of capacity for some time to come, and world steelmaking capacity will continue to increase, especially in the developing countries. The British steel industry, hampered rather than helped by successive governments and beleaguered by low productivity, looks set to continue its path of relative decline. Its problems are immense, but not insoluble. To overcome them will require effort and goodwill on the part of management and work-forces, and realistic and sustained policies on the part of government. In that, steel is the microcosm of the manufacturing sector.

NOTES TO CHAPTER 6

1. Much of the material of this chapter is drawn from the three reports of the Select Committee on Nationalised Industries on the British Steel Corporation published between November 1977 and February 1978 (SCNI, 1977a, 1977b, 1978), in the preparation of which the author was a specialist adviser. Statistical data come mainly from the Iron and Steel Statistics Bureau's *Annual Statistics* (ISSB, annually), the BSC's *Annual Statistics for the Corporation* (BSC, annually) and the *Iron and Steel Yearbook* of the Statistical Office of the European Communities (Eurostat, annually). Other material is derived from research supported by a grant from the Social Science Research Council, which is gratefully acknowledged.

2. A billet is a long bar of square lateral cross-section, in the range 2″ × 2″ to 5″ × 5″. See McGannon *ed.* (1964), page 631.

3. Minimum List Headings 311 to 313: Iron and Steel (General), Steel Tubes and Iron Castings etc.

4. As the result of an agreement effective from vesting day, one of the companies, Round Oak Steelworks, was jointly owned by BSC and Tube Investments Ltd, the former owner.

5. See Cmnd 3362 (1967), paragraphs 43–44, pages 19–20 and appendices F to G, pages 44–46.

6. For example, BSC sold its tool steel interests in 1972 and in 1974 took full control of Sheffield Rolling Mills Ltd, previously jointly owned with Thos. Firth & John Brown Ltd.

7. BSC sold the Brymbo Works at Wrexham, making chiefly forging steel, to GKN Ltd, its former owner, in 1974.

8. Unit labour costs measured in sterling increased by about two and a half times between 1973 and 1977. Column 6 of table 6.2 shows the increase adjusted for parity changes.

9. See SCNI (1977a), Q.17, page 55.

10. See SCNI (1977a), paragraph 188, page lx.

REFERENCES

Aylen, J. (1977) 'The British Steel Corporation and Technical Change' in SCNI (1977a).

Aylen, J. (1980) 'Innovation in the British Steel Industry' in K. Pavitt ed. (1980) *Technical Innovation and British Economic Performance*. London: Macmillan.

BSC (British Steel Corporation) (annually) *Annual Statistics for the Corporation*. Croydon: BSC.

BSC (1978) *Annual Report and Accounts 1977–78*. London: BSC.

Cmnd 2651 (1965) *Steel Nationalisation*. London: HMSO.

Cmnd 3362 (1967) *British Steel Corporation: Report on Organisation*. London: HMSO.

Cmnd 5226 (1973) *British Steel Corporation: Ten-Year Development Plan*. London: HMSO.

Cmnd 7149 (1978) *British Steel Corporation: The Road to Viability*. London: HMSO.

Cockerill, A. (1974) *The Steel Industry*. University of Cambridge, Department of Applied Economics Occasional Paper no. 42. Cambridge: Cambridge University Press.

Eurostat (annually) *Iron & Steel Yearbook*. Luxembourg: Statistical Office of the European Communities.

Gold, B. (1974) 'Evaluating Scale Economies: The Case of Japanese Blast Furnaces'. *Journal of Industrial Economics* 23, (1), 1–18.

ISSB (Iron and Steel Statistics Bureau) (annually) *Annual Statistics*. Croydon: ISSB.

McGannon, H. E. ed. (1964) *The Making, Shaping and Treating of Steel*. 8th edn. Pittsburgh, Pa.: US Steel Corporation.

Meyer, J. R. and Herregat, G. (1974) 'The Basic Oxygen Steel Process' in L. Nabseth and G. F. Ray eds. (1974) *The Diffusion of New Industrial Processes*. London: Cambridge University Press.

NEDO (National Economic Development Office) (1976) *A Study of UK Nationalised Industries*. London: NEDO.

SCNI (Select Committee on Nationalised Industries) (1977a) *The British Steel Corporation*. HC 26 of 1977/78. 3 vols. London: HMSO.

SCNI (1977b) *The British Steel Corporation*. HC 127 of 1977/78. 2 vols. London: HMSO.

SCNI (1978) *Financial Forecasts of the British Steel Corporation*. HC 238 of 1977/78. London: HMSO.

FURTHER READING

The Select Committee on Nationalised Industries' Report of November 1978 (*The British Steel Corporation*, London: HMSO, HC

26 of 1977/78) is a mine of information on both the public and private sectors. The development of the British steel industry up to nationalisation is described in J. Vaizey, *The History of British Steel*, London: Weidenfeld and Nicolson, 1974. The international structure of the industry is analysed in A. Cockerill, *The Steel Industry*, Cambridge: Cambridge University Press, 1974. A fascinating study of the politics of steel nationalisation is contained in K. Ovenden, *The Politics of Steel*, London: Macmillan, 1978. Basic statistics for the UK industry are in British Steel Corporation, *Annual Statistics for the Corporation*, London: BSC and Iron and Steel Statistics Bureau, *Annual Statistics*, Croydon: ISSB. Data for the European Communities are in Eurostat, *Iron and Steel Yearbook*, Luxembourg: Statistical Office of the European Communities.

7. Computers*

154-78

P. L. Stoneman

The computer – very much a product of the post-war world – has had its influence on everyday life recognised by the label the Information Revolution. Its effect has been compared with the Agrarian and Industrial Revolutions of the eighteenth and nineteenth centuries. Development has been closely tied in with the general advancement in electronics over the last thirty years although the principles of computing can be traced back to Babbage in the nineteenth century. The first modern electronic computers are generally considered to be the Z3, produced by K. Zuse in Germany during the Second World War, and the coding machines used by the UK at a similar time. The first commercial machine is usually considered to be UNIVAC I, produced by Remington Rand in the US in 1951.

Computer is a generic term covering a combination of inputs. Before these are detailed an initial useful distinction can be made between analogue and digital computers. The analogue machine is based on the principle of measurement and the digital on counting. As the analogue machines hold only a very small share of the overall UK market (2% in 1968) we shall concentrate on digital machines. The concept of a computer can be split between hardware and software. The hardware is the actual physical 'machinery', the software the set of instructions that make it work. Hardware consists of input–output devices, storage media, the arithmetic unit and the control unit, these two units plus the 'working' or fast access store usually being labelled the central processing unit (CPU). Software can also be divided into hard software, the set of basic instructions that are necessary for the hardware to function in a coherent manner; the compiler, which allows programs to be written in high level languages[1] (as opposed to binary forms); and the applications software, the actual programs making the computer perform the tasks for which it is required. It is usual for the hardware supplier to provide the hard software and the compilers for

*Much of the content of this chapter is based on Stoneman (1976).

the customer (usually included in the price of the machine) and the user to supply his own applications software. There is also a booming service sector providing applications software and other special software, specialist consultancy services and time sharing and other non-user owned computing facilities. In addition there is a separate leasing sector – the principle of leasing having a long history in the industry – and a myriad of suppliers of special stationery and other consumables, e.g. air conditioning equipment.

In many ways the importance of the computer cannot really be understood without some reference to the user sector. The actual manufacturing of the hardware [MLH 366 in the SIC (1968) classification] is not a particularly large sector but the operators, engineers, programmers and systems staff employed in users' installations considerably increase employment in the supply of computer services. In table 7.1 we give some detail on employment in the industry. The first column refers to the numbers employed in MLH 366 and the second to numbers in the computer services industry. It is

TABLE 7.1: Computer industry employment, 1966–76

Year	Computer manufacturing* (MLH 366)	Computer services	
		Full-time	Part-time
1966	35 800		
1967	41 600		
1968	45 100		
1969	48 800		
1970	52 400		
1971	47 700	14 387	1 114
1972	43 400	14 864	809
1973	45 700	16 957	1 023
1974	44 500	18 993	958
1975	43 300	19 048	1 135
1976	42 200	20 144	1 115
1977	42 900	20 460	1 073

Source: Trade and Industry, 24 June 1973, page 375; *Business Monitor, Electronic Computers; Business Monitor, Computer Services.*
Note: *End-year figures 1966–72; end-June figures 1973–7.

estimated that in 1971 this latter series covered only 25% of the companies in the service sector and thus a truer picture of employment may be gained by multiplying these figures by a factor of four. In addition there are the personnel employed in users' installations. A

National Computing Centre estimate gave a total of 194 000 persons directly involved with the computer industry in 1971 (SCSTA III, 1971, page 124). Even so these numbers represent little more than 0.7% of the total UK labour force (or only 0.2% in MLH 366). The industry is not therefore a big employer. We should state, however, that its products do make great demands on the electronics components sector but even there employment is not high. Table 7.1 shows that in the computer manufacturing industry employment has fallen in the early 1970s from its 1970 peak, whereas computer services has shown unbroken growth. The reasons for this are to a great extent attributable to changes in technology as we shall discuss below.

The net output of the computer manufacturing industry, i.e. MLH 366, rose from £20.5m in 1963 to £324.0m in 1974 (figures at current prices from the Census of Production). Thus although growing in importance over time the industry's contribution to total GNP was still less than 0.4% in 1977. In general we may say that the industry is not large in the total UK context.

The computer manufacturing function consists of assembling components provided from outside suppliers. This operation is supported by large development programmes on the design of computers and other ancillary tasks. Thus in 1971 of a total employment of 47 700, 18% were employed on research and development (R and D), 12% on sales, 33% on other tasks and only 37% on production. Moreover the actual assembly function has changed over time. The computer has gone through three distinct phases, usually labelled generations. In the first generation (essentially the 1950s) computers were constructed using vacuum tubes, the second generation (1960–64) used transistors, and the third generation (middle and late sixties) used integrated circuits. These circuits have been developed further in the latest machines which make use of large scale integration (LSI) or very large scale integration (VLSI), leading to the current marketing of microprocessors – or 'computers on a silicon chip'. It should be noted that these generations are defined with respect to the technology of the CPU, but there have also been advances in the production of peripherals and the quality of software that, although not so dramatic, are equally impressive. By one estimate (Bloch and Galage, 1978) advances in hardware have led to a sixteen thousand-fold improvement in cost–performance ratios in the period 1956–76. No commentator would however argue that any user has achieved such reductions in computing costs, especially given that they take no account of software, which, even prior to the advance of LSI, already accounted for a half of all computing expenses. A more realistic estimate, although by no means a precise one, is given in Stoneman (1976) and a fall in a price index (not accounting for general inflation) from 200 in 1956 to 50 in 1970 (1963=100) would seem to be of the correct order of magnitude, reflecting the fall in price for a whole computer system with some software and certain basic performance characteristics. Even this is quite dramatic considering that over the same period the general price level almost doubled. However these changes in basic technology have had implications for the computer producing sector. This has been most evident in recent years. The production of more compact integrated circuits has not only led to significantly smaller and more powerful computers but also to a simpler and smaller assembly function, electronic connections being made by component suppliers in the production of their silicon chips. Some reflection of this is that between 1963 and 1968 the proportion of total sales revenue of the industry spent on buying in electronic components rose from 16% to 35%. We can also ascribe the falling manpower requirements of the industry to this change in technology. Wages and salaries fell as a percentage of net output from 48.1% in 1970 to 28.8% in 1975. To match this however investment has steadily increased. Freeman (1965) argues that in the mid-1960s this industry had a very low capital intensity (less than £1000 per man) but the current pattern of capital expenditure indicates that this is changing. According to Census of Production figures, gross investment went up six times in money terms (slightly less in real terms) whereas employment only doubled between 1963 and 1968. With the increasing use of computers in the construction of computers this pattern is continuing, although even now it is still not a very capital intensive industry.

R and D – the importance of which has already been illustrated – involves the design of new hardware and software and no company can survive without a strong R and D facility. So heavy is the fixed cost of R and D that Honeywell argue that firms require 10% of the total world market to be competitive (SCSTA I, 1971, paragraph 93) for only then can the burden be spread across large numbers of machines. In 1972 UK expenditure on R and D in the computer industry was £27m (*Trade and Industry*, 2 July 1976, page 16), i.e. 10% of industry sales. However, as much R and D is undertaken by multinational companies overseas, this does not reflect the true extent of R and D expenditure behind the products being sold on the UK market. Imports represent a large share of the UK market. In 1972–3 only 35% of UK installed computer capacity was provided by British manufacturers (see below).

The actual installed capacity is not always easy to measure. A major problem is that the computer has changed dramatically in quality over time. However, from a stock of twenty machines in 1955, growth has proceeded through one thousand machines in 1964, 5500 in 1970, to an *addition* to the stock of twelve thousand machines in 1974 (see Stoneman (1976) and *Trade and Industry*, 18 July 1975, page 180). It is estimated (*The Times*, 14 September 1978) that the 1978 stock is ten times the size of the 1969 stock.

The market can be broken down by user to give a $\frac{2}{3}$ private, $\frac{1}{3}$ government division, this proportion having remained reasonably constant over time. In the private sector, most industries have some contact with computers. However the major users are the computer sector itself; engineering; chemicals, rubber, plastics, etc; and the financial sector. The export market is also quite buoyant with 1977 export sales of £355.4m (fob) i.e. about 40% of total sales by the UK computer industry. In computer services billings to foreign clients represented a meagre $4\frac{1}{2}$% of the total.

The phenomenal growth in the computer stock is a reflection of the diffusion process of a new technology which is more fully explored in Stoneman (1976). Major advances in computer ownership have occurred when generations changed. This fits in well with an hypothesis that the main propellant behind this growth in demand has been improvements in technology (which were in turn based on advances in components made outside the industry) and the consequent falls in price. This is reflected by the different concepts of computerisation attached to each generation – automated clerk, the integrated data processing system, and the management information system – as technology proceeded from the first to the third generation. As the area of application has grown so has demand, not only in the UK but worldwide.

7.1 MARKET STRUCTURE

Because of the worldwide nature of this industry and the importance of multinational companies within it, we should consider both national and international markets. It was estimated that in 1970 the total European and US computer market including services had a turnover of $14 500m split $\frac{3}{4}$ US, $\frac{1}{4}$ Europe (SCST, 1973a, Annex I). Of this market the dominant share is held by International Business Machines (IBM). In table 7.2 we present figures on company shares in the total value of the world computer stock as of 31 December 1977 which illustrate this dominance by IBM. If we look at the Western European market by company shares in the computer stock, we can see that the UK case is unique in the low value of IBM's market share and the large share of the indigenous producer International Computers Limited (ICL) (table 7.3).

To take the shares of computer companies as of the early 1970s does, however, hide much of the historical development of this industry. IBM has dominated the market since it entered computer production in the mid-1950s upon the base of its dominance of the office machinery market and has not engaged in any significant merger activity in the whole of this time. The other companies, however, are survivors of a development involving exits from and mergers in the industry as well as some entry. As can be seen in Stoneman (1976) the US industry in 1950 involved twelve major producers. By 1967 this had already been reduced to eight even though Control Data Corporation (CDC) entered in 1957. Of these eight, General Electric (GE) and Honeywell merged in 1971, the former having already incorporated Olivetti of Italy and Machines Bull of France.

TABLE 7.2: Share in value of the stock of installed computers (31 December 1977)

Company	% of value of world computer stock
IBM	71.0
Honeywell	8.3
Univac	7.5
Burroughs	5.7
CDC	2.4
NCR	2.3
DEC	0.8
Amdahl	0.4
Others	0.6

Source: Computer Weekly, 11 May 1978, page 13.

TABLE 7.3: Break-down of Western European computer market by manufacturer, 1972–3

	% of installed capacity 1972–3							
Company Country	IBM	Honey- well	Univac	Bur- roughs	CDC	ICL	Uni- data*	Others
Germany	57.0	8.0	3.0	3.0	3.0	0.5	16.5	9.0
GB	38.4	7.0	3.7	3.9	1.8	34.7	0.9	9.6
France	57.5	18.0	3.5	1.5	3.5	3.0	12.0	1.0
Italy	73.0	11.0	7.0	2.5	2.5	—	2.5	1.5
Benelux	60.0	9.5	5.0	4.0	4.0	3.0	8.0	6.5
Others	65.0	6.0	4.0	3.5	4.5	5.0	2.0	10.0

Source: SCST (1973a), Annex I.
Note: *A company formed on 4 July 1974 from the computer interests of CII (France). Siemens (Germany) and Philips (Holland). Disbanded in 1977.

RCA withdrew from the industry in 1971, its interests being taken over by Univac. SDS merged with Rank Xerox Data Systems (RXDS) in 1969 and RXDS itself withdrew from the market in the mid-1970s. This leaves IBM, Burroughs, CDC, Univac and Honeywell as the big five US companies. A similar pattern is evident in the UK. There were nine producers in 1950 but the merger process has left just one computer company of any size – ICL which was formed in 1968. Other companies in the market include National Cash Register (NCR) and the Digital Equipment Corporation (DEC), the latter entering via small computers and expanding into larger machines as time has proceeded. This picture of increasing concentration is, however, slightly misleading, for there are a large number of smaller firms that specialise in particular areas of the market. Thus, for example, Amdahl entered recently in the US with the avowed aim of competing directly with IBM in large central processors and is now ranked fourth or fifth in the league table of turnover. There are also a large number of specialist suppliers of 'plug-compatible' memories and other computer system components. It would however not be unreasonable to say that the world market is dominated by the big five US multinationals. The existence of ICL makes a six firm market in the UK. The software sector is nowhere nearly as concentrated. In 1971 there were about 750 software companies in the UK, although 3% of these accounted for 57% of the turnover (and 40% of the total ran at a loss). (SCST, 1973a, Annex I).

The cause of the increase in concentration is not difficult to find. The key factor is the speed of technological change in the industry. Pratten (1971, pages 218–225) shows that there are considerable economies of scale in computer production, mainly arising from the spreading of heavy fixed costs (including R and D) involved in computer manufacture. In fact it has been argued that with its long production runs IBM has unit costs of approximately half of its European competitors. Given this it would be impossible for any company to compete on price with IBM with its 60–70% world market share, across the whole range of machines. It may, however, be practical to compete with IBM through technological innovation. Even here the resources available to IBM put smaller companies at a distinct disadvantage unless they specialise. However, one may argue that technological competition is really the main strategy of companies in this industry. Such competition requires very high levels of R and D input and by its very nature is risky. Failure in innovation means the demise of the company, and thus changes in structure. Moreover, large R and D requirements imply large units and thus a tendency to a concentrated structure. Thus the stress on technological competition would seem naturally to imply a concentrated market structure. However the resources available to IBM are likely to allow it to maintain in the future the supremacy evident in the past.

Although it is difficult to obtain full data on R and D expenditure by company, it is estimated that in the 1970s IBM spent approximately £250m per annum (SCST, 1973b) and, in the US alone, Burroughs spent £19m, NCR £20m, and CDC £13m on R and D in 1970. It is estimated that the IBM investment in the development of the 360 series was $5000m. Between 1969 and 1971 ICL spent £45m on R and D. The size of the sums required has meant that governments in most countries contribute significantly to their computer industry R and D and we shall have more to say on this below. What we can do, however, at this stage is to attribute the demise of GE, RCA and RXDS among others to their inability, or unwillingness, to devote further funds to the R and D process when previous expenditures had not generated sufficient revenue to cover themselves.

The other aspect of the industry that is relevant to market structure is the question of compatibility. Compatibility essentially means that a product (either hardware or software) can be used with another manufacturer's machines. Thus, as IBM has such a large market share the production of computer system components that are not IBM compatible considerably reduces the available market. Therefore the commonest form of entry to this industry is by specialist suppliers of computer systems components that are compatible with IBM machines. By concentrating on a small sector of the market the benefits of specialisation and reduced R and D requirements make entry easy. It does not, however, seem to be a practical proposition for any company at this stage in the industry's development to enter the general purpose computer market to compete with the existing companies unless strong government backing is provided. What activity there is, as far as entry is concerned, comes from the Japanese sector, through their government-backed computer industry (plus shareholdings in Amdahl), and the government-backed attempts of Western European manufacturers to increase their market shares. However, as technology is always changing, the challenge to the big five may in fact come from a different direction. As VSLI has developed, the assembling function of the computer manufacturers has moved to the electronic component producers until we now have the 'computer on a chip'. It may not be too great a step for these producers actually to integrate forward into system manufacture. With the development of greater software capability they may be able to make significant inroads into the markets of the existing manufacturers.

In addition to the mergers, entry and exit that have occurred over the years there have been a number of other groupings in the market mainly involving the smaller general purpose computer manufacturers. Thus ICL has held technical exchange agreements with CDC and has recently arranged a similar agreement with one of the Japanese companies. Siemens has an arrangement with Fujitsu of Japan to market Fujitsu machines. The grouping of La Compagnie Internationale pour l'Informatique (CII), Phillips and Siemens as Unidata, to provide a major European computer producer, although only lasting three years was one attempt to produce a rival to IBM. ICL's apparent reluctance to join such a grouping may in fact long delay the appearance of a true, one-firm, European computer industry. ICL's latest move, the takeover of Singer Business Machines, indicates that their sights are set on the US market rather than the European. As we see from table 7.3 above, ICL's penetration into Europe is still not very deep.

The existence of multinational companies in this industry raises the question of the relationship between country of ownership and the distribution of production. Most of the multinationals do in fact have production and R and D programmes in the UK (and other countries as well as the UK) so market dominance by these companies does not solely mean importing, although as with IBM for example, products produced outside the US are not generally imported into the US but are replicated there. However most governments discriminate between computer producers by country of origin rather than country of production. Thus the UK government has an ICL preferred procurement policy and by the same token the 'Buy American Act' discourages importation into the US. There is also a $7\frac{1}{2}\%$ tariff on equipment imported into the US. The Japanese market is also protected and IBM have recently been forced out of India.

7.2 MARKET BEHAVIOUR

We have argued above that price competition is not the key to behaviour in this industry. The crucial relationship is that between machine performance and technology. Thus market behaviour mainly concerns innovative activity. Freeman (1965) provides a useful framework for analysing such activity. He classifies R and D into innovative, defensive and protective. Innovative may be described as R and D in the search for an advance that will attack a rival's market share, defensive R and D as directed towards thwarting an attack on one's market share and protective R and D as the process of developing products in case one's market is attacked. The motive for this latter category of expenditure is that while it may not be in a company's interest to launch a new product it is nevertheless unwilling to allow rivals to take its market. It therefore develops but does not market the product. Consider, for example, the position of IBM. With a 70% world market share and already under investigation by the US

Anti-Trust agencies, one can argue that it has no interest in increasing its market share. Moreover, if it launched a new product it would in the main be making inroads into a market held by its own existing products. As computer products have heavy initial fixed costs, the longer the production run the greater is the possible profit. A new product would therefore just reduce potential profit. However, by launching new products the other companies would be attacking rivals' markets rather than their own and thus have an interest in new products. IBM one can argue, therefore must undertake development to match these rivals but is not interested in upsetting the status quo. This would of course make it very difficult to reduce IBM's market share. Moreover such protective R and D represents a considerable barrier to entry.

Apart from innovative activity manufacturers may act to preserve or increase their market shares in a number of ways, some of which are outlined below.

(a) We discussed above the concept of compatibility. If a user wishes to change his machine for a new (more modern) computer, his total costs are lower if he can continue to use his existing software and perhaps his existing peripherals. Thus most manufacturers provide ranges of machines that are upward compatible (will run programs written for smaller machines in the range) and make new machines that can use the software of their less sophisticated forerunners. Compatibility also implies that one way to attack IBM's market share is to make products that are IBM compatible. ICL has chosen the route of non-IBM compatibility, although why it has done so does not seem very clear.

(b) Most computers need regular servicing; this is usually done through a service agreement with the manufacturer. ICL have in the past refused to honour a service agreement if non-ICL-approved elements are added to a computer installation during its life. IBM do not operate thus and the size of the market for IBM plug-compatible computer elements is much greater.

(c) A further ploy is to embody technological change in completely new systems rather than just to add new elements to the system thereby making the replacement market much bigger. The growth of the plug-compatible market has tended, however, to reduce considerably the efficiency of the procedure.

(d) Renting or leasing computers is common and thus the leasing terms offered can be a prime competitive weapon. The advantage to the customer of a leasing arrangement is that his own capital is not tied up and he has more flexibility in arranging a change to the latest technology. The usual monthly leasing cost is between 1/48 and 1/54 of the total cost of the installation. As this leasing finance is often arranged by the computer manufacturer he requires access to large sources of funds. This of course represents another barrier to entry.

(e) The software side of the market can also be important. It has been the practice for manufacturers to invest heavily in certain areas of applications software. Thus, for example, IBM and Univac have made great inroads into the airline market on the basis of their software expertise. Thus one must be careful not to identify market behaviour too closely with hardware technology alone.

(f) Finally there is the question of cross-subsidisation in the machine range. Most general purpose computer manufacturers deemed it necessary to have a whole range of machines (so as to gain custom from small users moving up) from the smallest to the largest. In the striving to produce very large machines a number of companies [e.g. Machines Bull (France), Ferranti and Phillips (Holland)] have come to grief. It has been argued that IBM have in fact cross-subsidised large machines with the revenues from its small machines. It has been estimated (*Sunday Times*, 13 May 1973) that the large 360/90 cost $172m to develop but only generated $58m in revenue, whereas the smaller 360/30 and 360/50 machines generated surpluses of 39% and 33% respectively on sales. By cross-subsidising large machines in this way a substantial share of a very influential market can be gained that yields benefits lower down the range. Such cross-subsidisation is usually considered socially undesirable.

7.3 PERFORMANCE

The performance of an industry can be discussed on a number of levels; for example, we might ask whether it is making excess profits, undertaking sufficient R and D expenditure or advertising too much or too little. In this industry, however, these are not really the interesting questions. As there is really only one computer firm of any significance in the UK – i.e. ICL – we must really ask ourselves the question: how is ICL performing relative to its competitors? Is it advancing technologically at a rate that will enable it to keep up with and make inroads into the markets of the US multinationals?

When ICL was formed in 1968 it inherited two series of machines, the 1900 series from ICT and the System 4 series from English Electric Computers Ltd. Its main task was to develop a new product line to replace these two. This was launched in 1973/74 with the 2900 series label and new machines in the range continue to be announced. In some earlier work (Stoneman, 1978), it has been shown that in terms of cost–performance ratios, in comparison with the machines of other companies, ICL machines have maintained their pre-merger position over the whole of the post-merger period without a drop in profitability. This would indicate that while ICL may not be gaining on its multinational rivals, it is not falling behind. The method used was to compare, on the basis of performance characteristics,[2] the price of ICL machines with the price of rivals' machines. As it was found that there was no secular change in this ratio over time, one could argue that as long as ICL was not achieving this performance by under-pricing its machines (i.e. by running at a loss), then it was maintaining its technological position in relation to its rivals. We are not saying that ICL is more or less technologically advanced than its rivals but only that it has profitably managed to market machines with relative price performance characteristics that have not deteriorated over time. The company has in fact increased its profitability, which may even reflect some catching up on its rivals (table 7.4). However the number of factors that influence profit levels are so great that one should be careful of such an interpretation.

Table 7.4:   Profit-turnover ratios, ICL, 1969–77

Year	Profit–turnover
1969	0.048
1970	0.059
1971	0.067
1972	0.022
1973	0.065
1974	0.067
1975	0.067
1976	0.080
1977	0.072

Source: Extel British Company Service, Annual Cards, Extel Statistical Services Ltd.

We turn then to two other performance characteristics, market share, and the trade balance. In table 7.5 we present details on shares of the UK market held by the major firms. To supplement these data, Peddar Associates estimate (*Datalink*, 22 May 1978, page 1) that in 1976/77 the percentage market shares of IBM and ICL were as follows:

	1976	1977
IBM	37.1	39.4
ICL	37.7	35.4

These figures are not strictly comparable with those in table 7.5. The figures reflect a gain in market share by ICL up to 1969 but a fall to below pre-merger levels in the 1970s. ICL also has a much better share

TABLE 7.5:   Market shares by notional value[3]

Company	1964		1965		1969		1974	
	Total	Private	Total	Private	Total	Private	Total	Private
ICL	41.4	34.6	32.0	29.1	49.4	39.9	31.7	23.7
Other UK	1.1	0.7	2.5	1.2	1.9	1.8	3.4	1.3
IBM	40.0	44.5	35.1	39.9	27.7	35.0	37.7	45.4
Honeywell	5.2	8.2	40.9	10.5	7.9	9.4	6.2	7.2
Burroughs	0.9	0.8	1.5	2.1	3.0	3.9	5.5	7.3
Univac	2.5	2.4	3.3	2.8	2.9	4.0	4.2	4.6
NCR	7.6	6.7	9.6	8.5	3.1	3.9	2.6	3.4
CDC	—	0	0.6	0.8	1.5	0.4	1.5	0.5
DEC	<0.1	<0.1	0.2	0	0.5	0.4	1.3	1.0
Others	1.3	1.8	4.2	5.1	1.5	1.1	3.7	3.8

Sources: SCSTD II (1970) page 4; SCSTA II (1971) page 25; and Trade and Industry, 18 July 1975, page 180.

in the total market than in the private market because of the government preferment policy (the private market representing about two-thirds of the total). We discuss the public sector market below. The fall in ICL's market share is almost exactly mirrored in the rise of IBM. One may argue therefore that ICL is gradually losing out to IBM. It should also be realised, of course, from the figures presented above that the UK performance of ICL is not reflected in any other world market – it is purely a domestic phenomenon. This performance ought to be looked at, however, in the light of the great differences between ICL and IBM in R and D input.

These share data do, however, only reflect market shares of manufacturers' systems, and these systems are not necessarily foreign produced because they have the names of US companies on them or are made up of UK parts because they have an ICL label on them. Thus we ought to consider the trade figures (these are detailed in table 7.6). These are supplemented in table 7.7 by a finer product breakdown for the first quarter of 1978. The first thing to notice is that the trade balance has deteriorated over time with imports growing faster than exports but computers and CPUs show a better ratio of exports to imports than other commodities. It would seem logical to argue that this reflects the strong indigenous mainframe manufacturing industry (ICL) and the relatively weak position of the peripheral and components manufacturing industry. Peripherals and components are not only imported for direct sale to users but also for incorporation in locally assembled products.

We do not have any figures for the imports of software so we cannot

TABLE 7.6:   Imports and exports of computer products, 1971–7

Year	Imports (c.i.f.) (£m)	Exports (f.o.b.) (£m)	Imports/exports (%)
1971	152.3	90.7	167.9
1972	170.4	137.8	123.6
1973	256.8	161.6	158.9
1974	345.6	208.6	165.7
1975	382.8	242.2	158.0
1976	552.5	318.2	173.6
1977	691.9	355.4	194.7

Source: Business Monitor, Electronic Computers, PQ 366, Quarterly Statistics, 1973–78.

TABLE 7.7:   Imports and exports by commodity: first quarter 1978

Commodity	Imports (£m)	Exports (£m)	Imports/exports (%)
Computers and CPUs	35.7	22.9	155.9
Peripherals	86.2	50.3	171.4
Parts	65.1	33.3	195.5
Related electronic equipment	13.1	4.3	304.6
Microelectronic circuits	26.3	13.9	189.2

Source: Datalink, 5 June 1978.

TABLE 7.8:   Software industry: productivity 1971

	West Germany	USA	France	GB
Turnover (million EUA)	75	300	51	40
Share of twelve biggest firms (%)	50	51	70	41
Data processing specialists employed	4 200	12 000	3 000	4 350
Turnover per man per annum (EUA)	17 850	25 000	18 500	9 100

EUA equals EEC unit of account.

Source: SCST (1973a), Annex I.

discuss the competitiveness of this industry in its international context. However in table 7.8 we present data on the productivity of the software industries of different countries in 1971 which do not reflect at all favourably on the British, although from 1972 to 1976 billings per full-time employee rose from £5355 to £10 956 at current prices. This low level of productivity may underlie the low level of exports of computer services. From *Business Monitor* figures, we know that in 1976 of total billings of £220.7m only £10.5m (4.79%) was to foreign clients (although this represents an increase from 3.4% in 1971).

We do not have any figures on the productivity of computer production in different countries, although net output per man employed in MLH 366 has risen (in current prices) from £1971 in 1963 to £10 983 in 1975 (*Census of Production* figures), which, in the absence of any reliable standard of comparison, seems a dramatic improvement.[4]

In summary, it appears that the UK service sector has lower productivity than in other countries although it is increasing. It also has a low proportion of billings to foreign clients, but again this proportion is slowly increasing (unfortunately we do not have any import figures). In MLH 366 ICL is managing to maintain its technological position relative to the multinational giants, although by computer industry terms it is still a very small company. Moreover it has only minimal market penetration in any major industrial country other than the UK but its position in the home market is superior to that of any of the other non-US computer companies in their home markets. This is a position achieved without incurring losses although the data tend to suggest a slowly declining market share. However as many components and peripherals used by ICL are of foreign origin, and the British company and peripherals producers are not so successful, this performance is unfortunately not reflected in the trade balance where the deficit is increasing over time. The relative success of ICL is therefore only part of the picture, which in its wider framework is not so encouraging.

7.4 PUBLIC POLICY

The present structure of the UK computer industry with its one dominant domestic producer, ICL, is the end result of a series of mergers the final stages of which were encouraged and promoted by the Industrial Reorganisation Corporation. With the formation of ICL the Government provided funds for the development of a new range of computers (the 2900 series) to replace the two ageing existing ranges. Since 1968 it has also operated a preferential procurement policy. Under this policy government departments and nationalised industries, but not local authorities, are expected to acquire all computers of a size greater than the Atlas (an early 1960s large machine) from ICL, subject to satisfactory price, performance and delivery terms. The effect of this policy can be seen in the different shares of ICL in the public and private sector shown in table 7.5 and in the data in table 7.9.

TABLE 7.9:   Central government orders placed between 1 April 1971 and 31 January 1973 for computers (£ thousand)

Company	Large computers		Small computers			Total
	Adminis-trative	Scientific	Adminis-trative	Scientific	Enhance-ments	
ICL	15 969	400	2 953	—	4 664	24 556
IBM	—	3 870	2 836	—	3 077	9 333
Honeywell	—	—	70	184	569	823
Burroughs	—	—	—	—	499	499
Others	—	—	—	358	498	956

Source: SCST (1974).

Direct financial assistance is provided by the British government to the computer industry, the majority of it to ICL. In fact of the total electronics industry R and D of £179.4m in 1972, £74m was financed by the British government. ICL received £57m from the government in the period 1968–77 and another £8.9m was provided as assistance to the rest of the industry (*Trade and Industry*, 27 May 1977, page 387). The computer industry is the third largest recipient after nuclear energy and aircraft of government finance for R and D. However, the funds provided are formally to be considered as loans rather than grants, e.g. between 1968 and 1976 £40m was provided by the government as a general support payment to ICL. The company is to repay any pre-tax profit in excess of $7\frac{1}{2}\%$ of turnover earned in the seven years from 1 October 1977 up to a maximum of 25% of profit each year to cover this sum. To date no sums have been paid by the company under this arrangement. Another £3.5m provided by the government for development contracts is to be recovered by a levy on sales, and to date £0.6m has been returned.

In addition, the government has provided a guarantee that it would, if necessary, help ICL fulfil its obligations to leasing companies in respect of equipment returned from leasing. It should be noted, however, that the majority of the government support to the industry has been to ICL for hardware development, although small sums have at different times been advanced for support of software projects (mainly outside ICL but not necessarily in the private sector). Prior to the formation of ICL practically no funds were provided by the UK government to support R and D in the computer industry. In the 1950s the total UK support was £10m distributed by the NRDC.

To put these sums in perspective it is necessary to look at government assistance to other national computer industries. In terms of European rivals this means France and Germany. Although different bases may make comparison difficult, it is estimated (SCST, 1973c, pages 180–3) that compared with UK government support to ICL of approximately £30m between 1971 and 1975, France provided £72m and Germany £93m for computers and peripherals development. Thus although strong support is being provided in the UK it is not excessive by West European standards. This makes the performance of ICL more impressive than would at first seem to be the case. Even these figures pale into insignificance beside US data. It is estimated that between 1951 and 1959 the leading firms in US electronics ventured $4206m of their own capital on R and D but this was supported by $4242m of government money. Between 1949 and 1959 IBM spent $254m of government money on R and D and after 1955 Sperry Rand spent about double that. Even as late as 1970 heavy support was still being provided (see Stoneman, 1976, page 96). However Honeywell argued in 1973 that such heavy support was no longer being given. In 1972 the US total general purpose computer R and D expenditure was $1000m (slightly in excess of £400m) of which less than 5% was government funded, and none of Honeywell's $110m (£45m) expenditure was government funded. These figures do not, however, allow for the special development contracts provided by the US government and from which the contractors must benefit (SCST, 1973b). Some idea of the current size of this support is given by the estimate that US government subsidies to R and D in electronics will total £200–£400m over the next five years (*Sunday Times*, 25 June 1978, page 55). The Japanese government, according to the same source, is providing £300m support over the next five years to companies developing VLSI electronic components. It is in this area of electronic components that it is argued that UK R and D support should now be directed. NEDO is currently advocating a £220m five-year programme of government support. These sums are far in excess of past support for the UK computer or electronics industry. It is estimated that only £10m has been directed to the micro electronics industry in the last six to seven years.

The question that arises from this widespread international support of indigenous computer industries is whether Britain should have an indigenous computer (or electronics) industry, and if so, whether it can survive and yield a social return on the government support provided for it. This question opens up the whole wider field of enquiry of the impact of the computer on the UK economy both to date and in the future, and it is essentially this question that is occupying the minds of many economists and policy makers at the present time. We start, however, with the more restricted question: should the UK have an indigenous computer industry?

One argument for establishing an indigenous industry is that it is necessary for military or defence purposes. Although this may well apply to the computer industry it does not provide an economic rationale. However the sentiment that underlies it is that only a nationally owned industry can be controlled by the national government. Production facilities owned by a multinational are not liable to such control. This must represent a strong argument for having a British-owned computer industry as opposed to a foreign owned industry with UK production facilities.

If we turn from the question of ownership to whether the UK should produce computers at all, the question really becomes one of opportunity costs. Could the UK obtain greater social benefits from deploying the industry's resources in another direction? It may be argued that as far as labour is concerned there is already excess supply so the opportunity cost is zero. This argument is flawed, however, for much of the industry's labour force is highly skilled and in the market for skilled labour there is no such surplus. For example, one can argue that by shifting labour from the production sector into the software sector there are social benefits to be reaped. There is no strong evidence in favour of this argument, so we shall in fact remain agnostic as to its virtues. The other main resource used in the industry is government funds for the support of R and D. That there are alternative uses for these funds is not in doubt; whether they would be more productive elsewhere is quite another matter. As foreign governments support their industries, the current pattern of expenditure allows the UK to keep up with its competitors. It is not clear whether there are non-computer related alternative uses where the application of these funds would enable the UK to overtake its competitors, and in which they may therefore be more productive, nor is this the place to try to compare the returns to R and D expenditure in the computer industry to the social returns available from the application of these funds to, for example, road-building. What we need is some idea of what the UK gains from having an indigenous production facility. The principal advantages are as follows.

(a) *Employment opportunities.* Although, as we have shown, this is not a labour intensive industry, it is one that is predicted to be a major force in most economies in the future and therefore computer production may provide more extensive employment opportunities later as the industry grows.

(b) *Balance of payments advantages.* The UK appears to suffer from continual problems with its balance of payments, and although we have shown that a deficit does exist for this industry the size of the deficit would be much greater without indigenous production facilities. If there were no local production facilities one might simply ask the almost unanswerable question: what should the UK produce to pay for its computer imports? In fact, however, considering the performance of ICL over time one might even argue that the UK has a comparative advantage in computer production, especially when ICL's performance relative to its rivals is compared with its relative R and D input.

(c) *Externalities.* It is argued that the existence of a thriving indigenous computer production facility encourages the application of computer technology in the economy in general. Thus the international competitiveness of a whole sector of British industry could be influenced by the existence of such a facility. This must be the main reason for having home production facilities.

These arguments however do not preclude some variation of the status quo. Two main modifications have been proposed.

(i) Greater support must be given to the non-mainframe manufacturing sector of the industry, i.e. components, peripherals and software. With regard to components we shall have more to say below. We have already discussed the poor UK performance in peripherals where the lack of government support is in marked contrast to that provided to ICL. The software industry has argued that the skills of its people and low wage costs give the UK a distinct advantage in this area. Although the export figures discussed above do not appear to reflect this, it would seem that the growing importance and size of the world software industry is a factor that ought to merit much further consideration.

(ii) Encouragement might also be given to greater European involvement. There have been overtures made to ICL by both European governments and computer firms for it to join in the formation of a single European computer manufacturer. ICL feel that the performance of the ill-fated Unidata venture is confirmation of the correctness of its reluctance to do so. However the Honeywell estimate that 10% of the world market is required for long-term viability would indicate that if ICL is ever to become a non-government-supported, independent, viable firm it must grow larger. It is difficult to see how this will be achieved through internal growth. The options are therefore for ICL to merge with either European, US or Japanese companies. For reasons detailed above the resulting company should remain UK-controlled. ICL's behaviour indicates that it does not view the European option with much interest. Its acquisition of Singer and the marketing of its 2903 machines in Canada suggest it has its sights set on the transatlantic market. Given the size of the US market in relation to the European this may well be the better strategy. It should be noted however that this would not preclude a joint US–UK–European venture.

Broadly the arguments would seem to be in favour of having a UK-based computer production facility under UK ownership, but with more extensive international linkages than at present.

Our next question is concerned with computer ownership. What have been and what are likely to be the effects on the UK economy of computer use?[5] This question has relevance in the sense of contributing to the debate on whether computers should be home produced and on whether the spread of computer use should be further stimulated by government action.

The computer is the embodiment of the automation concept that has for long concerned individuals and governments with its implication of mass unemployment. In Stoneman (1975), an attempt was made to evaluate the impact of computer use on the demand for labour in the UK. Concentrating on third generation computer technology, and comparing labour demands along the actual output path, it was argued that

(i) computers last for seven years before replacement;

(ii) in each of the seven years of their life in use they save twenty-seven man-years of labour over the previous technology (accepting however that the skill mix is also different); and

(iii) each computer takes two years to construct and requires forty-eight man years of labour in excess of that required by the previous technology.

These figures imply that if the diffusion process had been completed in 1970 with the economy using its equilibrium level of computers the demand for labour would have been reduced by 0.79% of the total labour force. This figure, however, hides the fact that as the economy follows its diffusion path from zero computer use it would utilise, for a while, more labour in computer construction than it would be saving by computer use. Thus if all UK computers installed had been produced in the UK the actual diffusion path would have implied an increase in labour demand from 1952 to 1969, after which the savings would have begun to outstrip the extra labour requirements. As many computers were imported and thus did not represent a demand on the UK labour force, the actual period of increased labour demand was in fact much shorter, the savings overtaking the increases by 1965. The moral is simple: the final position may be one where labour is being saved, but the transition path may be such that the actual effects are quite the reverse.

The procedure used for this exercise was based on a number of assumptions, of which the two most crucial were (a) that computer technology was of the third generation type and (b) that the output path of the economy was not influenced by the level of computer usage. The question that is currently meriting much consideration concerns the effect of the latest advances in technology, i.e. VLSI and the advent of microprocessors, on the UK economy and the degree to which the government should encourage the development of a home based microprocessor industry and stimulate the use of micro-processors. On the latter issue it is argued that unless British industry responds quickly to the opportunities presented by microprocessors and incorporates them in its products, it will lose out on market share to those countries who have entered the market and that this will cause losses of employment.[6] However it is also argued that the use of microprocessors will imply some unemployment, *per se*, so the supporting of microprocessor applications becomes a particularly difficult problem. The view that the use of microprocessors will mean unemployment is supported by observations of the limited (mainly US) applications to date (see *Computer Weekly*, 29 June 1978, page 2), namely:

(a) In the period 1970–75 NCR reduced its manufacturing workforce by more than 50% in making the transfer to cash registers based on integrated circuits.

(b) In the period 1970–76 the Western Electric manufacturing force dropped from 39 200 to 19 000 and a 75% cutback is expected in fault-finding, maintenance, repair and installation.

Hines (1978) estimates that such examples imply five million unemployed by the 1980s. We have in fact already illustrated similar effects in computer production. To offset such unemployment the following forces must be considered.

(i) The use of microprocessors can imply price reductions and quality improvement in output. The elasticities of demand with respect to price and quality should mean higher output and this should offset at least some of the labour demand reduction.

(ii) If UK industry is in the forefront of applying microprocessors there could be an increase in the world market share of UK producers, this increase in output providing further employment. This would however be only a temporary effect until others caught up.

(iii) The advent of the microprocessor could imply the production of new products or the performance of tasks previously not economically viable. This could have further employment implications.

(iv) The UK could alleviate the labour saving effects of micro-processor use by the development of a microprocessor construction industry, i.e. the stimulation of the electronics components industry. As to whether this should be just a production facility owned by a foreign company or a nationally owned industry all the arguments above concerning the computer industry proper apply. But above all, the externalities in terms of contact with the new technology and thus its implied earlier use is the key to the argument on whether there should be a production facility as such.

(v) The employment effects can be alleviated by developing an industry to supply the microprocessor industry. The key to cheap microprocessor production is a very advanced production technology with high environmental requirements, e.g. special dust free, vibration free buildings and 'machine tools'. An expertise here could be as important as in production itself.

(vi) Finally there are two areas requiring labour input: microprocessor design and software development. Although these are high skill content jobs, they may nevertheless be very important in numerical terms. Making the microprocessors perform the tasks for which they are required is both labour intensive and as necessary to efficiency as their use *per se*. If the reputed skill of the British software industry is as good as some commentators argue, this may be the key offsetting factor.

Thus the argument is that UK industries must use microprocessors, but in doing so this may cause unemployment. If they are not used, unemployment may well be even greater. However there may be some employment creating consequences as in the case of computer diffusion so that the net effect may even be an increase in employment rather than the reverse. But this effect can only be achieved if the UK seriously enters the microprocessor supply industry (with its associated intermediate inputs). To ignore both their use and production seems to be a recipe for failure. In June 1978 NEDO suggested a total investment of £220m (with £80m from the UK government) as a first step into microprocessor and microelectronic supply and support. At the time of writing the National Enterprise Board is funding the setting up of a company (Inmos) to produce microelectronic memory chips and the Department of Industry is funding a campaign to promote the use of microprocessors. GEC is discussing with Fairchild (of the US) the establishment of UK-based production facilities for microprocessors and Motorola is also considering production in the UK. ITT Semiconductors is also intending to fabricate microprocessors in the UK. However all this activity must be seen in the context of continued Japanese, US and European expansion within this area.

7.5 CONCLUSIONS

The one fact of life as far as the computer industry is concerned is that it never stands still. The force of technological change is so strong that it dominates the industry in all its aspects. This has certain disadvantages for the commentator in that it quickly dates his opinions.

However as of late 1978 it would seem that this industry is about to enter its fourth technological upheaval in the post-war period. The future will thus be as dramatic as the past. From the past the industry has inherited one indigenous mainframe manufacturer, a growing diverse software industry and a small weak peripherals and components industry. Just as the past has been mainly concerned with mainframes the future would seem to be the province of the latter. If the latter performs in the future as the former has performed in the past we should expect to see a continuing UK computer industry, serving mainly a home market, but requiring continued government support and competing with mainly US-based multinational companies. But such a future will be expensive. Only if the rest of British industry responds to the opportunities provided by the new electronic revolution can the support with public funds really be considered worthwhile.

NOTES TO CHAPTER 7

1. A high level language uses expressions closely resembling the users' vocabulary and in which one instruction may generate several machine operations.

2. The performance characteristics did not include any significant software dimension and it is in fact argued that 2900 series software has left something to be desired (*Computer Weekly*, 13 April 1978).

3. Notional value is an attempt to give each computer installation a value derived from the different prices charged for different configurations of the same system; it represents a sort of 'average' price.

4. Our use of current price figures is determined by the lack of an available, suitably defined price deflator.

5. This is a very involved question and we make no attempt here to detail fully all of its ramifications. We are simply indicating some of the major issues.

6. For example, in machine tools, Alfred Herberts were in 1978 already blaming the integration of microprocessors into machine tools by foreign producers for their own poorer than expected export performance.

REFERENCES

Bloch, E. and Galage, D. (1978) 'Component Progress, Its Effect on High Speed Computer Architecture and Machine Organisation'. *Computer*, Institute of Electrical and Electronic Engineers Inc. (April) 64–75.

Freeman, C. (1965) 'Research and Development in Electronic Capital Goods'. *National Institute Economic Review*, (34) 40–91.

Hines, C. (1978) *The Chips are Down*. London: Friends of the Earth.

Pratten, C. (1971) *Economies of Scale in Manufacturing Industry.* Cambridge: Cambridge University Press.

SCSTD I (1970) Select Committee on Science and Technology, Sub-Committee D, *UK Computer Industry, Vol. I, Minutes of Evidence,* Session 1969–1970. London: HMSO.

SCSTD II (1970) Select Committee on Science and Technology, Sub-Committee D, *UK Computer Industry, Vol. II, Appendices,* Session 1969–1970. London: HMSO.

SCSTA I (1971) Select Committee on Science and Technology, Sub-Committee A, *The Prospects for the UK Computer Industry, Vol. I, Report,* Session 1970–1971. London: HMSO.

SCSTA II (1971) Select Committee on Science and Technology, Sub-Committee A, *The Prospects for the UK Computer Industry, Vol. II, Minutes of Evidence,* Session 1970–1971. London: HMSO.

SCSTA III (1971) Select Committee on Science and Technology, Sub-Committee A, *The Prospects for the UK Computer Industry, Vol. III, Appendices,* Session 1970–1971. London: HMSO.

SCST (1973a) Select Committee on Science and Technology, UK Computer Industry Sub-Committee, *Minutes of Evidence, Minister for Industrial Development,* Session 1972–1973. London: HMSO.

SCST (1973b) Select Committee on Science and Technology, UK Computer Industry Sub-Committee, *Minutes of Evidence, Honeywell Information Systems,* Session 1972–1973. London: HMSO.

SCST (1973c) Select Committee on Science and Technology, UK Computer Industry Sub-Committee, *Second Report on the UK Computer Industry (First Part), Appendices to Minutes of Evidence,* Session 1972–1973. London: HMSO.

SCST (1974) Select Committee on Science and Technology, UK Computer Industry Sub-Committee, *Minutes of Evidence, the Rt. Hon. A. Wedgwood Benn,* Session 1973–1974. London: HMSO.

Stoneman, P. (1975) 'The Effect of Computers on UK Labour Demand'. *Economic Journal* **85,** 590–606.

Stoneman, P. (1976) *Technological Diffusion and the Computer Revolution.* University of Cambridge Department of Applied Economics Monograph, no. 25. Cambridge University Press.

Stoneman, P. (1978) 'Merger and Technological Progressiveness: the case of the British Computer Industry'. *Applied Economics* **10,** 125–140.

FURTHER READING

The interested reader can obtain some fascinating insight into this industry by reading the proceedings of the various Sub-Committees of the Select Committee on Science and Technology investigating the industry. Business Monitor (*Electronic Computers and Computer Services*) provides detailed material on the industry, which one can supplement from the *Census of Production*. Statistics on the computer stock can be found in *Computer Survey* (United Trade Press) and on computer performance in *Computers and Automation* (International Data Corporation). The publications of the National Computing Centre also provide a wealth of detail. Weekly publications, such as *Computer Weekly* (IPC Business Press) enable one to keep abreast of current developments. Company details can be obtained from *Extel* or various company reports. Other references are detailed above, with cross reference to the text.

8 Motor vehicles

179—206

D. G. Rhys

The products made by the British motor industry are a significant feature of the British economy and of society, and are likely to remain so for the foreseeable future despite the adverse effects of increased energy costs on the economics of the internal combustion engine. The car and the bus allow a virtually unprecedented freedom of travel, and for better or worse, the country's internal freight transport industry is wedded to road haulage. Significant social costs emanating from accidents, congestion and pollution do of course arise from the use of road vehicles. However, these factors do mainly arise from the use of road vehicles rather than from their manufacture. Obviously vehicle demand is directly related to vehicle usage but here we are mainly concerned with the structure, performance and behaviour of the motor manufacturing industry rather than with matters that belong to the study of transport economics.

8.1 POST-WAR DEVELOPMENTS IN THE INDUSTRY

8.1.1 The car industry

Because of the effects of the Second World War on Continental firms, US and UK firms dominated the world's car markets until the mid-1950s. However, by then the West German industry was beginning to compete in overseas markets and was followed by the French and Italian makers at the end of the decade. Britain's overseas marketing position was successfully challenged by this competition. At home successive UK governments used the motor industry and its market as an economic regulator. Both factors hampered the car sector's growth and prosperity.

By 1945 the car industry had already become fairly concentrated. However, the unstable economic environment of the post-war period led to further significant increases in concentration, and mergers saw the total disappearance of smaller firms. Indeed, as late as 1979 one of the largest firms, Chrysler UK (C UK), was sold by its US parent to the French Peugeot–Citroen group because of wider problems facing the Chrysler Corporation. The distribution of UK car production is shown in table 8.1.

TABLE 8.1:   Share of car production (%)

	Austin	Nuffield	Standard	Ford	Vauxhall	Rootes	Others	Total (thousands)
1946	23	20	11	14	9	11	12	219
1947	17	27	9	18	10	10	9	287
1950	17	22	11	19	9	14	8	523
	BMC							
1955	39		10	27	9	11	4	898
1960	38		9	28	11	11	3	1353
1964	37		7	28	13	12	3	1868
	BLMC					C UK		
1970	48			27	11	13	0.5	1641
1974	48			25	9	17	0.1	1534
1975	48			26	8	18	0.1	1268
1978	50			26	7	16	0.1	1223

Source: From data obtained from the Society of Motor Manufacturers and Traders (SMMT).
Note: Others cover the output of some eighteen firms. In 1980 the largest were Rolls-Royce, Lotus, Reliant and Aston Martin. The remaining firms were makers of either luxury cars such as Bristol, or workshop built high performance cars such as Davrian and TVR; from mid-1979 Peugeot marketed its Chrysler models under the Talbot name.

Unlike many car industries overseas, which had enjoyed strongly growing domestic markets over most of the 1946–80 period, the UK market experienced much more erratic progress. Indeed it stagnated over much of the post-1964 period. In terms of production the situation was worse for whereas foreign car industries showed almost continuous growth, the UK industry stagnated between 1964 and 1972, and then went into sharp decline. (See table 8.2).

8.1.2 The commercial vehicle industry

In the post-war period, the main UK commercial vehicle producers have been the four mass producers: Ford, Bedford (GMC), Rootes (C UK) and British Leyland. The last mentioned combines the quantity production facilities of BMC with the specialist vehicle making plants of the Jaguar Group and Leyland Motors. Unfortunately the creation of BLMC meant the cross-subsidisation of car investment from commercial vehicle (CV) profits with the ultimate result that the CV side suffered from underinvestment in new plant and models. In consequence it fell back in the European league to a position (in 1980) where its new heavy truck range represented almost the last chance for BL's CV activities as a whole to remain viable.

TABLE 8.2:   Trends in UK car production and exports, and total UK new car registrations per year (thousands)

Year	Total production	Total registrations	Exports
1946	219	122	84
1950	523	134	398
1955	898	511	389
1960	1353	820	570
1964	1868	1216	680
1970	1641	1127	679
1972	1921	1702	690
1976	1333	1308	496
1978	1223	1618	466

Source: SMMT. *The Motor Industry of Great Britain* (1979).

C UK's facilities have tended to be much smaller than the other makers. Ford and Bedford have been the traditional market leaders. By the late 1970s Ford had taken the leadership of most sectors of the UK CV market, a position which reinforced its newly regained leadership in the car market. Both Ford and Bedford use the UK as their main non-US CV design centre whilst Chrysler's UK CV facilities together with those in Spain, gave Peugeot an entry into the heavy CV market for the first time. The UK, perhaps uniquely in Europe, still has a number of prosperous independent specialist truck makers such as ERF, Foden and Dennis who make up to 5000 units a year. However, the largest specialist maker, Seddon Atkinson, is a subsidiary of the US International Harvester combine.

Although CV production in the UK reached a record 465 000 units in 1964 the industry still maintained an output in excess of 400 000 until 1974. Output has since slipped back to between 370 and 390 000. Since the post-1974 fall in UK output the French industry has been Europe's largest CV producer. However, West Germany has long had Europe's strongest and largest *heavy* CV industry.

8.1.3 The economic significance of the motor industry as a whole

Despite its decline as a world force the UK motor industry is still a major part of the economy. The motor industry as defined by the Standard Industrial Classification (MLH 381) accounts for about 2.5% of total employment. However, the inclusion of employment in raw material and component supplies in other industries directly dependent on the motor industry almost doubles this. Indeed the 1976 White Paper on the industry (Cmnd 6377, 1976) put employment in the motor and associated industries at 1.2 million, some 6% of total employment. About 8% of Gross Domestic Product, 16% of manufactured exports and 13% of visible exports are accounted for by the motor industry. In 1978 MLH 381 earned £3864m overseas with a net balance of £776m. If all the indirect effects of its operations are taken into account then the industry is responsible for some 12% of GDP, and indeed during its last major growth period in 1954–63 about 27% of the growth in industrial production could be explained by the growth of the motor industry.[1] The economic importance of the industry was fully understood by the Japanese, German and French authorities who used their motor industries as the main engines of economic growth and who, unlike their UK counterparts, avoided using them as short-term weapons of demand management in case their growth potential and hence their effects on the economy overall were harmed. Consequently, these authorities tried to maintain a steady growth of vehicle production. In the UK however the picture has, as we have seen, been very different.

8.2 SUPPLY AND DEMAND CHARACTERISTICS

The short-run elasticity of supply depends upon both the degree of capacity utilisation and the efficiency with which particular manufacturers can change output levels. The boom in demand in 1972–3 found the industry wanting and various production difficulties lost some one-fifth of achievable output. In the longer term the industry has traditionally responded to the growing vehicle market by new net investment. This was so in 1946–7, 1955–7 and 1962–5. However, the strong demand in the early 1970s did not produce increases in capacity. Indeed because of the financial difficulties of companies and the commitment of multinationals to export in kit form from the UK, final assembly capacity[2] fell from 2.5 million units in 1973 to 2.3 million in 1978.

8.2.1 Nature of technology; optimum size

The manufacture of motor vehicles mainly involves mass production assembly with the 'job' passing automatically from one piece of equipment to another. Hand building and even bespoke methods, however, are used in the production of premium heavy trucks and luxury cars. The *techniques* of mass production require large-scale production for the achievement of least unit-cost operation. Indeed, increased use of automation – involving, for example, the use of robots – has increased the optimum scale in assembly plants from 200 000 units a year to 300 000 on a two-shift basis.[3] However, more flexible equipment has at the same time reduced the model-specific assembly optimum. Another development has been the attempt to enrich the car worker's lot by introducing team assembly where either a team or a single individual can build an entire car or an engine or gearbox. However, such techniques have proved expensive in terms of unit costs and the substitution of labour by capital is seen as a better answer to the needs of mass producers in capital intensive but high wage economies.

If a manufacturer integrates production by carrying out the various distinct operations into which vehicle making is split, that is, pressing out sheet metal parts, casting, machining, assembly and painting activities, its overall optimum size will be dictated both by the maximum optimum of the various processes and by the need to balance correctly these processes. If it is impossible to achieve the output required to balance perfectly various processes with different minimum efficient scales, the car maker will attempt to minimise unit costs at its planned level of operations by using some plant at either above or below its optimum capacity. As far as can be determined from data supplied by manufacturers the minimum efficient scale (i.e. the scale at which unit costs are minimised) in the various operations involved in car-making are

Casting of engine blocks	1 million
Casting of other parts	100 000–750 000
Power train machining and assembly	600 000
Axle machining and assembly	500 000
Pressing of various panels	1 to 2 million
Painting (undercoats etc.)	250 000
Final assembly	250 000

It can be seen that to reach *maximum* efficiency in production a car firm would need to produce two million cars using at least some common body parts. For instance if two models are made at an annual rate of one million each the use of, say, a common floor pressing could optimise production.

As the parts needing the highest volume tend to be hidden from view, the skilful use of common body parts over a wide model range can occur. This has been achieved by firms such as GMC, Ford, Nissan, Toyota, VW and Peugeot. An increase in output from 250 000 units to two million units per year would produce unit cost savings of the order of 15–20%. In the range one to two million unit costs fall by around 6%, a significant saving in an industry where profits are often less than 5% of turnover (Rhys, 1977).

Over the range of European capacity bounded by Saab at the lower end and Peugeot at the upper we have the following unit cost estimates (Pratten, 1971). It can be seen that an annual production of 500 000 cars is likely to have a cost advantage per unit of around 25% over that of 100 000 units. (See also Rhys, 1972a). The estimates also indicate that further doublings of output would produce reductions in unit cost, albeit of only 5–6% each time.

Output per year	Index of costs
100 000	100
250 000	83
500 000	74
1 000 000	70
2 000 000	66

Table 8.3 illustrates the short-run unit cost structure of an average mass produced car at particular output levels. It shows the unit cost structure at both the break-even and standard output levels. The

TABLE 8.3:   Estimated typical cost break-down for an average car

	Unit cost break-down at break-even volume[1]	Costs at Standard Output[2]
Variable		
Direct production		
Materials	53.0	62.0
Warranty	2.0	} 14.0
Variable overhead	7.0	
Fixed		
Direct labour*	12.0	8.0
Fixed overhead	21.0	} 16.0
Capital costs	5.0	
	100.0	100.0

Sources: (1) CPRS, *The Future of the British Car Industry*, 1975.
(2) Various car firms.
Note: *In the modern car industry labour is only regarded as a variable factor in the long run.

former is the point at which total revenue equals total cost, with profits earned at greater output. Standard output is based upon average capacity utilisation. The output so derived is about 80% of maximum capacity, and is used as the basis for cost allocation. As standard output normally represents a profitable level of operation, this output is greater than that needed for break-even. Consequently an increase in output from break-even levels to standard volumes will increase total variable costs, but a given level of fixed costs will account for a smaller proportion of total unit costs.

In CV production the power train optimum requires annual volumes of 100 000 units a year while the cab manufacturing optimum is similar to that of car body pressings. However the cost penalty involved in producing cabs in much lower volumes is reduced by frequently changing dies in the stamping machines in order to increase utilisation and thereby engaging in a form of batch production. Engine castings for large diesels have an optimum of around 200 000 units a year while final assembly for large heavy complicated vehicles is around 30 000 a year for maximum weight vehicles and 50 000 for medium weight designs of 8–24 tons gross. As optimum volumes are large in relation to annual output, costs are spread over much longer model runs than are usual on the car side. For instance, Ford's main truck cab which was introduced in 1964 was still being made in 1980. Small truck makers have been able to keep costs near to the levels achieved by bigger firms. They have done this either by making items in materials which involve a lower optimum volume or by buying in from specialists who make cabs, engines, power train, axles and so on.

8.2.2 Organisation of labour

In the UK industrial relations problems have been important in preventing continuity of production and the full utilisation of resources. Indeed the proportion of production lost in 1972–4 – the years of boom demand – varied between 10 and 26% of capacity.

Unlike their counterparts in West Germany, Japan or the USA who have only to deal with one or two unions, UK makers have to bargain with over twenty, although the Transport and General Workers together with the Amalgamated Union of Engineering Workers (AUEW) account for about 80% of hourly paid workers. Ford and Vauxhall give equal pay for equal work in all plants and Chrysler by 1980 had largely achieved this objective. British Leyland planned to replace its 246 bargaining units by a common negotiating date and pay parity by late 1979. The UK motor industry suffers less, when compared with its Continental rivals, from absenteeism but more from strikes. Wage disputes are the greatest problem but the underlying causes are the inability of low productivity firms to pay higher wages, a mutual lack of trust between the two sides of the industry, decentralised wage bargaining, pay parity, payment systems, fragmented unions, shop floor militancy and a lack of confidence engendered by the many years of 'stop-go'.

8.2.3 Imports and exports

Apart from a short break in 1924–5 the UK import duty on vehicles remained constant at 33⅓% between 1915 and 1956. The Dillon Round of 1962–8 reduced duties to 22% while the Kennedy Round (1968–72) further reduced duties on cars and vans to 11% by 1972. The exclusion of CVs from this last cut resulted from pressure from the European firms who were fearful that they could not compete with the medium and medium-heavy UK truck sector. However, by 1968 EFTA duties on both cars and CVs had disappeared thereby benefiting Volvo and Saab–Scania cars and CVs, and by July 1977 the UK duty on EEC imports had been removed.

Although the UK was excluded from the EEC until 1973, the combination of the Kennedy Round, a belief that the UK would eventually enter the EEC, and a strong 'home' market which allowed Continental makers to load most overheads onto home sales, meant competitively priced imports. Further, the moribund nature of the UK motor industry persuaded the Japanese that the UK would be the easiest major European car market to penetrate. Consequently, Volkswagen which had been the only major established importer in the mass market in the early 1960s was joined, by the end of the decade, by Renault and Fiat, and in the post-1972 period, by the Japanese producers (Nissan's Datsun marque became the largest 'open' importer[4] in 1975–8.) In addition, the UK's entry into the EEC gave a boost to the multinational production and marketing activities of US firms so that by 1977 the largest importer was Ford. The growth in imports is shown in table 8.4.

TABLE 8.4:   Import penetration into the UK car market

	Total (Units)	Share of UK market (%)
1961	22 759	3.0
1969	101 914	10.0
1970	157 956	14.0
1972	450 314	26.4
1973	504 619	27.4
1976	533 901	37.9
1977	698 464	45.4
1978	800 772	49.3

Source: SMMT *The Motor Industry of Great Britain 1979.*

The surge in imports in 1972 was a reflection of the inability of the UK car industry to supply enough vehicles of the right type. The lack of investment in the 1960s had left the industry with uncompetitive facilities and an ageing model range. The UK consumer was now presented with a greater choice of vehicles, especially in the small to medium range in the mass market than he had enjoyed since the early 1930s, when some fifteen firms had offered their wares. By 1980 some eighteen domestic, West and East European, US and Japanese firms were competing in the bargain basement of the car market.

It can be seen from table 8.2 that the UK car industry's export performance has deteriorated since the mid-1960s. From a maximum of 772 000 cars exported in 1969 the total fell to 475 000 in 1977. The CV side held its own rather better with 181 000 units exported in 1969, 195 000 in 1971 and 177 000 in 1977.

The UK's poor trade performance was partly due to its exclusion from the EEC during a period of rapid economic growth and trade creation within the Six. During this period the multinationals used their smaller home market base in the UK to service their non-EEC markets. This often meant the sale of cars in kit (ckd) form for overseas assembly. Consequently the incentive to renew, let alone expand, UK assembly capacity was blunted. This incentive was further reduced by BLMC's preoccupation with almost continual re-organisations and short-term labour difficulties. Both factors interrupted the flow of production and new model programmes and alienated foreign dealer chains, harmed company finance, morale and product development. All these elements militated against any concerted export drive.

The overall result of these domestic problems and of the unprecedented strength and dynamism in the car industries of Continental Europe and Japan in successfully seeking out new sales was a fall in the UK's share of world car exports from 35% in 1955 to 6% in 1978. So, although cars imported by the USA rose from 700 000 in 1967 to 2.0 million in 1978, the UK's sales over the same period declined from 71 000 to 50 000, while Japanese sales increased from 66 000 to 1 350 000. The British car industry's share of new car registrations in Western Europe fell from 4.7 to 2.0% between 1966 and 1978. Even in markets where the UK was particularly strong, say in the Commonwealth or South Africa, its position was eroded by policies which encouraged local assembly and by Japanese competition. Land Rover's leadership of the four-wheel drive vehicle market and Chrysler UK's 50–60% hold on the Iranian market are exceptions to the general decline.[5]

Although buoyant home markets have given the Japanese, French and West German firms a solid base on which to attack export markets it is also true that exports are as important to the continued prosperity of the firms involved as the home market. Hence they have established first class dealer chains, backed by continual easy availability of good quality products, to consolidate overseas markets. Therefore, although the restrained UK market in the period 1965–71 did not help the industry to find overseas markets, the failure to overcome this handicap proved disastrous to the scale of activities in the UK.

Foreign competition in the UK market stems mainly from Western Europe and Japan, although low price imports from Communist Europe have captured 2% of the market. In 1980 some fourteen foreign firms operated in the mass market sector and eight foreign based concerns operated in the large volume quality market. As a result every sector of the UK market, with the possible exception of the niche held by Rolls-Royce, faces active foreign competition. The main preserve of the UK volume producers is the medium-sized saloon car sector: a sector with many non-private buyers.

Although foreign sales increased significantly in the 1970s import penetration of the CV market was held below 25%. The greater relative strength of the UK CV industry, especially in the medium van, medium heavy truck and bus markets, meant that keen UK prices, customer goodwill and relatively adequate stocks made the job of importers more difficult. However, the catastrophic decline in the competitiveness of BL's heavy goods vehicle products and operations in the latter half of the 1970s, the early EFTA competition in the booming heavy truck market of the 1960s, and later entry by EEC firms meant that by the end of the 1970s the very heavy truck market leader in the UK was Volvo of Sweden. Moreover, over 50% of this market was in the hands of various foreign producers. Indeed the prime concern of ERF, Foden and Seddon Atkinson became the restriction of imports rather than the increase in exports. In the car-derived van and medium pick-up markets the Japanese became very active, consequently most foreign competition was experienced at the extremes of the CV market. The UK-based firms – BL, Chrysler, Ford and Bedford (GMC) – dominate the medium truck and lightweight bus chassis sectors, and BL dominates the heavy bus sector.

8.2.4 Demand characteristics

Cars and CVs provide a flow of transport services. In the case of cars the product is also desired because it confers on its owner various attributes, not the least of which are prestige and status. The relevant dependent variable in the demand equation is not so much the demand for new cars as the demand for car ownership. The latter may involve the purchase of cars of vintages ranging from the new to, say, those over ten years old.

The main independent variables are price and per capita disposable income. Estimates of long run elasticity of demand for cars as a whole vary from –0.6 to –1.5 while income elasticities range from 1.1 to 4.2 (Rhys, 1972b). However, price elasticity estimates for the products of individual firms vary between 2.0 and –7.0 (e.g. Cowling and Cubbin, 1971). Advertising and demographic, locational and credit factors also influence car demand. Severe short-run changes in car demand are generated by changes in credit terms. For instance, it has been suggested that a fall in the minimum hire purchase deposit from 33 to 20% of the price of a car increases car demand by the same extent as a 2% growth in national income (Silberston, 1963).

Car demand tends to have three horizons: (i) the short run, which is greatly affected by market confidence; (ii) the medium term, which reflects the basic desire for car ownership and the normal replacement cycle; and (iii) the long run which covers the outcome of social and technical developments which may in turn be the result of basic changes in transport policy.

Although car buyers tend to be spread diffusely through the economy, the fleet users exert some countervailing pressure and are courted by the producers with special discounts. Such pressure is also present in the CV market. Although 122 000 of the 138 000 operators' licences cover fleets of five CVs or fewer, 39% of CVs are owned by fleets of six to sixty CVs and 10% of CVs are owned by fleets of over two hundred. In the bus field most new vehicles are sold to large operators, and sales are often obtained through tendering.

Long term demand estimates put the size of the UK car park in 2010 as between 21.9 million and 30.5 million depending on the growth of incomes and motoring costs (SMMT, 1978). However, this is based on a trend forecast and given the problems involved in extrapolating trends into the next century such figures must be treated with caution. Nevertheless, if it is conservatively estimated that annual scrappage remains at around one million cars a year, then annual registrations could vary around 1.5 million new cars a year.

8.3 MARKET STRUCTURE

The UK motor industry must now be viewed as a component of a wider European motor industry. Indeed, unlike the French, West German and Italian industries where most output comes from indigenous firms, three of the four large UK car makers are foreign owned. These owners have increasingly viewed the European market and the European industry as an integrated whole. Consequently Ford UK's main product and investment strategies are imposed on it by Ford Europe while GMC has integrated many features of its German and British controlled operations and model lines. Chrysler's integration is much less well advanced due to an early mis-specification of the problem. The company tried to make each of its European operations viable on an independent basis and then when the need to spread heavy fixed costs and to reduce operating costs was understood, the US parent did not have the money needed to invest in the necessary integrated products and facilities. However, the British government's rescue operation in 1975 provided money for integration to proceed, a policy which was continued by C UK's new parent, Peugeot. Therefore the product range and marketing strategy of these three firms is now European in context and leaves only an increasingly vulnerable BL as a British orientated company.

Thus, although output in the UK is concentrated in only four firms, the facilities of three of these are merely complementing other European plants. The market is less concentrated than output data would imply (table 8.5) because of intra-European free trade and Japanese penetration of about 11% of the market. (A figure constrained by the Japanese agreeing voluntarily to restrict exports to the UK). The integrated European-wide market (including the UK)

TABLE 8.5:   Shares of UK market, 1977 (%)

	Share of UK output (1977)	Share of UK market (1977)	Imports from European plants
BL	49	24.3	0.1
Ford	31	25.7	6.5
Vauxhall	7	9.1	3.0
Chrysler	13	6.0	1.1
'Tied' imports*	—	(10.7)	—
Other imports	—	34.6	—
Other British	0	0.3	—

Source: Derived from SMMT data.
Note: *'Tied' imports are those emanating from the other European plants of firms producing cars in the UK.

TABLE 8.6:   Share of European market, 1977 (%)

Peugeot–Citroen–Chrysler	18.0	GMC	10.7
Ford	13.2	BL	4.9
Renault	11.8	Daimler–Benz	2.5
Fiat–Seat	11.8	Others including	
Volkswagen	11.5	'imports'	15.6

Source: Derived from SMMT data.

displays an even greater degree of competition and a relatively low degree of concentration. The top three firms have less than 45% of the total (table 8.6).

8.3.1 Mergers

Merger activity in the UK motor industry has not been constrained by anti-trust legislation. Indeed many mergers have been officially encouraged.

The first major merger – which led to the formation of the British Motor Corporation – was that between Austin and Nuffield in 1952. This merger was a recognition that cut-throat competition between the companies was mutually harmful and that a merged combine would strengthen management, obtain scale economies, co-ordinate research and development, and strengthen the constituent firms' grip on the market. The merger was not a defensive move to combat Ford as the real threat from this firm was not understood until after BMC was formed. Subsequent mergers involving BMC, those with Pressed Steel in 1965 and with Jaguar in 1966, to form British Motor Holdings (BMH), were more defensive in nature. For example, the Jaguar company was used to cover deficiencies in BMC's vehicle range.

The creation of BLMC in 1968 resulted from both the aggressive growth of Leyland Motors and the decline of BMH and was allied to a desire by government to see the creation of a firm of size and strength to be internationally secure. Leyland had itself already absorbed various CV firms such as Albion, Scammell and the Associated Commercial Vehicle Group, as well as the financially embarrassed Standard–Triumph car firm (in 1961), and the efficient but small scale Rover company (in 1967). The Rootes group fell under complete Chrysler control between 1964 and 1967 only to be sold to Peugeot in 1979. In the area of specialist CVs Seddon bought Atkinson in 1971 only to sell to International Harvester in 1974 to obtain finance for a rapid model development programme. Further takeovers occurred on the components side, with US firms such as Dana, Eaton and Rockwell being extremely active.

8.3.2 Product differentiation

Although price competition has always been significant in the motor industry non-price competition concerned with the differentiation of products by style and model changes, and by technical, quality and other marketing variations and tactics is also important.

A style change every three years and a model change every six years can distinguish a firm's products from its own previous production and the unaltered offerings of its rivals. However, firms wishing to avoid the £15m needed for a facelift, the £70m for a rebodying and the £200m for a completely new car, aim to produce cars with advanced specifications and with function-based, rather than stylised, body designs. By these means they can obtain not only large annual output volumes but also long lived production runs as well. Firms try to avoid head-on competition by stressing differences in their product and by attempting to provide a different set of characteristics. The firms wedded to short product cycles are linked with huge European or world-wide organisations which can spread over-heads more thinly. The advanced specifications mass producers, however, although often both large and prosperous would find it difficult to engage in style and model competition of the US and Japanese kind without experiencing increased unit costs and lower profits.

The strategy of long production runs, allied to quality, durability or engineering specifications, has been followed by the 'Quality' car makers and specialist divisions of larger firms. Attempts have been made to separate this market from the more price conscious mass market by stressing a set of characteristics that imply cars are being built-up to a standard rather than down to a price. Nevertheless, even within the quality market the price variable cannot be ignored.

8.3.3 The degree of integration

UK car makers tend to have a greater degree of dependence on outside specialists than is the norm in the European motor industry. Therefore many major component makers have developed in the UK to supply the 65–70% of parts 'bought-in' by BL and Ford, the 71% by Chrysler UK and the 85% by Vauxhall. Although 8000 suppliers supply 7000 parts to a typical UK car firm, some 30% (by value) of the bought-in content is accounted for by a dozen major suppliers including firms such as Lucas, GKN, Automotive Products and Associated Engineering. On the CV side external economies are enjoyed by vehicle makers who buy-in as much as 90% of material costs. As a result quite small UK assemblers are able to reach unit cost levels competitive with those reached by much larger integrated producers.

As regards diversification all the UK-based car firms have CV facilities but diversification outside the motor industry has been slight. However, on the Continent firms such as Volvo, Renault, Fiat and VW are actively engaged in reducing their dependence on car making and aim at reducing car based turnover to less than 50% of the total by the early 1980s.

8.3.4 Barriers to entry

A new entrant would require large marketing outlays to challenge existing product differentiation and brand loyalty and to provide an adequate dealer system. However, such barriers have not proved insurmountable to any existing foreign maker wishing to enter the UK car market. Indeed, the various production and marketing weaknesses evident in the UK industry in 1969–79 actively *reduced* the marketing entry barriers facing well established foreign firms. An entirely new entrant would, however, face substantial difficulties.

The major barriers to entry are those stemming from economies of scale and from absolute capital needs. The minimum efficient scale for car manufacture would appear to be around two million units a year although entry might be risked in the mass market at one million units and in the quality car sector at 300 000 units. A firm such as Rolls-Royce survives making only 3000 units a year, while by utilising the supply infrastructure new makers have been able to enter the UK bus industry at 1000 units a year. Heavy CV manufacturers could prosper at either 10 000 a year when buying-in or 60 000 a year when integrated. The large car figures are partly due to economies of scale and partly due to the need to recover model-specific fixed costs as quickly as possible to reduce any vulnerability to model-change competition. The minimum efficient size is greater than the current output of the UK car industry, although C UK is now part of an organisation with a capacity of 2.6 million cars a year and Vauxhall and Ford are both within European enterprises which have capacities of around 1.6 to 2.0 million.

The absolute capital costs needed for car making are huge. A modern press shop for a volume car producer costs about £120m with each set of dies costing around £20m. An assembly plant costs in the region of £130m. A gearbox plant requires £90m. A complete engine plant would cost some £240m when all construction costs and working capital needs are added to tooling and development costs. The total of about £600m involved here is impressive, but a fully integrated and properly balanced optimum size firm would require much greater expenditures. For instance, two assembly plants would be needed to approach the full use of the output of an optimum sized engine plant. The £2.4bn envisaged as being needed to rescue British Leyland, an already established company, can perhaps be taken as an indication of the sums needed to enter the European motor industry at an optimum scale. Clearly such a sum, which was 2.4 times the original allocation to the National Enterprise Board, is beyond that which could be raised on a capital market.

8.3.5 The EEC and market structure

Within a European context the only autarchic UK producer is BL, which is relatively small scale in both car and CV making. The other producers are appended to US or French controlled European-wide operations. The unified home market of the European Community gave the multinationals the opportunity to change their scale of operations by rationalising and integrating their European activities.

The growth of Continental firms, and direct competition from them within the unified market, put the remaining UK-owned car maker in a vulnerable position as regards size and its potential for achieving economies of scale. In a world context its position is even worse (see table 8.7): hence BL's attempts in 1979–80 to project itself as one of the world's largest *specialist* vehicle makers; and its link with Honda.

TABLE 8.7:   Car industry's largest firms world wide, 1977

	Car production (thousands)	Car capacity* (thousands)
GMC	7 000 000	8 000 000
Ford	5 000 000	5 750 000
Chrysler	1 700 000	2 400 000
Peugeot–Citroen–Talbot	2 200 000	2 600 000
Toyota	2 100 000	2 350 000
Nissan	1 900 000	2 000 000
Fiat–Seat	1 800 000	2 650 000
VW	2 200 000	2 900 000
Renault	1 700 000	2 300 000
BL	800 000	1 100 000
Honda	600 000	700 000
Mitsubishi	500 000	700 000
Toyo-Kogyo	500 000	600 000
Daimler–Benz	420 000	450 000

Sources: Production based on SMMT data. Capacity based on information given by various companies.
Note: *This is an approximate maximum assembly capacity as defined in note 2.

8.4 MARKET BEHAVIOUR

Although the motor industry in the UK consists of only a few large producers and is oligopolistic in structure, there is little evidence of co-ordinated behaviour or collusion designed to earn a monopoly profit. Indeed, until the creation of BLMC, five firms competed vigorously in the mass market. Moreover the number of significant competitors increased dramatically with the huge influx of imports during the 1970s.

8.4.1 Prices and model changes

Although the 1970s showed indications of price leadership by either

Ford or BL, this was not so much evidence of collusive behaviour as of smaller firms following the barometric, rather than the dominant, price leadership of larger firms who were themselves subject to industry-wide inflationary cost pressures. The higher unit cost operation of smaller firms may have made them loath to lead the price round for any fall in market share would have had immediate adverse effects on their unit costs and profits.

The competitive nature of the car market ensures that the prices charged by various UK and foreign firms for comparable models are set close to each other with slight variations being possible because of product differentiation. However, the high inflation experienced in the UK from 1973 until the end of the decade saw effective list-price competition by firms as they absorbed inflationary cost increases to greater or lesser degrees. Ford, whose aim was to regain market leadership in the UK and thereby to increase its total European production reinforced its new model ranges by highly competitive pricing. However, all UK firms increased prices by far more than either the index of retail prices or earnings. Taking January 1974 as base 100, Ford prices had reached 263.7, BL 280.6, Chrysler UK 269.5, and Vauxhall 268.4 by January 1979. However, earnings and retail prices had barely passed the 200 point mark.

The result of this steep rise (rises which were not made by foreign car makers overseas), a result which was only partly explained by the UK's EEC entry in 1973 and the consequent phasing-out of tariffs, was the increased competitiveness of imports. Indeed, the takeoff of UK car prices in 1973 at a time when Datsun was charging comparatively low prices to help it enter the UK market, reduced further the barriers to Japanese entry. Continental firms enjoyed the same advantage if to a lesser degree. By January 1975 the price advantage of British over imported cars – around 10% in 1973 – had disappeared, a reflection of price increases in the UK rather than price cutting overseas. The main problem was the relatively high inflation in the UK, which was not reflected by exchange rates until 1977, and the reduction by UK makers of their standard output, upon which pricing decisions were based. The move to a lower level of capacity utilisation led inevitably to higher unit costs.

Despite the competitive nature of the car market all firms engage in the practice of price discrimination between home and foreign markets and, in domestic markets, between private buyers and fleet users. To this extent the niceties of marginal cost pricing are ignored but even so, dumping is rarely practised as prices more than cover variable costs (Rhys, 1978). An example of price discrimination across markets was given by Ford's Fiesta pricing in 1976 when the car sold for almost £400 less in Belgium than in West Germany even though VAT was 25% in Belgium and only 11% in West Germany.

Another pointer to the general lack of collusive behaviour in the UK motor industry was the considerable short and long-run fluctuations in the market shares held by domestic producers. For instance, between 1965 and 1978 the companies making up BL saw their share fall from 43 to 23%, Vauxhall's share fell from 12 to 8% and Chrysler's from 12 to 7%. On the other hand Ford held steady at around 26%.

Firms have also used non-price variables such as technical innovation, style and model changes in their competitive strategies. In the UK, BL has followed a policy of long product cycles of around ten years, partly because of the technical nature of the product and partly because of a lack of funds for replacement. Chrysler UK was forced to use long product cycles mainly because of the latter factor and was unable to offer advanced technology as an offsetting variable. Vauxhall, and Ford, have used a five-year product cycle for their European products but the gradual introduction from 1976 of advanced engineering models has forced these companies to lengthen their model runs in order to absorb mounting research, development and tooling costs. The specialist makers maintain styles for a decade and more. During this period they carefully husband resources to finance a model change which has to be correct or the companies' survival is in immediate jeopardy. Between model changes they stress the quality and exclusiveness of their products.

On the CV side light vans, medium trucks and buses retain their basic designs for between ten and twenty years. However, in the field of heavy trucks, rapid technical developments and the requirements of safety, environmental and other legislation reduced the product cycle from twelve to nine or ten years. In the late 1970s this reduction put medium-sized firms under pressure and was partly a cause of Leyland's declining market share as its trucks became out-dated.

8.4.2 Research, innovation and patenting

Although technical developments are continuous, it is difficult to foresee a short-term revolution in car design, although such a possibility on the heavy lorry front is more likely. There appears little prospect of change from the internal combustion engine in the near future, especially as improved petrol engines and driving habits, and the spread of diesel power to more and more cars could have considerable fuel-saving effects. The use of battery–electric technology may be the most viable alternative, but any social wish to see this replace internal combustion would have to rely on legislative and taxation measures to reduce the comparative advantage of oil as an energy source. Although many key patents exist for motor industry products, cross-licensing is so prevalent that no manufacturer appears able to maintain an advantage for long, especially if the patent is held by a component maker. However, to find funds and contain unit costs to meet new environmental regulations, European car firms may find it necessary to pool research facilities.

8.4.3 Advertising and marketing

The most immediate way of bringing products to the attention of the customer is by advertising. Longer term marketing strategies involve the nature and quality of the product, the dealer chain, product specification and prices.

Between 1968 and 1975 total advertising by car firms increased from £4.4m to £18.2m. However, this hid considerable fluctuations in expenditure by different firms. For example importers took a larger share as they tried to break into the UK market but UK firms subsequently reversed this trend as they endeavoured to preserve and indeed increase their market share. As prices are normally set in relation either to those of similar models made by other firms or to those needed to clear a firm's supply capacity, advertising strategies are seldom backed by changes in published list prices. Instead, the reinforcement comes from discounts, changes in specifications, adjustments in quality, more generous warranty and guarantee conditions and cheap credit. As the car buyer became more affluent the mass producers maintained their position, and often increased their prosperity by offering some better appointed and more expensive cars and by giving their dealers a wider model range.

Advertising on CVs only amounts to 5% of that on cars although CV registrations are 20% of car registrations. This is mainly because the CV buyer is more interested in ascertaining the basic economics of a particular vehicle and is totally unimpressed by generalised advertising aimed either at giving superficial information or at crude product differentiation.

With a product as expensive to buy and maintain as a car the distribution network's efficiency and accessibility can be a crucial competitive weapon. In order to try to establish dealers of nearer to optimum size, especially in terms of sales per outlet, UK car makers shed 7000 outlets between 1970 and 1977. BL accounted for 4600 of these. However, grateful importers snapped up 4000 of these outlets and the ease with which they established their networks illustrates how by this action UK car makers removed a barrier to foreign firms entering the UK market. By 1980 almost 50% of sales outlets were in the hands of importers. This is a major factor in explaining why the foreign car is in such an entrenched position in the UK market, especially in the private motorists' sector, where accessibility to a service point is often important.

8.5 PERFORMANCE

Although motor industry firms have some conception of marginal costs, long run prices are usually related to average total or incremental costs. However, these costs may not be the lowest possible, if the firms concerned are X-inefficient. Consequently the absence of abnormal reported profits in the motor industry is not necessarily sufficient evidence that monopolistic practices are not employed. However, given the competitive pressures that exist in the industry, it is probably true to say that there is little evidence of serious welfare loss from this source. (But see Cowling and Cubbin, 1971). This is not to say that some, albeit competitive firms have not suffered from various inefficiencies of their own. Indeed as rates of return have been low in relation to manufacturing industry's as a whole it may be questioned whether the use of resources *on their existing scale* by the motor industry is justified (see table 8.8).

TABLE 8.8:   Rates of return on capital employed (%)*

	1961	1965	1970	1973
Manufacturing industry	10.0	11.8	11.3	14.4
Motor industry	6.4	9.6	3.8	11.0

Source: Based on evidence contained in Fourteenth Report from the Expenditure Committee, Session 1974–5, *The Motor Vehicle Industry*, HC 617–1. London: HMSO, 1975, page 407.
Note: *Since 1974 the UK motor industry has been in the throes of reorganisation, so the previous years have been used for comparative purposes both here and in some subsequent tables.

In terms of the profitability of individual companies the UK motor industry has not presented a successful picture. Table 8.9 gives figures for 1965–77. Vauxhall and C UK were chronic loss makers and were saved only by their parent companies from disaster. BL found it impossible to match the real aggregate profits of the pre-merger constituent firms which made £54m in 1964 and £50m in 1965. Only Ford, Rolls-Royce and ERF amongst the vehicle makers reported adequate results with any consistency.

Table 8.10 gives data on returns to shareholders for both the vehicle producers and the main component manufacturers. Comparisons with foreign firms are particularly revealing here. It is worth noting that the component makers in general did rather better than the vehicle manufacturers. The low level of profits was symptomatic of low productivity, with even Ford suffering severely from this problem. Crude output per man figures are not favourable to the UK industry.

TABLE 8.9: Pre-tax profits (losses) for individual firms (£m)

	1965	1966	1967	1969	1970	1971	1972	1973	1974	1975	1976	1977
C UK	(2.5)	(3.4)	(10.8)	0.7	(10.7)	0.4	1.6	3.7	(17.7)	(35.5)	(42.9)	(21.5)
Ford	8.9	7.4	2.6	38.1	25.2	(30.7)	46.8	65.4	8.7	14.1	121.0	246.1
BL	50.0	44.0	16.0	40.0	3.9	32.4	31.9	51.0	2.3	(76.0)	70.5	3.1
Vauxhall	17.7	3.6	5.7	(1.9)	(9.7)	1.8	(4.3)	(4.1)	(18.1)	(12.7)	(1.8)	(2.0)
Rolls-Royce	0.1	0.6	1.3	2.1	2.4	3.8	4.0	4.8	4.9	6.3	11.0	15.0
ERF	0.3	0.4	0.4	0.4	0.7	0.9	0.4	0.9	0.6	(0.1)	1.7	3.3

Source: Company reports.

TABLE 8.10:   Return on shareholders' funds, vehicle producers and
component manufacturers (%): average 1970-3

C UK	-9.6	Lucas	6.7
Vauxhall	-8.4	GKN	7.2
BL	5.6	Associated Engineering	9.3
Ford (UK)	5.9	Automotive Products	13.5
Toyota	15.4	Birmid	13.5
Daimler–Benz	11.6	Smiths Industries	12.2
Peugeot	18.4	Chloride	14.0

Source: Central Policy Review Staff (CPRS) The Future of the British Car Industry. London: HMSO, 1975.

For instance, in 1975 the Japanese made 37 vehicles per man and the European Continentals averaged 12, while in the UK Chrysler made 11, Ford 9, and BLMC 5.5. Of course, differences in product mix and bought-in content reduce the validity of the above comparisons but value-added figures per man generate the same type of result (table 8.11).

TABLE 8.11:   Value-added per man, 1974 (£)

GMC (US)	8600	C UK	2765	Saab	4637
Opel	5875	Fiat	2259	Ford (UK)	3901
Volvo	4886	Ford (US)	7966	Vauxhall	2560
VW	4767	Daimler–Benz	5207	BLMC	2129
Renault	4133	Ford (Germany)	4883		

Source: Fourteenth Report from the Expenditure Committee, Session 1974–5, The Motor Vehicle Industry, HC 617–1. London: HMSO, 1975, page 428.

These unfavourable British results are reinforced by *direct* enquiries, such as those by the CPRS, which showed productivity in terms of the number of hours needed to assemble given items with nearly identical facilities. The results indicated that in various assembly operations the UK figure was twice the Continental. This was compounded by other problems such as high warranty costs and the poor utilisation of fixed capital arising from a fragmented model range and the consequent shorter production runs. All these inefficiencies increased unit car costs by in excess of 10% of the ex-works price (see CPRS, 1975, pages 77–94). The factors causing poor productivity can be put down to overmanning, interruptions to the smooth flow of production and under-investment in plant and capital equipment. It appears that BL and C UK are particularly under-invested. Ford and Vauxhall suffer mostly from the problems of overmanning, slow work pace and work interruption. Low productivity has been a long-term feature of the UK motor industry and has not just developed in the 1970s (table 8.12). The smaller size of UK motor plants, relative to those overseas may also be a source of inefficiency (see Jones and Prais, 1978). (Any tendency for industrial relations problems to increase with the size of plant-employment may be overcome by replacing labour by capital in the larger-output plants).

TABLE 8.12:   Vehicles produced per employee

	1955	1965	1973
UK	4.2	5.8	5.1
USA	11.1	13.9	14.9
West Germany	3.9	7.1	7.3
France	3.6	6.1	6.8
Italy	3.0	7.4	6.8
Japan	1.2	4.4	12.2

Source: CPRS *The Future of the British Car Industry.* London: HMSO, 1975.

The same results emerged when cash margins, expressed as a percentage of sales, were examined for the period 1970–3. Ford (UK) earned 8.6% but its German associate earned 11.3%, Chrysler earned 2.1% in the UK but 6.9% in France, and GMC earned 15.3% in West Germany and 6.0% in the UK.

Many explanations can be put forward for the industry's relative and, indeed, absolute decline. The lower per capita income growth in the UK, the highly cyclical and volatile nature of the economy, poor industrial relations, poor managerial and financial control of companies' activities, and the problems caused by the industry's role as an economic regulator, all played a part.

8.6 PUBLIC POLICY

To a minor extent government can influence the motor industry directly by its own purchases. For instance the public sector as a whole buys about two weeks' worth of Ford's UK production. So although a firm's viability would not be put in jeopardy by a loss of such orders, they nevertheless provide vehicle makers with a large amount of profitable business.

The motor industry on both the vehicle and component side has been subject to various Monopoly Commission enquiries. Some have examined conditions of supply involving dominant suppliers, while others have examined proposed mergers. Although some activities have been found to be against the public interest none of the Commission's recommendations could be interpreted as a major interference in the structure or behaviour of the firms or industries involved. None of the proposed mergers investigated by the Commission was found to be against the public interest, although the US takeover of Crane Fruehauf trailers produced a strongly worded minority report. Indeed the major structural changes in the motor industry (apart from BMC buying Pressed Steel) were not referred to the Commission at all. Moreover, mergers in the period 1966–70, especially those involving Rootes–Chrysler and BMH–LMC, received the tacit or active blessing of the Industrial Reorganisation Corporation, which was interested in seeing the establishment of large domestic firms able to compete successfully with the international competition. The policy objective here recognised that in the case of the motor industry, the appropriate criterion was not the effects of the merger on the structure of the UK motor industry, but the position of the merged firm in the European and, indeed, the world motor industry and market.

In the case of the Restrictive Practices Court the public watchdog did increase the degree of competition. In 1957 a test case showed that car firms could exercise a great deal of control over their dealers. In 1960 the manufacturers' regulation of discounts and minimum dealer standards and the discrimination against the non-franchised dealer were deemed against the public interest. Resale price maintenance did not stop dealers offering variable trade-ins or discounts off list price for cash sales, but the abolition of resale price maintenance (RPM) in 1964, followed by a deflated market, saw greatly increased price competition by retailers and indeed by makers. However, anti-trust legislation had a greater effect on the retail side of the car industry than it did on manufacturing.

8.6.1 Finance from the state

A significant feature of the post-1964 period was the emergence of the state as a source of selective financial assistance as distinct from the usual general assistance provided in the form of capital grants, allowances, employment premiums and regional help.

The Industrial Reorganisation Corporation (1966–71), established with a capital of £150m, was to bring about a reorganisation of parts of UK industry where organisational inadequacies were the cause of poor performance. It was, in effect, to encourage mergers. On only seven occasions did the IRC provide finance for individual companies, and two of these occasions involved vehicle makers. The IRC contributed £25m to help fund BLMC when it was formed in 1968. Later that year, when Chrysler took control of Rootes, it invested some

£3.0m in the company. This sum included the purchase of some 15% of the equity and thereby enabled Britain to retain a stake in the concern for a little longer. However, it was the rescue of BLMC that saw significant state involvement. In 1975 the Government agreed to help BL to the tune of £1,260m. This included a £50m guarantee given by the Department of Industry (DI) in late 1974 under section 8 of the 1972 Industry Act. As the rescue pre-dated the creation of the National Enterprise Board, BL was nationalised by Act of Parliament, with state control being passed to the NEB. The rescue of BL was in the form of equity and loans supplied either by the DI or by the NEB. However, such was the drain on the NEB's resources that its borrowing powers were increased in 1979 from £1bn to £3bn. The funds were for working capital, fixed investment and model development but no subsidies were allowed. (In 1979 the NEB filled a missing link in the BL rescue by helping to extend aid to the dealer chain). However, the rescue in December 1975 of C UK by the DI which put a contingent liability on the Exchequer of £162.5m, included payments of up to £72.5m to cover losses by direct subsidy. Smaller amounts of commercial money have been advanced to motor firms by the Scottish, Welsh and Northern Ireland Development Agencies. (The Scottish organisation helped the new Stonefield vehicles concern). The huge £65m investment package for the De Lorean car company in Northern Ireland had strong social overtones. Assistance to various firms associated with the motor industry has come from the varied provisions of section 8 of the Industry Act, while section 7 regional assistance added to general regional assistance provided Ford in 1977–8 with £148m to pay for a Welsh engine plant and related developments.

The industry has been amongst the greatest contributors to the creation of employment in development areas. In most cases the new locations appeared efficient (NEDO, 1969), although BL claimed in the early 1970s that making trucks at Bathgate imposed a penalty of £52 per unit, and at the same time C UK experienced operating penalties of £2m a year at Linwood. However, by the mid and late-1970s both firms were at pains to show that both locations were suitable, especially C UK when it justified transferring some production to Scotland under the post-1975 reorganisation.

8.6.2 The effects of policy on vehicle demand

Change in sales taxes and hire purchase regulations have severely affected the level of activity in the car market. CVs have not been as severely affected as sales taxes for most business users have had zero incidence since 1956.

The motor industry by making products whose demand is income elastic has been subject to the inherent fluctuations (and low growth) in the economy. This instability has been reinforced by governments' use of the industry as an economic regulator through variations in sales taxes and hire purchase conditions. The effects of fluctuations are to harm capacity utilisation and to make unit production costs higher than need be while destroying forward planning. Therefore the effects of government activities on the state of the market was a major factor in the harm done to the industry's profitability in the 1950s and 60s and hampered its ability to invest in new products and facilities, and to meet overseas competition. The harm done to the industry was officially recognised and resulted in sales tax incidence (and HP regulations after their re-introduction) remaining almost constant from 1973 until the general increase in value-added tax in mid-1979.

Other taxes and duties, such as those on fuel and vehicle licences, have been set either on amount of vehicle use or at low levels, so have had a smaller effect on the demand for cars and indeed CVs. However, a significant increase in fuel tax could affect the *incidence* of car demand, while a greater awareness by society of the net social costs of vehicle use could induce government to formulate a coherent policy in this area. This would include legislation on vehicle noise, noxious gas emissions, vehicle longevity, vehicle design, vehicle use and so on. Obviously, such changes and changes in general transport policy could affect vehicle demand. For instance, a policy to transfer freight to rail could adversely affect truck demand, while subsidised bus travel could increase the demand for buses. In addition the introduction of pricing schemes aimed at covering the marginal social cost generated by road users could curtail the use of and therefore the annual demand for vehicles.

8.7 CONCLUSION

The structure, performance and behaviour of the UK motor industry cannot now be properly studied outside a European context. The relatively fragmented European industry contrasts sharply with three massive producers in the USA and two clear market leaders in Japan. Consequently, the rapid growth of Peugeot from a firm making 750 000 cars a year to a combine capable of reaping the further economies of scale available at outputs of 2.6 million could be a forerunner of further full mergers or of increased co-operation among independent firms. This co-operation could involve European firms alone or more widespread alliances, say with the Japanese.

NOTES TO CHAPTER 8

1. For the period 1954 to 1963 it has been calculated that about 15% of the growth

in industrial production was due to the increased inputs into the motor industry. In addition the growth in output of the motor industry itself accounted for another 11.7% of the growth in industrial production. Consequently it was concluded that some 27% of the growth in industrial production over the period was attributable to the growth of the motor industry. See Armstrong (1967).

2. Except where stated otherwise, capacity refers to the maximum assembly capacity provided by working two shifts a day, five days a week and forty-six weeks a year. Therefore, the working of extra days and shifts would increase capacity.

3. In the early 1970s car makers in the USA began making small sub-compact cars. As the ratio of labour costs to total car costs varies inversely with car size, and as the US labour-to-capital cost ratio was then comparatively high, these cars were made in highly automated assembly plants with an optimum capacity of around 300 000 units a year. Elsewhere, lower wages dictated the use of less automated assembly tracks with an optimum capacity of around 220 000 units a year. However, many European and Japanese firms are finding it worthwhile to increase automation, so the assembly optimum can be expected to increase.

4. Many customers regard Ford, Vauxhall and Chrysler as purely British firms and are not always aware that these firms import cars from their Continental plants. These enterprises use the goodwill engendered by the consumers' perception of a firm's nationality to help sell cars on the UK market. To this extent they enjoy 'hidden' importing. Wholly foreign-based firms can only engage in obvious or 'open' importing.

5. In 1979, although substantial foreign earnings were made, the trade balance for the whole motor industry moved into deficit for the first time since the industry's infancy. There had been a deficit on cars since 1975.

REFERENCES

Armstrong, A. G. (1967) 'The Motor Industry and the British Economy'. *District Bank Review* (163), 19–40.

Central Policy Review Staff (CPRS) (1975) *The Future of the British Car Industry*. London: HMSO.

Cmnd 6377 (1976) *The British Motor Vehicle Industry*. London: HMSO.

Cowling, K. and Cubbin, J. (1971) 'Price Quality and Advertising Competition: an economic investigation of the UK car market'. *Economica* (New Series), XXXVIII (152), 378–394.

Economic Development Committee for Motor Manufacturing (NEDO) (1969) *Regional Policy and the Motor Industry*. London: HMSO.

Jones, D. T. and Prais, S. J. (1978) 'Plant-Size and Productivity in the Motor Industry: Some International Comparisons'. *Oxford Bulletin of Economies and Statistics* **40** (2), 131–151.

Pratten, C. (1971) *Economies of Scale in Manufacturing Industry*. London: Cambridge University Press.

Rhys, D. G. (1972a) 'Economies of Scale in the Motor Industry'. *Bulletin of Economic Research* **24** (2), 87–97.

Rhys, D. G. (1972b) *The Motor Industry: an economic survey.* London: Butterworths.

Rhys, D. G. (1977) 'European Mass-Producing Car Makers and Minimal Efficient Scale: A Note'. *The Journal of Industrial Economics* XXV (4), 313–320.

Rhys, D. G. (1978) 'Car Market Price Competition in the Mid 1970's'. *Management Decision* 16 (4), 217–231.

Silberston, A. (1963) 'Hire Purchase Controls and the Demand for Cars'. *Economic Journal* LXXIII (289 and 291), 32–53 and 556–558.

SMMT (1978) 'Forecasts of Car Ownership in Great Britain'. Unpublished research document.

FURTHER READING

Silberston, A. and Maxcy, G. (1959) *The Motor Industry.* London: Allen and Unwin.

Rhys, D. G. (1972) *The Motor Industry: an economic survey.* London: Butterworths.

Young, S. and Hood, N. (1977) *Chrysler UK: a corporation in transition.* New York and London: Praeger.

Fourteenth Report from the Expenditure Committee (Trade and Industry Sub-Committee), Session 1974–5 (1975) *The Motor Vehicle Industry.* HC 617, London: HMSO, plus volumes of evidence (1975), HC 617–I, HC 617–II, HC 617–III, London: HMSO.

Central Policy Review Staff (1975) *The Future of the British Car Industry.* London: HMSO.

SMMT, *The Motor Industry of Great Britain* (an annual publication). London: SMMT.

↗ Book Title

9 Synthetic fibres   207–30

R. W. and S. A. Shaw

9.1 INTRODUCTION

9.1.1 Early history

The synthetic fibres industry in the UK and Western Europe generally is essentially a post-Second World War phenomenon. Of the three main synthetic fibres nylon (a polyamide fibre) was first produced in the UK by British Nylon Spinners (BNS), a jointly owned ICI and Courtaulds subsidiary, in 1941; polyester fibre was first produced commercially in the UK by ICI in 1954; and finally acrylic fibre was first produced in the UK by Courtaulds and Monsanto (an American-owned firm) between 1957 and 1959. Synthetic fibres today have found their way into a wide range of clothing, household and industrial textile products.

Nylon was originally developed in two main forms: nylon 66 and nylon 6. The former was discovered and developed by the American Company Du Pont in the 1930s and was protected by patents. The latter was developed, again in the 1930s by I. G. Farben in Germany. British involvement began when ICI received an exclusive UK manufacturing licence for nylon 66 from Du Pont in 1939. Manufacturing licences were also granted in Europe to I. G. Farben, French Rhodiaceta, and Italian Rhodiaceta. Although ICI's chemical base provided know-how for on-going technical developments the firm lacked experience in the textile industry. Thus, in 1940 ICI formed a joint manufacturing company with Courtaulds who were able to draw on their experience in the textile industry. The jointly owned company was named British Nylon Spinners (BNS) and was owned 50% by ICI and 50% by Courtaulds. BNS enjoyed a patent protected monopoly for nylon 66 yarn production in the UK at least until 1961, although a second major patent concerning the manufacturing process (steam spinning) did not expire until 1964. However competition was still possible from imported nylon fabrics that were not protected. The only other nylon development in the 1950s was the introduction of a nylon 6 fibre by British Celanese. This company was acquired by Courtaulds in 1957.

Polyester fibre was discovered and initially developed in the UK by J. R. Whinfield and J. T. Dickson at the Calico Printers Association (CPA) in 1940. However as CPA's interests were mainly in the specialised area of the printing and finishing of fabrics the commercial development of polyester fibre was carried out by ICI, which was given an exclusive licence in the UK and the rest of the world except the USA, and by Du Pont which was given an exclusive licence in the USA. ICI subsequently granted sub-licences to producers in France, Germany, Holland and Italy; these gave the firms concerned exclusive rights in their own countries and non-exclusive rights elsewhere. Du Pont began commercial production in the USA in 1953; ICI followed in the UK in 1954. The basic UK patents expired in 1963, although a considerable degree of protection continued in Europe under the sub-licensing agreements until the end of 1966.

Acrylic fibre was first discovered and developed by Du Pont in the USA in the early 1940s, though commercial scale production did not begin until 1950. A variety of acrylic and the related modacrylic fibres developed by other firms in the USA and Europe were introduced in the 1950s: Courtaulds and Monsanto being the first to produce in the UK in about 1959. Unlike nylon and polyester fibres a competitive situation thus existed from the beginning.

9.1.2 Growth of the industry in the UK and Western Europe

Starting from an almost negligible usage in the immediate post-war period, by 1969 synthetic fibres had captured a 30% share of the Western European market for all textile fibres. By 1977, synthetic fibres' share had risen to over 45%, with cotton trailing far behind with only a 26% share, and wool and cellulosics effectively sharing the rest with 12 and 15% respectively.

Details of the growth of the UK industry from the early 1960s are given in table 9.1. As is readily apparent, UK industry production grew extremely rapidly in the 1960s – at an average annual rate of 19%. However in the 1970s there has been very little further growth overall and indeed a significant decline in output from the peak achieved in 1973. In addition it is clear that both imports and exports have become more important in the 1970s compared with the early and mid-1960s. Thus imports were 44% of domestic production in 1977 compared with only 15% in 1966. Similarly nearly 46% of domestic production was exported in 1977 compared with only 26% in 1966. Further these statistics underestimate the significance of foreign trade as they refer only to trade in staple fibre and yarn and omit trade in fabrics and finished textile goods (e.g. shirts).

TABLE 9.1: United Kingdom synthetic fibre production, imports, exports and net available supply (tonnes thousand)

Year	Production	Imports	Exports	Available supply
1962	84.0	11.4	22.7	72.7
1966	174.7	25.7	44.7	155.7
1970	336.8	53.8	120.2	270.4
1973	453.9	122.5	175.7	400.7
1974	396.1	135.9	165.5	366.5
1975	361.1	119.8	145.9	335.0
1976	414.2	146.0	177.3	382.9
1977	358.8	158.8	164.5	353.1

Source: Textile Organon.
Note: Imports and exports exclude spun yarn.

There are a number of reasons for the impressive growth and market penetration achieved by synthetic fibres. They include synthetic fibres' competitive advantage over traditional fibres such as cotton and wool arising from superior performance characteristics, e.g. easy care for clothes, and the sustained promotion expenditure emphasising such advantages. Diffusion was further encouraged by the improving price competitiveness of synthetics arising from cost reductions as a result of learning, technical improvements and economies of scale, and also price competition by synthetic fibres producers. In addition quality improvements and a broadening range of products widened the potential market. Finally, the possibility of lower production costs in the fibre-using industries as a result of substituting synthetic and other man-made fibres for natural fibres gave the first two a competitive edge over the natural fibres. For instance synthetics are more suitable than natural fibres for use in the machine knitting process which has lower conversion costs from fibre to fabric than the woollen–worsted type weaving system. Similarly, in the production of carpets, there has been a switch from woven carpets, traditionally using wool, to tufted carpets made by a faster, cheaper process and using predominantly man-made fibres especially nylon and the acrylics.

A further reason for growth, as opposed to increased market penetration, has been the increase in the overall textile market. The Food and Agriculture Organisation (FAO, 1971) estimated income elasticities of demand in the UK in 1971 for clothing to be 0.257, for household uses of fibres 0.131 and for industrial uses 0.064. Although small the elasticities are nevertheless positive. However, offsetting this there has been the growth in imports of fabrics and garments from elsewhere, especially the developing world.

The effects of changing relative prices on demand are difficult to assess. The overall price elasticity of demand for textile fibres is likely to be fairly low because fibre price represents only a small percentage of the final price of textile products. For example the yarn costs in fully fashioned knitwear represented only about one-third of manufacturers' selling price at the end of the 1960s (Hosiery and Knitwear EDC, 1970, page 44) and an even smaller proportion of retail price. Further, the price elasticities of demand for some finished products, e.g. clothes, are themselves low.

Although the overall price elasticity of demand for fibres generally may be low, the possibility of substitution may make the elasticity for any particular fibre quite high. No quantitative estimates are available for the UK but studies in the USA for the period 1949–68 (Minford, 1975) and Australia for 1975 (Tisdell and McDonald, 1977) suggest that the choice of textile fibre is sensitive to price – Minford estimated an elasticity of greater than 1 and probably around 2. In the UK, however, it is now believed that large-scale fibre substitution on price grounds is over and that choice of fibre type is now dictated mainly by technical considerations (e.g. the preference for synthetics rather than natural fibres in the knitting industry) and appearance of the garment in end uses where fashion is important.

9.2 THE CHANGING MARKET STRUCTURE

The discussion of market structure–conduct–performance relationships is dominated by the evolution of the industry in the post-war period. The latter includes the market introduction, early penetration, rapid growth and maturity stages of the synthetic fibres product life cycle. In line with these stages the market structures for particular fibres, and to a lesser extent for synthetic fibres generally, changed from monopoly, or near monopoly, protected by patent rights, to oligopoly and unprotected by patent rights. Further, the essentially isolated national markets, protected by patents, licensing agreements and tariffs, developed into a much more closely integrated Western European market as patent protection ended and tariff barriers were removed. These changes coincided with increasing buyer knowledge of the particular physical properties of the different fibres, and also of the generic similarities of the competing products of a single fibre type made by rival firms.

9.2.1 Seller concentration

The early history of the synthetic fibres industry has already been summarised in the introduction. As the innovators in the UK, ICI and BNS initially had a monopoly in polyesters and nylon respectively. In acrylics, where UK production started somewhat later, Monsanto, Courtaulds and Du Pont (with imports) were in early competition.

The monopoly in nylon was effectively ended soon after the sale of Courtaulds' share of BNS to ICI in 1963 following the failure of the latter company's takeover bid for Courtaulds in 1961/62. Courtaulds, which had previously taken over British Celanese, decided to develop its own brand of nylon 6 – Celon. By 1965 the two UK producers, ICI and Courtaulds, had been joined by British Enkalon, a subsidiary of the West German–Dutch firm AKZO and Monsanto.

ICI's monopoly in polyester fibres persisted in the UK until the end of 1966 when British Enkalon began manufacturing in Northern Ireland. Hoechst, a West German firm, at the same time began importing polyester into the UK and in 1969 established its own UK production facilities. Du Pont, which had been excluded from Western Europe by the continuing patent rights, built a major manufacturing plant in West Germany designed to serve the Western European market and began importing polyester fibre into the UK. Finally, in 1969 Courtaulds announced its intention to enter the polyester sector; production began in 1971.

In acrylics the UK market was oligopolistic virtually from its inception. Courtaulds and Monsanto both began production in the UK at the end of the 1950s and throughout the 1960s competition from imports was also significant. Du Pont, which had been importing for many years, was credited with a 30% share of the UK market in 1965 entirely from imports. Du Pont eventually built an acrylics plant in Northern Ireland at the end of the 1960s. Dow was also active in the UK market with imports from 1962 onwards.

The overall results of these developments in the 1960s are summarised in tables 9.2 and 9.3. Table 9.2 shows the estimated UK market shares and includes imports. Table 9.3 shows estimated UK production.

The penetration of the UK market by Western European and American synthetic fibre manufacturers was to a large extent paralleled in other markets. For instance ICI began manufacturing nylon and polyester fibres in West Germany for the EEC market in 1965 and 1967 respectively. Similarly Courtaulds began manufacturing acrylic fibre in France, also in the 1960s.

Although the major domestic firms have probably retained the largest market shares in their own countries, both the extent of their dominance and its significance in terms of market power have tended to decline in the 1970s. Several developments have been responsible. First, the number of firms active in each national sub-market has increased. Secondly, the loss of patent protection, the decline in tariffs and the increase in buyer knowledge have significantly reduced the isolation of national sub-markets. Finally, the existence of excess capacity in Western Europe and the world generally in most sectors for long periods during the 1970s has led to keen competition between established producers in any national market and foreign producers anxious to find some outlet for their products. However, even if it were appropriate to treat the whole of Western Europe as a single market, the degree of seller concentration remains high. Some indication of this concentration in Western Europe, based on synthetic fibre capacities in 1974, is given in table 9.4. Thus over 90% of Western European polyester capacity, for instance, is in the hands of ten firms, and four firms control over 70% of capacity. Although imports of fibre

TABLE 9.2:   Estimated market shares of total domestic consumption of synthetic fibres in the UK, 1969 (%)

Producer	Polyester	Acrylic	Nylon
ICI	75	—	56
Courtaulds	—	46	15
Monsanto	—	29	8
Du Pont	7	21	3
British Enkalon	7	—	13
Hoechst	9	*	—
Bayer	—	2	—
Others	2	2	5

Source: O'Neill, *Financial Times*, 2 September 1970.
Note: *Less than 1%.

TABLE 9.3:   Estimated UK production of synthetic fibres, 1969 (planned or current capacity in brackets) (tonnes thousand)

Producer	Polyester		Acrylic		Nylon		Total	
ICI	68	(104)	—	—	86	(123)	154	(227)
Courtaulds	—	(9)	54	(91)	18	(27)	72	(127)
Monsanto	—	—	27	(39)	12	(18)	39	(57)
British Enkalon	2	(7)	—	—	14	(20)	16	(27)
Du Pont	—	—	5	(18)	—	—	5	(18)
Hoechst	—	(7)	—	—	—	—	—	(7)
Total	70	(127)	86	(148)	130	(188)	286	(463)

Source: O'Neill, *Financial Times*, 2 September 1970.

TABLE 9.4: Distribution of European synthetic fibre capacity, end 1974 (%)

	Nylon 6	Nylon 66	Polyester	Acrylic	Total
AKZO	31.6	11.8	21.8	8.2	17.6
Bayer	12.7	—	4.3	16.4	8.3
Courtaulds	12.2	—	*	20.5	7.8
Du Pont	—	8.6	6.9	7.4	6.3
Hoechst	—	—	24.5	12.0	12.5
ICI	—	35.3	15.9	—	12.4
Monsanto	—	8.1	—	7.5	3.7
Montefibre	6.8	5.1	6.0	11.6	7.6
Rhone Poulenc	—	31.1	12.2	6.8	12.2
Snia Viscosa	20.8	—	2.7	5.5	5.8
Other	15.9	—	5.7	4.1	5.8
Total	100	100	100	100	100
Total capacity (tonnes per year)	395 000	467 000	940 000	732 000	2 534 000

Source: Montedison (parent company of Montefibre) estimates reported in *European Chemical News*, 10 October 1975.
Note: *Courtaulds were not credited with any capacity in Montedison's estimates. Courtaulds' 20 000 tonne plant in Northern Ireland began manufacturing in 1971.

from the Far East and Eastern Europe particularly have sometimes had a noticeable effect on the competitive situation, in general they have not been sufficiently large to alter the picture of concentration presented above.

9.2.2 Economies of scale and cost structure

There are variations in production costs between different types of fibre but there is broad similarity so that any figures quoted in this section can be regarded as generally representative of all fibres. The main structural distinction is between the production not of different fibres but between staple fibres and filament yarn.

(a) *Short-run costs* The estimated cost content of a kilo of polyester staple fibre in 1978 is given in table 9.5. These percentages are for fibre produced in a plant with an annual capacity of 10 000 tonnes. The average cost per kilo of filament yarn would be about 40% higher than that for staple fibre because the conversion process to yarn is more expensive.

Although variable costs form a fairly high proportion of total cost, largely due to the relatively high share of raw material costs, there are substantial fixed costs so that below capacity operations do cause significant unit cost increases. Additionally, there are quality control problems when output falls to around 70% of capacity. Finally it should be noted that closing down plant for short periods to escape these difficulties gives rise to re-start problems and hence is also unattractive.

TABLE 9.5:   Polyester staple costs per kilo of fibre

	(%)
Raw materials	38
Labour	10
Utilities	4
Maintenance, packaging, minor raw materials[1]	7
Depreciation and capital costs[2]	27
Selling costs	6
Other overheads	8
	100

Industry source.
Notes: (1) Catalysts, delustrants and spares.
(2) This is based on a ten-year life, some allowance for working capital and interest at 10%.

(b) *Long-run costs: economies of scale*   Economies of scale in production in the industry are significant in relation to total market size, largely because of the reduction in capital costs per unit as plant size is increased. The estimates in table 9.6 relate to the production of polyester staple fibre for plant sizes up to 100 000 tonnes per year (the largest currently being built).

TABLE 9.6:   Production economies of scale in polyester staple fibre

		Cost indices		
Annual capacity (tonnes)	Capital cost (£m)	Production cost excluding materials	Production cost including materials	Per cent of Western European polyester staple capacity, 1977 (%)
10 000	12	100	100	1.5
20 000	20	92	96	3
100 000	75	81	90	15

Industry source.

One factor which reduces the disadvantage of relatively small plants in practice is the tendency for the number of product lines to increase with the scale of plant (Pratten, 1971). The result is that potential economies from long production runs may not be realised. On the other hand, firms with relatively small plant(s) tend either to restrict their product range or to adopt plant specialisation so as to achieve long production runs in each plant.

9.2.3 Research and development expenditure

Research and development costs are very important, both because of the scale of expenditure and because capital may be tied up for long periods. In the case of nylon and polyester it took more than ten years from initial research to commercial scale production. Actual cost data are difficult to obtain but Pratten (page 63) quoted development costs 'of more than £20m for some new fibres introduced by an American manufacturer'. In recent years few completely new fibre types of any great significance have been introduced, but the process of developing new varieties of existing fibres continues. Production technology has also continued to advance: labour requirements for instance for a plant of given size are now about 25% of the level required in 1968. In order to keep pace with industry developments expenditure ranging from 3 to 5% of turnover for R and D has been quoted by industry sources for European companies. American companies, however, spend considerably more in absolute terms on R and D than their European counterparts but because of their larger output the American firms' R and D expenditure is probably only 1–2% of turnover. However firms faced with large short-term losses may cut back on R and D expenditure, thus protecting their short term financial position, though perhaps at the expense of their longer term competitive position. Finally, it is possible that indications of reductions in research expenditure in the 1970s by European firms reflected diminishing research possibilities, or 'exhaustion' of the technology.

9.2.4 Selling costs and product differentiation

An important feature of the synthetic fibres industry has been the emphasis by manufacturers on branding their products and using advertising as a means of promotion. This was particularly important during the 1950s and 1960s.

According to Census of Production data (HMSO 1969, 1974) advertising expenditure for the whole man-made fibre industry (including cellulosic as well as the synthetic fibres) in the UK was approximately £3.1m in 1963 and £5.1m in 1968. The resultant advertising–sales ratios were 1.47 in 1963 and 1.54 per cent in 1968. These

ratios indicate an unusual degree of advertising intensity for intermediate goods. By their advertising the synthetic fibres manufacturers were trying both to establish the brand names of their
particular products and to promote the demand for synthetic fibres
by final consumers, thus putting pressure on textile and clothing firms
to use synthetic fibres in preference to natural fibres and – in the case
of ICI – in preference to cellulosic fibres such as rayon.

In the 1970s, however, the volume of advertising expenditure and
the emphasis on manufacturers' brand names has declined. Fabric and
garment labels now have to specify generic product type (e.g. polyester) rather than brand names, and many retailers also have
emphasised generic rather than brand names in their promotional
activities. Also – and partly because of this – consumers have become
more knowledgeable about the properties of individual fibres, and thus
the power of the manufacturer's brand name has declined, thus
reducing the value of actively promoting it. Fibre manufacturers now
put their promotional emphasis on new fibre variants and in relative
terms spend more of the promotional budget on their textile rather
than final consumer customers. In addition, the losses being incurred
in the 1970s may have limited the money available to be spent on
promotion.

9.2.5 Diversification and vertical integration

In considering the extent of diversification by synthetic fibre producers
at least three means must be acknowledged. Firstly, there is the extent
to which individual firms cover the range of synthetic fibres. As will be
seen from tables 9.3 and 9.4 Courtaulds with its entry into the polyester sector at the beginning of the 1970s completed its range and thus
produces all the major synthetic fibres. ICI, on the other hand, has
remained out of the acrylics sector. Most of the other major Western
European producers such as AKZO, Rhone Poulenc, Montefibre,
Snia Viscosa, Bayer and Du Pont have adopted the Courtaulds
pattern of offering a complete range of synthetic fibres. Secondly,
some firms such as Courtaulds and AKZO also produce cellulosic
fibres and indeed are closely associated with the textiles industry
generally. ICI, on the other hand, has no interests in the cellulosics
sector of the fibres industry. Finally, all of the companies listed in
table 9.4 are major diversified chemical companies with the exception
of Courtaulds. In 1977, for instance, fibres accounted for less than
10% of ICI's turnover.

The degree and direction of vertical integration is related to the
pattern of diversification outlined above. Thus ICI, which manufactures the chemical intermediates for its synthetic fibre production,
generally sought to avoid forward integration into the textile fibre-

using industries – at least in the 1960s. In contrast with the ICI pattern, Courtaulds does not manufacture chemical intermediates for fibre production, but has pursued an active policy of vertical integration into the textile industry from the early 1960s (Knight, 1974). Thus by the early 1970s Courtaulds was responsible for about one-third of spinning output and one-quarter of weaving output in the UK cotton and allied textiles industry. Courtaulds is similarly heavily involved in the sector producing knitted fabrics.

9.2.6 Barriers to entry

Patent rights together with licensing agreements initially provided legal barriers to entry, at least to the nylon and polyester sectors of the industry. As this protection disappeared a limited amount of entry occurred. However the high capital costs for plant, substantial R and D costs, significant economies of scale and product differentiation advantages discussed above made entry unattractive to all but large chemical and man-made fibre firms. However, with the slowing down of growth of output in the 1970s and the emergence of excess capacity, the relative ease, or otherwise, of entry has for the present lost its significance.

9.2.7 Buyer concentration

The overall level of buyer concentration is on the surface extremely low as synthetic fibres find outlets in several fibre-using industries, some of them containing large numbers of firms. For instance in 1973 there were over two hundred firms each in the cotton spinning and weaving industries, and over eight hundred firms each in the woollen and worsted, and hosiery and knitted goods industries. However this picture is misleading. Firstly, specialised fibre products will only have access to a small proportion of total outlets. Secondly, a combination of moderate levels of concentration (e.g. five-firm concentration ratios of 50% in both cotton spinning and weaving in 1973) together with vertical integration by the fibre producers, especially Courtaulds, makes the market for synthetic fibres oligopsonistic (see section 9.2.5).

9.3 MARKET BEHAVIOUR

Associated with the fundamental changes in industry structure and growth outlined earlier were changes in market conduct. Initially price competition tended to be non-existent or unimportant because firms enjoyed monopoly positions (nylon and polyester) in their particular sectors and national markets, and market penetration was achieved largely by stressing the technical advantages of the fibres concerned. Later, as costs were reduced, and as further market penetration was sought, price competition with other fibres, e.g. cotton, rayon and wool, became more significant. However, simultaneously, actual and potential competition between synthetic fibres producers was developing as patent protection ended and the isolation of national markets diminished. Throughout these developments, however, a constant feature of the industry was the search for both product and process improvements.

In order to analyse the relationships between market structure and behaviour the discussion is divided into two sections covering the monopoly period for nylon and polyester fibre and the subsequent oligopoly phase experienced by all three major synthetic fibres.

9.3.1 The monopoly phase: nylon and polyester

Initially BNS and ICI were patent protected monopolists in the UK for nylon and polyester respectively. Competition was only possible from two sources: alternative fibres and imported fabric and finished goods made from nylon or polyester. In practice prices were at first set in the UK at a high level to recover the large initial R and D costs and as a reflection of the monopolists' uncertainty as to demand elasticities (Hague, 1957, page 126). Although synthetic fibres prices were competitive with each other, they were high compared with natural and other man-made fibres. For instance polyester staple, suitable for the cotton system, was four to five times as expensive as the comparable competitive alternatives, cotton and rayon. In general, apart from some list price reductions in the mid-1950s, probably caused by competition from foreign fabric and other fibres (Hague, page 111), prices remained stable until the early 1960s. Throughout this period market penetration was achieved by promotion on the basis of synthetic fibres' superior properties and not by overt price competition. Further, the association of these superior properties with particular brand names – BNS's Bri-Nylon (nylon) and ICI's Terylene and Crimplene (polyester) – was an important feature of the promotion activity.

Although the major patents for nylon 66 did not expire until 1961 and 1964, and for polyester until 1963, the established monopolists had to face the possibility that their profitability might attract entry on patent expiry. Hence the monopolists might have considered entry deterrent behaviour in the last few years of general patent protection. This could have taken several forms such as limit pricing, the maintenance of excess capacity, the development of a range of products and product differentiation and the creation of vertical links with customers.

In fact UK prices for both nylon and polyester were reduced between 1961 and 1963. However, it seems unlikely that entry deterrence was more than a marginal cause. In the case of nylon British Enkalon had already announced its plans to build a factory in the UK before the series of price cuts began. In the case of the smaller polyester fibre market (UK output was 24 000 tonnes of polyester compared with 50 000 tonnes of nylon in 1962) immediate entry was perhaps not a very serious threat as continued patent protection on the continent of Europe, together with licensing agreements, meant that the existing European producers would not invade the UK market at that stage, and any US producers would have found their sales largely confined to the UK. The threat posed by the US producers was more from imports than the setting up of manufacturing facilities in the UK. Finally, the most obvious UK potential entrant, Courtaulds, was in 1961/62 fending off a takeover bid by ICI and in any case was busy developing its acrylic fibre, Courtelle.

By the mid-1960s, however, the situation was substantially altered as patent rights in Western Europe generally were coming to an end, and by then further market growth had made entry more attractive. In practice ICI, which retained its monopoly up to the end of 1966, did lower polyester fibre prices progressively from 1961 onwards. Although these price cuts may have contained a small element of deterrence, other factors were almost certainly more important. Among these were cost reductions due to economies of scale and process improvements, the desire to extend the market penetration of polyester fibres and the threat of imports from the USA. Indeed a comparison of the timing and size of the UK list price reductions with movements in USA selling prices suggests that the import threat was a major factor (Shaw and Shaw, 1977).

As far as other possible competitive strategies are concerned it is difficult to distinguish between those aimed at entry deterrence and those aimed at both further market penetration for synthetic fibres and establishing a strong competitive position should entry sub-sequently occur. Thus the policies of developing wide product ranges to cover specialised end uses and promoting brand names are consistent with both market extension and making entry more difficult. One illustration of this problem concerns ICI's development of a textured (bulked) polyester filament at the beginning of the 1960s suitable for the fast, cheap knitting process, and ultimately used in the production of jersey fabrics, childrens' clothes and mens' suits. In its attack on the market ICI created the Crimplene Club, named after ICI's brand name for the fibre. Only the member firms of this club were licensed to bulk Crimplene yarn, and in return these firms agreed to buy exclusively from ICI. Further, jersey manufacturers were only allowed to sell fabric under the Crimplene name when it had passed

ICI quality tests. By creating an element of vertical control ICI was able at the same time both to develop the market rapidly and to establish entry barriers.

9.3.2 The oligopoly phase

In the acrylic fibre sector an oligopolistic market existed throughout the 1960s; for nylon the oligopoly phase did not begin until about 1964/65, and for polyester this phase only began in 1967. Despite these differences a common feature of all these markets was a decisive downward trend in prices in the 1960s and early 1970s up to 1973. Several factors contributed to this development: among them were the threat of imports, the achievement of economies of scale, technical progress and the desire to widen markets, as already indicated for polyester fibres in the period up to 1967. However, three interconnected factors: capacity extension, excess capacity and competitive price cutting merit special attention.

In the rapidly growing synthetic fibres market it was only to be expected that major firms would regularly announce expansionary investment plans. However the pattern of investment and pricing announcements on occasion suggested an apparently aggressive reaction by established firms to the entry and expansion of smaller rivals. For instance, after Courtaulds had announced its intention to become a major producer of nylon in the UK in April 1964, ICI, the dominant producer, announced early in June its own major capacity extension. Similarly, in July 1969 Courtaulds' announcement of its entry into the polyester fibre sector was followed virtually immediately by ICI's announcement of its own polyester expansion plans.

There is also some evidence for nylon and polyester that price cuts were initiated by major producers in an attempt to preserve their market positions in the face of new entry by rivals. For instance, in April 1965 ICI reduced its UK nylon prices following Courtaulds introduction of its nylon 6, Celon, earlier in the year. Indeed the Chairman of Courtaulds, referring to Celon's introduction, stated at a press conference: 'it is being produced during an increasingly cutthroat price war' (*European Chemical News*, 18 June 1965). In West Germany, in December 1966, Hoechst, the established firm, announced its intention to reduce polyester list prices by 25% in the face of entry by ICI and Du Pont. ICI immediately lowered its prices which forced Hoechst to bring forward its own price cuts. The result was that all producers' list prices moved substantially downwards. Similarly in the summer of 1967, under pressure of imports from Du Pont, Hoechst and British Enkalon, ICI, now the established firm, reduced its UK list prices again by about 25%. Du Pont, Hoechst and British Enkalon followed suit.

Although it is clear that the market leaders conceded market share only grudgingly, it would be incorrect to suggest that they were solely responsible for the emerging price competition in the 1960s and 1970s. A major factor was the often short-term, but rapid, build up of imports of a particular type of fibre leading to competitive price cutting and the disregard for official list prices. For instance, due to excess capacity in the USA import restrictions were imposed on fibre entering the United States in 1971. The effect on Western Europe was immediate. Japanese and other Far Eastern supplies of polyester filament were directed to Europe at the same time as demand for textured filament for the knitting industry was cut back. Prices tumbled as firms tried to protect their markets. From their high point at the beginning of 1971, prices fell by 50% by July 1972 (*European Chemical News*, 9 March 1973). When demand improved in the second half of 1972, however, and the pressure from imports eased, there was a sharp recovery in prices in Europe generally.

As indicated above the spasmodic emergence of excess capacity – and indeed in the mid-1970s, its persistence – has been an important feature of the industry. It has been experienced by all three major sectors, and in all of them it has led to severe price competition with list prices becoming meaningless. Between 1965 and 1967 when nylon filament capacity utilisation in Western Europe was below 75%, actual (as opposed to list) prices fell by about 40%. A similar reduction in acrylic staple prices occurred in roughly the same period (Berrini, 1973) again in the context of severe excess capacity.

Up to 1973 excess capacity tended to be a temporary phenomenon with industry sales rapidly catching up on capacity. However, from 1974 onwards the Western European industry has experienced persistent and severe excess capacity (capacity utilisation averaging 70% from 1974–6 for all synthetic fibres combined) because of a combination of increased imports of synthetic fibre fabrics and finished goods from elsewhere in the world, incompatible market share aspirations by the European producers, and the stagnation of industry demand.

The GATT Multi-Fibre Agreement of 1974 was intended to give protection to the European textile industry by persuading exporters of low cost textiles to the EEC to accept controls against their exports in return for a guaranteed share of the industrialised countries' markets plus some scope for growth. In practice, however, the accepted growth rates for imports were agreed on the basis of higher expected growth in the textile industry than actually occurred, and further the agreement did not cover all exporters. The EEC Commission estimated that from a position of overall trade balance in textiles in 1970, by 1976 imports of textiles exceeded exports by a fibre equivalent of 500 000 metric tonnes. If one makes the crude assumption that the loss of synthetic fibre outlets in Europe is in proportion to the present market share of synthetics (46%), this implies a loss of demand of about 230 000 metric tonnes. This accounts for roughly a quarter of the excess capacity in synthetics. The problems of imports were exacerbated by a swing back towards natural fibres from 1974 at a time when cotton became temporarily cheaper than polyester. As a result the overall textiles market penetration of synthetic fibres has hardly changed since 1973.

Although excess capacity, price competition and the resultant losses must dominate any discussion of the synthetic fibre market in the 1970s, other aspects of the competitive process in the oligopoly phase should not be neglected. One such aspect was the continuing search for high performance speciality fibres by firms seeking outlets unaffected by the increasing price competition in the main sectors. Indeed it has been argued that Du Pont's increased European profits in 1970, when other firms were suffering setbacks, were the result of its effective R and D and 'policy of extreme selectivity in choosing market . . . areas' (Trafford, 1971; see also Heller, 1971). Alongside this policy of developing high-performance speciality fibres the major firms continued to seek premium prices for their branded fibres wherever possible.

Another important aspect of market behaviour was the development of vertical control. Courtaulds in the 1960s was actively changing market structure by its vertical integration policy based on both internal growth and mergers. The initial moves were intended to protect Courtaulds' market for rayon. However other moves were directly related to the development of Courtaulds' synthetic fibre business. Sir Arthur Knight, later to become chairman of Courtaulds, listed 'the inadequacies of the existing market for dealing with a rapidly growing fibre on an adequate scale'; Courtaulds vulnerability to a switch of customers to US fibre competitors; and inadequate quality standards of some independent firms as reasons for vertical integration in acrylic fibres (Knight, pages 46–47). Vertical integration into the knitting industry was explained by the need to be close to buyers and because 'it is easier to promote the sale of Courtaulds fibre against US competitors, especially through the rapid translation of new development ideas into commercial products'. Finally, regarding Courtaulds' belated entry into the nylon sector, he commented that 'it was obvious that at that late stage it would be expensive to break into the market held by competitors, and a vertical attack would have more chance of success' (pages 47–48).

For ICI forward vertical integration into the textiles industry was much less important than for Courtaulds. Indeed despite giving some financial assistance to the textile industry through loans and minority shareholdings, ICI avoided direct involvement in the industry until the end of the 1960s. However, as already indicated, ICI did establish a degree of vertical control through its licensing arrangements with the Crimplene Club. Despite the reluctance to become involved ICI eventually acquired control of some textile firms such as Viyella International and Carrington and Dewhurst, though the reasons seem to have been primarily defensive as the viability of these major customers was threatened in the increasingly competitive environment. Finally, ICI used acquisition as a means of achieving vertical integration into the texturing industry. Here the major reason seems to have been the achievement of technical economies as integration offered the possibility of combining two stages in the production process (Gardner, 1972). However there was probably also a directly competitive reason as two of ICI's competitors – Courtaulds and British Enkalon – had already integrated forward into texturising and other firms such as Hoechst were threatening ICI's dominance in the UK polyester textured filament fibre market.

A final aspect of market behaviour concerns the investment and output reactions of firms to the severe excess capacity experienced in the 1970s. However, discussion on this point is deferred until the final section on the role of governments and competition policies in the EEC. At this stage it is sufficient to note that some major fibre producers cancelled expansion plans and shut factories and, significantly, sought permission from the EEC to carry out such actions in a co-ordinated manner.

9.4 PERFORMANCE

Comments on the performance of the UK synthetic fibres industry are peculiarly difficult to make not only because of the usual data problems but also because of the difficulty of evaluating performance in an excess capacity situation. For instance, excess capacity will depress figures for labour productivity but the spare capacity may be advantageously retained to exploit future demand growth or to attempt to increase market share. Similarly any assessment of firms' profitability must recognise that the industry is clearly in disequilibrium.

Turning initially to comparative productivity assessments, most of the available evidence refers to man-made fibres as a whole and not to synthetics alone. However production relationships for synthetic and cellulosic fibres are sufficiently similar to justify the inclusion of some data. An international comparison of output per employee is not reassuring. The UK industry performance falls far short of the levels achieved in the USA, Japan and West Germany with only Italy, of those reported faring worse (see table 9.7). At least four factors may account for the differences revealed: economies of scale, relative factor proportions, factor efficiency in use and product mix.

TABLE 9.7:   Man-made fibre production and employment: selected countries, 1976

Country	Employment	Man-made fibre production (thousand tonnes)	Output per employee (tonnes)
France	18 400	333.5	18.1
Italy	38 300	515.1	13.4
Japan	71 800	1 631.3	22.7
United Kingdom	43 000	632.9	14.7
USA	105 600	3 287.8	31.1
West Germany	40 200	909.6	22.6

Source: CIRFS – International Rayon and Synthetic Fibres Committee.

With respect to economies of scale at plant level and considering synthetic fibres only, table 9.8 shows the scale advantage enjoyed by American and, to a lesser extent, West German producers. It is probable that some part of the labour productivity differences reported is attributable to this scale factor. However, it would be

TABLE 9.8:   Number of synthetic fibre plants, total and average capacity, 1976

Country[1]	Number of plants (1)	Production capacity thousand tonnes (2)	Average capacity thousand tonnes (2)/(1)
USA	87	3524	41
Western Europe (total)	159	3230	20
Benelux	10	229	23
France	20	370	19
Italy/Malta	31	544	18
United Kingdom	24	590	25
West Germany	30	1003	33

Source: Textile Organon.
Note: (1) Data relate only to the acrylic, nylon and polyester groups of synthetic fibre in the case of the USA and Western Europe (total). For individual European countries the number of plants data again relates to the three main types of synthetic fibre. Production capacity includes other minor synthetic fibres leading to a small upward bias in reported average capacity.

incorrect to conclude that European firms in general and UK firms in particular opted for inappropriate plant sizes. The Western European market was historically subdivided into the relatively small national markets which effectively constrained the scale of plant built.

Some limited information on the three remaining influences on productivity referred to above has been provided by ICI in the form of manpower productivity comparisons between its synthetic fibre plants in the UK and West Germany (Lossius, 1977). Lossius reported that manpower productivity in West German plants rose by 7.5% per year between 1967 and 1976 whereas the annual increase was only 5% in UK plants. In 1976, for similar product groups, the number of men per unit of output was 40% higher in the UK than in West Germany. Lossius also reported that 'this ratio holds even across examples of identical new plant being used for exactly the same purpose in the two countries' (page 202). Finally, he noted that 'there is no evidence that the employees in either country are supported by a larger unit resource' (page 204). Despite the well known difficulties in making productivity comparisons it seems clear from this evidence that UK plants were less efficient technically than the West German plants. Offsetting this disadvantage higher wages were paid in West Germany.

The available evidence on profitability is extremely limited because most of the companies concerned are part of multinational, multi-product organisations which do not specify in many cases financial results for individual company sectors. For instance, Courtaulds, one of the two major UK companies, does not provide separate financial data for its synthetic fibre interests; the latter being combined with other man-made fibres and Courtaulds' important textile industry activities. Similarly, of the smaller UK producers, Du Pont, Monsanto and Hoechst do not identify their UK fibre results.

ICI, the second major UK producer, does provide separate financial data for synthetic fibres but this is limited to profits and turnover and there are no data for capital employed. Table 9.9 gives details of the financial results from 1970 until 1978. Although ICI's synthetic fibre interests have been loss-making between 1975 and 1978, this perform-ance has to be put in the context of general losses throughout the industry. It has been estimated that during the period 1975-mid 1978 the European man-made fibre producers lost over $2bn (Rhys, 1978). Although it is difficult to be precise about the scale of ICI's losses relative to other firms due to the combining of textile and man-made fibre results in some instances and the distorting effect of special non-recurring reorganisation expenses as firms cut back capacity, it is clear that major competitors such as AKZO, Rhone Poulenc, Du Pont and Hoechst were also making substantial losses. The losses reported for Montefibre, the largest Italian producer, however, deserve special mention. In 1975 and 1976 Montefibre's losses as a percentage of sales revenue amounted to about 50 and 30% respectively. The responses of the various firms to their losses and excess capacity is discussed in the final section.

TABLE 9.9:   ICI synthetic fibres profitability, 1970–1978[1]

Year	Profit (loss) (£m)	Sales (£m)	Profit (loss) as a percentage of sales (%)
1970	14	150	9
1971	5	149	3
1972	(9)	156	(6)
1973[2]	25	282	9
1974	29	331	9
1975	(30)	324	(9)
1976	(11)	422	(3)
1977	(16)	398	(4)
1978	(13)	420	(3)

Notes: (1) Sales in and exports from the UK only 1970–72; all fibre interests 1973–8.
(2) The results of the UK fibre interests in 1973 were profits £18m; sales £197m.

Two final comments on industry performance are appropriate. First, it is surely a considerable achievement for the synthetic fibre industry, which started virtually from nothing in 1945, to have captured over 45% of the Western European textile fibre market by 1977. This has been accomplished by a persistent search for new outlets, new products, quality improvements and cost reductions. Whether this performance could have been improved upon is a matter only for conjecture. Second, on the deficit side, there is the evidence of large-scale excess capacity. It is at least arguable that the competitive pressure to achieve economies of scale has contributed to some waste of resources as capacity far outstripped demand during the mid-1970s.

9.5 THE ROLE OF GOVERNMENTS AND COMPETITION POLICIES OF THE EEC

In the years of industrial prosperity there was little *direct* government involvement in the synthetic fibres industry in the UK. However, it should be apparent from the earlier discussion that UK and other governments' patent laws were a key feature in sustaining the monopoly positions of the pioneering firms. Further protection was also afforded by tariff barriers. Finally, within this protected environment the government's usual investment incentives were available for the synthetic fibres industry as for others, though in return the government exercised influence over some of the early plant location decisions to direct investment towards the development areas.

In the 1970s patent and tariff protection largely disappeared. The major patents had expired and with UK membership of the EEC, tariff barriers, at least within Western Europe, were progressively reduced. The resulting new entry and import competition was superimposed on the dramatic change in industry growth rate – from nearly 20% per year in the 1960s and early 1970s to stagnation and decline from 1973 onwards. As a result synthetic fibres became one of the 'problem' industries of the 1970s with the emergence of persistent excess capacity. The main issues with respect to government and EEC action relate to the role of governments in this context.

It is arguable that European governments through subsidies and investment incentives have contributed to the problem both by encouraging the expansion of capacity in their countries, and, along with trade unions, in resisting plant closures and rationalisation moves. For instance the Italian government gave continued support in the 1970s for the development of new large-scale plants in the south of Italy as part of its regional policy. In Belgium the state rescued Fabelta, a fibres subsidiary in the AKZO group, in February 1976 by taking majority control. In Italy, when Montefibre attempted to implement rationalisation plans the government transferred the 6000 workers to its own payroll. Similarly in France, rationalisation by Rhone Poulenc was delayed as a result of government pressure.

Partly as a result of such interventions, the speed with which rationalisation has taken place has varied among countries. West German firms have responded the most rapidly by rationalising production and closing old plant, followed by the British and Dutch firms. The main companies involved (AKZO, Du Pont, Hoechst, ICI, Monsanto and Bayer) are estimated to have cut back capacity by 500 000 tonnes by the end of 1977 and to have implemented cuts in their labour forces by 20–30% (Barron, 1978; *European Chemical News* 1977, 1978). At the same time, however, the Italian-based industry was proceeding with the development of new large-scale plants in the south of Italy and was also unable to withdraw 'obsolete' plant in northern Italy. Because of these diverse reactions those firms that cut back capacity may lose market share. Since, in the 1970s, it has been the relatively efficient low-cost producers which have made the reductions in capacity it appears that competitive pressure as distorted by government intervention is resulting in the survival of the weak.

In reaching such an assessment, however, it has to be remembered that the relatively efficient firms acquired their market positions and strength in a period of patent protection supplemented by accepted spheres of influence. The Italians argue that as a result of this history their industry has operated at a disadvantage, and that in any case their large modern plants will make them very competitive.

In an attempt to overcome the tendency to competitive over-investment, the European producers tried to persuade the EEC Commission to permit 'collective' arrangements as early as 1973. However, the attempt was unsuccessful. As the problems worsened, however, the EEC position changed, and after a second approach in 1977 the EEC Commission asked the governments of the member countries to stop giving aid towards creating additional production facilities for two years and asked the European Investment Bank not to grant any new loans to finance capacity increases. The Commission also undertook to obtain from the synthetic fibre manufacturers regular information on the capacity situation. These plans led to a proposal for a formal agreement for a series of measures designed to bring capacities into line with demand (*Financial Times*, 23 June 1978). New European capacity levels were set for all the main synthetic fibres. Non-Italian producers were expected to reduce their capacities by mid-1979 and to remain at the new level until 1981. Co-operation was obtained from the Italians by allowing them increases in some areas in return for cutbacks in others. A second part of the agreement concerned market shares. This aspect was regarded as necessary firstly to ensure that individual producers did not attempt to increase their market shares at the expense of competitors when the latter had cut back capacity, and, secondly to ensure an outlet for the additional Italian production provided for in the capacity agreement.

Eleven major producers in Europe signed the agreement in June 1978 even though it was realised that the provisions of the cartel agreement might infringe EEC competition rules. The American producers Du Pont and Monsanto were not party to it because the agreement would have brought them into conflict with American anti-trust law. The main hope for the participating European producers was that the agreement would be accepted as creating a 'crisis cartel' given the existence of chronic excess capacity and severe industry losses. The main stumbling block was article 85(1) of the Treaty of Rome which prohibits agreements between firms involving market sharing and 'the limiting or controlling of production, markets, technical development or capital investment'. However article 85(3) provides a possible loophole in that exemption may be made for an agreement that contributes to the improvement of production or distribution of the products or promotes technical or economic progress. A rationalisation agreement may thus be allowed. The difficulty is that the agreement must not enable the parties to eliminate competition in a substantial proportion of the goods concerned; and further the users must share in the benefits accruing from the agreement. Because one of the main purposes of the agreement is to provide conditions in which prices can be increased from their existing loss-making levels (1976–8) it seems likely that users would lose rather than gain at least in the short run.

At the time of writing early in 1979 the legality of the scheme has still to be tested despite protracted discussions within the EEC Commission and between it and the companies. These seem to have focussed on the possibility of obtaining agreement on the desired rationalisation of the industry but without the market sharing agreements. Whatever the outcome of the negotiations it is ironic that one of the main reasons for the cartel's existence is not a failure of market forces, but the fact that these market forces have not been allowed to work freely by national governments.

REFERENCES

Barron, C. (1978) 'The man-made carve up'. *Management Today*, (April) 51 ff.

Berrini, G. L. (1973) 'The prospects for man-made fibres in Western Europe'. Paper delivered at the October 1973 Congress, European Chemical Marketing Research Association.

FAO (1971) *Agricultural commodity projections 1970–1980* Volume 2. Rome: Food and Agriculture Organisation of the United Nations.

Gardner, K. (1972) 'ICI's links with the textile industry' in 'European fibres survey'. *Financial Times*, 1 February 1972.

Hague, D. C. (1957) *The economics of man-made fibres*. London: Duckworth.

Heller, R. (1971) 'Du Pont's delayed reaction'. *Management Today*, (September) 60 ff.

Hosiery and Knitwear Economic Development Committee (1970) *Hosiery and knitwear in the 1970s – a study of the industry's market prospects*. National Economic Development Office. London: HMSO.

HMSO (1969, 1974) *Report on the census of production, 1963*. London: HMSO; *Report on the census of production, 1968*. London: HMSO.

Knight, A. (1974) *Private enterprise and public intervention, the Courtaulds experience*. London: Allen and Unwin.

Lossius, T. (1977) 'A case study of international efficiency comparisons – ICI's synthetic fibres business' in C. Bowe *ed. Industrial efficiency and the role of government*. London: HMSO.

Minford, P. (1975) 'Textile fibre substitution and relative prices'. *The Australian Journal of Agricultural Economics* **19** (3), 175–196.

O'Neill, H. (1970) 'Synthetic fibres – what it will take to sustain profit'. *Financial Times*, 2 September 1970, 14.
Pratten, C. F. (1971) *Economies of scale in manufacturing industry*. Cambridge: Cambridge University Press.
Rhys, D. (1978) 'A prescription to make EEC fibres healthy again'. *Financial Times*, 23 June 1978, 20.
Shaw, R. W. and Shaw, S. A. (1977) 'Patent expiry and competition in polyester fibres'. *Scottish Journal of Political Economy* **24**(2), 117–132.
Tisdell, C. A. and McDonald, P. W. (1977) *Economics of fibre markets*. University of Newcastle, New South Wales, Australia.
Trafford, J. (1971) 'Du Pont bucks the European trend'. *Financial Times*, 13 January 1971, 8.

FURTHER READING

Business Monitor *Production of man-made fibres*. PA411 Business Statistics Office. London: HMSO.
International Cotton Advisory Committee *Report on inter-fibre competition* (annual). Washington, DC: ICAC.
Monopolies Commission (1968) *Man-made cellulosic fibres*. London: HMSO.
O'Brien, D. P. (1964) 'Patent protection and competition in polyamide and polyester fibre manufacture'. *Journal of Industrial Economics* **12**(3), 224–235.
Reader, W. J. (1975) *Imperial Chemical Industries – a history. Volume II. The first quarter century 1926–1952*. London: Oxford University Press.
Robson, R. (1958) *The man-made fibres industry*. London: Macmillan.
Shaw, R. W., Shaw, S. A. and Sutton, C. J. (1976) 'Price competition and excess capacity' in R. W. Shaw and C. J. Sutton, *Industry and competition*. London: Macmillan.
Textile Organon *World man-made fibre survey* (annually in the June issue).

10 :Construction*   231—53

M. C. Fleming

10.1 INTRODUCTION

The construction industry is responsible for the provision, repair, maintenance and demolition of buildings of all kinds, including their internal finishes and services, and also the wide variety of other types of structure embraced by the term 'civil engineering works' – e.g. roads, bridges, dams, etc. It also carries out related activities that require the use of contractors' plant and equipment, e.g. open-cast coal mining and the sinking of mine shafts etc.

In size the industry is one of the nation's largest, regularly contributing around 6–7% of gross domestic product. As a particularly labour-intensive industry, it employs an even greater proportion of the labour force (especially males) – around 9 or 10% of total male *employees* (i.e. excluding the substantial number of men, often not recorded in official statistics for the industry, who work – at least nominally – as self-employed). In these terms the relative size of the industry has remained remarkably stable over most of the period since the end of the Second World War. The economic significance of the industry, however, is even greater than these figures would suggest for it is pre-eminently responsible for providing the major part of national capital investment: buildings and works represent around half of gross fixed capital formation each year and constitute about two-thirds of the nation's accumulated capital stock. A substantial part of the activity of the industry is indeed devoted to the repair and maintenance of the existing stock rather than the construction of additions to it. For these reasons the industry occupies a position of central economic importance.

The demand facing the industry possesses two distinctive characteristics. First, the demand for the product is geographically dispersed but the product itself is not generally transportable. While some work

---

*I should like to thank Professor D. P. O'Brien who kindly gave me the benefit of his comments on the first draft of this chapter.

may be prefabricated in factory conditions, the building or other structure must ultimately be provided at a particular location, fixed as it were, to the site and, in the case of buildings, connected to mains services (electricity, water, sewers, etc.). Thus the advantages which firms in other industries may gain from centralised production in factory conditions do not apply in the construction industry. Second, productive activity cannot in general precede the receipt of orders: work has to be carried out under contract, to meet the individual requirements of a large number of separate clients. The only exceptions are in those areas of building where builders are able to undertake speculative development in advance of demand – in the main, private housebuilding. Contractors, therefore, are faced with a high degree of uncertainty: their workload is dependent upon their success in winning some of an essentially unpredictable number of highly varied contracts coming forward, the number and value of which can fluctuate very considerably. Differences between one site and another and the exposed conditions of the work itself also add to the uncertainties of contracting.

Together these factors help to explain the organisation and structure of the industry and also exercise an important influence on the market behaviour of firms and their economic performance in terms of productive efficiency and technical progress.

10.2 MARKET STRUCTURE

Unlike much of manufacturing industry in Britain, that has been subject to a pronounced trend towards higher and higher levels of industrial concentration, the construction industry remains, as it has long been, an industry comprised of a large number of predominantly small firms. The same is true in other countries (Fleming, 1977). In Britain it also consists of a not insignificant public sector: construction labour is employed in direct works departments ('direct labour') by most local authorities and by many other public bodies. Currently only part of this labour is officially classified to the industry but this part constitutes about one-fifth of the total labour force and provides about one-eighth of total output. Their work, however, is predominantly (all but a fifth) repairs and maintenance. Therefore, this chapter will concentrate mainly on the private sector of the industry which is responsible for the greater part of output, particularly of new work.

Table 10.1 shows the size distribution of the number of firms and their employment and output in 1977.[1] It will be seen that out of some 78 000 registered firms, over three-quarters employed fewer than eight persons. The importance of small firms, however, should not be over-emphasised: at the other end of the scale only 2% of firms (1682 firms

TABLE 10.1: Number of firms, employment and output by size of firm in Great Britain, 1977 (percentages)

Size of firm (No. employed)	Number of firms			Employment	Value of work done (third quarter)
	Main trades*	Specialist trades	All trades		
0–1	26.5	36.9	32.1	2.1	1.5
2–7	45.4	42.8	44.0	11.9	8.2
8–24	18.6	14.3	16.3	16.1	13.5
25–79	6.5	4.6	5.5	17.1	16.3
80–299	2.3	1.1	1.7	17.8	19.1
300–1199	0.7	0.2	0.4	17.8	22.9
1200 and over	0.1	—	0.1	17.1	18.6
All firms	100	100	100	100	100
	(35 586)	(42 056)	(77 642)	(1 029 100)	(£2717.8m)

Source: Department of the Environment, *Private Contractors' Construction Census 1977.* London: HMSO, 1978.
Notes: *General builders and building and civil engineering contractors.
— Less than 0.05%.

altogether) employed eighty persons or more, but these were responsible for more than half of output and employment. The structure of the industry at other times during the post-war period has been roughly the same (table 10.2). Although the number of firms has declined since the early post-war years (when it was inflated by the establishment of many new ones) and the size of the very largest firms has tended to increase, it appears that the mean size of firm (in terms of *operatives* employed) remains much the same now (nine operatives) as it was in 1948, and indeed, may even have declined over recent years.[2]

The multitude of small firms that persist in construction and its apparently unchanging methods of work are sometimes viewed as the cause of – what is held to be – inferior economic performance and are especially contrasted with manufacturing industry which has been subject to such pronounced changes in structure and production methods. The economic rationale for the structure of the construction industry, however, is not far to seek. It is to be found in factors associated with the nature of demand and the nature of the product itself to which we have referred.

The geographically dispersed pattern of demand and the non-transportability of the product naturally tend to produce a similarly dispersed organisation of construction enterprises and there is in fact a close correspondence between the regional distribution of firms and

TABLE 10.2: Sizes of firms in construction in Great Britain, 1948–77*

Date	Percentage distribution of number of firms by size							Mean firm size		
	Operatives per firm							Operatives per firm	Operatives and working principals† per firm	All persons per firm
	Nil	1–5	6–19	20–99	100–499	500–999	1000 and over			
February 1948	41.8	36.3	14.6	6.2	0.9		0.1	8		
May 1954	35.3	39.4	16.8	7.2	1.2	0.1	0.1	10	11	
April 1956	32.3	40.5	18.1	7.7	1.3	0.1	0.1	11	12	
April 1965	27.1	41.3	20.6	9.2	1.6	0.2	0.1	13	14	17

Date	Percentage distribution of number of firms by size							Mean firm size		
	Persons per firm							Operatives per firm	Operatives and working principals† per firm	All persons per firm
	Nil–1	2–7	8–24	25–114	115–599	600–1199	1200 and over			
April 1965	22.1	46.3	21.2	8.5	1.6	0.2	0.1	13	14	17
October 1973 (A)	24.8	45.4	19.8	8.1	1.5	0.2	0.1	12	13	17
October 1973 (B)	30.6	45.5	16.2	6.3	1.2	0.1	0.1	9	11	13
October 1977	32.1	44.0	16.3	6.2	1.2	0.1	0.1	9	10	13

Sources: Department of the Environment, *Annual Bulletin of Construction Statistics 1970; Private Contractors' Construction Census 1977* (London: HMSO, 1978) and unpublished data from censuses conducted by former Ministry of Works.

Notes: *The industry is classified in accordance with the *Standard Industrial Classification* from 1956; previously the classification was somewhat wider in scope (Fleming, 1980). In 1965 the size classification was changed from operatives to persons (operatives, working proprietors, administrative, professional and clerical staff) per firm – data are given on both bases for this year. In 1973 an additional 25 000 firms were added to the register – data are given on the basis of the old (A) and the new (B) registers.
†Working principals (i.e. proprietors who carry out manual work) until 1973 and then all working proprietors.

the regional distribution of work. The work itself is highly diversified by type, size, function, form and method of construction and in the materials used, and its execution requires the services of many different trades. These services are generally provided by specialist firms operating under sub-contract – few contractors carry out the full range of operations required. As table 10.1 indicates, less than half of the firms are general builders and contractors; the rest specialise in the work of particular crafts or services installations or in the provision of services to main contractors, such as plant hire or scaffolding erection, and most of these firms remain smaller than the general contractors.

Some firms, of course, are prepared to undertake large contracts (many of which would be beyond the capacity of localised builders) anywhere in the country – and indeed anywhere in the world – and these firms have grown to a substantial size (though nowhere near as large as the giants of manufacturing industry). But the number of large contracts available is small and most of the work may be handled by the small and medium-sized local contractors. The actual number of contracts available each year is very large (currently over 100 000 for new work – many of which are sub-divided into smaller sub-contracts – and possibly as many for repair and maintenance work) but only a small minority of these exceed £50 000 in value –

TABLE 10.3: Size distribution of orders for new work in Great Britain, 1977

Size of order (value range) (£ thousand)	Number (%)	Value (%)
10 and under 50	69.3	15.1
50 and under 100	13.5	9.3
100 and under 250	10.4	16.0
250 and under 500	3.8	12.7
500 and under 1 000	1.7	11.3
1 000 and under 2 000	0.9	11.9
2 000 and over	0.6	23.7
	100.0	100.0

	Total number and values (thousands)	(£m)
£10 000 and over	66.5	7 041
Under £10 000	na	363
All	na	7 404

Source: Department of the Environment, unpublished data.

itself a very low figure, equivalent to a mere three houses or so (table 10.3).

10.2.1 Conditions of entry and the growth of firms

The relative and absolute cost advantages which often favour large-scale operations and large established firms in manufacturing are of little importance as barriers to entry or as factors encouraging the growth of greater industrial concentration in construction. This is not to deny that some large contracts demand the technical expertise and resources possessed by large contractors but these are the exceptions rather than the rule and in practice their importance is further reduced by the technical conditions of production.

The site-based nature of construction, where each site is necessarily a temporary place of work, and the individuality of most projects ensure that the conditions necessary for the existence of many technical scale economies, namely the centralisation of production of standard products using specialised production techniques, do not apply. It is true that some types of scale economy exist but these are related to the size of individual contracts and the degree of repetitive work involved rather than the size of firm undertaking them. As we have seen, however, the majority of contracts are small, few provide any scope for large-scale repetitive work – housing would be the main example – and, apart from speculative housing, neither is within the control of the builder. The influence of these factors as entry barriers or in favouring the growth of established firms is therefore limited.

It is also true that specialisation of function – an important source of scale economies – does occur in building as elsewhere. But, as indicated above, in building it has been specialisation by trade – representing parts of construction work such as roofing, plumbing, etc. – and not by type of building. This fact reinforces still further the tendency towards small scale, because such firms undertake only part of the work on the contract, and facilitates the establishment of new firms by craftsmen in the relevant trades. It is the case that some firms do tend to specialise on particular types of work – for instance, civil engineering and housebuilding represent two sectors in which some firms specialise – but rarely do firms confine their activities solely to one type. There is no technical reason, generally speaking, for narrowing activities to one sector, for many of the basic processes involved in most types of construction work are similar, and the nature of demand itself provides good reason for not doing so. Specialisation would make firms more vulnerable to fluctuations in demand because the demand for particular types of work is generally less stable than the demand for construction work generally. There are sound commercial reasons, therefore, for a contractor to broaden his market by tendering for a variety of jobs within his technical and financial capacity. Moreover, it has been shown (DSIR, 1953) that specialist sub-contractors are generally more efficient than main contractors doing comparable items of work.

Thus, specialisation by trade represents a rational response to the fragmented, heterogeneous and uncertain nature of demand and the technical nature of the construction process itself. It provides great flexibility in coping with the highly varied demands placed upon the industry, for the ability to sub-contract parts of a contract as necessary enables contractors to take on jobs over the wide range of sizes that exist in practice with gains, rather than losses in efficiency.

Ease of entry and the existing structure are further sustained by low capital requirements both in terms of fixed and current assets. The buildings required for most manufacturing processes are not needed by contractors and plant requirements are also limited, because many building processes – especially the craft-based processes – are not amenable to mechanisation. On average the total accumulated stock of fixed capital in the industry is equivalent to little more than one year's wage and salary bill. But even this exaggerates the importance of fixed capital requirements for many firms. Much of the capital represents heavy equipment required for excavation, materials handling and concrete mixing for which the needs of many firms are met by a highly developed plant-hire sector and for which many of the specialist firms have no need at all. Working capital requirements are also limited for although construction projects may be large (relative to the size of a firm) and have to be financed over lengthy construction periods, the financial requirements are transferred to a substantial extent to the client through the mechanism of progress payments – generally made monthly on the basis of the value of work done less a retention – rather than total payment being withheld until completion. Many contractors increase the self-financing of jobs further by pricing early parts of the work at a high level in order to raise their net receipts in the early stages of the work. Of great importance too in reducing working capital requirements still further is trade credit extended for purchases of building materials – a large part of total costs – by producers and builders' merchants. The limited financial requirements also mean that the advantages sometimes conferred on large established firms by virtue of their size alone – namely an ability to raise finance more easily or cheaply than other firms (by virtue of the size of their requirements, their bargaining power and the security they can offer) – play a less important part in construction than in other industries. But in any case, because of the nature of demand, firms for whom size may confer some financial advantage will rarely be in competition with new entrants in the same sector of the construction market.

The scope for gaining competitive advantages by other means such as control over raw material supplies or by patent protection is also severely constricted or non-existent in construction. Materials account for a major part of total costs, but they are drawn from a wide range of extractive and manufacturing industries: no one material predominates. It is generally impracticable, therefore, for a contractor to meet his own general materials requirements and there is little advantage in providing for his own needs of a single material (indeed small-scale production could well be disadvantageous). For the materials producer, forward integration into construction provides little advantage because no one contractor is able to provide an adequate outlet, especially as many building materials industries are highly concentrated. The result is that vertical integration is of little importance in construction. There also appears to be little tendency for construction firms to diversify into non-related activities.

Patent protection in such a long-established assembly industry as construction in which traditional craft processes have proved difficult to replace is also of no significance as a barrier to competition. Similarly the nature of demand is such that firms in construction are not able to raise barriers to entry artificially by marketing strategies such as product differentiation and advertising which are so important for many manufactured products.

In summary then, no natural barriers to entry exist and the scope for artificial barriers is also virtually non-existent. This is not to say, of course, that a new entrant is able to enter and compete in any field of construction, tackling jobs of any size, type and complexity. But the availability of small-scale work which trade specialisation and a large volume of small repair and maintenance jobs provide and the limited financial and capital requirements ensure that construction is an industry of easy entry and, given free competition, it is possible for new entrants to extend the range and scale of their activities over time and challenge the larger existing firms.

Potentially, at any rate, domestic contractors are also open to foreign competition – a potential which has increased since the UK's accession to the EEC: public sector contracts above a certain size now have to be advertised in the *Official Journal* of the Community. In practice, however, foreign competition in the UK market is generally of no importance. The only exception in recent years has been in the construction of drilling platforms etc. in connection with North Sea oil exploration; in this area foreign contractors have won British contracts and vice versa. This is an area, however, in which the product is transportable and is thus a notable exception to the general rule. The large British contractors, however, compete successfully for contracts abroad over a wide front: those won in 1976/77 (valued at £1700m) were equivalent to one-quarter of domestic orders.

10.3 MARKET BEHAVIOUR

The large number of firms and the absence of barriers to entry (or exit) provide essential competitive conditions. These are strengthened by the fact that few of the marketing strategies which many manufacturing firms are able to employ to influence their level of sales are open to firms in construction. As we indicated earlier, advertising and product differentiation activities are largely ruled out because, apart from design-and-construct companies (discussed later) and speculative builders, contractors have no product as such to sell. Moreover, research and development activity, which is often important as the foundation for product and process innovation in manufacturing industry, also finds little counterpart as a competitive weapon in construction because the design and content of each job are normally outside the control of the builder. Similarly, market conditions are such that there is little or no opportunity or incentive for firms in construction to pursue market power through market dominance attained either by merger or by internal expansion. As we have seen, there has been no marked trend in the growth of firms in the industry and the wave of company acquisitions and mergers that affected much of manufacturing industry in the 1960s and early 1970s was scarcely felt in construction.

No contractor, therefore, is able to exert any control over the market environment in which he operates. Apart from speculative work and contracts obtained by negotiation, firms are dependent for their survival upon their success in competitive tendering. In principle, competitive tendering is a device which enables a client to select the most efficient contractor from among those willing to undertake his particular project. Disallowing the possibility of non-competitive behaviour by contractors in tendering (further considered below), it is the mechanism through which the resource allocation function of the market is performed in construction. The operation of this mechanism, therefore, deserves close attention.

In letting a contract, some clients may prefer to pre-select a contractor (on the basis of their own experience of working with him in the past or on the recommendation of others) and to negotiate the terms of the contract with him. The normal method, however, is to award the contract to the contractor submitting the lowest price in competition. Competition may be 'open' in which case any firm may submit a tender, or may be limited to a select list of contractors who are invited to tender.

It may be argued that open competition promotes efficiency because it allows each firm willing to undertake the work an equal opportunity of winning the contract. Many associated with the industry argue, however, that the expense involved in the preparation of tenders by an unlimited number of firms is unnecessary and raises the general level of construction costs – costs which are recouped in successful tenders. Further, it is argued that very low prices resulting from indiscriminate tendering lead to bad building, for any builder who has quoted too low a price and is faced with a loss if he does a good job is tempted to cut the quality of his work. Open competition is, therefore, said to be a system which encourages firms that work to the lowest standards and does not ensure value for money. This was the view of official committees in 1944 (Ministry of Works, 1944) and 1964 (Ministry of Public Building and Works, 1964). These committees recommended, therefore, that competition should be limited to a number of firms carefully selected as being capable of, and likely to do, work of the standard required.

Selective tendering is now in widespread use: in the public sector about two-thirds of building contracts and almost four-fifths of civil engineering contracts are let in this way; open competition is used for less than one fifth of contracts (NEDO, 1975). Open competition is also apparently little used in important parts of the private sector (Hillebrandt, 1974). The support for selective competition as a means of selecting a contractor, however, must be tempered by other considerations.

Firstly, a traditional argument in favour of open competition is that it satisfies, at least overtly, the requirements of public accountability for the expenditure of public money and is a safeguard against corruption through favouritism in the award of contracts. Selective tendering does not necessarily fail to satisfy these requirements but it needs explicit precautions to be taken. Secondly, such tendering may stultify the selective mechanism of the market by sustaining some firms with an established reputation but obstructing the development of others. Up-and-coming firms may be caught in the vicious circle of being unable to gain a place on a select list because they are unable to demonstrate their financial and technical capacity to handle certain types of project and this in turn may be due to their inability to gain contracts of the appropriate type because they are precluded from tendering in the first place. Much, therefore, depends on the way in which select lists of contractors are compiled and maintained. The list may be a standing list or an *ad hoc* list that is compiled specifically for a particular job. In either case it is essential that new firms should be regularly considered for admission to the list, and listed firms regularly considered for promotion or relegation to higher or lower categories on it or removal altogether if considered unsatisfactory. Unfortunately, it appears that current practices leave something to be desired in this respect (NEDO, 1975, paragraph 5.14). Thirdly, because selective tendering may restrict competition to a limited number of firms of a certain type, the possibility of collusion amongst them is facilitated. This is especially true where standing lists are maintained.

The resource savings that the greater use of selective tendering have produced are, of course, impossible to judge. But they should not be overrated. No information is available about how far the number of tenders submitted for each job has been reduced, although a recent study (Newcombe, 1978) has suggested that many local authorities, at any rate, still use fairly large select lists. The savings involved in obtaining satisfactory standards more readily, and the more timely completion of jobs, are largely intangible and certainly difficult to estimate. But against the savings which may arise for these reasons must be put the costs incurred by the client in operating a selective tendering system and also the economic costs involved when the system is not operated with sufficient flexibility to ensure that competition for a particular job takes place among the firms best fitted to carry it out and takes place without collusion. The danger is, therefore, that short-term gains here, as elsewhere, may be bought at the expense of greater long-term losses.

10.3.1 Non-competitive behaviour

Given the large number of firms in construction and the large number of contracts let each year, it is impossible for effective collusion to occur on a national scale. It may be easier to organise, however, where the number of potential competitors is limited either by the client – as in selective tendering – or where a natural limitation arises on account of the size, character or location of the work itself. Contractors may then learn the identity of their competitors and come to some arrangement among themselves about the prices each should submit, coupled perhaps, with some scheme of compensation to be paid to the unsuccessful tenderers by the successful one.

The best-documented example of a more generalised scheme of collusive tendering is one which was operated by the London Builders' Conference (LBC) and investigated by the Monopolies Commission in the early 1950s (Monopolies Commission, 1954). In the present context, however, it is notable that the effectiveness of this scheme was limited: out of 6903 competitions, LBC members won only 1687 and of these there were only 95 for which the pricing was organised through the Conference. Since 1956 restrictive arrangements of this kind have become subject to registration and investigation under the restrictive trade practices legislation including, since 1968, agreements simply to exchange information about prices. Not all registrable restrictions are in fact registered and in construction a number of unregistered arrangements among contractors tendering for electrical and mechanical engineering services contracts were detected in the 1960s, as a result of which injunctions were obtained against ninety-nine firms (Registrar of Restrictive Trading Agreements, 1973). The usual arrangement in these cases was for the exchange of information about prices and the joint determination of the bid to be submitted as the lowest, coupled with a scheme of compensation. Some of the arrangements also involved the giving and taking of 'cover prices' bilaterally. Cover prices are prices high enough to ensure that the firm quoting them will *not* win the contract but low enough to appear realistic. A firm may submit a cover price not only when it is a party to a restrictive arrangement but also when it does not wish to increase its workload but fears a loss of goodwill and possible removal from a select list by refusing to tender or by putting in a clearly unrealistic price.

Just how much collusive tendering still occurs and how much of it is encouraged by the greater use of selective competition is, of course, impossible to say. It is perhaps notable that all the cases of collusion referred to above were cases where a limited number of contractors had been invited to tender. Certainly the increased danger of collusion is one to which too little attention is now given by the proponents of selective competition. However, it remains true that selective competition does possess certain advantages in principle, and it would also seem impossible to sustain a general argument that the construction industry is conspicuously non-competitive. There would seem to be no reason to believe that generalised schemes of the type operated by the London Builders' Conference, if they now exist at all, are any more effective now than they were in the early post-war years. Moreover, while it is undesirable to underrate the importance of the collusive schemes revealed recently, it is notable that they all related to a specialised sector of the industry.

10.4 PERFORMANCE

The economic performance of the construction industry is often compared unfavourably with that of many other industries. It is clear, for instance, that much construction is still carried out in traditional ways and this is contrasted with the increasingly mechanised and automated processes that have transformed production in many other sectors. It is also clear that construction prices tend to rise faster than the prices of other goods: over the period since 1948 the prices of capital goods in general and also of goods and services in general have both increased by around five and a half times compared with a sevenfold increase for construction. This difference is mainly explained by the fact that productivity in construction has not increased at the same rate as elsewhere. It is not possible to measure changes in the productivity of the construction industry as a whole over time satisfactorily but it is clear that the disproportionate rise in prices cannot be accounted for by disproportionate increases in the unit cost of factor inputs.

It is a mistake, however, to equate the scope for productivity improvement in such a long-established industry as construction with that available in industries at earlier stages of development and where technological conditions are more favourable. It is also a mistake to regard the failure to increase productivity at a rate commensurate with that attained elsewhere as being a result either of the structure of the industry as such or of the behaviour of contractors themselves. While the price of a particular job and the level of efficiency with which it is carried out are determined by the contractor on that job, many factors which affect his performance – in particular design and technical constraints – are not within his control. The performance of the industry and the scope for improvement can only be considered, therefore, in the context of these factors, and it is these to which we devote most of our attention here.

As we indicated earlier, most construction projects have to be carried out in accordance with the individual requirements of particular clients. These requirements are normally translated into a particular design and specification by independent architects and/or civil and structural engineers and other consultants who are commissioned by the client. The contractor who is going to be responsible for the physical realisation of the project normally plays no part in this process, only appearing on the scene when the process is complete, or virtually complete, and the contract is ready to be let. This division between the design and production stages is a factor of great potential importance, for it precludes any interaction between design and production considerations except insofar as production aspects may be taken into account by the designer. Designers, however, can only do this in fairly general terms, for traditionally they have received little training in such matters and their practical experience is limited to that obtained indirectly in contract supervision – experience that involves transient relationships with different contractors on *ad hoc* jobs. Thus the separation of the design and production functions in construction precludes the close co-operation between designers and producers, which is important from a productivity point of view, and also limits the possibility of the feedback of production experience into subsequent design. This contrasts sharply with the close integration between design and production achieved in much of manufacturing industry where, typically, the main decisions – what to produce, in what volume and to what standards, using what methods and, moreover, where (in what location) – are all decided within the firm by its own managerial and technical (design and production) staff.

The organisation pattern in construction is one which has evolved over a considerable period of time in response to changes in demand

and technical developments. Demands for larger and more complex structures, the introduction of more mechanical and electrical engineering services in them, the use of new materials, and new uses for old materials (e.g. pre-stressed concrete) have been met by the employment of specialist design consultants and specialist sub-contractors (often nominated by the architect in order to safeguard the standards and performance of this part of the work). Thus considerable fragmentation of function and responsibility has developed on each side of the design–production divide. From the point of view efficiency it gives rise to a fundamental problem to which there is no easy solution. We consider various responses to it below.

Various ways of integrating design and production may be attempted. First, the client and his designer may select a contractor at an early stage of the design process so that he may work in close association with the design team. Since no finished design exists upon which contractors may be invited to tender in competition, the contract has to be negotiated with a selected contractor. The main disadvantage, of course, is the lack of competition and the difficulty facing the client in ensuring the negotiation of a 'fair' price. In the early 1970s about 14% of building (as opposed to civil engineering) contracts in the public sector were negotiated (NEDO, 1975).

Second, the builder himself may offer an all-in service – a so-called 'package deal' or 'turnkey' project – in which he takes over responsibility for the whole process from design to erection. An objection which is sometimes made against this solution is that the quality of design suffers because the builder may be more concerned with commercial considerations – subordinating design to production – and that the client forgoes the protection afforded by the architect representing his interests in dealings with the contractor. It also possesses the disadvantage that the client forgoes the benefits of competition again unless package dealers are prepared to compete on individual projects. Package deals are most used in the private sector for those types of work where requirements are fairly standardised. A recent survey showed that design-and-construct companies handle the design of about one-quarter of factory buildings and one-tenth of office buildings (NEDO, 1974).

Architects are unable to offer an all-in service because the rules of their professional institution do not allow them to be Principals of building firms. This is a contentious issue and one which is a matter of live debate within the profession at the present time. Problems arising from the division of functions on the design side itself among independent professionals has found a response in the development of multi-disciplinary practices. A difficulty here, however, is that such practices may not necessarily be able to provide the necessary expertise on all projects and may find it difficult to maintain a balanced workload for the practice as a whole.

A further solution to the design–production dichotomy is the supply of prefabricated 'systems' of construction by firms in manufacturing industry. Developments in this area, however, are best examined under the heading of 'Innovation' which is considered in section 10.4.2. In the context of innovation we may note here, however, one further disadvantage of the separation of design from production which has followed from the method used to determine contract prices. In arriving at his tender price, each contractor prices the items in a 'Bill of Quantities' which is drawn up by a quantity surveyor on behalf of the client for this purpose. The format of the Bill is such, however, that while it describes all the work that the construction of a particular building will demand, it does not directly provide information that enables the builder to assess the organisational implications of the job, for it does not indicate the sequencing of operations necessary to complete different stages of the work. It does not reveal, therefore, the extent to which different parts of the work will require contributions from many or few different men or gangs with, as a consequence, many or few potential disruptions to the flow of work. Thus the ease or difficulty of construction implicit in the design may not be recognised by the estimator, with the consequence that the design of buildings which are easy to build may not be rewarded with a correspondingly low price and vice versa. As far as this is the case, then it is clearly an important obstacle to innovation and rationality in design. A solution to this problem is the development of a new form of bill of quantities – an 'Operational Bill' (Forbes and Skoyles, 1963) – in which the requirements of the design are specified in terms of the sequence of operations required. Its adoption, however, which would represent a substantial change in well-established procedures is not one which can be quickly accomplished.

10.4.1 Site efficiency

A penetrating analysis of the multifarious factors that affect the efficiency of site work has been made by Bishop (1972). Each contract involves the establishment and control of an *ad hoc* organisation of many different gangs and sub-contractors who are required to carry out a large number of separate but interrelated operations. Within the constraints imposed by design, therefore, the efficiency of the process depends not only on the rates of output which can be attained in the execution of each of the operations but also on their smooth co-ordination so as to minimise non-productive time. Much therefore depends on the planning and programming of the work in the first place and, more important, on the effectiveness with which subsequent control is exercised on site for, as Bishop points out, 'on site one *force majeure* follows another' and the best plans and programmes have continually to be changed and updated. It is perhaps not surprising to find, therefore, that site studies reveal variations in the man-hours required on comparable work in the ratio of 3:1 or more (DSIR, 1953; Ministry of Education, 1955; Forbes, 1969).

Considerable attention has been devoted to planning, programming and control problems, especially by the Building Research Station, and although the early promise held out by the application to construction of techniques such as critical path analysis has apparently not been realised (Bishop), there is little doubt that the greater attention that has been devoted to these problems has been an important source of improvement. Mechanisation too has improved productivity either by replacing labour in direct substitution or because the introduction of a particular item of plant has involved the reconsideration of the programming and phasing of work with consequential improvements for that reason. However, it has proved difficult to mechanise many of the craft processes. We comment further on mechanisation below. Other sources of variation, and hence scope for improvement, reside not in the overall tempo of the work as a whole, but in the rate of output of individual men or gangs. Improvements here may be obtained by systematic on-the-job training in production methods and by the use of effective incentive schemes (Bishop). More dramatic sources of productivity improvement have been sought in innovation and it is to this aspect of performance which we now turn our attention.

10.4.2 Innovation

As we have indicated, product and process innovation in the construction industry is largely outside its own control as a result of its service character and the division in the production process between design, manufacture and construction. Innovation in the forms and methods of construction is largely in the hands of designers. Innovations in building materials are in the hands of the building materials industries and their introduction into building is again the responsibility of designers rather than builders. Generally speaking, the builders' responsibility only extends to the execution of work on site where the scope for innovation is limited to organisational matters and the introduction and use of mechanical plant. Innovation in contractors' plant as such, however, is again largely in the hands of manufacturing industry. The diffusion of plant innovations is, of course, more directly attributable to contractors, though yet again within constraints imposed by design.

The scope for the mechanisation of site work has proved very limited. Building remains a labour-intensive activity requiring the mixing, placing and fixing of a wide variety of materials and components on site and involving contributions from many different crafts. The major effect of mechanisation in the industry has been the replacement of much manual labour in the activities of excavation, materials handling and concrete mixing. As a consequence, civil engineering is more highly mechanised than building since it involves more of such activities. In building, apart from the development of powered hand-tools, the mechanisation of craft processes has made only limited progress and perhaps the main effect of innovations on their work has been through the introduction of new materials such as plastics, new methods of fixing and a greater degree of prefabrication. With regard to plant diffusion, lack of information makes it difficult to make a proper assessment. Perhaps the major development in the post-war period has been the introduction of tower cranes, but the criticism is sometimes made that British contractors were tardy in utilising them given the fact that they had been used on the Continent for twenty years or so before their introduction here in 1951. On the other hand, it must be remembered that the large programme of high-rise building, to which they are particularly suited, had scarcely begun at that time and that, once their safety and suitability in British conditions had been demonstrated, diffusion seems to have been quite rapid (BRS, 1971).

More ambitious attempts to 'industrialise' the construction industry generally involve the prefabrication off the site of as much of the work as possible, so that the work on-site becomes much more the work of assembly and erection rather than fabrication. There has, of course, been a long-standing trend for many components to be prefabricated – e.g. joinery, precast concrete goods, plasterboard, etc. – and these have all gradually been incorporated into traditional forms of construction. Similarly new materials have found their place in traditional forms. From time to time, however, special efforts have been made to take the trend towards prefrabrication much further very rapidly, especially for residential building purposes. These have taken the form of attempts to produce sets of parts or construction 'systems', which can be fitted together easily on site, and the development of larger individual components. Britain has witnessed three periods of experimentation in the development of such 'systems' – one after each of the two world wars and another in the 1960s – but few have proved to be successful economically. A more detailed examination of the reasons why many of the systems were not successful will be found in Fleming (1965). Briefly, studies showed that although many systems were successful in saving on-site labour, these savings tended to be confined to the superstructure, leaving a considerable part of the labour-intensive internal finishing work to be performed in largely traditional ways – with increased potential for disruption in the progress of work – and such savings in labour costs as were obtained were outweighed by the higher costs of prefabricated components. The costs of the few 'industrialised' housing methods that remain in use today are comparable with those of traditional houses of the same size,[3] but such methods now contribute less than 10% to the public authority housebuilding programme and a substantial part consists of 'rationalised traditional' on-site methods rather than prefabricated 'systems'.

It is fairly generally accepted that the way forward as far as the 'industrialisation' of building is concerned is more likely to be found down evolutionary rather than revolutionary paths. A key aspect of many potential sources of improvement is simplification and standardisation of design and production. As far as prefabrication as such is concerned, greater potential appears to be offered through the development of 'component building' – i.e. standardisation of a range of components which are sufficiently interchangeable in use as to meet general building needs – rather than unique proprietary 'systems' with a limited range of uses. This requires as a prerequisite an underlying system of 'dimensional co-ordination' – i.e. a generally agreed set of dimensional constraints within which all designers work. Much has been done to lay the foundations for this approach (DOE, 1978), but it yet remains to be seen how successful it will prove to be in practice.

10.5 PUBLIC POLICY

The government influences the performance of the industry both directly and indirectly in important ways. Particularly important is the government's control and influence over the level of demand on the industry. Direct control is extensive because around half of total output is carried out for public sector clients. Indirectly, the pre-eminence of construction as an investment goods industry, and the fact that the level of investment is more volatile than demand in general, means that construction is particularly vulnerable to changes in the general economic climate. The effects are usually intensified in construction, for building investment is often postponable because building needs may be satisfied by the existing stock rather than new construction. A persistent criticism through much of the post-war period has been the extent to which a succession of 'stop–go' demand management policies operated by successive governments has had a particularly marked impact on the construction industry. This is not always evident in output statistics because the long construction periods of many projects mean that the fluctuations in the flow of orders may be absorbed to some extent by variations in the construction periods rather than in output in any period of time. No more revealing indication of the vulnerability of the industry, however, can be given than its experience during the recession after 1973 when cuts in public expenditure, coupled with the general decline in economic activity, led to a fall in construction output of 17% in the period to 1977 – compared with a fall of 9% for manufacturing industry (within manufacturing only two industries were more severely hit) and 3% for the economy as a whole over the period to 1975 (by 1977 GDP had overtaken its 1973 level in real terms). The flow of orders into construction was much more severely hit, falling – according to official statistics – by 34% over the period from 1972 to 1977.

Alternate booms and slumps in activity are likely to have a particularly adverse effect on the industry in view of its labour-intensive, craft-based nature and the value to a firm of retaining men who are used to working as a team; moreover experience seems to show that recessions often lead to trained men being lost from the industry altogether as they find employment elsewhere. The particularly high degree of uncertainty which faces construction firms must preclude forward planning of any worthwhile kind and thus retard investment in plant and labour training. Labour may also be dissuaded from entering the industry in the first place – a factor which may be especially important with regard to the quality of managerial staff attracted to it.

The influence of the government on the level of demand on the industry has, to date, been far more concerned with macroeconomic objectives than with the effects on the industry itself. The government has taken a direct interest in labour supply and training matters, however, by the establishment in 1964 of the Construction Industry Training Board which finances and encourages training by means of a levy/grant system. However, the activities of such a body cannot be expected to overcome the problems associated with fluctuations in the level of demand of the size recently experienced.

Direct steps have also been taken by the government to foster innovation. Buildings are required to have a long life and have to satisfy stringent performance requirements – many of which are laid down in official regulations concerning public health and safety – but it is not easy to show that new materials and components possess all the performance characteristics required, with the result that designers, the drafters of national standards and the institutions responsible for the provision of finance or insurance cover, all tend to adopt a conservative attitude. This in turn retards innovation and, especially, the diffusion of innovations. With the aim of helping to overcome these obstacles the Government established the Agrément Board in 1965 to test new building products and to issue certificates of approval. However, fundamental difficulties remain in the way of demonstrating the likely performance of products in use and perhaps inevitably, cautious attitudes are still prevalent. Government influence is also felt in a more diffuse way through its responsibility for building research. This is carried out by a central Building Research Station (part of the Building Research Establishment) which covers the whole field of relevant technical and operational matters from soil mechanics and the properties of materials to building economics, user requirements and town planning. As we indicated earlier, the government has also sought to achieve efficiency and economy in building through its encouragement of selective tendering, rather than open competition, as a means of selecting contractors, through the stimulation of 'industrialised' building and also by support for the formation of public sector purchasing consortia which achieve economies through the bulk-ordering of standardised components.

Direct government intervention in the construction industry by means of price controls, financial support or 'restructuring' has been notable for its absence. It is, of course, difficult to exercise control over contractors' tender prices as each price is a unique price for work yet to be done. However, the industry has not escaped the incidence of price controls altogether: if a tender price is not quoted as a 'fixed price' contractors may recoup increases in costs that occur during the construction period, but for a time during the 1970s only part of labour costs increases could be recouped in this way. In contrast with manufacturing industry government assistance to firms in financial difficulties in construction seems to have been restricted to companies which were engaged on public sector work at the time of their difficulties.

The industry has also been little affected directly by the intervention of government anti-trust agencies. The control of restrictive trade practices, particularly collusive tendering, is of most relevance, but the only known instances are the cases referred to earlier and a registered price-fixing agreement between members of the British Constructional Steelwork Association which was abandoned in 1958. Such practices, however, are difficult to detect and it is impossible to judge how widespread they are in the construction industry or what effect the legislation may have had.

In conclusion, we turn to look ahead. It is always hazardous to predict the future but in this industry it is difficult to reject the view that the future path of development will be very similar to the old. In principle, public policy towards an industry, if a 'policy' is thought to be necessary, can focus its attention on structural matters or on matters more directly relating to its behaviour and performance. In the construction industry, public policy to date has been largely concerned with matters relating to behaviour and, especially, performance. The actions with regard to restrictive practices, the placing of contracts, the finance of research (and the dissemination of results), the encouragement of innovation, labour training and attention to the organisation of demand (as opposed to its level) may all be interpreted in this light. No revolutionary improvements have been brought about and, given the nature of the demands that the industry exists to satisfy and the nature of the technical processes that have to be performed to satisfy these demands, it would be unrealistic to expect any in the near future. Obviously attention must continue to be devoted to these areas. A major objective in the future, however, must be to stabilise the level, or the rate of growth, of demand on the industry as a means of creating a more favourable economic environment in which it may operate by removing some of the worst excesses of uncertainty from which it has suffered recently.

Given the nature of demand, the product and the process, the scope for structural change as a means of improving performance must remain limited. Proposals for the extension of public ownership and control, either by the nationalisation of construction companies or by the expansion of public direct works departments, are not clear about how the industry's economic performance would be improved given that the techniques of production and the problems of managing and controlling work on unique projects on numerous dispersed sites would remain the same. The organisation of the industry has adapted to cope flexibly with the demands placed upon it, and it is questionable how far greater administrative control over productive enterprises in this industry, without attention to demand, can be expected to provide economic benefits.

NOTES TO CHAPTER 10

1. For a discussion of the problems involved in measuring the industry's size, capital stock etc. see Fleming (1980).

2. The apparent decline is probably explicable, at least in part, by the growth in the practice of employing 'self-employed' labour under labour-only sub-contract, rather than as direct employees.

3. The tender prices of traditional and industrialised two-storey five-bedspace houses for local authorities in England and Wales amounted to £95 per m^2 and £97 per m^2 respectively in 1976 (unpublished data supplied by the Department of the Environment).

REFERENCES

Bishop, D. (1972) 'Productivity in the building industry'. *The Philosophical Transactions of the Royal Society, London, A272* (1229), 533–563.

BRS (1971) *BRS News* (18). Garston, Watford: Building Research Station.

DOE (1978) *An Introduction to Dimensional Co-ordination.* Department of the Environment. London: HMSO.

DSIR (1953) *Productivity in House-building, Second Report.* National Building Studies, Special Report no. 21. London: HMSO.

Fleming, M. C. (1965) 'Economic aspects of new methods of building'. *Journal of the Statistical and Social Inquiry Society of Ireland* XXI (III), 120–142.

Fleming, M. C. (1977) 'The bogey of fragmentation in the construction industry'. *National Builder* 58, 134–137 and 284–286.

Fleming, M. C. (1980) *Reviews of UK Statistical Sources, Vol. 12, Construction and the Related Professions.* Oxford: Pergamon Press.

Forbes, W. S. and Skoyles, E. R. (1963) 'The operational bill'. *Chartered Surveyor* 95 (8), 429–434. Building Research Station Current Paper Design Series 1.

Forbes, W. S. (1969) 'A survey of progress in housebuilding'. *Building Technology and Management* 7 (4), 88–91. Building Research Station Current Paper 25/69.

Hillebrandt, Patricia M. (1974) *Economic Theory and the Construction Industry.* London: Macmillan.

Ministry of Education (1955) *Site Labour Studies in School Building.* Building Bulletin 12. London: HMSO.

Ministry of Public Building and Works (1964) *The Placing and Management of Contracts for Building and Civil Engineering Work. Report of the [Banwell] Committee.* London: HMSO.

Ministry of Works (1944) *The Placing and Management of Building Contracts.* London: HMSO.

Monopolies Commission (1954) *Report on the Supply of Buildings in the Greater London Area.* House of Commons Paper 264, Session 1953–4. London: HMSO.

NEDO (1974) *Before You Build.* London: HMSO.

NEDO (1975) *The Public Client and the Construction Industries.* London: HMSO.

Newcombe, Robert (1978) 'Cost of competition'. *Building* 234 (7041), 95, 97.

Registrar of Restrictive Trading Agreements (1973) *Restrictive Trading Agreements, Report of the Registrar 1 July 1969 to 30 June 1972.* Cmnd 5195. London: HMSO.

FURTHER READING

The following texts provide useful surveys of the history, economics and organisation of the industry.

Stone, P. A. (1976) *Building Economy.* 2nd edn. Oxford: Pergamon Press.

Bowley, Marian (1966) *The British Building Industry.* Cambridge: Cambridge University Press.

Hillebrandt, Patricia M. (1974) *Economic Theory and the Construction Industry.* London: Macmillan.

Ministry of Works (1962) *Survey of Problems Before the Construction Industries* [Emmerson Report]. London: HMSO.

For a comprehensive review of the sources and nature of the statistical data available see

Fleming, M. C. (1980) *Reviews of UK Statistical Sources Vol. 12: Construction and the Related Professions.* Oxford: Pergamon Press.

11: Rail transport

K. M. Gwilliam

11.1 INTRODUCTION

11.1.1 The creation of a nationalised rail monopoly

During the Second World War the four private railway companies, which were responsible for the vast majority of rail transport in the UK, were integrated operationally under the management of the Railway Executive Committee. Protected from road competition by fuel rationing, they demonstrated their effectiveness despite serious losses both of staff and equipment in meeting the greatly increased demands made upon them. At the end of the war, both the successful experience of integration and the physically poor state of a system deprived for so long of adequate maintenance, made further state intervention probable. In 1945 the election of a Labour government with a longstanding commitment to the nationalisation of rail transport finally determined the form that this intervention would take. By the Transport Act 1947 the whole railway system, together with the bulk of the public road transport industry, was taken into public ownership, to be managed by a newly created British Transport Commission (BTC).

Although a belief in integration through common ownership underlay the 1947 Act, the Act itself gave no guidance to the BTC as to how this should be achieved. In the event, the BTC managed the industry through five separate Executives, responsible respectively for Rail, Road Transport, London Transport, Docks and Inland Waterways and Hotels. Thus, operationally, rail transport remained in competition with the other modes of transport. Denationalisation of road haulage after 1953, and the change to a philosophy of co-ordination through the market mechanism, which was introduced by the Conservative administration in the early 1950s and survived subsequent changes of government, strengthened this institutional and operational independence of the rail mode. The 1962 Transport Act completed this separation by splitting the BTC into five completely autonomous transport bodies, including the new British Railways Board. Thus, effectively since 1948, the rail transport industry in Great Britain has been a state monopoly, operating independently of, and in competition with, other modes of transport, both public and private.

11.1.2 Rail as a declining industry

The recent history of the railways has been very troubled; the successive major Transport Acts (in 1953, 1962, 1968, 1974 and 1978) have all tried to meet the growing 'problem of the railways'. As table 11.1 shows, rail carryings have fallen, both relative to other modes and in absolute terms; this fall in sales has been accompanied by a reduction in network size, labour force and amount of rail service offered. Even

TABLE 11.1:   Rail transport, 1948–76

	Thousand million passengers km	% of all passengers km	Thousand million ton km	% of freight ton km	Thousand km network size	Thousand* labour force	Million 'train' km
1948	34.2	na	35.4	na	31.5	648.7	588.3
1955	32.7	18.6	36.2	37.3	30.7	565.0	584.6
1960	34.7	15.6	30.5	30.6	29.6	514.5	604.2
1965	30.1	10.5	25.2	20.9	24.0	365.0	518.8
1970	30.4	8.8	26.8	19.4	19.0	274.3	469.9
1976	28.6	7.4	23.1	10.0	10.0	247.6	445.9

Sources: Transport Statistics of Great Britain; Union International des Chemins de Fer: International Rail Statistics.
Note: *Includes rail workshop, shipping and other staff.

at this aggregate level, however, two features of the decline in traffic are apparent. Firstly, particularly in the 1960s, the absolute decline in rail transport is much less startling than the relative decline in terms of market share. Secondly, the reduction in labour force and network size greatly exceeds that in train miles, or in traffic carried. The railway system has thus adjusted to a new diminished role within the transport sector with a more intense use of physical assets and a more productive use of labour. This interpretation can be supported by observing improvements in most of the simple physical productivity indicators (see section 11.4). Moreover, for the remaining rail system the quality of service offered has substantially improved. Average speeds of freight trains and mean delivery times of freight traffic have improved; the frequency of passenger services on major inter-city

TABLE 11.2:   Passenger transport: consumer cost indices (1970 = 100)

	1960	1965	1970	1976
Rail fares	57	77	100	270
Bus and coach fares	53	70	100	240
Purchase price of motor vehicles	98	85	100	204
Running cost of motor vehicles	68	80	100	216
Total consumer expenditure on goods and services	69	79	100	208

Sources: Passenger Transport in Great Britain; Transport Statistics Great Britain.

routes has increased and journey times have fallen by about 30% over the last twenty years. For London surburban services both journey times and frequencies have been reduced slightly.

In terms of the cost to the consumer, the picture is less favourable to rail transport. As table 11.2 shows, the price of rail transport has increased more rapidly since 1960 than that of competing modes, or than the average prices of all consumer goods and services. Moreover, this relationship has not been altered significantly by the oil price increases of 1973–4. Indeed, only for a very short period – between 1973 and 1975 – were rail fares increasing less rapidly than running costs of motor vehicles, and this was predominantly due to government intervention to prevent the increase in rail costs being fully reflected in prices during this period of high inflation.

The most obvious, and politically most troublesome, consequence of this history has been the mounting financial deficit of the railways. Immediately after nationalisation the Railway Executive, although showing a surplus on operating account, was not able to meet its allocated share of the central charges of the BTC (administration and capital charges). This situation improved during the next four years so that by 1952 the railways produced its first overall surplus. The success was shortlived. In the next decade the operating results deteriorated steadily and in 1956 the railways went into deficit on operating account, a deficit which reached the level of £104m for the year 1962, giving an overall deficit in that year of £156m.

Several factors contributed to this situation. Increased competition from road haulage after 1953 brought about losses in freight traffic and revenue. The recession of 1957–8 hit the staple rail traffics of coal and iron ore particularly harshly. Above all, it was argued at the time, the lack of adequate investment in rail transport prevented the railways from achieving increases in productivity to offset increasing costs.

11.1.3 Recovery by investment: the modernisation plan

This latter argument is worth some attention. There is little doubt that rail investment was inadequate. It has been estimated that there had been a net disinvestment of £440m in the railways during the period 1937–53 (Redfern, 1955). Unfortunately when the Government set out to rectify this situation in the mid-fifties the outcome was not as expected.

In 1955 the Government accepted a Modernisation Plan presented by the BTC which had an estimated cost of £1240m (HMSO, 1956). The programme had four main investment components: improvement of track and signalling, replacement of steam locomotion by electric or diesel traction, modernisation of passenger rolling stock and stations, and remodelling of freight services using continuously braked wagons and modernised depots. In the event, it soon became apparent that the capital costs of the programme would be greater than anticipated and the benefits slower to accrue. Technical difficulties with early diesels and problems of finding a satisfactory form of continuously braked wagons were compounded by association with inaccurate forecasting of traffic and price trends. The result was that by 1962, originally quoted as the year by which the programme should have restored the railways' profitability, the deficit had reached a record level.

11.1.4 Recovery by retrenchment: the Beeching era

The mounting rail deficits focussed political attention on the railways. In 1960 the Select Committee on Nationalised Industries reported very critically both on the general way in which the railways were being run and on the modernisation plan in particular (Select Committee on the Nationalised Industries, 1960). In 1961 a special committee set up under the chairmanship of Sir Ivone Stedeford advised a thorough reorganisation of nationalised transport.

The 1962 Transport Act implemented this reorganisation. The BTC was divided into five separate boards and the newly created British Railways Board was given a remit to break even as soon as possible. To this end the BRB was given a capital reconstruction which purported to leave the Board the responsibility for servicing only the book value of assets created since 1955. Nearly £500m of capital debt was written off and a further £700m was suspended. It was expected that, on this basis, the railways would be able to break even after five years. Grants of up to £450m were provided for this interim period.

There were two other major elements in the strategy to revitalise the railways. The 1962 Act removed the remaining historic restrictions that required them to act as common carriers and, with the exception of London area fares and charges for services competing with coastal shipping, gave the Board commercial freedom.

This freedom was rapidly and dynamically used. In June 1961 Dr Richard Beeching, who had been a member of the Stedeford Committee, was appointed as Chairman of the British Railways Board. In late 1961 and through 1962 he undertook a thorough review of the rail business; this was published in March 1963 (British Railways Board, 1963).

The Beeching Report disclosed a grossly over-extended, and under-utilised, rail system. One-third of the route mileage carried only 1% of the traffic. One-third of the stations produced only 1% of the traffic. Almost half of the passenger rolling stock was operated solely for high peak requirements. Stopping services for passengers were seen to be highly unremunerative whilst general merchandise traffic was seen to be responsible for about two-thirds of all losses on freight. On the other hand, inter-city express services were shown to be potentially profitable and the mineral and coal traffics, despite their decline in quantity in the late fifties, still remained profitable.

The proposals to repair this situation were radical. Over two thousand stations and five thousand route miles of track were suggested for closure to passenger traffic. The carriage and wagon fleet was to be reduced and workshops rationalised. More positively, the conversion from steam to diesel traction was to be continued and freight traffic, both bulks and sundries, was to be increasingly concentrated to produce a freight service operating essentially in full-train loads. To this end a new type of service – the liner train – was to provide combined road and rail movement of containerised merchandise.

The investment costs of the plan were of the order of £250m, implying £25–30m in annual depreciation and interest charges which would be offset by the net revenue improvement predicted to be in the range £115–147m per annum. The proposals did thus seem to give the railways some chance of eliminating their operating deficit.

These hopes were disappointed for a number of reasons. The government did not, in the event, permit the rate of withdrawals envisaged in the Report. Liner trains failed to make the expected impact, and wagon load traffics were not cut as rapidly as proposed. The sundries traffic became more rather than less unprofitable. The continued stagnation of the basic industries prevented the expected growth in profit from coal and coke traffic.

Finally, two defects of forecasting must be mentioned. Many of the proposals implied increases in labour productivity without making any allowance for the share of those increases that labour would be certain to demand. Moreover, the extent of the financial turnover required for the railways to break even was probably underestimated through inadequate attention to the depreciation requirements to maintain the new situation (Gwilliam and Mackie, 1975, pages 240–243).

11.1.5 Objectives and subsidies

Despite Beeching the financial position of BR continued to deteriorate so that by 1968 the deficit had once more reached £150m per annum. So the 1968 Transport Act, the product of a comprehensive review of transport policy undertaken under the then Minister of Transport Mrs Barbara Castle, once more reconstructed rail finances. A further £1262m of capital debt was written off, leaving the Board with a book value of only £365m. This alone improved the accounts by £54m in servicing charges in 1969. In addition the transfer to the newly formed National Freight Corporation of the loss-making sundries services, and half of the Freightliner Company improved the accounts by £18m.

But that was still insufficient to attain financial balance. The residue was to come from two kinds of direct grant. Firstly, it was accepted that there remained a substantial element of surplus track; a grant of £15m per annum was therefore provided for a five-year period to finance the elimination of this surplus capacity.

The second type of grant was much more important. The Act accepted that some unprofitable railway services were nevertheless socially desirable and that specific subsidies should be paid to the railways for their continued provision. The grant on these services was to be the difference between the expected total costs and total revenues. Inevitably, because of the complexity of railway cost structures and particularly the high degree of jointness in costs, this required some essentially arbitrary conventions of allocation.

The philosophy of this regime was simple. The railways were to compete in the market and were expected to be commercially viable. Any obligations thrust upon them by government would be the subject of a specific grant. The small surplus shown in 1969 seemed to indicate the correctness of the calculation.

Again, however, the out-turn belied the expectations. The surpluses of 1969 and 1970 turned into escalating deficit. Increasingly it became apparent that the commercial remit of 1968, even with its social service subsidy provisions, could only be met at the expense of a very substantial reduction in size of network. Indeed, in the Railway Policy Review exercise of 1973, both BR and the Government appear to have been convinced that no acceptable pruning exercise could restore financial viability within the existing framework. Moreover, BR argued, more investment would also be needed even to contain the deficit in operating the existing network.

Having reached this conclusion the government again changed the statutory provisions accordingly. The 1974 Railways Act – using the powers and terminology suggested by EEC regulations on railways – specified a 'public service obligation' (PSO) on British Rail to maintain its network and services broadly at their 1974 level. The system of specific subsidies was replaced by a blanket subsidy of about £300m per annum for the next five years, to cover operating deficits and new capital investment. Rail capital was again written down from £439m to £250m.

Even this regime has proved very difficult to live with. Government restraints on the prices of the nationalised industries from 1973 contributed to further financial deterioration so that by 1976 the total cash requirement of railways from government had risen to £450m. British Rail management continued to emphasise the needs for further capital investment, arguing that if the government wished to maintain the specified network of rail services it would have to provide financial resources adequate for the task (British Railways Board, 1978). The 1974 settlement, which took no account of the particular difficulties of the inflationary years to follow, was not seen as such a provision.

In 1976 and 1977 this problem was put back into the context of a comprehensive review of transport policy. The 1977 White Paper (HMSO, 1977) restated rail objectives in terms of their distinctly separate markets – freight, intercity passenger services, London suburban, etc. A continuing public service obligation subsidy was provided for – to be negotiated annually – and the separate markets given targets in terms of covering full allocated costs (e.g. for Intercity) or avoidable costs (e.g. for freight). Some greater security of investment funding was promised. Despite the claim of the White Paper to have provided a firm foundation within which rail management could operate, by itself it seems to have solved nothing. Everything, in future, would turn on the annual PSO negotiation (Beesley and Gwilliam, 1977).

11.2 THE RAIL TRANSPORT MARKET

11.2.1 The nature of the product

Rail transport, like all transport services, cannot be stored; if not consumed at the time of production it is wasted.

In some markets, such as that for large bulk freight consignments, it is possible to tailor the production to the demand. By the end of 1977 nearly 85% of the freight tonnage of BR was conveyed in trainloads. This reflects not only the policy of BR management to concentrate on this kind of carriage but also the composition of rail freight traffic which is heavily concentrated in a small number of bulk commodities, especially coal and coke and iron and steel.

For rail passenger traffic such a fine adjustment of supply to demand is rarely possible, and the art of management is to plan and market services, and to set prices, in such a way as to match demand and services most profitably. The complexity of scheduling rail services means that there can be a lead time of up to eighteen months on revision of timetables, leaving railways very vulnerable, in their adjustment of service, to unforeseen increases or reductions in demand.

11.2.2 The supply characteristics

Joint costs and the problem of allocation
This inherent inflexibility can also be observed very clearly in rail cost structures. Track, signalling and terminal facilities are subject to great indivisibilities and these costs cannot be easily adjusted to variations in the level of utilisation. About 40% of rail expenses fall in these categories (see table 11.3).

An important corollary of this characteristic is that it is not possible

TABLE 11.3:   Summary of BR consolidated profit and loss account

Expenditure	£m	Income	£m
Rail infrastructure costs		*Fares and charges*	
Track maintenance	244	Passenger	593
Signalling, operating and		Freight	348
maintenance	115	Parcels	110
Associated administration		Miscellaneous	16
and general expenses	39		**1067**
	398		
		Payments by government	
Rail operating costs		*and other agencies*	
Train services	620	PSO payment	364
Terminals and		Payments for level	
miscellaneous	200	crossings	10
Administration and		Grants for rail non-	
general expenses	192	passenger sector	−3
	1012		**371**
Corporate expenses	**4**	Exchange gain	**4**
Interest	**43**	Other income (net) from	
Net surplus	**27**	subsidiary activities	**42**
	1484		**1484**

Source: British Railways Board *Annual Report and Accounts*, 1977, page 11.

to allocate all costs between freight and passenger services, or even between units of operation within one of these categories, except on an arbitrary basis. Hence BR has introduced a costing system based on the principle of 'contribution accounting'. Revenue and expenditure is broken down into some seven hundred major sub-sectors, called profit centres. These profit centres are defined so that the resources allocated to each of them can be specifically identified, with a minimum need to allocate common or jointly used resources. They may consist of single flows of traffic, groups of flows, or specific passenger services. But, even for these profit centres, the indirect costs of track and signalling and administration cannot be objectively allocated. So, for each profit centre, the accounts present the surplus of revenue over directly attributed expenses as a 'contribution' to the indirect costs.

It is sometimes possible to go a little way towards allocating the costs of jointly used infrastructure. This is done by trying to answer two questions. How much are costs altered by changes in outputs? And, if one activity were to cease – all others continuing – what costs would be avoided? This 'avoidable cost' approach is already incorporated in the freight sector objective for BR set by the government, that requires rail freight to cover its avoidable costs.

Of course, the sum of avoidable costs for all sectors will not add up to total accounting costs. There will still remain a residue that BR have called the 'basic facility cost' of the business as a whole. As BR have argued

> Although the basic facility cost will have to be met by the business as a whole, or otherwise supported (e.g. Government support for rail infrastructure), this separate identification of costs unique to sectors ensures a high level of certainty in profit assessment. It is therefore well suited to businesses with a high proportion of indirect joint costs, such as the railways. (*Annual Report and Accounts*, 1976, page 15)

Labour

Despite the importance of indivisibilities in infrastructure being the dominant characteristic of rail costs it should still be remembered that rail transport remains a labour-intensive industry. Over two-thirds of the operating expenditure is accounted for by staff expenses, a proportion only slightly less than the 70% of the nationalised bus industry, but considerably higher than the 45% of the nationalised road haulage undertaking, the National Freight Corporation.

There are three rail unions. The National Union of Railwaymen (NUR), the general union, has a total membership of about 180 000, of whom about 133 000 work for BR. The Amalgamated Society of Locomotive Engineers and Firemen (ASLEF) has a total membership of around 29 000, all except 2000 of whom are at BR. The Transport and Salaried Staffs Association (TSSA) has a membership of 74 000, 54 000 of whom are at BR. As their names imply there is some functional specialisation amongst the unions, with TSSA being the union of the non-manual labour and ASLEF that of the footplate staff. But the lines are not clearly drawn and NUR has a large membership in both of these areas. Because of this inter-union division conflict may arise among unions, as well as between unions and management. ASLEF, particularly, has on occasions acted militantly to the chagrin of NUR. But whilst NUR (as the biggest union) has favoured amalgamation to form a single industrial union the other two have not.

As we have already shown, the labour force of BR has been reduced drastically over the last twenty years. But it has been suggested that futher reductions may be achieved through the elimination of the second man in the driving cab and of guards on freight trains fully fitted with air brakes, increases of average driving time per shift for footplate crew, reduction of station and ticketing staff by mechanisation and reduction of official headquarters staff (Select Committee on Nationalised Industries, 1977). Such suggestions may be conceded at a general level, but the real argument concerns the size of such further cuts, the political acceptability of redundancy, the effects on the age and skill structure of reduction by natural wastage and the safety effects of reducing manning levels.

Capital Investment
British Rail have consistently argued that the best – and possibly the only – way to secure such staff reductions is through new investment. Some of the sources of reduction in manpower, such as the increased mechanisation of ticketing and station control, imply that directly. But there are others, such as network electrification, that are equally important. There is no doubt that electrification increases labour productivity in a number of ways. More intense use of track and rolling stock is possible, whilst the added maintenance of fixed electric track equipment is offset by reductions in maintenance on electric locomotives compared with diesel. It is not without significance that the Western European railways showing labour productivity higher than that achieved by BR all have significantly higher proportions of electrified activity.

British Rail have also argued that – at least on Inter-City Passenger Services – there is already a *financial* advantage in electrification. Moreover, they argue, the case improves over time: 'firstly because wages tend to rise faster than other costs and secondly, because energy costs are forecast to rise more rapidly for diesel than for electric traction' (*Annual Report and Accounts*, 1977, page 29). On this basis it is argued that a good case can be made for electrification of a further 3000 route miles over a period of twenty to thirty years. Commitment to such a programme would certainly provide a stable basis for employment in the railway supply industry and would give to rail transport a high degree of flexibility in choice of primary fuel source.

Track electrification is not the only means by which BR have or could improve both their quality of service and their productivity. Where track is suitable the High Speed Train (HST), available in either diesel or electric version, allows speeds of 125 mph (200 kph) to be achieved. In the first full year of operation of HSTs on the route from London to Bristol and South Wales long distance average timings approaching the 100 mph level became the norm and the rail share of the passenger market on the routes rose by 30%. HST now also operates on both the East and West Coast main lines to the North.

Even HST was initially seen as an interim solution pending the introduction of the technologically more radical Advanced Passenger Train, which, by virtue of its revolutionary pendular suspension, was designed to be capable of extremely high speeds even on poor track configurations. Under the 1973 interim rail strategy 120 APT sets – some electric, some gas turbine – were to be in operation by 1981. The HSTs were then to be 'cascaded' from the major to the minor trunk routes (e.g. London–Norwich). In the event it appears that the APT will only be introduced, in the electric form, on the West Coast main line; if the original intentions to provide high speed are to be met this will involve further investment in HSTs and possibly also in track improvement.

Maintaining the quality of the passenger services will also require other rolling stock investment. Over 75% of the electric and diesel multiple unit sets that provide the bulk of suburban and local services were over fifteen years old at the end of 1977. Replacement of this stock, particularly with sliding door stock suitable for one man operation, will not only improve reliability and quality of service but also reduce costs and increase labour productivity.

In the *rail freight* business we have already remarked on the large proportion (80% of tonnage) handled in full trainload consignments. Many of these movements are closely integrated into the production processes of their customer industries. For instance the 'merry-go-round' trains maintain a continuous supply of coal to power stations. But there is also an increasing range of goods carried in this way including, at one extreme, movement of refuse out of Greater London for disposal, and, at the other, full train movements of containerised car components.

The emphasis on this trainload movement did, for some time, seem to imply a limitation of interest in less than trainload traffic to the Freightliner business. The carriage of containers by rail was developed as a concept in the Beeching report in 1963. By 1978 the Freightliner Company made over 600 000 container movements and carried over six million tons of traffic.

Two recent developments have been aimed at developing this less than wagon load business, however. The nationwide computerised wagon monitoring system, TOPS, enables rail management to pin-point any wagon on the system immediately. This makes it possible to reduce delays and to give a better service to customers. It also improves the usage rate of rolling stock, hence reducing costs. The system completed its first full year in operation in 1976.

Towards the end of the following year the Board launched a network of twenty-nine fast daily services linking the main industrial and market areas with high capacity, airbraked, wagons operating at up to 75 mph. In 1978 these Speedlink services have been increased to sixty per day and are carrying an estimated four million tons per year. A total investment of £67m is involved, including the building of a further 3400 wagons.

The final major sector of rail business is *parcels*, defined as individual packages which are carried partly on special parcels trains and partly on passenger trains. The main components of this traffic are newspapers, mail, mail order carriage and an expanding premium express parcels service, marketed as 'Red Star'. In total parcels generated revenue of £110m in 1978, about 10% of receipts from traffic.

11.2.3 The demand for rail transport

As we have seen, rail transport is very heterogeneous. It is therefore both difficult and dangerous to make generalisations about the characteristics of demand for such a set of differentiated products. But we can make some introductory observations which may help in understanding the market performance of BR.

For *passenger transport* three factors are of paramount importance: income, price and quality of service.

The effects of income are complex. Increasing income is associated with increasing car ownership, which would normally be expected to militate against the use of public transport. On the other hand rail transport is a 'superior' good and as incomes rise there is a tendency for the amount of personal transport demanded to increase more than proportionately and certainly for rail transport to be substituted for bus, and for long journeys, for car transport. Thus, as the 1976 Consultative Document showed, the higher income groups are responsible for a disproportionately large share of expenditure on rail transport. Of course, this is partly accounted for by the fact that business travel, more than any other category of travel, is taken at full fares.

The evidence on price elasticities fits well within this pattern. For business travel, price elasticity appears to be low, whilst for other purposes higher elasticities prevail. In particular, recent evidence of competition between rail and express bus services for the custom of students and old age pensioners suggests fairly high elasticities and cross-elasticities in these markets.

Competition between rail and the private car, and to a lesser extent between rail and air seems to depend more on quality of service. The ability of accelerated rail services to compete with air on the routes from London to Leeds, Birmingham and Manchester and with the private car for transport to the South-West has demonstrated relatively high service elasticities. Similarly improved speed and reliability associated with electrification has contributed to the expansion of the long distance commuting market in the South-East.

For *freight transport* service factors also have been shown to be important in the modal choice studies (Edwards and Bayliss, 1969). Whilst price is clearly not irrelevant it seems that the ability to provide a quality service, well integrated with the rest of the production and distribution system of the sector concerned is paramount.

11.2.4 Market structure

BR has an effective statutory monopoly in rail transport. The interesting questions of market structure are thus not internal to railways but concern its relationship in the transport market with its customers and competitors.

As table 11.1 showed, the rail share of both the freight and passenger markets in the UK has been falling steadily. But in recent years this has represented increasing specialisation of function and a growth of road transport rather than an overall decline in rail traffic. Between 1972 and 1977, the rail freight business increased in a number of major bulk categories (coal and coke, earths and stones, chemicals). Similarly in the passenger market, Inter-city has maintained, and very recently increased, its market. For instance, the introduction of the HS125 services increased the rail share of the London–Bristol market by nearly 10% between 1976 and 1977. Similarly, despite fare increases, BR maintains its leading role in providing for commuters into London from the South-East.

One of the dominating characteristics of the transport sector is that the road network is substantially more dense than the rail network (250 000 route miles compared with 11 000). Thus rail transport is dependent either on traffics that both originate and terminate very close to the sparser network or on adequate arrangements for modal transfer. In the passenger market the history of competition between bus and rail has often meant that bus stations and railway stations were far apart and there has been relatively little attempt to co-ordinate services or timetables. Interesting comparisons can be made with Sweden and the Netherlands where closer co-ordination of public passenger modes is achieved. For instance, the new Central Station at the Hague is a combined station designed to permit very rapid and convenient transfer.

The problem has been even more intense for freight where the costs of terminal handling are a large proportion of total costs, hence militating against multi-modal transport. The traditional rail response to this has been to offer its own road collection and delivery services, hence attempting to offer a door to door service at least within the one organisation. Even this device was eliminated when, in 1968, rail collection and delivery services were transferred to National Carriers Ltd, an operating subsidiary of the road dominated National Freight Corporation (NFC). Whilst NFC was charged, as far as possible, to use rail transport for trunk haulage, many rail operators considered that their own marketing power was unfortunately and unfairly reduced.

A second type of solution was pursued by the development of the Freightliner system. Because the transfer of whole containers from road to rail vehicles was much cheaper than the manhandling of goods, and because it gave improvements also in speed and security, this was felt to be the best way of maintaining the railways' general merchandise market. Again, however, the transfer of the majority holding in Freightliners to the National Freight Corporation in 1968 may have weakened the BR marketing effort and in 1978 the company was transferred back to BR.

Even more crucial than the co-ordination among modes of transport may be the co-ordination between the transport function and the rest of the production and distribution system. In this respect the own account road haulage fleet has an obvious initial advantage in terms of total control over distribution management. The corollary of this is that BR has also had to seek means of providing services equally closely linked to the rest of the production and distribution process.

In some markets it has succeeded brilliantly. The 'merry-go-round' trains carting coal between mines and power stations are physically well integrated with both the mining and power supply industries. More generally, government support for investment in private sidings under section 8 of the 1974 Railways Act is selectively redressing a trend that has seen the number of private sidings reduced from 6000 to 2000 over the last fifteen years. Increasingly the evidence on freight transport suggests that the crucial decisions are not decisions by customers concerning what proportion of their traffic they should send by different modes or by the railways on freight pricing, but decisions both by the railways and their customers on investment in facilities, terminals and fleet that will effectively tie consignors to one mode or other for the bulk of their traffic. It is clear, for instance, that once a firm has committed itself to a trunk road haulage fleet it is likely to be cost efficient to keep it fully employed and only to use public modes to smooth out peaks.

In addition to its central function of providing rail services, BR inherited, and has further developed, a range of subsidiary activities that diversify its product. Its ships, hovercrafts and harbours offer an integrated service for international travel; British Rail Engineering Ltd (BREL) and its consultancy organisation, Transmark, have developed substantial export markets; whilst the hotel, rail catering services, advertising and property subsidiaries enable BR both to make its main product more attractive and to develop its assets appropriately.

11.3 MARKET BEHAVIOUR

11.3.1 Railway business objectives

It is paradoxical, at a time when the government has agreed to a financial arrangement involving a large global subsidy payment, to argue that the recent history of BR is that of an increasingly commercial, market-oriented, enterprise. But that is what recent developments in the relationship between the government and BR suggest. The 1968 Transport Act granted certain specific subsidies to BR but, on this basis, required BR otherwise to act commercially. This led BR to consider carefully both the kind of services and the level of fares necessary to satisfy this requirement. It was the government, as much as BR management, that found the likely consequences of pursuit of that objective unacceptable. The 1974 Railways Act introduced the public service obligation and its corollary global compensation payment. But this new regime has been subsequently developed to set BR sector targets that require a very commercial approach. Thus freight has to meet all of its avoidable costs and inter-city passenger services are expected to meet both the avoidable costs and an allocation of the indirect costs of the business.

11.3.2 Costing

The two dimensions of the commercial approach are product development and pricing. But the basis for either type of policy to be used sensibly and purposefully is an adequate, systematic understanding of the costs of railway operation and of the market potential of proposed services.

So long as BR were subject to the common carrier obligation to accept all traffic offered and to control on fares and charges, they had little incentive to develop sophisticated costing systems. Internal management control could be based on physical productivity objectives. Once freed from these obligations by the 1962 Transport Act an efficient costing system became a necessity. In the event BR have developed a system of Cost and Profit Centre Analysis which compares favourably with any railway accounting system in the world. This system allows management to identify accurately the effect on costs of any proposed change in service, and, through the attribution of expected revenues accruing from such changes, to decide what different alternatives will contribute to meeting the overall financial objectives of the enterprise.

11.3.3 Marketing and pricing

As far as marketing is concerned the major development has been the splitting of the rail activity into a number of separate 'businesses' – sometimes defined geographically, sometimes by product moved – to allow specialisation of responsibility. Thus there now exist product marketing functions which both allow, and positively encourage, product development.

In *freight* the major successes have been in the train load movements of bulks. More recently there has been a renewed interest in wagon load traffic for which TOPS, the computer based wagon control system, has given a new dimension in security from loss and Speedlink has given a new dimension in speed and certainty of delivery.

Increasing recognition of the need for closer integration of the transport function with the rest of the production and distribution system has led to a renewed interest in private sidings traffic. This almost inevitably means substantial capital investment in private terminal facilities. BR may be unwilling to enter into such commitments without any guarantee of the continued traffic at rates adequate to justify the investment, whilst users tend to be unwilling to make the investment without some guarantee of adequate future service at reasonable rates. Consequently an increasing proportion of the rail freight business is effectively secured by commitment of resources on one side and obligations to buy or sell at agreed terms on the other, on long-term contracts. Thus the relevant price considerations are these long period contract terms.

In the *passenger* business the emphasis has been on speed and reliability. Electrification is seen as a key to both qualities and BR are now re-emphasising the merits of a substantially electrified system. But the introduction of the High Speed Train, whether electrically or diesel-powered, has already boosted the major Inter-City markets, and there are plans to extend it to less prime routes.

Product improvement in the passenger market has been associated with very positive pricing policy. Having identified market segments with differing price elasticities BR has set out energetically to exploit those characteristics. Increases in standard fares, even in real terms, have increased revenue from peak inter-city (predominantly business) travel. At the same time, however, a range of discriminatory promotional fares have succeeded in increasing off-peak utilisation. The student and senior citizen fares appear to have been particularly successful in this respect.

11.4 PERFORMANCE

11.4.1 Financial and physical indicators

In the 1978 White Paper on the Nationalised Industries the Government required each industry to devise and construct indicators of performance that could be reported and monitored. In doing so it recognised that publicly-owned industries are subject to varied, and variable, constraints. If profit maximisation is not the most desirable objective, then financial results will not be the most appropriate indicator of performance.

To exhort railway organisations not to judge themselves solely on gross profitability is to preach to the converted. None of the major railway of Western Europe has been profitable (in the sense of covering all its costs from direct revenue from customers) since the early 1960s. Nor are the slightly more sophisticated financial measures, such as proportion of costs covered by revenue, or loss per unit of traffic, any more helpful. For, both in international comparisons and in comparisons in one country over time, differences in these indicators may reflect the variations in the tightness of government control over price levels or levels of service to be provided rather than variations in the efficiency with which railways perform the tasks assigned to them. Although BR have recently shown (see table 11.4) that rail support as a proportion of GDP is lower and the number of passenger and freight ton kms per £1 of support is substantially higher for BR than the average for the main European railways, it is more for the political purpose of demonstrating that there is nothing unusual in the BR situation than because such measures are believed to be good performance indicators.

The obvious alternatives to financial indicators are physical productivity indicators. For instance, in their 1977 annual report BR show their performance over a ten-year period on six such measures (table

TABLE 11.4: International rail performance comparisons

	British Rail		Average of main European railways	
	1975	**1976**	1975	**1976**
Train kilometres per member of staff employed	2363	**2395**	2009	**2070**
Passenger kms plus freight/tonne kms per train km	113	**110**	160	**163**
Passenger and freight/tonne kms per £1 support from public funds	101	**101**	79	**66**
Support from public funds as proportion of Gross Domestic Product (%)	0.50	**0.40**	0.88	**0.84**

Source: BR *Annual Report and Accounts*, 1977, page 14.

11.5). Whilst BR, on the basis of these figures, suggest that their performance has been acceptable, other selections show a less favourable picture. In particular both the Consultative Document on Transport Policy (HMSO, 1976) and a report of the Select Committee on Nationalised Industries (1977) have shown BR to produce a lower output per number of staff employed than most of the Western European railways. There are, however, a number of very serious problems in interpreting such comparisons as a commentary on the 'efficiency' of BR.

TABLE 11.5: Physical productivity in BR, 1967–77

	1967	1972	1976	1977
Passenger miles and net tonne miles per member of staff employed* (Rail and Rail workshops) (thousands)	114.3	142.2	146.8	151.1
Passenger mile per loaded passenger train mile	96	99	93	94
Net tonne miles per wagon (thousands)	28.6	51.1	69.7	76.2
Net tonne miles per loaded freight train mile*	227	275	330	349
Loaded train miles per total route mile (thousands)	20.0	21.7	21.9	22.0
Average wagon load* (tonnes)	14.12	19.29	22.47	22.99

Source: BR *Annual Report and Accounts*, 1977, page 14.
Note: *Includes an estimate for National Carriers and Freightliner traffic.

11.4.2 Problems of measuring output

Firstly, there are severe difficulties involved in measuring output.

(a) *Adding together freight and passenger traffic*
The standard measure of output, the traffic unit, gives an equal weight to one passenger km and one freight tonne km. However, analysis of the results of several European rail undertakings suggests that passenger traffic is more costly to provide for and that a different set of weights should be used in computing the simple output measures (Webb, 1979). The implication of reweighting would be to narrow the apparent differences in productivity among systems; on an appropriate basis the Swedish productivity is only about 30% better than BR rather than 120% better.

(b) *Product mix*
Examination of the same problem of output measurement can be taken a little further by looking at the different composition of passenger or freight tonne kms. For instance, disaggregated analysis of costs of BR show labour productivity in production of passenger kms on Inter-City services to be 1.6 times that in production of inner surburban services in London. Similarly, in freight the labour productivity in production of tonne kms of trainload traffic is twice that of production of wagon load tonne kms. Unfortunately for BR their proportion of freight carried in trainloads is very high by European standards, so it is difficult to explain (or excuse) their performance on this count.

(c) *Length of haul*
Because of the high costs of terminal activities one would expect the costs per tonne or passenger km to be inversely related to average length of haul. Thus, for instance, the fact that much of the trainload traffic for BR is the short haul of coal between mines and power stations would somewhat explain the absence of high productivity associated with high proportion of trainload traffic.

11.4.3 Traffic and the utilisation of capacity

Rail transport infrastructure exhibits such indivisibilities that high levels of labour productivity are likely to be associated, *ceteris paribus*, with intense utilisation. In that the characteristics of the economy are not favourable to rail transport, then relatively low traffic levels and low productivity may be outside the immediate control of management. There are three respects in which this might be argued to apply to British Rail.

(a) *Income and car ownership*

High income and high car ownership might be expected to bias the passenger modal split against public transport. But Sweden, with high car ownership and high incomes still manages to achieve a higher annual public transport usage per head than does the UK associated in this case with high labour productivity. In contrast, West Germany, with high incomes, also has higher public transport usage per head than the UK but with labour productivity in rail transport much more comparable with BR levels.

(b) *Economic structure*

A similar argument might be applied to freight haulage. If a country has a good deal of long distance transport of bulk commodities suitable for rail transport one may expect its share of the freight market and its absolute freight traffic level per worker employed to be high. Britain certainly has a favourable commodity structure for rail freight transport. It also has an above average share of the domestic freight market. That this share is still not as high as might be expected given the Commodity Structure may perhaps be explained in terms of the statutory environment in which BR operates, to which we now turn.

11.4.4 Government intervention and rail transport productivity

Government impinges on the productivity of railways in three important ways: as the source of capital, as the source of revenue support and a powerful influence on prices and as the ultimate determinant of the nature of the competitive environment in which railways operate. In each of these dimensions it may be argued that the international comparisons of productivity depend on factors beyond the control of management.

(a) *Capital investment*

On general economic reasoning one would expect labour productivity to be high in cases where the capital–labour ratio is high. Given the heterogeneity and great age of rail assets it is very difficult to arrive at any satisfactory valuation of capital stock to allow meaningful international comparisons of this ratio. For this reason 'total factor productivity' measures cannot be used as a way of adjusting for capital stock differences. There do appear to be some signs, however, that maintenance and operating costs of new locomotives (particularly electric) and rolling stock are less than for old stock. Thus the average age of stock and the recent levels of investment may give some indicators of advantage. On this basis the high productivity of both the Netherlands and Sweden, with high levels of electrification, and

France with high recent levels of rolling stock investment may be associated with capital factors. In contrast, Italy, with the worst labour productivity figures has a very aged fleet and has had little recent investment.

(b) *Prices and subsidies*
Whilst financial measures are not satisfactory indicators of productivity, the level of subsidy per rail traffic unit, particularly where competing modes are operated purely commercially, may be an important influence on mode share and hence on labour productivity. In 1971 Britain had the second highest passenger fares of the European rail networks and, alone of the more expensive networks, these fares increased in real terms over the following six years to make BR the highest fare railway in Western Europe. These high average prices, which are associated with relatively low unit subsidy levels, are clearly related to the level of rail usage per capita (Webb). On the other hand, the *structure* of fares may be as important as the general level. BR uses price discrimination more extensively than most other railways and may therefore be in a better commercial position than the average fare levels suggests.

(c) *The competitive environment*
Governments influence the competitive situation of railways in two main ways. First, the way they define the objectives of the rail undertaking (and the financial support offered to secure those objectives) may significantly affect both physical productivity in producing train miles and load factors. For instance, in the Netherlands the government requires the railways to maintain high minimum frequency levels on nearly all its passenger services. This produces high utilisation of infrastructure and high labour productivity. In Sweden co-ordination between rail and bus operation enables the railways to withdraw from some local stopping service without losing the feeder traffic potential. In Italy, at the other extreme, railways are expected to maintain the existing network without any co-ordination with other modes or protection from them. Taken with the use of railway public service employment obligations this produces very low levels of labour productivity.

Second, in most countries government controls entry to, and conditions of operation in, public road transport. This normally involves capacity control on public road haulage and sometimes (as in France) control over road haulage charges. However, the effectiveness of this protection is substantially weakened if, as in most countries, entry to the own account haulage sector is unconstrained. It is doubtful whether BR have received any very effective protection from road haulage on this account.

In some respects it may even be argued that the conditions of competition have militated against BR. Safety standards and hours of work legislation have always been more tightly enforced for rail than for road transport. Moreover, whilst in total it would appear that road users do pay in taxes more than sufficient to meet the costs of provision and maintenance of the road infrastructure, the same does not appear to hold for the heaviest categories of vehicles (HMSO, 1976). Even within these categories it is the highest mileage, heaviest vehicles which are most competitive for potential rail traffic, for which taxes fall most below attributed cost.

11.5 PUBLIC POLICY

11.5.1 The nature of the public policy problems

Rail transport is importantly affected by public policy in two ways. Firstly, it is subject to those general industrial policies, such as price restraint, that affect all industries and also to those general obligations that are put on all nationalised industries. The obligation on the nationalised industries to limit price increases to 5% per annum in 1974/75, when cost inflation ran at five times that rate, meant that it was impossible to satisfy financial obligations under which they were supposedly operating. For British Rail it produced an imbalance between their prices and those of the modes predominantly in private operation (particularly road haulage) which would subsequently have to be rectified. The difficulty, in such circumstances, of knowing what part of the deficit was caused by general price control inevitably attentuated the sense of management responsibility.

Secondly, the transport sector has always been a sector subject to more detailed public policy intervention than most. This intervention originated in the control of a rail monopoly in the mid-nineteenth century; continued in the mid-twentieth century in the belief that price competition between modes with such different cost and market structures as road and rail transport would lead to waste of resources; and has now been extended on the belief that there are strong social arguments for ensuring the maintenance of some minimum network and level of public transport service.

The central problem of public policy for rail transport is to reconcile the desire to support the maintenance of those rail services that provide a public service function with the need to secure efficient co-ordination among modes. After attempting to achieve this by specific subsidy within a general framework of a competitive market the 1974 Railways Act required BR to satisfy the 'public service obligation' of maintaining services broadly at the level prevailing at the time. In return the government gives BR a global compensation payment.

11.5.2 The government as purchaser

The global compensation payment, referred to by BR as the contract price for fulfilling the obligations, is calculated initially on the basis of the Board's budget. The net requirement for compensation is equal to the estimated total cost of operating the system, less the estimated passenger and associated revenue, a contribution from the freight and parcels sector representing the avoidable costs of their use of the system and payments by the Passenger Transport Executives. The price, wage and economic parameters on which the estimates are calculated are agreed in advance with the Department of Transport and the contract price may subsequently only be varied for a limited range of specified variations in circumstance, which include subsequent government interventions affecting the costs of operation.

The nature of this contract arrangement has already been affected by the existence of cash limits. In June 1975 the Secretary of State informed Parliament that he had set the Board a short-term target of keeping the passenger support payment constant in real terms for the following year. In February 1976 this limitation was extended to apply to subsequent years. In June 1977 the White Paper on Transport Policy both tightened this constraint and made it more specific. It stated the objective of containing, and then reducing, the subsidy to revenue account for the operation of passenger services. A reduction of £20m was foreseen by the end of the decade. It was asserted that after the current year the Board should eliminate any continuing requirement for support of other rail services. The consequences of these judgements were subsequently incorporated in the Public Expenditure Estimates (HMSO, 1978).

Both in 1976 and 1977 BR were able to report that they had met the terms of this financial arrangement. But they also had to comment that the linking of the support level to an arbitrary datum could only represent a short term solution to the problem of financing social passenger services. Whilst the Board's own intention to publish financial results for each principal sector of the passenger business, and to develop methods of relating financial inputs to measures of social output and impact, might provide a basis for discussing a revised arrangement, it will not guarantee any satisfactory outcome. As it stands, the logic of the situation implies increasing use of price discrimination to achieve simultaneous satisfaction of the level of service and budget constraints. Whilst the Inter-City business traveller may be 'soft' politically for such exploitation, the London commuter, the other obvious source of increased revenue, probably is not. Hence it appears likely that government will soon have to go even further than at present and introduce specific price constraints for which specific subvention is payable in addition to the global PSO payment.

11.5.3 Government control of the transport sector

Control of entry to the road transport market and determination of the levels of vehicle and fuel taxation have traditionally been the central instruments in policy for co-ordination of public transport modes.

In *passenger transport* the provision of bus services and the fare levels at which the services are offered are controlled by the quasi-independent Traffic Commissioner. There has been some dispute on the fairness of the basis for competition between buses and rail in that BR are able, through representations to the Traffic Commissioner, to influence what bus services are provided without the bus operators having any reciprocal influence.

More recently, however, it has been through the use of discriminatory pricing policy that BR have most significantly implemented their competitive strategy. In particular they have offered attractive prices to compete for the traditional student and senior citizen bus passengers. So long as prices do not fall below escapable costs, and this leads to a more intensive utilisation of rail infrastructure, this would appear to be perfectly sensible arrangement.

The danger, however, is that the global PSO gives no inducement to consider whether rail service should be provided at all on particular routes. For some links in the public transport network one might question whether it would not be more efficient to withdraw the rail subsidy, and hence service, completely and concentrate on a serious co-ordination of bus and rail modes. In the absence of any institutional means of ensuring that such solutions are considered the onus would seem to lie on central government to appraise the costs and benefits of such alternatives and, if necessary, to force the pace on the matter. If it were to do so, of course, it would move even further away from the traditional 'arms length' relationship between government and the nationalised industries, from which it has already departed substantially.

In *freight transport*, the 1968 Transport Act effectively eliminated any control on entry. The main residual distortions in competition would appear to be twofold. Firstly, safety requirements are more rigorous and their enforcement far more effective for rail than for road. Secondly, taxation of the very heaviest and highest mileage road goods vehicle categories is not adequate to meet a proper allocation of road track costs to these vehicles. Even if an increase in these taxes did not lead to any great transfer of traffics from road to rail it would allow BR to increase its revenue from freight and ensure that its existing services did not come under further pressure.

Thus, by means of a complex set of regulations and administrative interventions, the government is centrally engaged in the attempt to reconcile the objectives of public service and economic efficiency in rail transport. In this the British problems reflect those faced in rail transport in most of the developed countries of the Western world. Only the details of the policy responses differ. British Rail, contrary to popular mythology is amongst the most commercial, the least protected and the least subsidised of Western European railways.

REFERENCES

Beesley, M. E. and Gwilliam, K. M. (September 1977) 'Transport Policy in the UK'. *Journal of Transport Economics and Policy* **XI** (3).
British Railways Board (1963) *The Reshaping of British Railways.* London: HMSO.
British Railways Board (1978) *Railway Electrification.* Discussion paper.
Edwards, S. L. and Bayliss, B. T. (1969) *Transport for Industry.* London: HMSO.
Gwilliam, K. M. and Mackie, P. J. (1975) *Economics and Transport Policy.* London: Allen and Unwin.
HMSO (1956) *Proposals for the Railways.* Cmnd 9880. London: HMSO.
HMSO (1976) *Transport Policy: A Consultative Document.* London: HMSO.
HMSO (1977) *Transport Policy.* Cmnd 6836. London: HMSO.
HMSO (1978) *Public Expenditure.* Cmnd 7049. London: HMSO.
Redfern, P. (1955) 'Net Investment in Fixed Assets in the UK'. *Journal of the Royal Statistical Society,* series A, **118** (2).
Select Committee on the Nationalised Industries (1960) *British Railways.* London: HMSO.
Select Committee on the Nationalised Industries (1977) *The Role of British Rail in Public Transport* First Report Session 1976/77. London: HMSO.
Webb, M. (1979) *Variations in the Performance of European Railway Systems: Economic Demographic and Geographic Explanations.* Unpublished MA thesis, University of Leeds.

FURTHER READING

Aldcroft, D. H. (1968) *British Railways in Transition.* London: Macmillan.
Allen, G. Freeman (1966) *British Rail after Beeching.* London: Ian Allan.
Pryke, R. and Dodgson, J. (1975) *The Rail Problem.* London: Martin Robertson.

Bonavia, M. R. (1971) *The Organisation of British Railways*. London: Ian Allan.

White, P. R. (1976) *Planning for Public Transport*. London: Hutchinson.

Joy, S. (1973) *The Train That Ran Away*. London: Ian Allan.

International Union of Railways *International railway statistics*. Paris.

12 Retailing

F. Livesey

12.1 INTRODUCTION

Retailing is a major industry. In June 1978 the number of employees in retailing in Great Britain was 1 850 000 or $8\frac{1}{2}$% of the total in all industries (*Department of Employment Gazette*, October 1978) while its share of GDP is probably around 8%.[1]

Although retail sales have risen with the overall level of economic activity, they have tended to account for a diminishing share of total consumers' expenditure and of GNP, as shown in table 12.1. This table also shows changes in the composition of retail spending. The share of consumers' expenditure accounted for by spending on food has declined, reflecting a relatively low income elasticity of demand. Declines have also occurred in the shares of clothing – also believed to have a low income elasticity of demand – and tobacco, where the link between consumption and ill health has probably affected demand. The biggest increase in the share of expenditure was achieved by alcoholic drink. A substantial increase in the share of durable goods also occurred during the first part of the period, but this increase was subsequently reversed, mainly, perhaps, because of the decline in incomes towards the end of the period.

One would expect changes in the pattern of spending to be reflected in the turnover of different kinds of retail business, and it can be seen from table 12.2 that the share of grocers and provision dealers, other food retailers, and clothing and footwear shops fell between 1961 and 1971, while that of household goods shops and other non-food retailers rose.

Unfortunately this series cannot be continued beyond 1971. The results of the retailing inquiry, which replaced the Census of Distribution from 1976, cannot be compared directly with the results of that Census.[2] However the main trends of the earlier period appear to have continued (see table 12.3).

Changes in turnover are often associated with changes in the

TABLE 12.1: Consumers' expenditure at current prices

	1966 (£ million)	(%)	1971 (£ million)	(%)	1977 (£ million)	(%)
Food	5 297	21.8	7 025	19.9	16 268	19.5
Alcoholic drink	1 626	6.7	2 593	7.3	6 539	7.8
Tobacco	1 504	6.2	1 691	4.8	3 632	4.3
Clothing	2 154	8.9	2 990	8.4	6 838	8.2
Durable goods	1 757	7.2	3 074	8.7	6 400	7.7
Other household goods	732	3.0	1 031	2.9	2 310	2.8
Books, magazines	349	1.4	526	1.5	1 212	1.5
Chemists' goods	345	1.4	581	1.6	1 425	1.7
Miscellaneous recreational goods	507	2.1	846	2.4	1 961	2.3
Other miscellaneous goods	318	1.3	455	1.3	1 166	1.4
Total retail spending	14 589	60.1	20 812	58.8	47 751	57.2
Total non-retail spending	9 477	39.1	14 610	41.3	37 097	44.1
Adjustments (e.g. tourism)	194	0.8	−52	−0.1	−1 318	−1.6
Total consumers' expenditure	24 260	100	35 370	100	83 530	100
Gross National Product	38 369		57 617		140 898	
Total retail spending as % of GNP	38.0		36.1		33.8	

Source: National Income and Expenditure, HMSO.

number of establishments. However the relationship is by no means exact. Table 12.2 reveals that the fall in the share of grocers and provision dealers was much greater in respect of the number of establishments than turnover. This is no doubt due mainly to the increase in the average size of shop, which has been much greater in groceries than in other kinds of retail business. (It can be seen that the grocers' share of the labour force declined only slightly). Conversely the increase in the share of household goods shops was greater in respect of the number of establishments than turnover (or employment).

Changes in the number of shops during this period are shown in table 12.4. Perhaps this table demonstrates even more clearly the different experiences of grocers, food retailers and confectioners, tobacconists and newsagents (CTNs) on the one hand, and non-food retailers on the other. Tables 12.2 and 12.4 also show that a substantial fall occurred in total retail outlets during this decade. At first this

TABLE 12.2:   Market shares for UK retailing by kinds of business (%)

Kind of business	1961			1971		
	Turn-over	Estab-lish-ments	Labour force	Turn-over	Estab-lish-ments	Labour force
Grocers and provision dealers	26.6	27.1	21.8	26.2	22.2	21.6
Other food retailers	19.6	21.1	20.1	17.1	19.4	17.3
Confectioners, tobacconists and newsagents	9.0	12.9	8.5	8.5	11.1	8.3
Clothing and footwear shops	15.4	16.0	15.6	14.8	16.7	15.9
Household goods shops	10.7	11.1	11.7	12.7	15.2	12.6
Other non-food retailers	8.0	11.0	9.8	10.3	14.5	11.9
General stores	10.5	1.0	12.5	10.3	1.0	12.4

Source: Census of Distribution 1961–1971, HMSO.
Note: Turnover is at current prices, and the labour force is adjusted to full-time equivalents.

reduction was mainly confined to small independent retailers. More recently the multiples have increased the rate of closure of their smaller branches, especially in groceries. In its annual survey of shopping provision the Institute of Grocery Distribution found that in the twelve months to the end of April 1976, multiple and co-operative grocers closed 1315 shops and opened only 247. Nevertheless the net result was that the total area occupied by these retailers *increased* by 800 000 sq. ft.

Retailing is on the whole a low wage industry. The *New Earnings Surveys* undertaken by the Department of Employment reveal that earnings for both men and women are substantially below the average for all industries and services and are also below those in wholesale distribution. Moreover for most categories of worker the number of hours worked is above average in retailing, so that an even bigger gap exists in hourly earnings. The low earnings are probably largely due to the fact that there are few barriers to the entry of workers into retailing – for most occupations relatively little training or experience is required in a new entrant. Moreover, retailing offers many opportunities for part-time work, especially suited to married women; this again influences the balance between demand and supply in the labour market and thus wage rates, including those of full-time workers. However, despite their low average level, wages and salaries still constitute the most important item of expense apart from the cost

TABLE 12.3: Retail trades in 1976: analysis by kind of business

Kind of business	Businesses (no.)	(%)	Outlets (no.)	(%)	Persons engaged (thousands)	(%)	Turnover (£m)	(%)	Gross margin (% of turnover)
Grocers and general food retailers	56 021	21.4	69 717	17.7	431	17.0	6 899	20.0	17.0
Other food retailers	47 947	18.3	73 824	18.8	338	13.4	4 499	13.1	22.6
Confectioners, tobacconists, newsagents	38 949	14.8	48 521	12.3	262	10.4	2 673	7.8	16.8
Clothing, footwear and textile retailers	39 355	15.0	72 786	18.5	327	12.9	3 468	10.1	38.4
Household goods retailers	39 530	15.1	60 892	15.5	315	12.5	4 816	14.0	40.1
Other non-food retailers	38 295	14.6	50 809	12.9	247	9.8	2 860	8.3	32.8
Mixed retail businesses	2 259	0.9	17 141	4.4	608	24.0	9 214	26.8	29.0
Total retail trade	262 356	100	393 690	100	2 528	100	34 429	100	27.5

Source: Retailing inquiry, 1976, *Trade and Industry*, 22 September 1978; *Business Monitor SDA 25*.

TABLE 12.4:   Number of retail outlets by kind of business (%)

	1961	1971	Percentage change
Grocers and provision dealers	151 154	108 282	–28
Other food retailers	127 304	100 806	–21
Confectioners, tobacconists, newsagents	70 662	52 751	–25
Clothing and footwear shops	96 612	93 644	– 3
Household goods shops	63 476	72 877	+15
Other non-food retailers	64 349	71 646	+11
General stores	3 750	4 775	+27
Total retail outlets	577 307	504 781	–13

Source: Census of Distribution, 1961, 1971, HMSO.

of goods purchased. For most trades wages and salaries are between 30 and 40% of gross profit (turnover minus the cost of goods purchased). This means that retailers have a strong incentive to reduce labour inputs by such means as the introduction of self service.

12.2 MARKET STRUCTURE

One of the most striking features of retailing in the post-war period has been the increase in the market share of the multiples at the expense of independent retailers and, to a lesser extent, the co-operative societies. (See table 12.5). Multiples are defined in table 12.5 as retailers owning ten or more outlets. The 1976 retailing inquiry classified these retailers as large multiples, and made a further distinction between retailers with two to nine outlets (small multiples) and

TABLE 12.5:   Share of retail sales by form of organisation (%)

	1961	1966	1971	1972	1973	1974	1975	1976
Independents	53.9	49.9	48.1	46.7	45.6	44.8	44.2	43.0
Multiples	28.2	33.0	36.4	37.4	38.4	39.1	39.6	40.1
Co-operatives	9.5	7.7	5.8	5.6	5.5	5.5	5.7	6.2
Departmental stores*	5.9	5.7	5.8	6.0	5.9	5.8	5.8	6.0
Mail order	2.5	3.7	3.9	4.3	4.5	4.8	4.7	4.7

Source: Census of Distribution 1961, 1966, 1971; Business Monitor SD series 1972–6, HMSO.
*Note: * Including co-operative department stores.

retailers with single outlets. Table 12.6 shows that the share of this last category was around only one-third in 1976. There is, however, a wide range around this average figure. At one extreme the share is 65% in CTNs, a trade in which a high proportion of sales (especially of newspapers) is made by shops serving local residential markets. At the other extreme the share is 15.7% in mixed retail businesses, a trade dominated by large multiples such as Marks and Spencer, Woolworth and British Home Stores.

TABLE 12.6: **Share of retail sales by kind of business and form of organisation, 1976** (%)

	Single outlet retailers	Small multiple retailers	Large multiple retailers*
Grocers and general food retailers	33.8	8.5	57.7
Other food retailers	42.5	18.0	39.6
Confectioners, tobacconists, newsagents	65.0	12.0	23.0
Clothing, footwear and textile retailers	29.3	22.9	47.8
Household goods retailers	35.5	20.5	44.0
Other non-food retailers	53.3	26.9	19.8
Mixed retail businesses	15.7	9.2	75.1
Total retail trade	33.9	14.9	51.2

Source: Retailing inquiry 1976, *Trade and Industry*, 22 September 1978.
Note: *Includes co-operative societies, whose share of total retail trade was 7.0%.

In recent years the greatest increase in the market share of the larger multiples has occurred in groceries, a trade in which price competition has been very marked (see below). By contrast the co-operative societies steadily lost market share between 1961 and 1973. [Since then they have enjoyed a period of stability and even a slight revival in their fortunes, although estimates indicate a further loss of market share in 1977 (Economist Intelligence Unit. *Retail Business*, May 1978)].

This loss of market share when other multiple organisations have benefited from economies of scale is, perhaps, surprising, especially in view of the fact that the co-operative movement encompasses retailing, wholesaling and manufacturing. However, the financial relationships that link these three activities have not led to an organisation which is fully integrated in trading terms. The retail societies, each of which is owned by its own customer shareholders, exercise their right to buy from sources outside the movement with the result that the potential economies of vertical integration are not fully exploited. Moreover each retail society has the right to buy independently of the other retail societies with the result that some of the potential advantages of horizontal integration – and in particular economies of supply – are lost.

The high degree of centralised control that exists in other large multiple retailers facilitates the quick adoption throughout the organisation of the best management techniques. By contrast the co-operative movement has been characterised by considerable differences in managerial ability between one society and another. While some societies have been pioneers in such developments as self-service, supermarkets, own labels and freezer centres, others have proved unwilling or unable to innovate and so have lost sales, sometimes to the extent of having to amalgamate. The number of societies operating in the UK fell from 988 in 1953 to 201 in 1979. Although this represents a considerable measure of rationalisation, there is a long way to go before the target of twenty-six regional societies, agreed at the national level in 1974, is reached.

The stability of the market share of department stores shown in table 12.5 reflects a balance of conflicting forces. On the one hand these shops provide a high level of service, which may be demanded by an increasing number of consumers as incomes rise. On the other hand this level of service is reflected in higher prices, and this makes the department stores vulnerable to competition from several sources: the specialist multiple chains selling clothing, furniture, etc., variety stores such as Marks and Spencer that have gradually upgraded their image and appeal and the superstores and hypermarkets which come increasingly close to the department store in the range of goods offered (often at lower prices and also, in some instances, at locations more convenient to the car-borne shopper).

Mail order selling steadily increased its market share until 1974, as shown in table 12.5. Perhaps the most important factor favouring the growth of mail order sales in the early part of the post-war period was the offer of extended credit at a time when most consumers found it difficult to obtain substantial credit facilities from conventional retail outlets. Another advantage of mail order is that customers are able to try out merchandise in the privacy of their own homes and outside conventional shopping hours, an advantage which assumes greater significance with the increase in the number of working wives and increasing traffic congestion in town centres.

Although table 12.5 does not necessarily indicate that the growth in the market share of mail order has come to an end and indeed further growth in 1977 is indicated by some estimates (Economist Intelligence Unit, *Retail Business*, August 1978), this must, of course occur eventually. This may happen either because the mail order companies have reached all the consumers who are attracted by their particular competitive mix or, alternatively, because they are unable to increase the number of agents.

The small retailers have tried to combat the competition from the multiples either by reducing their costs and so trying to narrow the gap in prices – or at least prevent the gap increasing – or by means of non-price competition, especially for instance by offering the consumer greater convenience. An institution which has played an important role here is the voluntary group. Retailer-sponsored voluntary groups are formed mainly in order to centralise buying activities and thus to obtain better terms from suppliers. Centralised buying is also an important feature of wholesaler-sponsored groups. In addition these groups provide (via the central offices and/or the wholesalers), assistance and advice with respect to advertising and promotions, site location, shopfitting, stock control, etc. Voluntary groups are most prominent in groceries and during the period 1961–76, while the market share of the non-group independents fell from 40 to 16%, that of retailers affiliated to groups grew from 13 to 21%. This growth was due partly to an increase in the number of shops affiliated to the groups and partly to an increase in turnover per shop.

In recent years many grocery retailers have begun to stock an increasing proportion of non-food items. One factor encouraging this diversification may be the relatively low income elasticity of demand for foodstuffs. Another may be the low gross margins (see table 12.3). However there are several reasons for thinking that these may not be the most important factors. First, several major retailers, such as Marks and Spencer and Woolworth, have moved *into* food retailing. Second, few of the major grocery retailers have attempted to move into non-foods by making major acquisitions. (One of the exceptions is Associated Dairies which in 1978 took over Wades and Allied Retailers, operators of chains of furniture and carpet stores. But even this might have been due at least partly to the fact that government controls on dividends, combined with a substantial cash flow from its supermarket business, had left Asda with liquid assets of around £25m). Third, there are positive advantages in stocking a wide range of products, in terms of attracting consumers who wish to make a large number of purchases in one shopping trip. The number of such consumers tends to increase as real incomes and car-ownership increase.

Many other examples of diversification are to be found including Boots, whose traditional chemists goods account for a much smaller proportion of sales than previously (a proportion that would have been further reduced had the proposed merger with the House of Fraser succeeded), and Burtons who sought to counteract the fall in their traditional menswear business by taking over a chain of shops selling office equipment.

However, the age of the specialist retailer is by no means dead. Indeed some of the more spectacular successes in post-war retailing have been achieved by specialists. A good example is Mothercare, the chain of shops that stocks articles for babies, young children and mothers. Mothercare's first shop opened in 1961, and by the end of 1977 the company operated 315 shops in ten countries, together with a substantial mail order operation.

There has been a considerable debate as to how retailing might be most appropriately classified in terms of the traditional market forms (Tucker and Yamey, 1973, part 2). It is agreed that neither perfect competition nor monopoly would be an appropriate classification (although local monopolies may be found) and therefore the debate has centred on the choice between oligopoly and monopolistic competition.

If a structural approach were adopted the decision would depend upon whether the market was supplied by a few or many retailers. This approach is particularly unsatisfactory when applied to retailing because of the problems of defining the market – in terms of both the geographical area and the kind of retail business – and hence the number of suppliers.

A somewhat different approach is to examine alternative market forms in terms not of their initial structural conditions but of their alleged consequences. George (1974, page 176) stresses the existence in retailing of excess capacity, a characteristic of monopolistic competition. However, there is nothing in economic theory to suggest that excess capacity cannot exist in oligopolistic (or, of course, monopolistic) markets. Moreover much of the excess capacity that exists at certain times may be due to the substantial fluctuations in demand that occur in retailing. If peak demands are to be met it is inevitable that excess capacity will exist at other times.

Yet another approach is to consider whether the *behaviour* of firms is consistent with that assumed in the various models. In this context a distinguishing feature of oligopoly is said to be that in his decisions each supplier takes into account the possible reactions of his competitors; this is advanced as an explanation of why prices are 'sticky' and why the price structure (the relationship between the prices of competing products) tends to be stable. Retailing is frequently characterised by unstable price structures for individual products. But we cannot conclude from this that retailers do not take the reactions of competitors into account. It is common practice to reduce the prices of products whose prices are *not* reduced by competitors, in order to differentiate one's offer to the consumer. The price war in grocery retailing sparked off by Tesco in 1977 (and discussed in more detail below) suggests that the main suppliers do react to each other's policies, and this would again be thought of as being characteristic of oligopoly.

However, although the decisions of retailers are consistent with the assumptions of oligopoly models, there is, perhaps, little to be gained by applying this particular label in preference to others. As we shall see in the following sections, the traditional models that are applied to manufacturing industry are of only limited assistance in explaining behaviour or performance in retailing.

12.3 MARKET BEHAVIOUR

In this section we adopt the usual distinction made in economic analysis between price and non-price competition. Moreover we make the usual assumption that price competition requires the firm to choose between alternative price–output combinations (i.e. the demand curve is taken as given), while non-price competition is designed to alter the position and/or the slope of the curve. However, the concept of the retailer's demand curve is by no means straightforward.

12.3.1 Price competition

Retailers' pricing decisions are usually made on the assumption that some (and often most) consumers who enter a shop purchase more than one item. If such multiple purchases form any part of a retailer's trade we cannot in principle analyse that retailer's operations in terms of a series of demand curves for individual products. If a retailer stocks a range of products A, B, . . ., n, the demand for A will be influenced by the number of products which comprise the set B, . . . ,n, and by the characteristics, including the price, of each of these products.[3] It is, in fact, more helpful to an understanding of competition in retailing to think of the demand for the overall output of the retailer, for the totality of his products, although even here there are very strict limits to the usefulness of the concept of the demand curve.

If the demand curve relates to all the retailers' products, price must be interpreted as an average for all the products. It would be easiest to calculate an average price where all the products were measured in the same units, e.g. kilos. This would also enable us to calculate a total volume of sales (per period) at that price, and thus to identify a point on the demand curve.

However even in this situation we could not go on to derive a unique demand curve for that retailer. There would be various combinations of price changes that would enable the retailer to change his average price level by, say, 2%, but the change in the volume of sales would probably differ from one combination to another. This is illustrated in fig. 12.1 where the initial price and quantity are P_1 and Q, and a reduction in the average price to P_2 would result in an increase in the volume of sales to N in one instance and to M in another.

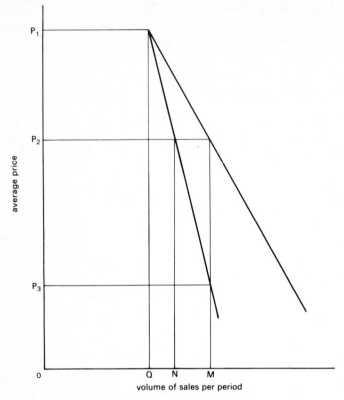

FIG. 12.1: Demand with alternative pricing strategies

Although our inability to derive a unique demand curve prevents us from following the usual line of analysis, it helps us to explain the nature of price competition in retailing. The pricing policies of retailers can be explained in terms of a search for the *most efficient* form of price competition. If the firm has decided to reduce its prices and if, for the moment, we assume that marginal cost is identical for all products, it will be concerned to obtain the greatest increase in sales volume for a given price reduction. In terms of fig. 12.1, when it reduces price from P_1 to P_2 it will hope to expand sales to M rather than N. Putting the matter the other way round, if the firm wishes to increase sales volume by a given amount, say from Q to M, the more efficient policy is that which requires the smaller reduction in average price – to P_2 rather than P_3.

We can make a broad distinction between two basic alternative strategies that have been adopted by retailers in the search for the most efficient policy: selective and across-the-board price reductions. A policy of selective price reductions involves large reductions – usually with respect to both the retailer's own normal price and the price currently being charged by competitors – on a small number of products. A supermarket stocking several thousand lines would typically reduce the price of less than a hundred.

The basic justification for this policy is that the consumer is able to remember the prices of only a limited number of products, so that there is no point in reducing the prices of a large number. By making a (limited) number of large reductions the retailer seeks to create a low-price image and thus attract more shoppers (Nystrom, 1970). He will reduce the price of those items which he believes have a high cross elasticity of demand, or 'transfer effect' to use the term adopted by Holdren (1960). (The transfer effect refers to the change in the *value* of sales of other products following a reduction in the price of one product).

Items are most likely to have a high transfer effect if their price is high enough to permit a reduction that is easily perceptible, if they account for an appreciable proportion of consumers' expenditure, and if they have been so heavily advertised as to make consumers highly price conscious. A much lower transfer effect is likely to be attached to products whose price is seen by consumers as an indicator of quality or whose price is subject to frequent fluctuations so that there is no well established market price.

Another important factor influencing the selection of products for price reductions is the offer of special terms by the manufacturer, including an allowance towards the cost of advertising the price reduction. (When selective reductions are advertised, the policy is known as promotional pricing).

The alternative policy which might be adopted by the retailer who wishes to make pricing an important part of his competitive strategy is to reduce the margins on all his products in an attempt to price below his competitors 'across-the-board'. The prices that are set will not, of course, be lower on those items selected for large reductions by competitors following the alternative strategy. But it is hoped that an across-the-board policy will also create a favourable price image and so attract consumers.

The operation of these two alternative strategies has been witnessed most clearly in grocery retailing. In the 1950s and 1960s the major gains in market share were made by retailers who adopted a policy of selective price reductions, e.g. Tesco and Fine Fare. However, in the 1970s the pendulum began to swing. Firms such as Asda and Kwik Save, operating on the basis of modest reductions across the board, grew very rapidly. At first this growth was largely at the expense of smaller independent grocers who were unable to compete on price. However from about 1973 or 1974 they also began to eat into the market share of some of the major multiples, including the market leader, Tesco (see table 12.7).

TABLE 12.7: Leading multiples' estimated share of total grocery market, Great Britain (%)

	1970/71	1973/74	1976/77	16 September 1978
Tesco	7.2	8.6	8.3	12.4
Sainsbury	6.1	7.0	7.7	10.6
Allied Suppliers	7.9	7.0	5.7	5.1
Fine Fare	4.8	4.2	4.0	4.3
International	3.2	3.0	3.7	4.5
Asda	1.5	2.5	4.7	6.3
Kwik Save	0.3	0.6	1.4	4.0
Total	31.0	32.9	35.5	47.2

Source: Audits of Great Britain Ltd.

It seems that, in addition to the lower overall prices charged by Asda and Kwik Save, two other factors might have led to this swing of the pendulum. First, more information was provided to consumers about the average price levels of different retailers. This information consisted partly of advertising by retailers, and partly of reports by such institutions as the Consumers' Association. Second, the first half of the 1970s was characterised by an increase in the rate of inflation, which might have reduced consumers' awareness of 'normal' prices and hence dampened the impact of selective price reductions. Eventually the success achieved by retailers who reduced prices across the board caused their competitors to modify their policy of selective reductions in several ways. First, some of these competitors reduced prices across-the-board in a proportion of their outlets. For example Fine Fare converted some of their small shops into discount stores under the name Shoppers Paradise. These stores stock fewer than four hundred lines, compared with the two to three thousand stocked by the normal Fine Fare supermarket. They also have very simple fittings and virtually no choice of brands. However in compensation their prices are about 10% lower. Allied Suppliers announced plans to increase the number of Presto discount stores from 45 in 1976 to 140 in 1981, either by building new stores or by converting existing ones.

The Presto stores operate on a gross margin of about 14%, compared with 20% in Allied's conventional outlets.

Second, pricing policies were modified in the remaining outlets, which constituted the majority. The number of products whose prices were reduced was extended. Tesco, the first major retailer to change its policy, did so at the time they abandoned Green Shield trading stamps, and they were able to reduce their overall price level. This move by Tesco led to a further intensification of price competition. It appeared that Sainsbury might be especially vulnerable to this competition. They had previously reduced the price of about twenty products at any one time, but had not promoted these very heavily, preferring to rely more on their reputation for good general value. In order to combat the increased competition Sainsbury put *more* emphasis on selective price reductions. In 1978 they introduced a 'Discount 78' programme, under which they reduced the price of around one hundred big selling lines by about 10%.

The success of these new policies in reversing the fall in the market share of the selective price cutters can be seen from table 12.7. However it will be noticed that the share of the across-the-board pricers has continued to rise, the losses in market share having been suffered by retailers not represented in this table, and especially the small independents.

As a consequence of these and other changes, the distinction between firms adopting the two alternative strategies is now less clear in practice than it was at the beginning of the 1970s. This is especially true if one takes account of the fact that a retailer may adopt entirely different policies in different outlets. Nevertheless it is useful to retain the distinction as an expository device.

In many other retail trades the transfer effect is lower than in groceries, and consequently selective price reductions have been less common. Price competition has more often taken the form of across-the-board reductions. Numerous reports from bodies such as the Prices and Incomes Board, the Price Commission and the Consumers' Association have revealed a substantial range in the prices of given brands of television sets, refrigerators, paint, wallpaper, etc. For example the Consumers' Association (*Which?* January 1978) found that the range of prices of colour televisions was frequently over 20%. The prices of consumer durables are usually lowest in multiple retailers such as Comet and Currys, and highest in specialist independent shops and department stores. (These differences are due partly to the buying economies enjoyed by the multiples, and partly to the fact that they are willing to accept lower gross margins).

In some retail trades a substantial proportion of products are sold under the retailer's own label. Own labels are frequently cheaper than the corresponding manufacturers' brands, and they may play an important role in a retailer's pricing strategy. Retailers are able to set lower prices for own labels because they themselves buy at lower prices from manufacturers. These lower purchase prices may reflect the fact that manufacturers are willing to accept lower margins in order to obtain a guaranteed (or at least a more secure) outlet, and/or the fact that an own label contract enables the manufacturer to operate with lower costs; savings may be made in selling costs (including advertising), packaging and, perhaps, in raw material costs. It appears that the cost savings to retailers are such that even though they resell at lower prices they often earn higher margins than on comparable manufacturer brands. (See table 12.8). (Note that if the manufacturer's margin had been assumed to be lower on own labels, as frequently occurs, there would have been further scope for a higher retailer's margin and/or a lower price to the consumer).

TABLE 12.8:   Own label and manufacturer brand prices for typical grocery product

	Own label	Manufacturer brand
Manufacturer's cost	100	112
Manufacturer's margin (%)	15	15
Price to retailer index	115	129
Retailer's margin (%)	25	20
Price to consumer index	144	155

Source: Economist Intelligence Unit, *Own Labels*, 1975.

12.3.2 Non-price competition

This can take many forms, but a common characteristic is that they all tend to increase the firm's average cost at any given level of output. Another characteristic is that, by comparison with price competition, non-price competition is often more dificult to match (i.e. by competitors) exactly and quickly. It is therefore analogous to the activities adopted by manufacturers in the attempt to differentiate their products from those of competitors. We examine in turn each of the main forms of non-price competition, beginning with service.

Service has numerous aspects, several of which relate to the retailer's staffing policy. Assuming a given size of shop and range of goods stocked, the more staff are employed the less time each customer has to spend on searching for goods, waiting to be served or waiting to pay. The technical expertise of staff may also be important; staff can advise on such matters as the freedom from distortion of radio sets, the probable durability of carpets, the best way to clean different kinds of clothes, etc (Woodside and Davenport, 1976). Finally, the attitude of staff may, of course, have an important influence on the decisions of consumers as to which shop to patronise.

The rising cost of transporting goods has led to a fall in the number of firms offering a delivery service, especially for low-price items such as groceries. However delivery remains important for bulky items such as furniture and other consumer durables. Some firms, e.g. many department stores, provide a free delivery service while others, usually those retailers who offer the lowest basic price, charge. Making a delivery charge enables retailers to discriminate between those consumers who need the service and those who do not.

Credit is an aspect of service that has received increasing attention. At one time credit was offered to all customers only by the mail order houses, but now credit is available from a wide variety of sources, including the credit cards issued by the major banks and by individual retailers such as Marks and Spencer, Woolworth, Tesco and Fine Fare. The existence of so many sources of credit makes it impossible to measure precisely changes in the importance of credit. However it seems likely that credit-financed sales have accounted for an increasing share of total sales in recent years.

After-sales service has different aspects whose relative importance depends upon the type of business and product. Purchasers of such products as television sets and washing machines are interested in the speed and reliability of the retailer's maintenance and repair service, especially when facilities are not provided by the manufacturer (Livesey, 1971–2). Some of the multiple retailers who made early gains in these markets on the basis of very low prices, subsequently introduced added maintenance facilities as part of the 'package' offered to consumers. For other products a more important aspect of after-sales service may be the opportunity for the consumer to have her money refunded should the product prove to be unsuitable, e.g. clothing that does not fit.

We have already mentioned trading stamps and they can be considered either as a form of price competition or as part of the package of services offered by the retailer. (The dividend stamps issued by the co-operative societies are probably best seen as a deferred price reduction; the societies insist that dividend stamps should be differentiated from trading stamps.) Retailers giving stamps have to recoup the cost either by charging higher prices or by increasing their sales volume (or by reducing other costs, such as advertising expenditure). The required increase in sales is most likely to be achieved in the earlier years of the stamps' history when fewer competitors give stamps. As the market matures, gains in sales volume become more difficult to attain. Moreover the retailer may become vulnerable to price competition offered by lower cost rivals, a danger that influenced Tesco's decision to drop Green Shield stamps.[4]

The second major form of non-price competition is *stock assortment*, the first aspect of which is the number and type of commodity groups stocked. By increasing the number and type of commodities stocked, retailers obviously hope to gain revenue from the sale of the additional commodity groups. Moreover the sales of their existing products are also likely to increase as additional customers are attracted by the prospect of being able to find an increasing proportion of their requirements under one roof. The second aspect is the volume of stock held for any given range of goods. The retailer has to balance the extra costs of high stockholding against the loss of potential revenue and of goodwill that he may suffer if he cannot meet his customers' requirements. The final aspect of stock assortment is the quality of the goods sold. This can obviously be an important competitive weapon and may be of overriding importance in some instances, e.g. sales to consumers in the highest income groups.

Expenditure on *furniture and fittings* is especially important in department stores, which often seek to make a strong appeal to consumers in the higher income groups. This expenditure may be intended to add to the convenience of shopping, to create a pleasant atmosphere or to enable the goods to be presented in a striking manner.

Location is undoubtedly an important determinant of store patronage as has been shown by studies at both the micro (e.g. the effects of pedestrian traffic flows within a shopping centre) and the macro level (e.g. city centre versus suburban and rural locations).

For many years retailers spent less money on *advertising* than manufacturers, being content in the main to use low-cost media such as window-stickers, hoardings and local newspapers. More recently the advertising expenditure of retailers has risen dramatically. The Economist Intelligence Unit estimated that expenditure by retail shops on press and television advertising increased from £17.5m in 1971 to £115m in 1978 (*Retail Business*, April 1979); in 1978 Marketing and Economic Research Ltd. found that the largest ten spenders on press and television advertising were all retailers (*Financial Times*, 1 February 1979).

Advertising is sometimes designed to draw attention to a particular aspect of the retailer's policy. For example when Tesco abandoned trading stamps and reduced its prices, it spent a considerable amount of money drawing the attention of consumers to this fact; its advertising expenditure was estimated by the EIU to have increased from £1.6m in 1976 to £3.2m in 1977. Marks and Spencer advertise mainly in order to draw attention to new store openings and the introduction of new products. (Incidentally their total advertising expenditure at below £1m, is less than 0.1% of sales revenue, indicating that heavy advertising is not essential to success in retailing). Other retailers, such as Fine Fare in groceries, and many department stores, adopt a more general approach in their advertising, with the aim of creating a favourable overall image in the mind of the consumer.

The effect of non-price competition is illustrated in fig. 12.2 in which AC_1 and D_1 denote the initial average cost and demand curves, and P_1 the initial price level. An increase in non-price competition causes an increase in both average cost (AC_2) and demand (D_2). The firm might choose to maintain price P_1 and increase sales from M to N. Alternatively it might choose to maintain its existing volume of sales, M, at the higher price, P_2. (Or it might, of course, choose another alternative). The first reaction would be typified by the grocery multiples who spend heavily on advertising, the second by the

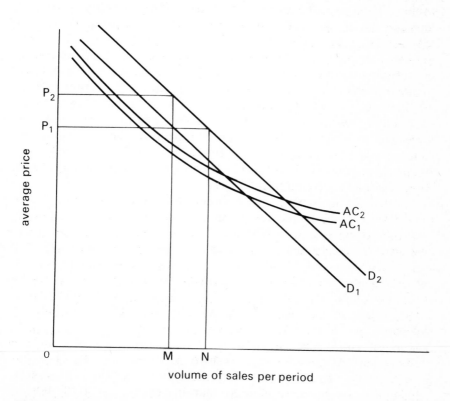

FIG. 12.2:   **Non-price competition and demand**

department stores who spend heavily on furniture, fittings and a high level of personal service.[5]

12.4 MARKET PERFORMANCE

In this section we consider several alternative indicators of market performance, although none of them can be applied entirely satisfactorily to retailing. We begin with productivity.

In order to identify changes in productivity or efficiency, we require measures of inputs and outputs. Some writers have used a volume index, such as retail sales at constant prices, as a measure of output (see, for example, Ward, 1973). A volume index is a satisfactory measure only if the retailer is seen as selling goods rather than a 'bundle' of goods and services. We would, however, reject such a view because – as we showed in the previous section – retailers provide a wide variety of services to which many consumers attach positive values. Unfortunately the value of sales, although sometimes used, is also an unsatisfactory index, especially when retail prices are rising rapidly. Difficulties of measurement also exist in relation to inputs, particularly, of course, if one attempts to construct an index of total input. Ward used the number of persons engaged as his input index, arguing that previous studies had tended to show that movements in output per person engaged give a fairly good indication of variations in overall factor productivity. Ward found that for the period 1954 to 1970 labour productivity in retailing increased at much the same rate as in manufacturing, and at a faster rate between 1965 and 1970. The acceleration in the latter period might have been due to a combination of factors including the imposition of Selective Employment Tax, the progressive abolition of resale price maintenance and some deterioration in retail service.

An analysis of Census of Distribution data reveals that during the period 1961 to 1971 the average annual growth in the ratio of turnover (at current prices) to labour was 6.14 for multiples, 5.46 for co-operative societies and 4.58 for independents. The average growth for different trades ranged from 6.17 for household goods shops to 1.87 for CTNs. Despite the deficiencies of the data it is clear that there were substantial differences in the rate of change in productivity as between different forms of organisation and different kinds of business.

The same problems arise in the use of gross margins as an indicator of efficiency. After reviewing Census of Distribution data, Hall and Knapp (1955) concluded that 'It is clear from this that the Census information on percentage gross margins cannot, in itself, tell us anything conclusive about the comparative efficiency of firms even when the data refer to a single trade defined in a fairly narrow way.'

Market performance is often evaluated in terms of the rate of return on capital employed. The results of an analysis of the accounts of large public companies, undertaken by the Department of Industry, showed that the rates of return of large companies have been consistently higher in retailing than in manufacturing, even when due account is taken of the data limitations (*Trade and Industry*, 22 September 1978).

This could be taken to indicate that the large retailers had taken advantage of their dominant market position to earn unduly high profits. On the other hand many commentators have suggested that after providing for stock appreciation, and valuing capital at replacement costs, profits have been too low in manufacturing. Moreover the higher rates of return earned by the large retailers can be seen as an indication that they have succeeded in meeting consumers' needs. This conclusion would, of course, be consistent with their increase in market share discussed above.

An alternative approach to market performance is via an examination of firms' operating procedures, and especially the extent to which they take advantage of economies of scale. However measurement problems again arise, relating for example to the definition of output, the fact that some retailers provide a higher level of service than others and so incur a higher proportion of the total costs involved in shopping (the remaining costs being incurred by the consumer) and the difficulty of holding non-scale factors constant (Tucker, 1973). The difficulties of precisely measuring economies of scale would alone make it impossible to decide how near to the ideal is the existing size distribution of shops or firms. Additional problems arise when changes in the size of shop involve changes in location, and thus in the pattern of shopping provision (see below).

12.5 PUBLIC POLICY

The decisions and policies of retailers are constrained by numerous aspects of public policy. Location decisions are subject to the approval of the planning authorities. Applications for planning permission have to be made in the first instance to District Authorities, but the Secretary of State has the power to call in for investigation any application which in his opinion warrants special consideration. In practice, many of the applications called in for investigation have been for very large stores, and two special development control policy notes have been issued in respect of these.[6]

On the whole the authorities have tended to adopt a restrictive attitude towards planning applications for very large shops, especially for rural or semi-rural locations. Until the end of 1976 the Department of the Environment asked to see all applications for stores with selling areas in excess of 50 000 sq. ft and twenty-two out of twenty-eight investigations resulted in a refusal of planning permission. Since the 1977 development policy note was issued, restrictions have been eased slightly and the Department of the Environment now only calls in automatically applications for more than 100 000 sq. ft of selling area. The policy note also stated that 'retailing developments which extend choice in shopping, allow more efficient retailing, enable a better service to be given to the public as a whole, and make shopping more convenient and pleasant are, in general, to be welcomed'. Moreover, an annex to the policy note concluded that 'research currently available suggests that the larger food stores offer significantly lower prices than other retail outlets for some food products as well as convenient shopping facilities; . . . the lower prices charged by the larger food stores spring from relatively lower cost levels that can be expected to continue in the future'.

Given the change in central government procedures and the tone of this policy note, many retailers expressed the belief that planning permission would be easier to obtain in the future. However the attitudes of many local planning authorities appear to have remained as rigid as before, reflecting a belief that the advantages of large shops may be outweighed by their disadvantages. If the competition from new, larger shops in out-of-town locations leads to the decline of existing town centre shopping centres, the revenue of some local authorities may fall. In addition, shopping will become less convenient for people without cars, who are often the poorer, older members of the community. (These people also tend to suffer most from the closure of local 'corner' shops).

In recent years governments have introduced a substantial body of legislation designed to protect the consumer, and this has increased the obligations laid on retailers (and also on manufacturers). Under the Sale of Goods Act 1893, as amended by the Supply of Goods (Implied Terms) Act 1973, consumers are entitled to buy goods which correspond to their description, are of merchantable quality and are fit for the purpose for which they are bought. Under the 1973 Act these rights apply regardless of whether the goods are bought for cash, by hire purchase or by conditional sale agreements. Moreover consumers can no longer lose as a consequence of signing away, or of notices exhibited in a shop or on the back of the receipt, the rights they have under the 1893 Act. The Trade Descriptions Act 1968 made it an offence to give false descriptions of goods orally, in writing or in advertisements. The Act also bans false indications about the price of goods; for instance where a retailer claims a price reduction, he must have charged the old price for at least twenty-eight days in the previous six months. Under the Consumer Credit Act 1974 it is a criminal offence to carry on a credit or hire business without a licence; this condition is aimed at protecting consumers from unscrupulous traders. Consumers must also be provided with more information than previously, including details of both the total charge for credit and the annual percentage rate of charge. Other protection for consumers includes a cooling-off period to allow for a change of mind when a credit agreement is signed at home, and the right to be given the name of any credit reference agency consulted about their credit-worthiness.

The Fair Trading Act 1973 provided for the establishment of the Office of Fair Trading under the guidance of the Director General of Fair Trading. The Director General is charged with safeguarding consumers' interests. He can investigate both general consumer trade practices and the activities of individual traders. Where a practice is thought to be unfair, for example because it misleads or puts undue pressure on consumers, it can be referred to the Consumer Protection Advisory Committee with recommendations for government action. The Director General is also responsible for screening all proposed mergers and for recommending references to the Monopolies and Mergers Commission where there is a possibility that a merger will operate against the public interest. A reference can be made where the assets acquired exceed £5m, or where a monopoly (defined as a situation where one firm controls at least 25% of the market) would result. Only six proposed mergers involving substantial retailing interests have been referred to the Commission. Perhaps the main reason for the relatively low reference rate is the fact that few retailers would meet the market-share criterion.

The introduction of so much legislation in recent years has meant that the interests of consumers are now better protected in many respects. However this has also entailed an increase in costs on the part of both the authorities and retailers. Eventually, of course, at least part of these costs is likely to be borne by individuals, in the form of higher taxes and prices.

NOTES TO CHAPTER 12

1. The *National Income Blue Book* shows that in 1977 the distributive trades as a whole accounted for 10.3% of GDP.
2. The basis of the retailing inquiry is outlined in *Trade and Industry*, 3 February 1978.
3. This elementary point has been ignored in much of the previous literature. See, for example, Clemens (1951) and Holton (1957).
4. For an assessment of the economics of trading stamps during an earlier period see Pickering (1973–4).

5. This model is, of course, highly simplified. The assumptions underlying models of this type are discussed at length in Livesey (1979).

6. Department of the Environment, Development Control Policy Notes: *Out of Town Shops and Shopping Centres*, 1972, and *Large New Stores*, 1977.

REFERENCES

Clemens, E. W. (1951) 'Price Discrimination and the Many Product Firm'. *Review of Economic Studies* **xix**, 1–12.

George, K. D. (1974) *Industrial Organisation*. 2nd edn. London: Allen and Unwin.

Hall, M. and Knapp, J. (1955) 'Gross Margins and Efficiency Measurement in Retail Trade'. *Oxford Economic papers* (New Series) **7** (3), 312–326.

Holdren, B. (1960) *The Structure of a Retail Market and the Market Behaviour of Retail Units*. Ames, Iowa: Iowa University Press.

Holton, R. H. (1957) 'Price Discrimination at Retail: the Supermarket case'. *Journal of Industrial Economics* **vi** (1), 13–32.

Livesey, F. (1971–2) 'The Marketing Mix and Buyer Behaviour in the Television Rental Market'. *European Journal of Marketing*.

Livesey, F. (1979) *The Distributive Trades*. London: Heinemann Educational.

Nystrom, H. (1970) *Retail Pricing: an integrated economic and psychological approach*. Stockholm: Swedish Institute of Economic Research.

Pickering, J. F. (1973–4) 'Trading Stamps and Retail Prices'. *European Journal of Marketing*.

Tucker, K. A. (1973) *Economies of Scale in Retailing*. London: Saxon House.

Tucker, K. A. and Yamey, B. S. *eds.* (1973) *Economics of Retailing*. Harmondsworth: Penguin.

Ward, T. S. (1973) *The Distribution of Consumer Goods: Structure and Performance*. London: Cambridge University Press.

Woodside, A. G. and Davenport, J. W. (January 1976) 'Effects of Price and Salesman Expertise on Customer Purchasing Behaviour'. *Journal of Business*.

FURTHER READING

Dalrymple, D. J. and Thomson, D. L. (1969) *Retailing: an economic view*. London: Collier–Macmillan.

Distributive Trades EDC (1976) *The Measurement of Labour Efficiency in Retail Stores*. London: HMSO.

Holdren, B. (1960) *The Structure of a Retail Market and the Market Behaviour of Retail Units*. Ames, Iowa: Iowa University Press.

Robinson, O. and Wallace, J. (1976) *Pay and Employment in Retailing*. London: Saxon House.

Thorpe, D, ed. (1974) *Research into Retailing and Distribution*. London: Saxon House.

Tucker, K. A. (1973) *Economies of Scale in Retailing*. London: Saxon House.

Tucker, K. A. and Yamey, B. S. *eds.* (1973) *Economics of Retailing*. Harmondsworth: Penguin.

Ward, T. S. (1973) *The Distribution of Consumer Goods: Structure and Performance*. London: Cambridge University Press.

Some basic statistical sources are

Business Monitor SD series. London: HMSO.

Gower Publications *Retail Trade Developments in Great Britain*. London: Gower Press.

Nielsen Researcher. Headington, Oxford: A. C. Nielsen Co. Ltd.

Results of the Retailing Inquiry. London: HMSO.

Retail Business. London: Economist Intelligence Unit.

13: Insurance   304-29

R. L. Carter

13.1 INTRODUCTION

The insurance industry traces its origins back to various crude forms of risk sharing practised amongst merchants of the ancient world and the burial clubs of Rome. Today it plays an important role in the economy of every country. Essentially insurance is a mechanism for sharing (or spreading) risks, but in doing so insurance companies acquire secondary, though important, functions in relation to savings and investment.

Uncertainty is an inescapable feature of life. Firms face the uncertainties of future supply and demand conditions and other entrepreneurial risks which may lead to large profits or losses. Equally firms and individuals are exposed to other uncertain events which cause only loss; obvious examples are accidents in the home, at work or on the road, fires, floods and disease. Insurance is designed to deal with this latter class of so-called 'pure' risks through the pooling of individual risks. Each insured (or policyholder) pays into a fund administered by the insurer a premium related to the expected value of the losses he may incur during the ensuing period of insurance due to the occurrence of any event specified in the policy. In return the insurer undertakes to pay in whole or part any such loss suffered by the policyholder. This process was explained in the preamble to the first Act to regulate insurance business in Britain, as follows:

> ... by means of which policies of assurance it cometh to pass on the perishing of any ship, there followeth not the undoing of any man, but the loss lighteth rather easily upon many than heavily upon few ... [1]

A broad distinction can be drawn between short-term and long-term insurance business. The latter consists mainly of life insurance where the insurer spreads the risk over time in that the policyholder enters into a contract which undertakes to pay either a certain sum upon the death of the life assured (life assurance)[2] or an annuity during his life-time. Although the mortality risk increases with age, a life policy-holder is normally charged a level annual premium: in the early years of the contract the premiums exceed the expected value of the risk transferred so that the insurer builds up a fund which, with accumulated investment earnings, will be sufficient to cover the premium short-fall in later years. (Clayton and Osborn, 1965).

Non-life insurances typically are for periods of only one year (hence the label short-term) but even then the insurer accumulates a pool of premiums from which to pay losses. Moreover, for some classes of non-life insurance several years may elapse between the receipt of premiums for any block of business and the final claims payment.

Consequently, insurance companies accumulate substantial funds representing their liabilities to policyholders. Life funds are further boosted by the writing of endowment and other contracts with a large savings element in addition to the protection afforded against early death. The life offices, therefore, are important financial institutions.

Theoretically, only risks that an insurer can measure objectively, that give rise to losses capable of monetary valuation and that are fortuitous so far as the policyholder is concerned, are suitable for insurance. However, few risks fully measure up to such conditions, and insurers are constantly extending the classes of insurance they offer.

The aleatory nature of insurance contracts makes them different from most commodities. At the time of purchase, the consumer receives in exchange for the premium only a promise by the insurer to pay a certain or determinable sum if some chance event occurs. Unlike gambling contracts, however, the law requires a policyholder to have an insurable interest in the subject-matter of the contract, i.e. he must stand to suffer financial loss if the insured event does occur. Also, apart from contracts on human life, the policyholder is only entitled to an indemnity for any loss he incurs. Although it is illegal for a policy-holder to seek to profit from an insured loss, the problem of moral hazard remains. Few policyholders may deliberately try to bring about an insured loss, but carelessness and the inflating of losses are problems that insurers seek to control by surveys, policy conditions and the investigation of claims.

The value of an insurance contract depends entirely upon the insurer possessing sufficient funds to pay all claims arising on policies it has written. Therefore governments take a special interest in the solvency of insurers.

Before anyone can consider buying insurance he must first know about the nature and severity of the risk to which he is exposed. He then has the choice of accepting the uncertain cost of possible losses, or of paying a fixed premium. Generally, the larger the possible loss the more likely he is to prefer insurance.

13.1.1 The British insurance industry

Insurance business typically is domestic in character; that is, it consists mainly of locally incorporated insurers handling the insurance of local residents. However, since the early nineteenth century British insurers have conducted their business on an international scale. Besides their domestic operations all the major British companies operate abroad through local agents, branch offices, subsidiary and associated companies and large volumes of overseas insurances and reinsurances are underwritten in London.

Lack of adequate statistics prevents a detailed description of the development of the industry. Separate premium income figures for UK and foreign non-life business have been published only since 1969, and all premium income figures are net of reinsurance transactions.[3] The figures in table 13.1 therefore cover the world-wide premiums of British companies and Lloyd's for insurances and reinsurances accepted, less premiums for reinsurances ceded.

TABLE 13.1:   World-wide net premium income of British insurers, including Lloyd's

	1948		1958		1968		1977	
	(£m)	(% of total)	(£m)	(% of total)	(£m)	(% of total)	(£m)	(% of total)
Ordinary life and annuities	173.0	23.1	438.3	25.4	1224.8	30.9	4067	31.5
Industrial life	123.4	16.4	177.9	10.3	276.8	7.0	513	4.0
Total life	296.4	39.5	616.2	35.7	1501.6	37.9	4580	35.5
Marine and Aviation	118.2	15.8	203.4	11.8	499.0	12.6	1402	10.8
Other non-life	335.2	44.7	907.3	52.5	1958.9	49.5	6929	53.7
Total non-life	453.4	60.5	1110.7	64.3	2457.9	62.1	8331	64.5

Sources: 1948–1968: *Annual Abstract of Statistics;* 1977: *Policy Holder Insurance Journal* **96** (49), 1978.
Note: Industrial life premiums include the Collecting Societies.

A significant part of the growth of premium income over the twenty-nine years covered by table 13.1 is attributable to the combined effects of inflation and the fall in sterling's foreign exchange value.

TABLE 13.2: World-wide premium income of British insurers as percentage of GNP (at factor cost)

	1948 (%)	1958 (%)	1968 (%)	1977 (%)
Life	2.84	3.06	3.98	3.70
Non-life	4.34	5.52	6.51	6.73

Sources: As for table 13.1 and *National Income and Expenditure.*

TABLE 13.3: Total investments of financial institutions at end of year at market values

	1957 (£m)	1967 (£m)	1977 (£m)	% of total	Annual growth rates 1956–57 (%)	Annual growth rates 1967–77 (%)
Insurance companies						
Life	4 042	10 086	33 088	44.8	9.6	10.7
General	399	1 872	6 723	9.1	16.7	11.9
Total insurance	4 441	11 958	39 811	53.9		
Superannuation funds	2 093	6 246	24 100	32.6	11.6	14.5
Investment trusts	1 142	4 022	6 563	8.9	13.4	5.0
Unit trusts	65	788	3 432	4.6	28.3	15.9
Total	7 741	23 014	73 906	100.0		

Sources: 1957: *Report of the Committee on the Working of the Monetary System.* Cmnd 827.
1967 and 1977: *Financial Statistics.*
Notes: (1) Insurance companies' figures exclude balances held by agents, the 1957 and 1967 figures relate to British Insurance Association members only and are at book values. Also the growth rates for 1967–77 are based on book values.
(2) Superannuation funds: holdings of local authority funds are as at 31 March of the following year.
(3) Investment trusts figures for 1957 apply to a sample of 256 out of some 300 trusts.
(4) Unit trust figure for 1957 is an estimate as at 30 June 1958.
(5) Between 1967 and 1976 the Inland Revenue estimated that the aggregate wealth of individuals in current prices increased at an average annual rate of 10.4% compared with an annual rate of 10.3% for life office funds (at book values).

Table 13.2 provides a better indicator of the development of the industry compared with the UK economy as a whole. Throughout the 1950s and 1960s, life premiums, of which over four-fifths relate to domestic business, increased faster than national income. In the 1970s, and particularly after the 1973 oil crisis, real growth of life insurance was adversely affected by inflation and the economic recession so that premium income fell as a percentage of national income.

Overseas business accounts for almost two-thirds of non-life premiums. The post-war economic growth has caused a substantial increase in demand for all classes of non-life insurance. Motor insurance business in particular grew rapidly in the 1960s.[4] Although like life business, non-life insurance has been adversely affected by the post-1974 economic recession, premium income measured in sterling has continued to rise as a result of inflation and the fall in the external value of sterling.

The steady real growth of the industry until the early 1970s parallels the experience of most other countries. The evidence points to the probability of the income elasticity of demand for insurance exceeding unity at least until standards of living reach very high levels. (Swiss Reinsurance Co., 1971). Therefore it is no surprise that the post-oil crisis recession interrupted the growth of premium expenditures.

As noted earlier, premium income generates funds for investment so that the post-war period has also witnessed a substantial increase in

TABLE 13.4:   **Distribution of insurance companies' UK funds by class of asset at 31 December 1977**

Class of asset	Long-term funds (£m)	(%)	General funds (£m)	(%)
British government securities	8 664	26.2	1 895	28.2
Local authority securities	599	1.8	186	2.8
Company securities:				
Debentures	2 141	6.5	306	4.6
Preference shares	143	0.4	212	3.2
Ordinary shares	9 747	29.5	2 180	32.4
Unit trusts	957	2.9	1	—
Loans and mortgages	2 904	8.8	308	4.6
Property	6 574	19.9	579	8.6
Cash and other short-term assets	1 075	3.2	887	13.2
Other (including overseas government securities)	284	0.9	169	2.5
Total	33 088	100.0	6 723	100.0

Source: Financial Statistics, January 1979.
Notes: (1) All holdings are at market values except Loans and Mortgages and part of 'Other' which are at book value.
(2) Agents' balances have been excluded.

TABLE 13.5: The contribution of insurance and other services to the UK balance of payments (£ million)

	1970	1971	1972	1973	1974	1975	1976	1977
At current prices								
Insurance companies	111	137	160	157	148	138	307	345
Lloyd's	136	157	157	139	164	200	334	379
Insurance brokers	50	55	58	60	76	104	154	185
Total insurance (including portfolio investment income)	297	349	375	356	388	442	795	909
Banking	90	71	122	123	46	215	416	254
Merchanting	87	100	125	165	220	299	309	229
Other financial	131	106	128	160	233	292	316	355
Total City services	605	626	750	804	887	1248	1836	1747
Other services, net earnings	-194	-91	-164	-182	-84	-97	146	1054
Total services	411	535	586	622	803	1151	1982	2801
At constant 1975 prices								
Insurance	550	556	590	524	494	442	692	698
Total services	761	906	921	915	1021	1151	1724	2152
Insurance earnings as % of								
Total 'City' services	49.1	55.8	50.0	44.3	43.7	35.4	43.3	52.0
Total services	72.3	65.2	64.0	57.3	48.4	38.4	40.1	32.4

Source: UK Balance of Payments 1967–1977.
Notes: (1) The National Income deflator is used to calculate constant prices.
(2) Insurance earnings include all income on direct investment overseas and on portfolio investment. For foreign insurances written in UK only net earnings on marine and aviation risks are included; earnings from other classes of insurance are thought to be small. No allowance is made for the UK earnings of foreign companies.

the investments of insurance companies. Again available data are not as good as one would desire. In particular, details of market values have only been published since 1976 so that prior to that date precise comparisons cannot be made with the other institutions in table 13.3.

During the uncertain market conditions of 1974 to 1977 insurance companies, like other financial institutions, substantially increased the proportion of liquid assets in their investment portfolios. Consequently the proportions of cash and short-term assets shown in table 13.4 are higher than they had been in the early 1970s. The table, however, does reveal the extent to which insurance companies seek to diversify their funds between fixed and variable interest securities, mortgages, and property. Also it shows the extent to which the companies match their assets to their liabilities, with the general (short-term) funds being far more liquid than the long-term (life) funds.

Finally, table 13.5 provides an indication of the contribution that British insurers and brokers make to the balance of payments. A major criticism of the figures is that they do not allow for the UK earnings of foreign insurers. Like Switzerland, Britain is still a major net exporter of insurance services but over the last decade over sixty foreign insurers have been newly authorised to write insurance in Britain, though their interest is mainly in the international business placed on the London market.

13.1.2 The supply of insurance

There are five features of insurance business that have an important bearing on supply. Each one will be considered individually.

(a) *Variable costs*. These comprise a large proportion of total costs (Carter, 1979a). The largest cost item is claims payments which on non-life business account for 60% or more of premiums. The expected aggregate size of such payments is directly related to the volume of business transacted, as is also the amount paid to agents and brokers as commissions. Though labour, which typically accounts for over 10% of total costs, cannot readily be readjusted to fluctuations in the amount of business transacted in any one year, some of the other management expenses are variable. Thus, from a cost standpoint, an insurer has considerable flexibility in the volume of business he writes.

(b) *Uncertainty*. Uncertainty at the time of sale as to the final cost of a contract is not unique to insurance business, though with insurance it is the *raison d'être*. The possibility that an individual policyholder may incur a loss provides the reason for insuring, so that there must always be uncertainty as to the outcome of writing one more insurance contract. However, insurance operations are based on the principle of risk combination: the larger the number of independent exposure units that an insurance company insures, the smaller will be the variation in its actual from its expected aggregate claims costs. Insurers provide for the risk of fluctuations in claims costs by reinsuring to reduce the range of possible outcomes and by maintaining free reserves to meet claims in excess of expected aggregate costs net of reinsurance recoveries. As an insurer increases the volume of business he writes, so he can afford to retain more for his own account and/or to operate with relatively smaller free reserves: herein lies one of the economies of scale for insurers.

(c) *Government.* Governments regulate both the entry of new insurers to their domestic markets and the operations of established insurers. In Britain supervision is exercised by the Insurance Division of the Department of Trade under the provisions of the Insurance Companies Act 1974 and regulations issued thereunder.[5] Amongst the various constraints imposed on insurers, the solvency regulations limit the amount of business an insurance company can transact relative to its capital reserves.

(d) *Investment income.* This is generated by reserve funds, the size of which is determined by the amount of business underwritten and is an additional source of revenue for an insurer. Therefore, the cash flow characteristics of different classes of insurance business and capital market conditions have an important influence on the rates of premium at which an insurer is prepared to supply different classes of insurance.

(e) *Ancillary services.* These are often supplied by insurers to their policyholders. They carry out surveys of industrial and commercial premises and other large risks and advise policyholders on loss prevention. Collectively, insurers support bodies like the Fire Protection Association and the Motor Repair Research Centre. After losses have occurred they can often advise on minimising the extent of damage and business interruption. The costs of such services are built into premium loadings though there is a good case to be made for insurers charging separately for such services.

13.1.3 The demand for insurance

The demand for insurance is directly related to the demand for economic security. Thus the price an individual is prepared to pay for insurance, measured in terms of the premium loading on top of the loss expectancy, is determined by his degree of risk aversion. (Friedman and Savage, 1948). Similarly firms make their insurance purchasing decisions in the light of their corporate objectives and attitudes to risk (Carter and Doherty, 1974a and Carter, 1978).

The strength of demand is related to the size of possible loss. To insure against very small losses is neither necessary nor economic in that the premium loading an insurer must charge to cover the costs of dealing with small claims will be high.

The price elasticity of market demand for the different classes of insurance has not been adequately researched and remains debatable. The Monopolies Commission (1972) argued that for fire insurance total market demand is relatively inelastic, though nowadays large buyers probably are not so insensitive to premium rates as the Monopolies Commission believed. Increases in premium rates do induce firms to devote more resources to loss prevention (Doherty, 1976) and to consider partial insurance arrangements whereby they carry part of their own risks.

At the level of the individual insurer, demand tends to be highly responsive to price. The best evidence for the British market relates to private motor insurance, and some insurers certainly try to take account of the effect of a change in premium rates on the amount of business they can expect to transact (Reynolds, 1970). A 1977 survey of motorists has indicated that, *ceteris paribus*, the average British motorist would change to another insurer that offered a 13% cut in premium (Louis Harris International, 1977). Of the respondents 27% indicated that a 5% reduction would be sufficient to persuade them to change.

Reference has been made already to the high probability that the income elasticity of demand for insurance exceeds unity.

Life insurers operate in both the insurance and savings markets. Only a small part of the premium for an endowment policy relates to protection, the remainder is devoted to paying a sum at maturity. Competition between life offices and other savings institutions was highlighted in the late 1950s by the entry of unit trusts into the insurance market through the issue of unit-linked life policies. The success of the new savings policies forced the established life offices either to co-operate with unit trusts or to form their own trusts. In 1977, almost half of the premiums paid for new ordinary life assurances in the UK related to linked life policies.

13.2 THE STRUCTURE OF THE BRITISH INSURANCE MARKET

At the end of 1977, 632 British registered companies and 169 foreign registered companies were authorised to transact insurance business in Britain. In addition London is the home of that unique institution known as Lloyd's which comprises over 17 000 underwriting members (including 1650 foreign nationals) operating through approximately 400 underwriting syndicates. Sixty-four friendly (or collecting) societies also participate in the writing of industrial life insurance.

Companies are authorised by the Department of Trade to transact specific statutorily defined classes of insurance (including reinsurance) business. Most of the major British registered companies transact both life and non-life business: they are referred to as composite companies. Other companies specialise in just one or two classes of business. The specialists are particularly important in life and marine business: in the life market, specialist life offices account for over 40% of total business. Many of the specialist life offices and a few other companies are organised as mutual companies which have no shareholders, the company being owned by its policyholders.

If 173 small companies, mainly mutual associations that write business only for their members, are excluded, the structure of the market at the end of 1976 was as shown in table 13.6. Approximately one hundred of the British registered companies are subsidiaries of the major insurance groups. The insurance market is less concentrated than many other industries but as shown in table 13.7 a few companies still write substantial shares of the total business. A series of mergers in the late 1950s and 1960s increased the proportion of non-life business controlled by the major company groups.

TABLE 13.6:   Numbers of companies authorised to transact insurance business in Great Britain, end 1976

	UK registered	Foreign companies	Total
Companies writing only life and personal accident insurances	152	34	186
Companies writing only general insurance	233	127	360
Companies writing life and general insurance	67	6	73
Total	452	167	619

Source: Department of Trade.

Only a few of the foreign insurers established in Britain write a significant amount of UK business. They are mainly interested in overseas direct and reinsurance business placed on the London market. A few major foreign companies have owned British registered subsidiary companies for many years, e.g. the Zurich, and one of the recent trends has been for foreign companies, especially American insurers, to take over established UK insurance companies.

The origin of Lloyd's dates from the merchant underwriters of the seventeenth century who gathered in the coffee house of Mr Edward Lloyd to transact insurance business. (Gibb, 1957). Today, Lloyd's

TABLE 13.7:   Concentration ratios in British insurance 1976

	General insurance (%)	Ordinary life (%)
(a) *World-wide premium income of British insurers* (including Lloyd's)		
3 largest companies	36.4	30.9
6 largest companies	53.0	46.9
Lloyd's	21.7	—
(b) *UK domestic business* (excluding Lloyd's)		
3 largest companies	26.3	24.6
6 largest companies	44.3	36.2

Source: Policy Holder Insurance **95** (50), 1977.

provides a major world market for the insurance and reinsurance of large and unusual risks in addition to run-of-the-mill motor insurances etc., but its organisation essentially remains the same as that established in the late eighteenth century. The Corporation of Lloyd's writes no insurance business itself but provides the facilities for the individual underwriting and broking members to carry on their business. Today the underwriting members are organised into separate, competing syndicates, each managed by an underwriting agent. Each member remains individually responsible for his underwriting debts to the full extent of his business and personal means.

Generally the market is highly competitive. The cost and other advantages of the large companies are not so large as to shield them from competition from either the smaller companies or from new entrants which often have the backing of large foreign insurance companies. Also the Lloyd's market is a major competitive force in the market and a source of many product innovations. Richards and Colenutt (1975) have shown how new entrants have quickly gained substantial shares of the life market.

13.2.1 Insurance intermediaries

Insurance is marketed in various ways. Some insurance companies sell direct to the public through their own full-time salesmen. The major companies maintain branch organisations throughout the country where they deal with the public both direct and in most cases, through part-time agents and brokers. Lloyd's syndicates accept business only through registered Lloyd's brokers: if another broker handles the business it still must be channelled to Lloyd's through a Lloyd's broker.

There are no firm figures as to the number of sole traders and firms operating as insurance brokers and consultants. The best estimates put the total number of firms at around 6000. The extensive development of provincial brokers over the last twenty-five years has helped to reduce the barriers to entry for new insurance companies by providing them with access to a nationwide marketing network.

Like the insurance companies, fewer than a dozen major broking firms control over half of the total business handled by brokers. All of the major firms are active in overseas markets and most have branches or subsidiaries in many parts of the world. Recently a number of mergers or working relationships have been arranged between large British and American broking firms which will give the latter easier access to the Lloyd's market.

In the mid-1960s the clearing banks extended their activities into insurance and all of them have formed broking subsidiaries or divisions. It is probably the smaller provincial brokers that are encountering most of the competition from the banks.

Under the provisions of the Insurance Brokers (Registration) Act 1977, the use of the term 'insurance broker' after 1980 will be confined to persons and firms registered by the Insurance Brokers Registration Council.[5]

The purpose of the legislation is to protect the public by restricting the handling of insurance business to suitably qualified and experienced persons who possess adequate financial resources and conduct their business in an ethical fashion. It was the Labour Government's intention to extend registration eventually to all insurance intermediaries.

13.2.2 The London market

London is the world's leading international insurance market. In addition to Lloyd's which obtains three-quarters of its premium income from abroad, the large firms of international brokers bring in large amounts of direct and (more important) reinsurance business where it is placed with both British and foreign companies.

Originally, the direct insurers placed all reinsurances between themselves, and Britain with its large direct companies was slow to form specialist reinsurance companies. Today there is still only one major British reinsurance company, the Mercantile and General Reinsurance Company: the leading international reinsurance companies are German, and Swiss (Carter, 1979b). Since the 1970s, in response to changes in international insurance trade, the large British direct insurance companies have strengthened their reinsurance interests by forming reinsurance subsidiaries, and by participating in the formation of international joint-venture reinsurance companies.

13.3 MARKET BEHAVIOUR

13.3.1 Pricing

For very large industrial and commercial risks the insurer may negotiate a special premium related to the characteristics of the particular risk and the firm's loss experience. In the majority of cases, however, the individual risk forms one of a group of similar risks and the insurer then proceeds to calculate a rate for that class.

The first task is to obtain an estimate of the expected cost of claims under each contract. Here the life insurer has a marked advantage by having access to mortality tables derived from observations of large numbers of lives. Moreover, a life policy undertakes to pay a certain sum upon the death of the insured life (or at maturity in the case of endowment policies). The main element of uncertainty is in the rate of interest which the insurer can expect to earn on funds and so in the discount rate to be used for calculating premiums. The principles employed are now well-established, and premium rating for life insurance is a relatively precise process using conservatively low discount rates.

Matters are more complicated for other insurers. They have two elements to consider: the probability of one or more losses occurring and the size of such losses. For some classes of non-life insurance, notably private car insurance, a well-established insurer can draw upon a large volume of past loss statistics, possibly supplemented by data collected from a large section of the market. In other cases because of the heterogeneity and/or limited number of exposure units, the underwriter may have a very limited past loss experience from which to estimate loss expectancies. Moreover past experience can never be more than a guide to the future. Changing economic, social, legal, technological and other factors can over time significantly affect the probability or the severity of loss or both. Inflation in particular has been a major worry to insurers during the 1970s in that it has substantially increased average claims costs for many classes of insurance, and in fixing premiums the insurer has to allow for inflation up to the date when the last claim arising on a block of business is finally settled (Carter, 1979a). In the case of liability insurances covering claims brought by third parties for injuries or damage caused by the action of a policyholder or employees, claims may remain outstanding for several years increasing in cost the whole time.

Although progress has been made in the statistical analysis of risk factors and in the application of actuarial techniques to the fixing of non-life premiums, subjective judgement inevitably still plays a far more important role than in life insurance. A matter of debate is the extent to which interest that an insurer will earn on his funds should be brought into account. For the so called 'long tail' classes of insurance (i.e. those subject to long claims settlement delays), even if interest is not explicitly taken into account, market pressures will ensure that premiums are adjusted accordingly. After fixing the pure premium rate the insurer will load it to provide for his management expenses, to make a contribution to reserves for claims fluctuations, and to provide a profit. The rating process, therefore, is of a cost-plus pricing type, but insurers then modify the premiums they quote in the light of market competition (B. Benjamin, 1977).

Only a few years ago many classes of insurance were subject to minimum price agreements, known as tariffs, to which most large insurance companies subscribed. Under the pressure of intense competition from new cut-price companies in the 1960s, the motor insurance tariff was abandoned in 1968, shortly followed by all but one of the other tariffs. Despite a recommendation by the Monopolies Commission (1972) that the commercial fire tariff should be terminated, the Government still has to make up its mind. In the meantime the tariff continues, though latterly the tariff companies have been facing increasing competition from American insurers who are more willing to enter into partial insurance arrangements for very large cases. Although there is a good case for abandoning price fixing agreements, there is much merit in the collective pooling of loss statistics to provide a sounder statistical base for rate making than would be available to any individual insurer (Carter and Doherty, 1974b).

13.3.2 Marketing

Apart from industrial life assurance where the offices employ full-time agents to solicit new business and to collect premiums at, usually, monthly intervals from the homes of policyholders, most insurance business is marketed through part-time agents and brokers. As noted earlier, only authorised Lloyd's brokers are permitted to place insurances at Lloyd's, and brokers handle most large industrial and commercial insurances and insured pension schemes (Economist Intelligence Unit, 1971).

An undesirable feature of the market is the ownership links between some insurance companies and brokers. In 1976 the Department of Trade issued regulations requiring an intermediary to inform any person with whom he is dealing of any such connection.

Perhaps the three most significant developments that have occurred in the marketing of insurances over the last decade are the use of direct selling sales forces by some of the new life offices marketing unit-linked policies; the entry of the clearing banks into insurance broking; and the increased use by insurance companies of press and television advertising and the sponsorship of sporting and other events. It is frequently said that insurance is sold and not bought in the sense that there is a lot of consumer resistance. Consequently some of the advertising has been of an informative character undertaken by various insurance associations. At the competitive level although insurance companies have engaged in more extensive advertising campaigns to promote their own names and products, expenditure is still relatively very low compared with many consumer industries.

Finally, most large industrial, commercial and local authority buyers of insurance have formed their own insurance departments to handle the purchase of insurance, often dealing direct with the insurance companies. Some companies have formed their own broking subsidiaries and some have set up their own insurance companies, known as captive insurers.

13.4 PERFORMANCE OF INSURERS

The performance of insurance companies may be judged in the same ways as for other firms, i.e. in terms of their growth of business, efficiency, profitability, innovative record and so forth. In addition, because their *raison d'être* is to provide security for policyholders, their solvency is an important question too.

(a) *Business growth*. This is normally measured on the basis of premium income, but as explained above, inflation and exchange rate fluctuations make it very difficult to measure real growth. A further complication arises with life business where policyholders enter into long-term contracts so that a large part of a year's premium income consists of premiums paid on policies effected in earlier years. Therefore, a better measure of a life office's progress can be its premiums for new business, though they can be subject to wide fluctuations due to the incidence of single premium business. As shown by Richards and Colenutt (1975), there can be significant differences between the growth of life business judged in terms of total premium income and new premium income.

(b) *Efficiency*. This is never an easy concept to measure. Part of the problem for the insurance analyst lies in the limitations of published data but there are conceptual difficulties too (Monopolies Commission, 1972, appendix). The most widely employed partial measure of efficiency is the ratio of management expenses plus commissions to written premiums. Care is needed in interpreting such ratios in that the relative costs of handling different classes of insurance vary considerably, and differences between two insurers may be attributable to the differing standards of claims handling services, loss prevention advice, etc., which they may provide. Nevertheless time-series data do give some guide as to whether insurers are becoming more or less efficient in handling their business. For example, over the period 1968–77 the average combined expense and commission ratio for fire and accident insurance business of the nine largest British insurance companies was cut from 35.2% of premiums to 32.0% despite the large increase in salaries and other expenses that occurred due to inflation.

(c) *Claims payments*. These could be considered the end product of an insurance company, and so various claims ratios are employed by analysts. The main ratio used is the claims: premiums ratio, but its apparent simplicity is a trap for the uninitiated for reasons too long to explain here.[6] As a comment on performance the claims ratio is not entirely unambiguous. A low ratio indicates that the insurer is returning to policyholders little by way of claims payments of the premiums they have paid – though a new life office would not expect many claims in its early years. A very high claims ratio on the other hand may indicate that unless remedial measures are quickly taken the company will soon be insolvent, or if the high claims ratio applies to only one class of insurance, that those policyholders are being subsidised by others.

(d) *Profitability*. The problems of measuring the profitability or otherwise of insurance business differ somewhat between long-term (mainly life) and short-term business. The result of a long-term insurance contract, or even a block of such contracts, will only become clear many years after inception. Therefore the profitability of a life office can only be judged on the basis of periodic actuarial valuations of its assets and liabilities.

Although short-term insurance contracts typically have a life of only one year, at the end of a financial year some of the policies issued or renewed during that year will still be in force, and claims arising thereon may not be finally settled for two, three or even more years hence. Consequently the calculation of the profit earned in any financial year will again depend to a large extent upon the valuation of unearned premiums and outstanding claims, and profits (or losses) calculated according to the normal accounting conventions will be affected by under- or over-reserving in earlier years.

In the case of non-life insurance a distinction is usually drawn between so-called underwriting profit and total profit. Essentially the underwriting result consists of

premiums – (claims + expenses)

Investment income earned on the funds is added to obtain the total profit, though whether realised capital gains should be counted too is a matter for argument. (Carter, 1979a, chapter 7, and National Association of Insurance Commissioners, 1970).

The difference between the two is substantial. For example, the average non-life underwriting results of the ten leading British insurance companies over the period 1972–6 expressed as a percentage of written premiums was –1.85% but investment income converted that loss into a profit of 6.54%. If these results are converted into a return on capital employed, over the last decade the profitability of insurance business has been low. There are now grave doubts regarding the ability of the industry to raise the additional capital required to finance the growth of premium income caused mainly by the effects of continuing inflation (Kelly, 1978 and Plymen, 1977).

(e) *Innovation.* Innovation provides a better picture of the industry's performance. Many product and process changes have been made over recent years. Computers are changing organisation and working systems and have enabled the major companies to handle a larger volume of business with smaller staffs. New types of insurance have been desigٍed to meet new types of risk ranging from atomic energy to hang-gliding, and new forms of contract have been devised to allow larger buyers of insurance to retain part of their own risks. Brokers have played an important role in such developments.

(f) *Solvency.* The ability of an insurance company to meet its liabilities to policyholders is of primary importance. The provision of security is its *raison d'être*, and it may be argued that the failure of an insurance company may have far more serious consequences than the failure of most other types of firm. Therefore most governments require insurance companies to maintain a certain minimum balance of assets over liabilities relative to the size of business transacted.

The 1970s have been a difficult period for insurance companies world-wide. Non-life premiums have increassed rapidly but generally have tended to lag behind inflationary increases in claims costs. Although stock prices have recovered from the stock market collapse in 1974, asset values have not increased in line with inflation. Consequently between October 1974 and December 1977 the ten leading British companies have had to raise additional share capital of £461m (equal to 14% of total shareholders' funds at market values at end-1977) to maintain reasonable levels of solvency.

13.5 PUBLIC POLICY AND INSURANCE

13.5.1 Supervision

Throughout the world, regardless of political ideologies, governments regard insurance business as requiring special supervision. The reason for buying insurance is to obtain financial security. If an insurance company fails, not only is the performance of its insurance contracts frustrated but also policyholders and others can suffer far more serious financial losses than would be caused by the failure of most other types of firm. Life policyholders may lose most of their savings, and other policyholders and third parties such as road accident victims may incur large losses for which they can obtain no compensation.

Until the mid-1960s the principle of British supervisory legislation was 'freedom with publicity', i.e. the government did not intervene in the way insurers conducted their business but they were required to submit detailed accounting returns to the Department of Trade. The failure of a number of cut-price entrants to the motor insurance market in the 1960s, persuaded the government to pursue a more stringent supervisory role. The present rules are laid down in the following statutes and regulations issued thereunder:

The Insurance Companies Act 1974
The Industrial Assurance Acts 1923 to 1958
The Policyholders Protection Act 1975
The Insurance Brokers (Registration) Act 1977

The provisions regarding insurance companies are concerned with (i) reducing the probability of an insurance company failing, but (ii) if it does so, minimising the losses suffered by policyholders.

The Companies Act 1967 introduced the control of new entrants through the official authorisation of companies wishing to transact any class of insurance subject to certain requirements regarding capital, solvency, the fitness of its management and adequate reinsurance arrangements being observed. Moreover the Secretary of State was empowered to impose on newly authorised companies and companies in financial difficulties certain requirements regarding the conduct of their business, including their investments, and the regular provision of information, and to make regulations dealing with the annual returns to be provided by all companies. Following the collapse in 1971 of the Vehicle and General Insurance Company the Government introduced further regulations which are now contained in the Insurance Companies Act 1974 and regulations issued thereunder. (Carter, 1973, chapter 1.2). Well-founded, established companies still have considerable freedom in their pricing, marketing, claims handling and investment policies, but on the strength of detailed returns they must make each year to the Department of Trade their performance, and particularly their standards of solvency, are more closely scrutinised than in the past.

The entry of Britain to the European Community has required its participation in the programme for the creation of a common market in insurance. France, Germany and Italy traditionally have imposed tighter control over their insurance industries than Britain (or the Benelux countries), and harmonisation of insurance law as part of that programme is likely to lead to more control in Britain too. Progress has been slow but in 1973 the Directive on Freedom of Establishment for Non-life Insurance was ratified (Skerman, 1976). The Directive required Britain to adopt in 1978 the more stringent Common Market solvency rules for non-life insurance.

However detailed the rules and their supervision are, it is impossible to guarantee with absolute certainty that an insurance company will never fail. Therefore in 1975 the government passed the Policyholders' Protection Act. The name is self-explanatory. If an insurance company fails, a Board appointed under the Act can impose a levy on the industry to indemnify or otherwise assist personal policyholders or other people prejudiced by the failure of the company.

However desirable it is that the government should seek to protect policyholders and others from the consequences of fraudulent or incompetent insurance management, there are costs which have to be paid. The more detailed supervision has substantially added to the expenses of both the Department of Trade and of insurers. Also the Policyholders' Protection Act in effect penalises companies that run their businesses on sound lines in that they have to meet the costs of companies that fail, while competition is distorted as the Act removes the potential penalty of insuring with less reputable companies.

13.5.2 Control of investments

Insurers are largely free to invest their very substantial funds as they desire, subject to the constraints imposed by the nature of their liabilities to policyholders (See Clayton and Osborn, 1965; Dickinson, 1971; and Committee to Review the Functioning of Financial Institutions, 1978). In recent years they have encountered increasing criticism about the way they have distributed their funds, particularly in regard to levels of investment in industry generally and in small firms in particular, and their acquisitions of land and property. Also there has been concern regarding the concentration of financial power in the hands of insurance companies and pension funds. Over the period 1963–75 personal holdings of ordinary shares have fallen from 54.0 to 37.5% of the total market value of quoted shares while insurance companies' and pension funds' holdings have increased from 10.0 to 15.9%, and from 6.4 to 16.8% respectively (Erritt and Alexander, 1977). It must be emphasised that those holdings are spread over many hundreds of independent, often competing, institutions so that there is little fear of collusive action to control industry.

Evidence gathered by the Committee of Inquiry on Small Firms (1971) showed that as a general rule the size of individual investments preferred by life offices precludes the provision of finance except for the largest of 'small' firms. A number of life offices, however, do provide finance either directly or through specialist intermediary companies: as the result of its experience in providing small loans, one life office has acquired a banking subsidiary. Substantial support for small firms has been provided too through the amounts subscribed to Finance for Industry Limited and its subsidiary the Industrial and

Commercial Finance Corporation Limited, and some of the property developments financed by insurers have provided accommodation for small firms in industry and commerce. Undoubtedly the difficulties involved in lending to small firms deter some investment managers, but if there does exist a large unsatisfied demand for finance at terms reflecting the higher transaction costs and risk involved, there is every incentive for life offices, which largely compete on the basis of the yields they can obtain on their funds, to meet it.

The counterpart to the criticisms relating to small firms is that by favouring larger firms, life offices and other financial institutions have contributed to the increasse in industrial concentration in Britain. In particular Prais (1976) claims that the supply of relatively cheap debenture funds to large firms during the 1950s and 1960s helped to finance the merger boom. That may be so, though it certainly was not the intention of the life offices when, in order to increase yields and obtain a hedge against inflation, they set out to increase the proportion of corporate securities in their investment portfolios.

More recently, institutions have been criticised for investing too little in industry. Table 13.8 shows the basis for such complaints:

TABLE 13.8:   Net acquisitions by life offices

	(as % of total net acquisitions)		
	1963–7	1968–72	1973–7
Cash and short-term securities	0.7	2.8	4.1
British government securities	16.5	22.5	53.1
UK local authority	1.6	–0.9	2.7
Overseas government securities	–0.2	–0.2	0.3
Debentures and preference shares	30.5	13.2	–1.1
Ordinary shares	15.6	32.2	12.7
Unit trusts	—	—	3.5
Loans and mortgages	21.3	11.9	4.5
Land and property	14.0	18.5	20.1

Source: Financial Statistics.

during the period 1973 to 1977 the life offices each year invested on average only 15% of their new funds in corporate securities (including unit trusts) compared with 46% ten years earlier. Undoubtedly, following the 1974 stock market collapse, corporate securities have lost some of their former attractiveness, so that life offices are unlikely to want to increase the proportion of their total funds held in loan stocks and ordinary shares. On the other hand the demand from industry for new funds has been depressed in line with new capital investment. In particular, companies have been unwilling to raise new loan capital at the high rates of interest required to give investors the prospect of earning a real return on their funds, and to compete with the yields on long-dated government securities.

The TUC has recommended to the Wilson Committee that there should be official direction of the investment of institutional funds. Insurance companies and the other institutions in their evidence to the Committee expressed vigorous opposition to direction arguing that it would lead to the inefficient use of capital resources. Nevertheless it is possible that the Committee may recommend that a small percentage of institutions' new funds should be subscribed each year to a body such as Equity Capital for Industry Limited for investment in situations where a company may have difficulty in obtaining funds through the normal market channels.

Finally, life offices have been criticised on many occasions for allegedly failing to become involved in the companies in which they invest but simply selling their shares when things go wrong. In practice the size of their investments is such that often they are locked into companies and cannot readily dispose of their shares. Moreover evidence presented by the insurance companies to the Wilson Committee and the findings of other researchers (Midgley, 1975), show that they are more active than it would appear. Further involvement would necessitate access to information not available to other shareholders, so raising considerable problems in relation to insider dealing and market competition.

13.5.3 Nationalisation

As early as 1948 the Labour Party considered the nationalisation of insurance, and the issue was seriously raised again in a Green Paper issued by the party's Home Policy Committee in 1973. In 1976 the party's National Executive Committee modified the nationalisation proposals in its paper *Banking and Finance* which proposed that the government should take into public ownership only the seven largest companies which collectively write 37% of the life premiums and 55% of the non-life premiums of all UK insurers. The case for such action was based mainly on the alleged need to control the investment of their funds which has been examined already.

However, far more arguments can be marshalled against the proposals. (Carter, 1976 and Committee to Review the Functioning of Financial Institutions, Second Stage evidence from Insurance Companies, 1978, paragraphs 157–167). There is no evidence that a state-run insurance corporation would be run more efficiently than the existing companies. Indeed after ten years' experience of nationalised insurance companies, the Egyptian government in 1977 decided to re-admit private companies in order to improve service to policyholders.

It is doubtful whether life policyholders would welcome the prospect of some notion of the 'public interest' replacing their interest in determining the investment of life funds. The overseas business of the companies would suffer particularly in the United States where government-owned or controlled foreign companies are prohibited from operating in half the states. No mention was made of what would happen if the remaining private companies grew faster than the nationalised companies to regain a major share of the market; if EEC insurers took advantage of the situation it is hard to see what a British government could do.

13.5.4 International trade

International insurance transactions are conducted in two ways. An insurance company may establish branch offices or subsidiary companies in countries where it wishes to transact business, or it may underwrite insurances and reinsurances of foreign risks at its head office. Local establishment is necessary for a direct insurer for production reasons; only by having a local staff can it provide on a large scale the standard of service, including claims handling services, which policyholders require.

Over the last twenty years many countries, particularly amongst the developing nations, have imposed severe restrictions on international insurance transactions (Carter and Dickinson, 1979; Griffiths, 1975). Many have either totally excluded foreign insurers from their domestic markets or have made it very difficult and/or costly for foreign companies to remain. Also in many instances local residents have been prohibited from placing their insurances abroad.

Apart from countries that have nationalised insurance for political reasons, other countries have been anxious to develop their own insurance industries, to retain insurance funds for internal investment and to reduce the balance of payments costs of insurance imports. Such policies have received the support of UNCTAD which has exhorted developed countries to provide new local companies with assistance in training and technical services.

The effect of such developments on the British insurance industry has been twofold. Companies have been forced out of many of their traditional overseas markets, and international trade in insurance services has increasingly taken the form of reinsurance. Whereas over the last thirty years there has been considerable liberalisation of international trade in goods, the service industries such as insurance have encountered increasing barriers to trade. It must be emphasised, however, that the problem should not be seen simply as a North v. South issue; few if any countries impose no restrictions and many developed as well as developing countries pursue highly protective policies. The EEC insurance programme is an important step forward in trade liberalisation in Europe.

Although the desire of governments for self-sufficiency in insurance is understandable, like other protective policies, the costs in many cases may far exceed the benefits. Until recently there has been little research into international insurance transactions so that policies have been formulated with little theoretical understanding of potential consequences and on even shakier empirical evidence. Even in the case of the insurance for very large industrial complexes, giant tankers, jumbo jets and suchlike, or catastrophe risks (e.g. earthquakes, hurricanes and floods), where there are obvious advantages in spreading potential losses, and the funds to meet those losses, as widely as possible, some governments have still sought to retain a high proportion of the insurance locally (Carter and Dickinson). Balance of payments effects are even less well understood: even when attempts are made to quantify the various elements, the results are often confused and incomplete (Dickinson, 1977). Even if, in the long term, a country found that it was incurring a net foreign exchange cost due to its level of insurance imports, this would not be a sufficient reason for restricting trade. On the one hand it may be a reasonable price to pay to avoid the disruptive effect on its balance of payments of large fluctuations in insured losses. However, insurance transactions should not be considered in isolation: resources that otherwise would be employed in producing insurance services may be better used elsewhere in the economy to produce import-substitutes or commodities for export. There is no reason why some countries should not possess a comparative advantage in the production of insurance services. Finally, there are the indirect costs of protection. Access to the type of insurance and ancillary services which international insurers can provide is important to many technologically advanced industries, and at the margin the lack of such facilities may deter a multinational company that is thinking of setting up a manufacturing plant in a country.

There are signs that some governments are coming to appreciate the economic costs of the barriers to international trade in insurance and that before long the restrictive trend may be reversed (Carter and Dickinson). Although British insurers would stand to benefit from liberalisation, insurers in America, Europe, Japan and other countries are also looking for opportunities to participate in overseas markets, so that British insurers can expect to meet increasing competition at home and abroad.

NOTES TO CHAPTER 13

1. 'Act touching policies of assurance used among merchants, 1601'. See Raynes, 1964, page 53.

2. The three main forms of life assurance are (a) whole-life where the sum assured is payable only on death; (b) term assurance where the insurer only pays if the life assured dies within a specified period; and (c) endowment assurance which is a combination of a term assurance plus an undertaking to pay the sum insured if the life assured survives until the end of the term.

3. Reinsurance is a system whereby one insurer can transfer to another insurer, known as a reinsurer, part of the liabilities he has accepted under contracts of insurance he has written. Thus insurers can further spread large risks which exceed their own underwriting capacities.

4. In all countries motor premium income tended to grow faster than other classes of business, so that in many countries by 1970 it accounted for over a quarter of all premiums: see Swiss Reinsurance Company (1976).

5. For a brief account see Carter (1973).

6. A good account of the problems involved can be found in Benjamin (1976).

REFERENCES

Benjamin, B. (1977) *General Insurance*. London: Heinemann.

Benjamin, S. (1976) 'Profit and other financial concepts in insurance'. *Journal of the Institute of Actuaries* **103**.

Carter, R. L. (1973) *Handbook of Insurance*. London: Kluwer (updated).

Carter, R. L. (1976) 'Insuring for the future'. *Policy Insurance Journal* (December).

Carter, R. L. (1978) 'Risk Management: a British point of view'. *Zeitschrift für die Gesamte Versicherungswissenschaft* 1/2.

Carter, R. L. (1979a) *Economics and Insurance*. 2nd edn. Stockport: P.H. Press.

Carter, R. L. (1979b) *Reinsurance*. London: Kluwer.

Carter, R. L. and Dickinson, G. M. (1979) *Barriers to Trade in Insurance*. London: Trade Policy Research Centre.

Carter, R. L. and Doherty, N. A. (1974a) *Handbook of Risk Management*. London: Kluwer (updated).

Carter, R. L. and Doherty, N. A. (1974b) 'Tariff control and the public interest'. *Journal of Risk and Insurance* **XLI** (3).

Clayton, G. and Osborn, W. T. (1965) *Insurance Company Investment*. London: Allen and Unwin.

Committee of Inquiry on Small Firms (1971) *Financial facilities for small firms*. Research report No. 4. London: HMSO.

Committee to Review the Functioning of Financial Institutions (1978a and b) First stage evidence of the Insurance Companies, Evidence on the Financing of Trade and Industry, Volume 3; Second stage evidence of the Insurance Companies.

Dickinson, G. M. (1971) *Determinants of Insurance Company Asset Choice*. Hove: Withdean Publications.

Dickinson, G. M. (1977) 'International insurance transactions and the balance of payments'. *Geneva Papers on Risk and Insurance* no. 6.

Doherty, N. A. (1976) *Insurance Pricing and Loss Prevention*. Farnborough, Hants: Saxon House, D. C. Heath Ltd.

Economist Intelligence Unit (1971) *Insurance: profile of an industry*. London: Corporation of Insurance Brokers.

Erritt, M. J. and Alexander, J. C. (1977) 'Ownership of Company Shares'. *Economic Trends* (September) (287).

Friedman, M. and Savage, L. J. (1948) 'The Utility Analysis of Choices involving Risk'. *Journal of Political Economy* LVI, 279–304.

Gibb, D. E. W. (1957) *Lloyd's of London*. London: Macmillan & Co.

Griffiths, B. (1975) *Invisible Barriers to Invisible Trade*. London: Macmillan for Trade Policy Research Centre.

Kelly, P. (1978) 'The profitability of insurance companies'. Paper presented to the 1978 annual conference of the Chartered Insurance Institute.

Louis Harris International (1977) *A survey of motor insurance*. London: Sentry Insurance Co.

Midgley, K. (1975) *Companies and their shareholders – the uneasy relationship*. London: Institute of Chartered Secretaries and Administrators.

Monopolies Commission (1972) *Report on the supply of fire insurance*. London: HMSO.

National Association of Insurance Commissioners (1970) *Synopsis of the Report on the Measurement of Profitability and Treatment of Investment Income in Property and Liability Insurance*, NAIC proceedings, Volume II. New York.

Plymen, J. (1977) 'Profitability and reserve strength of non-life insurers'. *Journal of the Chartered Insurance Institute* (new series) **2**, part 1.

Prais, S. J. (1976) *The evolution of giant firms in Britain*. Cambridge: Cambridge University Press.

Raynes, H. E. (1964) *A History of British Insurance*. 2nd edn. London: Pitman.

Reynolds, D. I. W. (1970) 'Motor Insurance Rate Fixing'. *Journal of the Institute of Actuaries Students Society* **19**.

Richards, K. and Colenutt, D. (1975) 'Concentration in the UK Ordinary Life Assurance Market'. *Journal of Industrial Economics* **XXIV** (2), 147–159.

Skerman, R. S. (1976) 'The Development of a Common Market in Insurance'. *The Three Banks Review* (110).

Swiss Reinsurance Company (1971) 'An international comparison of the development of the gross national product, of private and State consumption as well as expenditure on insurance from 1955–1968'. *Sigma* (April).

Swiss Reinsurance Company (1976) 'Structural changes in the insurance industry 1950–1973'. *Sigma* (April).

FURTHER READING

Carter, R. L. (1979) *Economics and Insurance*. 2nd edn. Stockport: P.H. Press.

Carter, R. L. and Dickinson, G. M. (1979) *Barriers to trade in insurance*. London: Trade Policy Research Centre.

Clayton, G. (1971) *British Insurance*. London: Elek.

Committee to Review the Functioning of Financial Institutions (1978) Evidence on the Financing of Trade and Industry, Volume 3. London: HMSO.

Committee to Review the Functioning of Financial Institutions (1979) Second Stage Evidence, Volume 2. London: HMSO.

Doherty, N. A. (1976) *Insurance pricing and loss prevention*. Farnborough, Hants: Saxon House, D. C. Heath Ltd.

Monopolies Commission (1972) *Report on the supply of fire insurance*. London: HMSO.

The following are useful statistical sources:

Annual Abstract of Statistics. London: HMSO.

Business Monitor M5. London: HMSO.

Financial Statistics.

Insurance Business: Annual Report. London: Department of Trade, HMSO.

Insurance Facts and Figures. London: British Insurance Association.

Life Assurance in the UK. London: Life Offices' Association *et al*.

14. Medical care

I. Papps

14.1 INTRODUCTION

14.1.1 Post-war development of the industry

The post-war history of medical care in the UK is essentially the story of the National Health Service (NHS).[1] The 1946 National Health Service Act nationalised one thousand voluntary hospitals and two thousand local authority hospitals, made provisions for universal free access to a GP and provided for free dental and ophthalmic services as well as free supplies of dentures, spectacles, medicines, etc. Thus, when the NHS was set up, all services could be obtained free at the point of use. These services were to be paid for by a combination of National Insurance contributions, rates and general taxation but (contrary to popular belief) the National Insurance contribution has never provided a large proportion of the finance for the NHS. It has, in fact, provided only about 15% of the NHS funds throughout the history of the NHS.

The system set up in 1948 was administered by the Ministry of Health and, latterly, by the Department of Health and Social Security (DHSS) and contained three administrative entities: (i) the Regional Hospital Boards which allocated funds to hospital management committees and controlled the hospital sector, with the exception of that part of the finance of teaching hospitals which was the responsibility of the University Grants Committee; (ii) the Local Executive Councils which were concerned with non-hospital medical services such as those provided by GPs, dentists, pharmacists and ophthalmic services; and (iii) the Local Authorities which had the responsibility of providing support services such as antenatal and postnatal care, midwives and so on. Although this structure survived for twenty-six years until the reorganisation of the NHS in 1974, problems of co-ordina-

---

*This chapter was completed before the Report of the Royal Commission on the National Health Service was released. See Further Reading on pages 355–356.

tion among the three entities were almost inevitable. For example, the decision on whether to discharge a patient from hospital will depend, among other things, on the level of support services which will be available to him at home, but because decisions about the amount and type of resources allocated to hospitals and support services were made by different authorities, there was no reason to expect that the mix of hospital and domiciliary services would be efficient. For such reasons, the reorganisation of the NHS emphasised centralisation by placing all health services in a given area under the control of the Regional Health Authority which was in turn made responsible directly to the DHSS.

The history of the NHS has not on the whole been one of steady growth. Table 14.1 shows that although total expenditure at current

---

TABLE 14.1: **National Health Service expenditures, selected years 1948–78**

| | Years ended 31st March | | | | | | |
	1949/ 50	1952/ 53	1957/ 58	1962/ 63	1967/ 68	1972/ 73	1977/ 78
£ million	463	518	717	1002	1589	2786	7157
% of GNP	4.2	3.7	3.7	4.0	4.5	5.0	5.8

Source: Annual Abstract of Statistics.

---

prices has grown since 1948, the proportion of GNP devoted to the NHS has grown only from 4.2% in 1949/50 to 5.8% in 1977/78 and, moreover, that most of this growth has occurred since the late 1960s after a fall during the 1950s. On the other hand table 14.2 shows that manpower in the NHS has been growing rapidly both in absolute terms and as a proportion of the labour force, the most dramatic increases being in the manpower used by hospitals. While manpower used by the NHS as a whole has approximately doubled between 1951 and 1976, hospital medical staff have more than trebled while the number of GPs has increased only by about 25%. The large increase in hospital manpower compared with the 13% decrease in hospital beds shown in table 14.3 suggests that there has been considerable substitution between factors of production in the hospital sector. Indeed, tables 14.2 and 14.3 taken together suggest that the factor mix (and possibly the output) in the NHS is now very different from that used when the service first started.

It was originally thought that expenditure on the NHS would eventually fall as a healthier population required less medical care. However, initial expenditures were much higher than expected and continued to grow during the earlier years in absolute terms (though

TABLE 14.2: Manpower in the NHS, selected years 1951–76 (Great Britain, number or whole-time equivalent)

	1951	1956	1961	1966	1971	1976
Hospital medical and dental staff	11 495	14 969	16 486	19 281	32 901	40 214
Hospital nursing and midwifery staff	183 937	207 106	242 145	294 661	343 642	414 961
Other hospital staff	208 801*	264 464	294 251	331 180	375 065	439 119
GPs	20 411	21 980	23 015	22 504	24 668	26 418
Dentists and ophthalmic practitioners	10 948†	10 590†	11 498†	11 354†	19 734	21 021
Other non-hospital staff	na	na	na	na	3 663	4 144†
Total	435 592	519 109	587 395	678 980	799 673	945 877
Total as % of total labour force	1.88	2.15	2.37	2.65	3.26	3.71

Source: Annual Abstract of Statistics.
Notes: *England and Wales only.
         †Dentists only.
          na   Not available.

TABLE 14.3: Hospital beds, selected years 1951–76 (Great Britain, thousands)

1951	1956	1961	1966	1971	1976
527.6	546.5	541.6	531.4	516.1	479.4

Source: *Annual Abstract of Statistics.*

not as a proportion of GNP). As a result, there was a demand for the introduction of charges both to inhibit 'frivolous' demands for medical services and to raise some revenue. In spite of protests by some Labour MPs, charges for spectacles and dentures were introduced in 1951 and prescription charges in 1952. With various minor changes, such charges have persisted for most of the subsequent period.

Although the NHS provides almost all medical care in the UK, a private sector has persisted. Largely in order to persuade doctors to support the NHS, private beds were allowed in NHS hospitals after 1948. There has also been a small amount of private non-hospital medical care. This private sector has always been small in the post-war years. In 1977, about 4% of the population were covered by private medical insurance plans and private expenditure on medical care accounted for about 1% of total expenditure (Lee Donaldson Associates, 1978). In spite of its size, the existence of the private sector has generated substantial political heat.

14.1.2 The nature of the product

There are several distinctive features of the medical care industry.

(a) Most service industries produce an output which is very difficult to measure and the medical care industry is no exception. The real output of the industry is ultimately an improvement in the health status of the patient but it is extremely difficult to measure this output directly. The output of an industry producing services which are marketed – for example, hairdressers – is measured by its value. This solution is clearly not entirely satisfactory. One still has great difficulty in defining price per unit of output because the quality of services is certain to vary a great deal. Such problems are multiplied for the output of the NHS because as medical services are not marketed, one has no direct information about the value which consumers place on them. Therefore, it is usual to measure the output of the industry in terms of inputs – for example, number of patients treated by a GP or number of patient-days spent in hospital. As a result, it is possible to record changes in such measures which do not necessarily reflect a change in the output of health but a change in the mix of factors of production used to produce a given amount of health. For some purposes, this difficulty is of little importance. For example, we may well be interested only in the supply of and demand for GPs' services and so the distinction between inputs and outputs can be ignored. However, when it comes to measuring the performance of the industry, suitable measures of output become extremely important.

(b) Another feature of the medical services industry that makes it necessary to take some care before applying simple economic analysis is the very close connection between supply and demand factors – particularly in the case of hospital treatment. Doctors not only supply medical services but also, to some extent, demand them by acting as the patient's agent because the patient seldom has sufficient technical knowledge to make a decision about the treatment he needs. Typically, he will go to a doctor for advice and this doctor will demand services on the patient's behalf while at the same time supplying some of the services. Such an interaction makes it possible that the usual assumption of the independence of supply and demand curves will not be as useful as it has been in the analysis of other industries.

(c) Because modern hospital care involves large and often unexpected expenditures, most countries have evolved a system of finance which provides medical care free at the point of use. The NHS does so by government finance and provision of medical services; in the US, there is some government finance but most medical services are provided by the private sector and financed by private insurance; most other countries have schemes which consist of various mixes of these two types. The common feature of all of these schemes is that, for at least some medical services, the price faced by the patient when he is making his decision about the amount and type of care which he will demand is less than the marginal cost of care. This implies that a misallocation of resources in medical care is likely to result unless some additional allocative mechanism is introduced.

Moreover, the fact that the service is free at point of use introduces some elements of moral hazard. Because some close substitutes for medical care (such as more sensible life styles and some proprietary medicines) are still priced at marginal cost, the patient has an incentive to substitute medical care for these alternatives, some of which may be more efficient from a social point of view.

(d) Like most other services, nearly all the output of the medical services industries is geographically immobile and must be consumed at the point at which it is produced. This feature of the industry has obvious implications for the regional distribution of consumption of medical care.

14.1.3 Supply characteristics

One of the reasons for the unexpected increase in NHS costs is the advances in medical techniques made over the last thirty years that were unanticipated by the founders of the NHS. Advances in the treatment of cardiac cases and the development of spare-part surgery, for example, provide effective treatment for patients who would otherwise have died or lived much more restricted lives. Because these techniques are very expensive, they have increased the average cost per case. On the other hand, some innovations have decreased the average cost per case. The development of an effective drug treatment for tuberculosis replacing the long and costly treatment of the disease in sanatoria is a case in point. However, new medical techniques which have increased costs have almost certainly predominated.

Partly as a result of changes in medical techniques, the mix of cases treated in hospital has changed as shown in table 14.4. There has been a dramatic fall in the proportion of beds devoted to diseases of the chest and sexually-transmitted diseases, probably due to the development of antibiotic drugs, while there has been a similarly large pro-

---

TABLE 14.4: **Proportion of beds occupied in each specialty, 1959 and 1976 (%)**

	1959	1976
All specialties	100	100
Medical		
General medicine	6.97	8.04
Paediatrics	1.37	1.32
Infectious diseases	1.64	0.35
Diseases of the chest	4.79	1.45
Neurology	0.21	0.45
Cardiology	0.08	0.29
Sexually transmitted diseases	0.06	0.00
Other	0.71	1.03
Geriatrics and chronic sick	12.04	16.89
Surgical		
General surgery	7.06	7.37
Ear, nose and throat	1.41	0.93
Traumatic and orthopaedic	3.66	5.34
Neurosurgery	0.19	0.35
Gynaecology	1.91	2.32
Other	2.39	2.96
Obstetrics and GP maternity	4.08	4.12
Psychiatric	44.92	42.66
Other	6.51	4.02

Source: DHSS, *Health and Personal Social Service Statistics for England;* and DHSS, *Digest of Health Statistics for England and Wales.*

portionate rise in cardiology and neurology, probably as a result of the availability of new techniques. It should be noted that the largest single category, apart from psychiatric, is geriatric and chronically sick which in 1976 accounted for about 17% of all beds. Because there is little that modern medicine can do for such patients, one could ask whether one should provide the necessary care for them in relatively expensive medical establishments. It may well be less expensive to organise geriatric and chronically sick care on another basis.

It is difficult to say much of any interest about the supply of medical services in the UK. If we are concerned with the output of medical services as a whole, we cannot examine the response of the NHS to changing prices and, thus, identify a supply curve.[2] By its very nature there are no prices for NHS output to which the service could respond, even were that considered desirable. More seriously, we probably cannot examine the reaction of the NHS to changes in the relative prices of its inputs in order to infer the form of the production function which the service faces. There is nothing in its organisational structure which would ensure that the NHS operates on its production frontier and many reasons, derived from the literature on the economics of bureaucracy (Niskanan, 1971), to believe that it does not.

One can, of course, discuss the supply of various factors of production to the NHS and this is an interesting and fruitful field for research which has, unfortunately, been poorly worked so far. Obviously, for non-specialised factors of production, such as ancillary workers, the supply could be expected to be perfectly elastic at the going wage, for the NHS, even though a large employer, can scarcely be large enough to affect the wages of unskilled labour. A similar argument may well be relevant for drugs. Because the market for pharmaceuticals is international and the NHS is a small buyer in world terms, one might expect the supply of pharmaceuticals to be perfectly elastic at the world price. However, because of patents, each pharmaceutical company has a monopoly over its own drugs, and if it can combine this with control over resale, then it can engage in discriminatory pricing.[3]

The more interesting questions concern those of the supply side of medical manpower. We have very little information about the supply curves of doctors and nurses in the UK although we can suggest some factors which should be considered in any investigation. First, and especially in the case of doctors, the manpower tends to be internationally mobile. For example, the rate of emigration of doctors has been about three hundred per year while their rate of immigration has been approximately three thousand per year so that far from experiencing a net outflow of doctors, the UK has had a large net inflow. It would be foolish to think that a change in relative salaries in different countries would not affect these figures but, as yet, we have no information on their sensitivity to such changes.

Second, the NHS has a major role in training doctors as well as using them. As long as there is an excess demand for places in medical schools, the supply of doctors will depend not only on individual decisions but also on decisions taken by NHS administrators about the number of medical school places. Perhaps because of this, most of the work concerning the supply of manpower to the NHS has been concerned with manpower planning.

14.1.4 Demand characteristics

It is tempting to interpret table 14.1, corrected for inflation, as providing information about the income elasticity of demand for medical care in the UK. Of course, this interpretation would be mistaken for two reasons.

First, it is difficult to argue that the government's decision about spending on medical care is the same as that which would result from the sum of individual decisions if the NHS did not exist. Indeed, the rationale for the NHS is that it does provide a pattern of medical services which differs from that resulting from individual choice. Thus, although it may be argued that decisions about NHS expenditure reflect some kind of public income elasticity of demand, it will be unlikely to be comparable with the income elasticity of demand that is estimated for marketed goods.

Second, and probably more important, there is some reason to think that the relative price of medical care has changed over the period. Lee Donaldson Associates (1978) show that in 1976 costs per claim for private medical care were three and a half times larger than they were in 1966 while the retail price index was only 2.8 times larger. Although this is by no means conclusive evidence, it does suggest, when taken together with the experience of other countries where the index of prices for medical care has been rising faster than the retail price index, that table 14.1 reflects substitution as well as income effects.

More sophisticated techniques are, therefore, needed to estimate price and income elasticities of demand.

Cairns and Snell (1978) summarise much of the work that has been done on own price elasticity of demand for medical services. Although all of this work refers to US data, the results are sufficiently consistent to be interesting. Almost all studies conclude that the own price elasticity of demand is negative as expected though small.[4] Most estimates for various types of services are found to be numerically less than unity and, indeed, are seldom significantly different from zero.

Moreover, the work of Newhouse and Phelps (1974) and Anderson and Benham (1970) finds that the income elasticity of demand for various services is also less than unity (seldom significantly different from zero) although they are found to be positive as expected.

Newhouse and Phelps also provide information about cross-price elasticities of demand between hospital treatment and visits to a doctor's surgery and find again that they are small and frequently not significant. This suggests, somewhat surprisingly, that patients do not see these services as very close substitutes. On the other hand, because a visit to a GP is often a necessary prerequisite to hospital referral, the services may be complements in a large number of cases. The small and insignificant cross-price elasticities of demand may not, on closer inspection, be so surprising.

Some other interesting work has also been carried out by Kleiman (1974) and Pryor (1968) on the interaction between the public and private provision of medical care. Pryor argues that they are perfect substitutes so that changes in public provision will be exactly offset by changes in private provision. Using cross-section data on sixteen countries, Kleiman develops a model which suggests that only 20% of changes in public provision are offset by private provision – but again his results are not statistically significant.

Indeed, one of the striking features of the large amount of work on the estimation of price and income elasticities of demand is that, although similar results are obtained by using different data sets, few of these results are statistically significant.

14.2 MARKET STRUCTURE

14.2.1 Concentration

With the NHS supplying 98% of hospital throughput and most GP services, the degree of concentration in the supply of medical services in the UK is clearly very high. Although there has been some attempt to allow choice in general practice by making it legally possible for patients to change their GP without changing their place of residence, it is, in practice, quite difficult to do so. There is also the possibility of competition among different areas of the NHS — for example, the use of a Casualty Department of the local hospital rather than one's own GP — but such possibilities are likely to be few and one cannot avoid the overwhelming impression of the NHS as the monopoly supplier of medical services, a position which allows very little choice to patients.

The degree of concentration among the suppliers of factors of production is also of interest. The British Medical Association (BMA) represents the majority of doctors in the NHS and not only engages in negotiations about salary and conditions of work but also has considerable influence, as an expert pressure group, over the determination of the number of medical school places. The BMA, therefore, has important monopoly power and, because the NHS is almost the sole employer, we have the interesting spectacle of bilateral monopoly tempered only by international flows of medical manpower.

14.2.2 Barriers to entry

The NHS maintains its monopoly position largely because of the advantage it enjoys as a result of its method of finance. There is no way by which a patient can opt out of the NHS. He has to pay his national insurance contribution and other taxes whether he uses the NHS or private medical services. Thus, a patient pays a price for private medical care *in addition* to the amount he has already paid for the NHS and not *instead of* this amount, as would be the case in most other industries with competing firms. This price advantage enjoyed by the NHS has been reinforced by an increase in the standard of services provided by the NHS — for example, the move toward smaller wards which has increased patients' privacy. In this way, the services provided by the NHS and those of the private sector have become more homogeneous and the incentive to enter the private sector has been reduced. This is not to say that the product of the private sector is not differentiated from that of the NHS. There are virtually no queues in the private sector while one could wait for up to two years to obtain a minor operation in the NHS and some people are willing to pay in order to secure treatment at a time convenient to them.

However, such 'queue-jumping' by private patients has raised considerable political storms and led to calls for the removal of private beds from NHS hospitals – if not for the total abolition of private practice. Although there has been little evidence that the abolition of private beds would reduce waiting lists significantly, the political arguments have concentrated on this aspect. However, a more cogent argument may be that private patients receive a subsidy from the NHS. Culyer and Cullis (1974) suggest that, on the basis of average cost pricing, private patients do not bear the full capital costs of their beds in NHS hospitals. If this is the case, the abolition of private beds from NHS hospitals would increase the cost for private patients who would then have to be treated in private hospitals. These increased costs would tend to decrease private practice.

14.2.3 Cost structures

Because it is so difficult to measure the ultimate output of medical services – a change in health status – most of the research on costs has concentrated on measuring the costs of intermediate outputs such as costs per patient week in hospital, cost per case, etc.

In one of the few studies using UK data, Beresford (1972) examines the behaviour of costs per patient week and costs per case as a function of throughput. (Throughput is defined as the number of cases per occupied bed per week. Therefore, multiplying the reciprocal of throughput by seven gives the average length of stay in days.) He finds that costs per patient week rise with throughput. The early days of any course of treatment are relatively costly and, because by increasing throughput one is increasing the number of 'early days', this positive relationship is hardly surprising. On the other hand, he finds that costs per case at first fall rapidly with increases in throughput and then tend to level off at a throughput of about 0.7. This suggests that hospital costs per case could be minimised by speeding up throughput so that the average length of stay was fewer than ten days. However, we must be careful not to infer from this evidence that hospitals 'should' speed up their throughput to this level. Beresford's evidence, while useful, refers only to *hospital* costs. By reducing length of stay in hospital, one would be shifting the costs of care from the hospital to the domiciliary health services and, perhaps more importantly, to the family. It is not obvious that social efficiency would be increased by reducing hospital stay.

Beresford's study refers only to optimal use of existing resources but it would also be useful to have some information about the optimal pattern of investment in new hospitals. Unfortunately, the information about the size of hospital that minimises average costs is inconclusive. Feldstein (1967), correcting for the effects of case-mix, concludes that the optimal size of hospital is either 310 or 900 beds (the latter figure is relevant if the larger hospitals which had a lower throughput could achieve the throughput of the smaller ones) while Culyer *et al.*[5] conclude that the optimal size is about 500 beds. Similarly conflicting results are obtained when data from other countries are used.

The paucity of information about economies of scale has not, of course, prevented policy recommendations about the optimal size of hospitals. Gray and Topping (1945) recommended that a District General Hospital should ideally have about 800 beds in order to take advantage of economies of scale while some time later, the Bonham-Carter Report (1969) argued that the optimal size was even larger (about 1000–1750 beds).

The same lack of evidence underlies the policy with respect to health centres and group practice. The thinking behind these innovations is that they 'must' provide economies of scale and, therefore, be more efficient than the single GP practice. As a result, they have received considerable official encouragement. Bailey (1970), however, casts some doubt on this faith. Using US data, he finds no evidence of economies of scale of this type. While his methodology is open to criticism, his conclusions do point to the necessity for more work in this area. For the NHS in particular, it is most important that we have better estimates of the underlying cost structures in each part of the service so that planning can be carried out on a firmer basis than has been possible hitherto.

14.3 MARKET BEHAVIOUR

14.3.1 Resource allocation in the NHS

Waiting lists for hospital beds have been a problem since the early days of the NHS. Table 14.5 shows that the waiting list per thousand

TABLE 14.5:   Waiting lists, average length of stay and throughput capacity, selected years 1955–71

	1955	1959	1963	1967	1971
Total waiting list (thousands)	444.0	466.2	468.2	531.1	520.0
Total waiting list per thousand population	10.0	10.3	10.0	11.0	10.7
Average length of stay (days)	22.9	20.1	17.6	15.7	13.9
Throughput capacity	11 546.6	13 042.6	14 772.7	16 579.4	18 543.7

Source: Culyer (1976).

of the population remained remarkably constant between 1955 and 1971. It is tempting to argue that the persistence of waiting lists demonstrates that the NHS is failing to allocate resources efficiently and that the waiting lists measure the excess demand for medical care generated by zero pricing. Fig. 14.1 illustrates the argument with a familiar supply and demand diagram. P_1Q_1 is the demand curve for medical care and Q_2S is the supply curve which would be relevant if there were no NHS. Note that a finite amount, OQ_1, is demanded even at a zero price because, for a given state of medical knowledge, the net value of the marginal product of medical care goes to zero. The assumption of finite demand at a zero price is necessary if waiting lists are to be used as a measure of excess demand. The supply curve is drawn on the assumption that some small amount OQ_2, would be supplied even at a zero price – that is, there would be some medical charities. This is not a necessary assumption but it seems reasonable enough. OQ_3 shows NHS provision and as it is provided at a zero price, there will be an excess demand equal to Q_1Q_3. This excess demand, so the argument goes, will be measured by the waiting list.

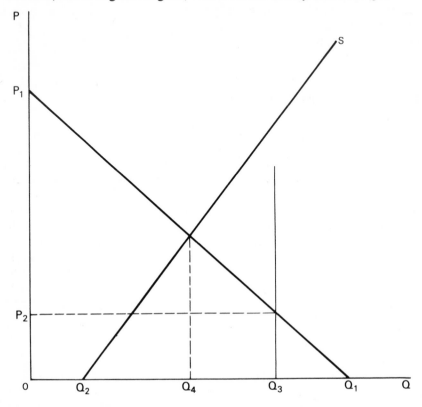

FIG. 14.1:   Supply and demand curves for medical services

Would pricing reduce the waiting list? Clearly, if this analysis is correct, it will. By allowing price to rise, the excess demand will be eliminated at price OP_2 but this does not mean that pricing alone will lead to an optimal allocation of resources. It is true that by pricing at OP_2 the excess demand will be eliminated (and waiting lists disappear) and the available supply, OQ_3, will be allocated to those placing the highest value on it. However, the optimal allocation of resources is achieved at an output OQ_4 where the marginal cost of resources is equal to the marginal value placed on them by patients. Theoretically – though probably not very easily in practice – the NHS could produce an output OQ_4 and allocate it to users who place the highest value on it but if it priced the services at zero there would be an even larger waiting list equal to Q_1Q_4. Thus, the existence of a waiting list does not by itself prove that there is an inefficient allocation of resources. It only shows that a decision has been taken not to allocate resources by using the price mechanism. Several points should be made about the use of this diagram.

First, many would argue that by the very nature of medical care OQ_4 does not reflect the optimal output of medical services. They would argue that the whole purpose of the NHS is to overrule market decisions and that the market demand curve, based as it is on the existing distribution of income, is not an adequate reflection of social valuation.[6] Thus OQ_3, which could be based on social valuations, is in fact the optimal output and the real problem is how to ration the excess demand.

Second, table 14.5 suggests that waiting lists cannot be used as a measure of excess demand. Between 1955 and 1971, the supply produced by the NHS (its throughput capacity) increased by about 60% while waiting lists increased by about 17% and population by about 9%. Thus, although output was increasing rapidly relative to the population (that is, Q_3 was moving closer to Q_1), waiting lists did not fall and, therefore, do not appear to measure the excess demand which would have been falling over the period. There are several possible reasons for this. One possibility is that waiting lists are equal to or less than the excess demand for hospital care such that, if excess demand is very large, GPs and specialists practise rationing by not referring the less serious cases to hospital, by making arrangements for domiciliary care, or by other methods. Thus, as output increases and some of the existing excess demand is satisfied, some of the previously unexpressed excess demand is allowed to be registered by appearing on the waiting list. Such a process will continue until all of the quantity demanded is being treated or appears on a waiting list. Thereafter, further increases in output will reduce waiting lists. Of course, the demand for medical care at a zero price may not be finite. In this case waiting lists could remain constant while output increases indefinitely and yet excess demand would be falling, in the sense that, if appropriate allocation procedures could be introduced, the available output would be allocated to increasingly lower valued uses.

Another possible interpretation of the constant waiting list is that 'supply creates its own demand'. Because doctors demand care on behalf of their patients as well as supplying it, the demand curve, it is argued, will not be independent of the supply curve. The most extreme form of this argument is that the quantity demanded at any price will depend not only on the price of care, the income of patients and other demand variables but also on the quantity supplied; so that the quantity demanded at any given price will be different for, say, supply OQ_4 than OQ_3. In a non-competitive market such as the UK, doctors will therefore have an incentive to 'create' waiting lists in order to create a demand for their own services. The possibility of this interaction between supply and demand exists wherever one needs advice from an 'expert' who also provides the services he advises – for example, solicitors and motor mechanics. Clearly, the possibility for the 'expert' to affect the demand curve depends on the availability of other advice and the market conditions under which it is given. If, for example, a motor mechanic consistently advises more maintenance than others in the area, customers who compare their cars with others which have been to other mechanics will change their mechanic if they feel that their own cars are not significantly better as a result of the extra maintenance. Such comparisons and the possibility of changing one's expert depends on the competitiveness of the market in which the experts operate.

Other versions of the 'supply-creates-its-own-demand' argument are not significantly different from the conventional supply and demand analysis. For example, improvements in medical knowledge make new techniques available. Because this increases the marginal product of medical services, the demand curve shifts to the right. We do not need arguments that doctors have a new technique which they 'want' to use; we have simply a demand curve shift. Similarly, if excess demand exists and resources are unequally allocated geographically, we would expect areas that have more facilities for a certain type of treatment to treat more cases even if there is no reason to expect the incidence of that particular type of case to vary across areas. Thus, one area may have supply equal to OQ_3 while another may have OQ_4. The first area will give more treatment than the second, but there is no reason to think that the underlying demand conditions have been affected by different provision.

14.3.2 Regional allocation of resources

Culyer (1976) argues that fig. 14.1 is seriously misleading when used to illustrate the optimal allocation of resources for the NHS. He claims that the market demand curve for medical care is irrelevant by the very nature of the NHS and that, for these purposes, the concept of *demand* should be replaced by a concept of *need* which he develops based on the idea that individuals as a group would like to make medical care available to everyone whether or not they would have purchased it themselves in a free market. There are some problems with this view, but it does appear to be consistent with some popular opinion. If this is in fact the case, one might expect that an important aspect of a NHS based on need would be equal access to health producing facilities.[7] Note that this does not necessarily imply equal access to medical care because some environments are more unhealthy than others. Thus, where medical care is not equally accessible, the concept of need would require it to be concentrated in areas of greatest need – that is, in areas of highest incidence of disease and illness. Ideally, this concept would apply to individuals but data on individual access to medical care are very scarce.[8] However, we do have regional statistics on medical care which give a fairly comprehensive view of the regional distribution of resources.

Table 14.6 gives examples of hospital spending that show very large regional variations in medical care which do not appear to be related in any systematic way to medical 'need'. Table 14.7 shows that there is little significant correlation between various indicators of medical need and NHS expenditure and that there is some significant *negative* correlation as in the case of the birth-rate. Moreover, Culyer (1976, page 115) claims that the 'general pattern in the early 1960s was, it would appear, in proportionate terms not so very different (as far as the hospital services are concerned) from what it was after the First World War'.

It seems, therefore, that the introduction of a NHS based on need has not changed the regional distribution of medical resources from that which existed under a system based primarily on demand. It was the recognition of such persistent regional inequalities which led to the setting up of the Resource Allocation Working Party (RAWP) in 1975. Its Report (1976) confirmed the existence of these inequalities and proposed a formula to relate future financial allocations to need in such a way as to penalise currently well-endowed areas and favour those whose facilities are poor relative to their needs.

14.3.3 Manpower planning

Because of the abolition of market signals in medical care in the UK and because the NHS trains a large proportion of the specialised manpower which it uses, the NHS has from the start engaged in various manpower planning exercises.[9] Such exercises have been *ad hoc* rather than part of a continuous planning procedure and have come to very different conclusions. The Goodenough Report (1944) suggested only a cautious increase in the stock of doctors. The government ignored this advice and increased the number of doctors by over 20%. The Willink Report (1957) came to the conclusion that there was a potential surplus and recommended that medical school admissions should be reduced by 10%. This recommendation was followed but Lafitte and Squire (1960), using somewhat different assumptions, concluded that the Willink requirements had been underestimated by about 17%. Partly because of this criticism of the Willink report, the Government set up yet another Working Party to review its data and conclusions. The Platt Report (1961) made suggestions about the career structure of doctors and expressed concern about the shortage of British doctors. Paige and Jones (1966) using a somewhat different

TABLE 14.6: Variations in hospital spending by area, 1971/72

| | Population (thousands) | Current expenditure | % variation from national average for provision per capita | | | | |
| | | | | Beds | | | |
			Total	General medicine	General surgery	Maternity (adjusted)†	Geriatric and chronic sick (adjusted)‡
Mersey							
Cheshire	865	−11	39	−25	0	−18	65
Liverpool*	607	62	38	192	130	105	36
St. Helens and Knowsley	377	−34	13	5	−25	−44	−55
Sefton	425	−15	−6	71	23	−10	−19
Wirral	355	−10	−2	60	85	21	−40
Oxford							
Berkshire	624	−10	1	−11	1	20	1
Buckinghamshire	477	−29	−24	−29	−33	5	−9
Northamptonshire*	468	−32	−15	−36	−9	−8	53
Oxfordshire	505	3	24	−21	−19	2	−5
South Western							
Avon*	901	14	23	33	−7	37	−9
Cornwall	378	−30	−7	−38	−41	4	−6
Devon	896	−14	14	−32	0	18	−11
Gloucestershire	467	−36	−18	−45	−22	21	9
Somerset	386	−17	21	−44	−38	26	40
South-West Thames							
Croydon	334	na	35	na	na	na	5
Kingston and Richmond	250	na	30	na	na	na	−44
Merton, Sutton and Wandsworth*	680	na	58	na	na	na	17
Surrey	1111	na	32	na	na	na	−20
West Sussex	627	na	−19	na	na	na	−56

Source: Buxton and Klein (1975).
Notes: *Teaching area.
† Beds per female in age group 15–44.
‡ Beds per person in age group 65 and over.
na Not available from profile.

TABLE 14.7:   Correlations between health and social status indicators and
health service spending

	Community health expenditure per capita	Hospital revenue expenditure per capita	Hospital capital expenditure per capita
Birth-rate	–0.6388	–0.5242	–0.0580
Death-rate	0.2420	0.0324	–0.3318
% population over 65	0.3600	0.1227	–0.1268
Infant mortality rate	–0.4458	–0.3305	–0.2626
% of population managerial and professional	0.8307	0.7937	0.4700
% of population semi-skilled and unskilled manual	–0.7455	0.7822	–0.2314

Source: Noyce *et al.* (1974) page 556.
Note: Coefficients >0.78 are significant at 0.1% level,
>0.6614 at 1% level, and
>0.5325 at 5% level.

methodology estimated that 'a shortage of doctors in 1975 is unavoidable'. The next official exercise was contained in the Todd Report (1968) which also estimated a shortage.

Table 14.8 shows forecasts of requirements with actual outcomes. In each case the forecast requirements of GPs is greater than the actual amount while for hospital doctors the reverse is the case. It would be difficult to argue that manpower planning in the NHS has been a success. Forecasts have been made on the basis of *ad hoc* assumptions about future trends. Such 'ad hockery' is illustrated by the definition of 'shortage'. The manpower planners' shortage has no close relationship with the economists' concept of excess demand which refers to the differences between quantities demanded and supplied at a particular price. The planners calculate the required number of doctors in some future time period as a function of population and, perhaps, the distribution of population and project the estimated number of doctors available at that time as a function of net migration rates, output of medical schools, etc. The difference between the two is the shortage (or surplus) of doctors. Notice that neither the required number of doctors nor the estimates of those available depends on doctors' salaries. That is, there is no attempt to adjust the projected factor mix used by the NHS in response to changes in the relative price of different factors of production nor to

TABLE 14.8:   Forecast requirements and outcomes: physician stock movements (hospital doctors and GPs)*

Year	Willink	Paige and Jones	Todd	Actual‡
1955	(a) 24 841	—	—	24 216
	(b) —	—	—	20 484
1965	(a) 25 591	—	—	24 260
	(b) 23 684	—	—	24 734
1970	(a) 25 966	—	—	24 458
	(b) 24 484	—	—	29 043
1975	(a) —	—	29 260	26 135
	(b) —	(29 346)**	33 034†	35 316
1980	(a) —	33 700	—	—
	(b) —	32 400	—	—

Source: Maynard and Walker (1978).
Notes: *(a) General practitioners (including trainees and assistants), and
(b) hospital physicians.
**Estimate based on their assumed annual growth rate of 2% to 1980.
†Based on 1975 actual estimate and Todd additional requirements for 1965–75.
‡*Health and Personal Social Services Statistics*, 1975, and Department of Health and Social Security.

allow for the individual response of doctors to changes in salaries – particularly relative to salaries abroad. For example, planners have seriously under- or over-estimated emigration and immigration of doctors and this has led to errors in forecasts. Moreover, the sporadic nature of the exercise has made it impossible to improve the forecasts by making gradual adjustment to the plans.

14.4 PERFORMANCE

There are very great difficulties involved in measuring the performance of the medical care industry in the UK. Because the output of the NHS is not marketed we cannot use a simple measure, such as the ratio of profits to net book value as an estimate of the rate of return on capital. Moreover, because the true output of the industry is a change in health status, the output itself is difficult to measure and even more difficult to value. In addition, part of the activities of the NHS are research into and development of new medical techniques along with the training of a new generation of medical personnel and these activities are often inseparable from the day-to-day work of treating patients. Therefore, some effects of inputs used at present will not be felt until the future and we have the problem that exists in all firms producing joint products of how to allocate the costs among its various activities.

Because of such difficulties, it is impossible to produce a single measure of performance for the NHS and it is necessary to examine the suitability of various measures which have been used.

14.4.1 Indicators of health status[10]

Indicators of the health status of the country as a whole – such as the infant mortality rate or life expectancy rates – have been used to show the performance of the country over time or compared with other countries. For example, table 14.9 shows that the UK's infant mortality rate has fallen dramatically since 1930 but that this country's performance is poor relative to others such as Denmark and Japan.

TABLE 14.9: Infant mortality rates (number of deaths of infants under 1 year of age per 1000 live births), selected years, 1930–75, for ten countries

	1930	1940	1950	1960	1970	1975
US	64.6	47.0	29.2	26.0	19.8	16.1
Japan	124.5	90.4	59.8	30.7	13.1	10.1
Austria	104.1	74.2	64.0	37.5	25.9	20.5
Denmark	79.6	50.2	30.7	21.5	14.2	10.4
France	78.2	90.5	47.4	27.4	15.1	11.3
Germany*	84.7	64.1	55.4	33.8	18.8	19.8
Italy	105.5	102.7	62.9	43.9	29.2	20.7
Netherlands	50.9	39.1	25.2	17.9	12.7	10.6
UK	63.1	61.0	31.4	22.5	18.4	16.0
Australia	47.2	38.4	24.5	20.2	17.9	14.3

Source: UN Demographic Yearbook.
Note: *Post-war figures refer to the German Federal Republic.

However, we cannot interpret these figures as telling us anything about the relative performance of medical care in the UK because they do not provide any information about expenditure on medical care. Moreover, we cannot be sure that all – or even most – of the improvement in these indicators can be attributed to changes in medical care. Some (Hartwell, 1974; and Perlman, 1974a) indeed, would argue that the changes reflect better nutrition, better living conditions and so on rather than improved medical care.

Even if we could disentangle the effects of medical care from those of other factors, the health indicators we have discussed so far are much too crude. After all, most modern medicine is not about saving or prolonging life (life expectancy has scarcely changed since the war) but about making life more comfortable by relieving pain, increasing mobility and so on. There has been much recent work on the production of a more satisfactory index of health status taking such factors into account but much still remains to be done.

14.4.2 Measures of inputs

Comparisons can be made of inputs – such as expenditures on medical care as a proportion of GNP or number of doctors per thousand population – but such figures cannot, of course, tell anything about the effectiveness with which the country is using the inputs to produce changes in health status. Moreover, a low proportion may reflect lower prices as a result of the monopsony power on the part of the NHS rather than a lower *quantity* of inputs. Therefore measures of inputs can tell us nothing about the relative *performance* of the medical industry in different countries.

14.4.3 Cost–benefit analysis

Instead of attempting to measure the performance of the NHS as a whole, cost–benefit analysis could be used to calculate the rate of return to particular types of treatment. This approach raises difficult problems because it necessitates the placing of values on human life[11] and on the reduction of pain and suffering. It also requires information about the probable effects of the treatment. Eventually, the development of this approach may enable us to move toward some kind of evaluation of the NHS as a whole but, even if it does not, it is valuable for planners in the NHS to obtain some idea of the relative rates of return being earned by various treatments.

Because of the difficult problem of the evaluation of benefits and because so little is known by the medical profession about the natural history of or the effects of treatment on many diseases, it is difficult to find satisfactory examples of cost–benefit studies in the NHS.[12] Most so-called cost–benefit analyses are really cost-effectiveness studies: that is, they measure the effectiveness of different ways of achieving the same goal without considering whether the attainment of the goal is worth even the lowest costs.

14.5 POLICY

Obviously, much of what happens in the industry is a result of government policy. The discussion in this section will, however, concentrate on an examination of the effects of possible changes of policy toward the NHS and the interaction between the NHS and policy in other areas.

14.5.1 Charging for medical services

It is unlikely that any government in the near future will change the NHS so radically that health care in the UK would be provided largely by the private sector, but it has often been suggested that a larger proportion of medical services should be financed by user charges. For example, it is suggested by some that charges should be raised to cover more – or perhaps all – of the cost of the prescription. At present, there is a charge of 45p per item on prescription while the average cost to the NHS is almost £2. It has also been suggested that a charge should be made to hospital patients to contribute towards the residential costs of hospital care. Such charges to patients are justified on the grounds that although there may be good reason for the social provision of *medical* care, there is no good reason why those in hospital should receive food, laundry and so on for no charge while those not in hospital (some of whom are also ill) have to finance these items themselves. To give some idea of the amounts involved, if each hospital patient were charged £1 per day, then £175m per year could be raised (or about $2\frac{1}{2}$% of the total NHS expenditure).

The arguments for user charges are that they will both raise revenue for the hard-pressed NHS and help to reduce pressure on NHS services by inhibiting demand. A little thought suggests that these two aims are not consistent. If demand is price elastic, then charges will be more effective in limiting demand than in raising revenue while, on the other hand, if demand is price inelastic, charges will be more effective in raising revenue than in inhibiting demand. Because what little evidence we have suggests that the demand for medical services is relatively inelastic,[13] the introduction of charges would be expected to increase revenue to the NHS, without having any substantial effect on the pressure of demand.

14.5.2 Substitutes for medical care

It was argued earlier that one of the problems encountered in manpower planning is the tendency to assume fixed coefficients of production. A related difficulty may arise when considering the NHS as a whole. When medical need is observed, it is tempting to meet this need by expanding the NHS. However, it may be more efficient to allocate resources so as to avoid the medical need ever arising. For example, it may be more efficient to increase resources for health education and medical research rather than for medical treatments of often dubious efficacy.[14]

Moreover, some activities, which involve care rather than cure, for example a large amount of geriatric provision, are carried out by the NHS. It is possible that such activities could be carried out more cheaply and perhaps more effectively by some other body. It would probably be widely agreed that society has a resonsibility to provide such caring activities, but it is not at all clear that the NHS should be its agent. A searching examination of the role and scope of the NHS could well yield surprising and useful results.

14.5.3 Illness and the UK economy

In 1974, a bad year for strikes, the UK lost 14.8m working days because of strikes. In the same year, more than 300m working days were lost through illness. The effect of illness on the economy is, therefore, very large. Indeed, some of the earlier arguments for the creation of the NHS were that it would 'pay for itself' by improving the health of the working population. Unfortunately such hopes have not been fulfilled. Working days lost through illness have actually risen since 1948 (when they were about 140m). We cannot, however, conclude that the NHS has failed to improve the health of the working population. The increase in working days lost may be due to more generous sick pay arrangements or to an income effect which means that more prosperous workers are prepared to take longer periods of sick leave at lower pay rather than to return to work at full pay before they feel completely well.

This brief discussion illustrates some of the difficulties of measuring the value of the output of the NHS. Not only is it difficult to place a *value* on health, the concept of health itself is not unambiguous. Whether people feel well enough to go to work depends not only on the medical care they receive from the NHS but also on a range of other factors – some of which may be policy variables such as sickness benefit – that change the relative costs of sickness. Policy toward the NHS cannot therefore be viewed in isolation from other policies. The development of efficient services to meet the health needs of a modern population with rising incomes requires a hard look at what those needs are, whether they are being met by the NHS or, indeed, whether they can be met by conventional medical care, and to what extent more efficient substitutes are available. The fact that medical care in the UK is almost entirely provided by the public sector makes it all the more necessary that policymakers know as much as possible about both the interaction between individual behaviour and demands on the health services (for example, smoking and lung cancer) and the interaction between other government policies and use of the NHS (for example, sickness benefits and demand for sickness certificates). Without such awareness, increasing expenditures on the NHS could well be, at best, inefficient or, at worst, useless.

NOTES TO CHAPTER 14

1. For more detailed description of the history of the NHS, see Maynard (1975), Watkins (1978) and Abel-Smith (1978).

2. The NHS pays GPs' fees for special services such as cervical smears, and one might be able to estimate supply curves for such services in response to changes in the real value of the fees. No such estimates are available so far as I know.

3. See chapter 5 for a more detailed discussion of the structure of the pharmaceuticals industry.

4. However, Feldstein (1974) argues that price elasticities of demand will be biased downward if a correction is not made for quality differences.

5. Quoted without publication details in Culyer (1976).

6. See Culyer (1976) for a good exposition of this view. However, it does not really provide convincing reasons why 'need' as defined by Culyer should not be used in the allocation of other goods as well as health. Why, for example, should the market be allowed to allocate resources to food and clothing but not to medical care?

7. 'Health producing facilities' consists not only of medical services but also of the environment in which the patient lives and works.

8. Le Grand (1978) provides some information about access to medical care by different social classes.

9. See Maynard and Walker (1978) for a more detailed discussion of manpower planning in the NHS.

10. See Culyer *et al.* (1972) for a discussion of the problems of existing indicators and of the way in which more satisfactory indicators may be developed.

11. See Jones-Lee (1976) for a summary of earlier attempts to value human life and for his own estimates.

12. Culyer *et al.* (1977) provide references to several studies most of which deal with the methodology of applying cost-benefit analyses to health rather than actually analysing quantitatively the rate of return to particular programmes in the health service.

13. See, however, chapter 5 in this book for evidence which suggests that the demand for drugs may be price elastic.

14. Cochrane (1972) provides an interesting discussion of how little is known about the efficacy of common treatments for common diseases.

REFERENCES

Abel-Smith, B. (1978) *National Health Service. The first thirty years.* London: HMSO.

Andersen, R. and Benham, L. (1970) 'Factors Affecting the Relationship between Family Income and Medical Care Consumption' in Klarman (1970).

Bailey, R. M. (1970) 'Economies of Scale in Medical Practice' in Klarman (1970).

Beresford, J. C. (1972) 'Use of Hospital Costs in Planning' in M. M. Hauser *ed. The Economics of Medical Care.* London: George Allen and Unwin.

Buxton, M. J. and Klein, R. E. (1975) 'Distribution of Hospital Provision: policy themes and resource variations'. *British Medical Journal.* 8 February 1975.

Cairns, J. A. and Snell, M. C. (1978) 'Prices and the Demand for Care' in Culyer and Wright (1978).

Cochrane, A. L. (1972) *Effectiveness and Efficiency: Random Reflections on Health Services*. Nuffield Provincial Hospitals Trust.

Culyer, A. J. (1976) *Need and the National Health Service*. London: Martin Robertson.

Culyer, A. J. and Cullis, J. G. L. (1974) 'Private Patients in NHS Hospitals: Waiting Lists and Subsidies' in Perlman (1974b).

Culyer, A. J., Lavers, R. J. and Williams, A. (1972) 'Health Indicators' in A. Shonfield and S. Shaw *eds. Social Indicators and Social Policy*. London: Heinemann.

Culyer, A. J., Wiseman, J. and Walker, A. (1977) *An Annotated Bibliography of Health Economics*. London: Martin Robertson.

Culyer, A. J. and Wright, K. G. *eds.* (1978) *Economic Aspects of Health Services*. London: Martin Robertson.

Feldstein, M. S. (1967) *Economic Analysis for Health Service Efficiency*. Amsterdam: North–Holland.

Feldstein, M. S. (1974) 'The Quality of Hospital Services: An Analysis of Geographic Variation and Intertemporal Change' in Perlman (1974b).

Gray, A. N. H. and Topping, A. (1945) *London Hospital Survey*. Ministry of Health and Nuffield Provincial Hospitals Trust. London: HMSO.

Hartwell, R. M. (1974) 'The Economic History of Medical Care' in Perlman (1974b).

Jones-Lee, M. W. (1976) *The Value of Life: An Economic Analysis*. London: Martin Robertson.

Klarman, H. E. *ed.* (1970) *Empirical Studies in Health Economics*. Baltimore: Johns Hopkins.

Kleiman, E. (1974) 'The Determinants of National Outlay on Health' in Perlman (1974b).

Lafitte, F. and Squire, J. R. (1960) 'Second Thoughts on the Willink Report'. *The Lancet, 2.*

Lee Donaldson Associates (1978) *UK Private Medical Care. Provident Schemes Statistics, 1977*. Report for the Department of Health and Social Security.

Le Grand, J. (May 1978) 'The Distribution of Public Expenditure. The Case of Health Care'. *Economica* **45** (178), 125–142.

Maynard, A. (1975) *Health Care in the European Community*. London: Croom Helm.

Maynard, A. and Walker, A. (1978) 'Medical Manpower Planning in Britain – A Critical Appraisal' in Culyer and Wright (1978).

Newhouse, J. P. and Phelps, C. E. (1974) 'Price and Income Elasticities for Medical Care Services' in Perlman (1974b).

Niskanan, W. A. (1971) *Bureaucracy and Representative Govern-*

ment. Chicago: Aldine.
Noyce, J., Snaith, A. H. and Trickey, A. J. (1974) 'Regional Variations in the Allocation of Financial Resources to the Community Health Services'. *The Lancet.* 30 March 1974.
Paige, D. C. and Jones, K. (1966) *Health and Welfare Services in Britain in 1975.* Cambridge: Cambridge University Press.
Perlman, M. (1974a) 'Economic History and Health Care in Industrialized Nations' in Perlman (1974b).
Perlman, M. *ed.* (1974b) *The Economics of Health and Medical Care.* London: Macmillan.
Pryor, F. L. (1968) *Public Expenditures in Communist and Capitalist Countries.* London: George Allen and Unwin.
Report of the Committee to Consider the Future Numbers of Medical Practitioners and the Appropriate Intake of Medical Students. (Willink Report) (1957) London: HMSO.
Report of the Committee on the Functions of the District General Hospital. (Bonham-Carter Report) (1969) London: HMSO.
Report of the Inter-Departmental Committee on Medical Schools. (Goodenough Report) (1944) London: Ministry of Health.
Report of the Joint Working Party on the Medical Staffing Structure in the Hospital Service. (Platt Report) (1961) London: HMSO.
Report of the Resource Allocation Working Party. (RAWP Report) (1976) London: HMSO.
Royal Commission on Medical Education. (Todd Report) (1968) Cmnd 3569. London: HMSO.
Watkins, B. (1978) *The National Health Service. The First Phase.* London: George Allen and Unwin.

FURTHER READING

Culyer, A. J., Wiseman, J. and Walker, A. (1977) *An Annotated Bibliography of Health Economics.* London: Martin Robertson.
Culyer, A. J. and Wright, K. G. *eds.* (1978) *Economic Aspects of Health Services.* London: Martin Robertson.
Hauser, M. M. *ed.* (1972) *The Economics of Medical Care.* London: George Allen and Unwin.
HMSO (1979) *Report of the Royal Commission on the National Health Service.* Cmnd 7615. London: HMSO.
Klarman, H. E. *ed.* (1970) *Empirical Studies in Health Economics.* Baltimore: Johns Hopkins.
Perlman, M. *ed.* (1974b) *The Economics of Health and Medical Care.* London: Macmillan.

Some statistical sources:

Department of Health and Social Security (annual) *Health and Personal Social Service Statistics for England.* HMSO.
Department of Health and Social Security (annual) *Hospital Costing Return.* HMSO.
Lee Donaldson Associates (1978) *UK Private Medical Care. Provident Schemes Statistics, 1977.* Report for the DHSS.

357-80

15 : Tourism

A. J. Burkart

15.1 INTRODUCTION

15.1.1 What is tourism?

A contemporary definition of tourism will be used in this chapter:

> Tourism denotes the temporary, short-term movement of people to destinations outside the places where they normally live and work and their activities during the stay at these destinations. (Burkart and Medlik, 1974)

For many purposes it is usual to restrict the term 'tourist' to visitors who stay at least twenty-four hours but not more than one year at the destination. Tourism may thus be regarded as being bounded by day trips or excursions on the one hand and by migration on the other.

Tourism is not restricted to holidays. Business travellers, students, people on pilgrimage or simply visiting friends or relatives, spend money at the destination and make demands on its resources equally with the holidaymaker, and must be regarded as tourists. A distinction may be made between those travelling to and from sovereign states, i.e. international tourists, and those travelling away from home but still within a single sovereign state, i.e domestic tourists. When residents of a country travel abroad, this may be seen as import tourism and the reception of visitors from abroad as export tourism. To encourage residents to stay at home effects an import saving and to encourage visitors from abroad is to engage in a kind of export trade. Tourism involves travel to the destination, accommodation at the destination, entertainment and other services. The organisations providing these services make up the tourist industry. Of particular importance are the airlines, tour operators[1] and hotels. Many of these organisations are not exclusively concerned with tourists and are often large diversified groups so that it is not always easy to separate out their interests in tourism. In this chapter, the main concern will be with accommodation, passenger transport (mostly airline) and tour operation, because these account for the major part of the tourist industry. But the use of the private car, particularly in domestic tourism, is a significant phenomenon.

15.1.2 Historical development

In 1946, 203 000 overseas visitors (excluding visitors from the Republic of Ireland) came to the United Kingdom, and by 1977 the number of visitors, including those from Ireland, had reached 11 490 000 (see tables 15.1 and 15.2). The propensity of British residents to take a holiday at all has risen from 26 million holidays in 1951 to 45 million in 1976 (British Tourist Authority, 1977). This growth in tourism is due principally to two factors: the rise in real incomes since World War II has stimulated demand for both business and leisure travel, and the suppliers of some tourist services, notably the airlines, have succeeded in reducing their prices in real terms as table 15.3 shows. While changes in the patterns of trade have given rise to increased business tourism, the dramatic increases have come in holiday tourism.

TABLE 15.1:   Visitors to and from the UK, selected years 1946–69 (thousands)

Year	Overseas visitors excluding the Republic of Ireland	Visits overseas by UK residents
1946	203	na
1950	618	na
1955	1037	na
1960	1669	na
1965	2895	6472
1969	5057	8083

Source: British Tourist Authority *Digest of Tourist Statistics* (annually).

Two particular aspects of this growth deserve further mention. First, the private car has played an increasing role. By 1977 it was used as the means of transport in 71% of all holidays taken in the UK by British residents, public transport, i.e. the coach and the train, accounting for a mere 11% each. Second, air transport has developed a central role in holidays abroad by British residents: it now accounts for 62% of holiday transport, a figure reflecting both the island situation of Britain and the development of air inclusive tours (English Tourist Board, 1978). Air travel across the North Atlantic exceeded the volume of sea traffic for the first time in 1957. A year later, the

TABLE 15.2: Visitors to and from the UK, 1970–77 (thousands)

| Year | Visits to UK | | | Visits by UK residents | | | |
	from North America	from Western Europe	from rest of world	Total	to North America	to Western Europe	to rest of world	Total
1970	1 975	3 718	999	6 692	256	7 462	764	8 482
1971	2 074	3 838	1 061	6 973	301	8 273	852	9 426
1972	2 163	3 856	1 148	7 167	341	9 201	991	10 553
1973	2 059	4 459	1 207	7 723	409	10 244	869	11 522
1974	1 755	4 820	1 379	7 954	420	9 179	890	10 489
1975	1 817	5 431	1 596	8 844	492	10 109	1 006	11 607
1976	1 967	6 352	1 752	10 071	547	9 485	1 047	11 079
1977	2 215	7 295	1 980	11 490	573	9 529	1 027	11 129

Source: *International Passenger Survey*: Business Monitor M6 HMSO (annually).
Note: Western Europe includes the Republic of Ireland.

TABLE 15.3:   The diminishing cost of air travel

	1948	1958	1968	1974
Average weekly earnings (UK male)	£7	£13	£23	£46
Price of small car (UK)	£300	£500	£673	£1026
No. of weeks' work to buy car	42.7	38.4	24.9	22.0
Scheduled air fare London–				
New York	£156	£203	£166	£236
No. of weeks' work to buy ticket	22.2	15.5	7.2	6.1

Source: The Economist, 12 October 1974.

introduction of jet aircraft and economy class fares produced a combination of increased speed and relative cheapness that led to the explosive growth of air travel in the 1960s and early 1970s.

The invention in the UK of the air inclusive tour made a major contribution to the growth of holiday traffic to destinations abroad and has been widely copied in Western Europe. Its origins lie in the need of many private sector airlines to seek charter operations when their access to scheduled services was strictly limited. The chartering of aircraft capacity for combining with hotel accommodation into an inclusive tour meant that the total price of such a holiday could be significantly reduced, often to only a pound or two above the scheduled air fare alone. A new form of travel organiser appeared, the tour operator, and the 1960s saw the beginnings of the massive flows of holiday tourism to Spain and the Mediterranean, from both Britain and a large part of northwestern Europe.

The accommodation sector of tourism was a slow starter in postwar growth. A large part of the British stock of hotel and other accommodation was (and is) in coastal resorts and it was a relatively long time before many resorts recovered from requisitioning, minelaying and other effects of war. However, new hotels began to appear in London and also to some extent in other non-coastal cities in the 1960s, but even now little new construction has taken place on the coast. After experimental schemes, the hotel development incentive scheme embodied in the Development of Tourism Act 1969 triggered off, over the period 1970–73, a major increase in the accommodation stock of 54 772 bedrooms. This represented some 10% of the total stock but about 20% of the higher priced sector in which development was mainly concentrated.

The Hotels and Catering Economic Development Committee in 1968 was in no doubt that 'the industry will not realise its potential contribution, either to foreign currency earnings or to regional development, unless it is given a greater incentive to invest in hotel development' (Hotels and Catering EDC, 1968). While some investment would no doubt have taken place anyway, it is probable that a number of investment plans were 'firmed up' by the inducements of the hotel development incentive scheme. The question remains, however, of how far the scheme encouraged firms to invest in capacity beyond what they would otherwise have regarded as an optimal level.

The British government in recent years has shown increasing interest in tourism, both from the importance attached to tourism earnings in the balance of payments (table 15.4) and because of the prospect of developing tourism as an instrument of regional policy. Under the 1969 Act four co-equal tourist boards were established to oversee the promotion of Britain as a tourist destination in worldwide markets (through the British Tourist Authority), to supervise the provision of tourist facilities and to conduct the marketing of each country within Britain (through the English, Welsh and Scottish Tourist Boards). The tourist boards have remarkably few actual powers and rely on their appropriate sponsoring ministry for finance. Yet their influence has been considerable and as a result both the tourism phenomenon and the tourist industry have come under close scrutiny.

TABLE 15.4: Contribution of tourism to the UK balance of payments: the leading six exports in 1977

Visibles	Invisibles
1. Non-electrical machinery £6078m	
	2. Interest, profits and dividends £3873m
3. Chemicals £3867m	
4. Transport equipment £3749m	
	5. Sea transport £3378m
	6. Tourism (including fare payments to British carriers by overseas visitors) £2763m

Source: British Tourist Authority *Annual Report*, 1978.
Note: A recent discussion of the effect of tourism on the balance of payments is to be found in Airey (1978).

15.1.3 Tourism supply

The tourist industry within the UK has to supply, first, the demand created by British residents travelling away from home but staying in this country, and, second, the much smaller (in numbers) demand arising from overseas visitors. A large part of the tourist industry is also engaged in meeting a third kind of demand, namely that created by UK residents wishing to go abroad. An airline for example is as interested in taking British residents abroad as in bringing overseas visitors to Britain.

The accommodation sector consists of a relatively small number of large establishments that are located mainly in the large cities and towns and which, in total, account for a substantial part of the supply of accommodation, and of a large number of small establishments, e.g. pensions, guest houses. Estimates of the number of establishments of different types depend on the chosen definition, but in 1976 the Hotels and Catering Economic Development Committee estimated the figure to be 33 700. Of these, half of the accommodation stock (56% of establishments and 49% of the bedrooms) was in coastal resorts with a marked geographical concentration in Bournemouth, Torquay and other large resorts, and 62% of all establishments were between four and ten bedrooms in size.

Some 820 000 persons are employed in the whole catering and hotel industry, not all of whom are involved in tourism – for example, the staff of catering contractors are mostly outside our definition. But roughly half that total may be said to be wholly or partly employed in tourism enterprises. Employment is often seasonal and a large part is part-time employment. Women employees over the whole industry outnumber men. (For a full examination of employment in the accommodation sector, see Medlik, 1978).

The supply of tourist services is often quite elastic even in the short run, as for example in the case of accommodation at the lower end of the price range: guest houses, bed and breakfast establishments and so on. The supply of some tourist attractions, for example snowfields and beaches, may be regarded as fixed or very nearly so, although improved management may make better utilisation possible. It may be pointed out that the economic use by tourism of the involuntary supply of otherwise largely unproductive and intractable natural features is often used as an argument for the development of tourism.

The supply of all forms of transport, unlike that of accommodation, is highly regulated and in particular the price or fare is determined by some authority other than the operator's or at least requires the approval of some outside authority. This situation applies both to international and domestic operations. Regulation tends also to extend to various forms of non-price competition, but on the whole regulation has stopped short of predetermining the capacity to be offered.

15.1.4 Demand in tourism

Generally, demand for tourism is held to be markedly income elastic.

Sauran (1978) reviews a number of recent estimates. The International Union of Official Travel Organisations (IUOTO), precursor of the World Tourism Organisation, published a study in which global income elasticity was estimated at 1.5 (IUOTO, 1966). However, the value of such global estimates is doubtful, and for the developed countries which are the main generators of tourism demand, an income elasticity of 2 or more seems realistic (Sauran).

Three broad categories of tourism demand may be identified.

(a) *Demand created by business travellers.* Business demand for travel to any given destination tends to be relatively price inelastic. For first-class air travel across the North Atlantic which may be assumed to be mostly business traffic, Straszheim (1978) has estimated a coefficient of –0.65. The cross-elasticity of such demand, with respect to fares to *other* destinations, is likely to be low, but the cross-elasticity of business demand for any one carrier to the given destination with respect to the fares of others on the *same* route will be high.

(b) *Demand created by common interest travellers,* that is, persons whose travel is motivated by a close common interest with the destination, e.g. visiting friends or relatives, attending a school or university. This type of demand for any given route or destination is likely to be relatively price elastic, although in relation to cross-elasticities, it is likely to display similar characteristics to those of business demand.

(c) *Demand created for holiday and leisure purposes.* This type of demand is highly price elastic, and recognition of this has led to the rapid development of the inclusive tour. For the UK inclusive tour market, Green (1978) gives values of –3.0 to –2.5, and for a group of promotional fares on the North Atlantic, Straszheim (1978) calculates a coefficient of around –2.0. The cross-elasticity of such demand for travel to a particular destination with respect to fares to other destinations is high. Within a given route, travellers will be highly responsive to variations in price between carriers.

Wheatcroft (1978) has stressed the importance of examining elasticities disaggregated by types of demand and by seasonal characteristics. This is especially important in the context of the marketing of tourist services and merits some further discussion. The supplier of tourist services typically will face several different types of demand for those services. These different types will display varying degrees of price elasticity. If he can discriminate between the different types on the basis of their price elasticity, he will be able to increase his revenue; for example, groups of customers with relatively price inelastic demand will be prepared to pay higher prices. However, in order to discriminate successfully among the different types of demand, the supplier needs to ensure that those with relatively inelastic demand are prevented from buying at the lower prices. To this end, he may attach special conditions to the sale of his services which will deter those for whom the lower prices are not intended.

This segmentation of customer groups on the basis of their price elasticities has been widely practised in tourism. Airlines especially, but also tour operators and hotels, have been encouraged to offer a range of differential fares and prices with special conditions of validity attached – for example, by requiring advance booking in the case of the cheaper fares or by attaching a minimum stay requirement. It is assumed that the business traveller (whose price elasticity of demand is low) needs to be able to travel whenever he wishes at short notice and without the imposition of a minimum stay requirement. On the other hand, the holidaymaker who is highly responsive to price will not be deterred from travelling by the need to commit himself in advance. Thus the attachment of special conditions enables the supplier effectively to split the market according to the price elasticities of the different classes of consumer. The business traveller will then be charged a higher price than the holidaymaker, even though the service each receives is in physical terms identical.

The high price elasticity of holiday demand has led to intense rivalry in pricing, particularly by the leading tour operators. It must be remembered that in air transport the price is subject to considerable regulation, but the less regulated environment of tour operation has made keen competitive pricing possible. The attention of governments has been invoked by the high price elasticity of holiday demand, because this type of demand can apparently be readily managed by appropriate pricing policies.

15.2 MARKET STRUCTURE

15.2.1 Passenger transportation

British Airways, the main UK air carrier, is now one of the largest airlines in the world. However, it has been government policy to encourage a private sector in civil aviation, and following the recommendation of the Edwards Committee (1969), British Caledonian was assured of a share of scheduled traffic. More recently, Laker Airways began operating in 1977 very low fares across the North Atlantic under the name of Skytrain. There are a number of smaller scheduled airline operators, such as Air Anglia, which offer regional and some international services. Other airlines concentrate on non-scheduled operations – in several cases for their parent or affiliated tour operator. Britannia Airways and Thomson Holidays, and Monarch Airlines and Cosmos are examples of the interdependence of large tour operators and their airlines. British Airways competes for holiday traffic with the private sector and runs a tour operating–charter wing.

A feature of civil aviation in the UK is the apparent ease of entry and exit from the industry. An air operator's certificate (AOC) is needed in order to trade as an airline or otherwise offer public air transport for sale. The list of holders of AOCs in September 1978 (Civil Aviation Authority, 1978a) contained 162 names. While this list includes operators of air taxis and specialised helicopter services as well as conventional airlines, the figure bears witness to the intensity of interest in providing air transport at levels well below the Olympian heights of British Airways.

It is perhaps surprising in a regulated industry that entry is apparently so easy. Since the early 1960s, the government has adopted a liberal licensing policy (particularly for non-scheduled services) and has viewed failures with equanimity. Ease of entry has been facilitated by the rapid technological evolution of the aircraft itself. This has led to an active market in secondhand aircraft which has made it easy for new entrants to acquire a fleet and to escape a large part of their costs on exit from the industry. With buoyant demand for aircraft, the substantial capital outlays have been financed on the security of the aircraft, and the rapid growth of demand has encouraged new entrants and their financial sponsors to take an optimistic view of the traffic available.

The principal alternative mode of transport for travel to and from Britain is the car ferry. Ferry services, which also carry foot passengers, operate all around the coasts principally across the English Channel in the arc from Plymouth to Felixstowe, while other services operate across the Irish Sea, the North Sea and to the outer Scottish Islands. The cross-Channel routes are dominated by a consortium of British Rail and its French, Belgian and Dutch partners (trading under the name of SEALINK) and by the largest private operator, European Ferries Ltd. Since the abandonment of the Channel Tunnel project, new entrants Brittany Ferries (French) and Olau Line (Danish) have established themselves. P & O Group are represented by Normandy Ferries. Hovercraft services have been deployed by Hoverlloyd (Swedish) and by SEASPEED, the trading name of the British Rail hovercraft operations, and in 1977 P & O inaugurated a hydrofoil service from Tower Bridge across the Channel.

15.2.2 Accommodation for tourists

During the post-war period, there has been a steady shift of demand, as far as domestic holiday trades are concerned, from the traditional guesthouse–boarding house type of accommodation towards self-catering modes. For the foreign visitor, however, the full-service hotel is still important. Concern is occasionally voiced at the apparent dearth of accommodation at the lower tariffs. At current levels of costs, it would certainly be impossible to build purpose-built new accommodation that would be profitable at the £5 a night level (1978 prices). However, accommodation at the bed and breakfast end of the market is plentifully available at around that price level.

The accommodation sector did not escape the trend to mergers in the post-war period. Medlik (1978) records twenty substantial mergers in the period 1960–75. The most significant was the merger between Trust Houses and Forte in 1970, because Trust Houses was already something of a market leader by virtue of its widespread network of establishments. Much merger activity has revolved around the brewing industry; Grand Metropolitan acquired Truman, Hanbury and Buxton in 1971 and Watney Mann in 1972. This large group has also diversified into milk distribution and into entertainment. The justification for these mergers seems to lie in diversification rather than in integration. One possible motive for much of this merger activity may be the attempt to reduce the seasonal sensitivity of cash flows.

15.2.3 Tour operation

Although the idea of combining accommodation and transport into a single product sold at an all-inclusive price is not new, the 1960s and 1970s have seen the emergence of tour operation as a major force in tourism particularly by air (Burkart, 1972). In the UK a tour operator is required to hold an air travel organiser's licence from the Civil Aviation Authority in common with other kinds of organiser. In 1978 licences were in force for 8.35 million seats, twenty-one operators accounting for 2.8 million (Civil Aviation Authority. 1978b).

The largest tour operators display a marked degree of vertical integration: Thomson Holidays are served by Britannia Airways, both companies being subsidiaries of the Thomson Organisation, which also owns the Lunn–Poly chain of retail travel agents as well as a number of hotels in European resorts. Cosmos and Monarch Airlines are subsidiaries of their Swiss parent Globus, and the most recent arrival in the leading group of tour operators, Intasun, is forming its own airline, Air Europe. British Airways already owns a large number of retail outlets and has several tour operating subsidiaries. For the larger operators, much of their product range is vertically integrated.

There appear to be few barriers to entry in tour operation, except the need to hold the appropriate licence. There are however some deterrents to successful growth. One of these is the difficulty of matching seats of aircraft to beds in hotels in such a way that all seats and all beds are fully occupied. The trend to vertical integration – and also computerisation – makes the task easier. Marked seasonality of demand is another obstacle to successful growth because of the need to support a lean winter by summer's profits. The development of winter tours has gone some way towards mitigating this imbalance, but the larger tour operators tend to be owned by organisations whose other activities are able to offset the travel company's weak winter cash flow.

Another barrier to growth has been the lack of capable management. The record of the larger tour operators has been one of ambitious firms outgrowing the capability of their managements, and the largest survivor, Thomsons, has reached its leading position in part by acquiring several large but unsuccessful competitors.

It must also be added that the success of tour operation depends on the attainment of a very high percentage of available seats and beds being occupied. Success is highly geared to high load factors[2] and occupancy rates and there is considerable volatility in tour operators' profitability as a result.

15.2.4 Foreign competition

Foreign competition exerts continual but background pressures. There is a sense in which every tourist destination competes with every other, but there is little evidence to suggest that for example a British resident sees a holiday in Spain as a direct alternative to one in Devon.

Within the individual sectors of the industry foreign competition is more overtly present. It is almost axiomatic to say that any given route will be flown by airlines of each country at each end of the route. This concept that the traffic 'belongs' in some way to the two national carriers is probably a major cause of the excessive capacity supplied to many routes. International hotel interests have operated in the UK for many years. Hilton (owned by TWA), Intercontinental (owned by Pan Am), Holiday Inns, Sheraton and others now occupy prominent positions in London and some other large conurbations. In tour operating, the prospects in Britain, still the largest generator of tour traffic, have induced entry by Tjaereborg (Danish) and by Vingresor (Swedish). At present only working on a small scale, it may be expected that these two Scandinavian tour operators will attempt to gain a firm foothold in the UK market.

15.3 MARKET BEHAVIOUR

During the later years of the 1970s, it has been possible to detect a change of climate in tourism away from regulation and *dirigisme* in favour of market forces. The most notable case has been the impetus in the USA to de-regulate air transport, but in the UK and in Europe there has been a trend in the same direction. However, much regulation remains, licences to operate are still required and minimum and maximum prices are still set.

15.3.1 Air transport

In international air transport, the fare-determining activities of IATA (International Air Transport Association) have become notorious as examples of cartel behaviour. This trade association of most of the world's scheduled international airlines has been charged by governments with the task of setting international air fares, and a provision to that effect has been incorporated in most of the bilateral air service agreements that regulate international air transport. There has been an understandable ground swell of opinion in IATA that the large (particularly American) airlines should not come to dominate the world's civil aviation and that care should be taken to minimise injuries to smaller, weaker airlines which for example may only be able to acquire modern efficient aircraft some years after their larger competitors. Fares have accordingly been tightly regulated as have service conditions which might be regarded as transformations of fares. The one factor not regulated has been capacity and as far as IATA has been concerned, member airlines have been free to fly as much or as little capacity as they wished.

The fares determined by IATA thus tend to a kind of average for the industry, not as low as the most efficient airline would want nor as high as the least efficient would seek, but at some compromise level which is acceptable to all the airlines concerned. Thus the essentially political aim was secured, that the weaker airline, probably that of a developing country, would be protected for a time against the inevitable consequences of the fact, for instance, that the world fleets cannot all be re-equipped instantaneously with Boeing 747s.

The combination of a regulated fare and of unrestricted capacity has led the airlines into flying excess capacity. (Some excess capacity is inevitable; for example, airline capacity is supplied in planeload lumps, some traffic is highly directional and return journeys may be lightly loaded). But the effect of regulation which sets fares at a level higher than the equilibrium level is to tempt out excess capacity, especially since there is some evidence that the higher the frequency of service, the greater the traffic attracted. Fig. 15.1 illustrates the effect of regulated high fares on capacity. If fares were unregulated, the capacity and fare level would settle to an equilibrium at e. In fact, the fare is regulated at P. A fare so high reduces the quantity demanded to Q_1, but tempts the airlines to supply capacity at Q_2. Excess capacity is represented by $Q_2 - Q_1$, and the revenue load factor is represented by the ratio of the areas generated by PQ_1 and PQ_2.

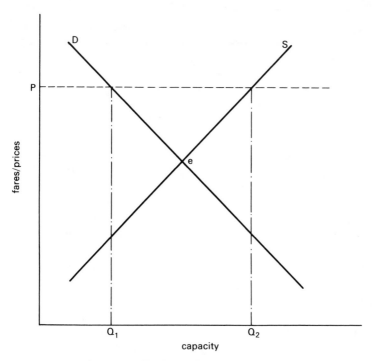

P

fares/prices

Q_1 Q_2

capacity

FIG. 15.1:   The effect of regulating fares

A similar kind of situation appears to have existed in tour operation in the 1960s. The regulatory authority believed that the tour operators would drive very hard bargains with the charter airlines, and accordingly it determined minimum prices for inclusive tours in order to protect their financial well-being. The effect was to generate excess capacity, as new and existing operators put on capacity in the knowledge that they could not be undercut.

In Europe, the rationalising of capacity has been attempted by a type of commercial agreement known as a revenue pool. For example, the two airlines flying between the UK and Ruritania may agree to schedule a given capacity for a stated period and to pool their joint revenue for sharing on a 50/50 basis, irrespective of which airline has actually provided the capacity. Proponents of pools argue that this permits each airline to secure scheduling economies and better utilisation of the fleet. Its critics claim that it limits competition. But at the end of the pool period, the airline not achieving its 50% of the pool revenue is recompensed by its more successful partner, who in turn will threaten to renegotiate the pool basis to, say, 53/47. Each partner will thus still, it is claimed, compete vigorously to maintain its pool share. Any discussion of pooling must take into account the historical background. For at least fifteen years after the Second World War, for example, the scheduled British airline (British European Airways) enjoyed an advantage of some kind, technical or other, over at least some of its European competitors. Germany and Italy in particular developed their airlines later. Politically, it would have been impossible to have given a free rein to BEA. Today, most intra-European routes are the subjects of pooling agreements.

Such agreements are not possible on the other principal tourist routes, those between the UK and the USA, due to the US fair trading and anti-trust legislation. On these routes, recourse has been had to a series of low-priced promotional fares of the kind discussed above. Despite the high price elasticity of demand, this solution did not at first prove successful in terms of profitability. Several reasons contributed to this state of affairs: scheduled carriers tended to reduce their scheduled capacity, and to employ it in the charter field instead, thus nullifying its effectiveness as a solution to the problem; recovery in traffic was slow after the set-back at the time of the energy crisis in 1973–4; and possibly the low-fare market simply did not apprehend the full extent of the low-fare opportunities. Certainly, the introduction of the Laker Airways Skytrain service in 1977 was accompanied by publicity on a massive scale gratuitously generated by the media for a fare which at the time was not in fact the lowest one available. It must also be noted that by that time some recovery in demand had taken place generally. It remains to be seen whether the Skytrain service to Los Angeles, started in 1978, proves as dramatically successful as the earlier service to New York.

15.3.2 Tour operation

Success in tour operation has depended on identifying a large, highly price elastic demand for holiday tourism and on supplying that demand with the low-priced products that are made possible by chartering aircraft and contracting with hotels for relatively long periods of time. This time-chartering of both seats and beds has enabled tour operators to offer a complete holiday package at a price often well below the cheapest available fare alone. That demand for inclusive tours is highly price elastic may be inferred from a statement made by one of the larger British tour operators: ' . . . Price is everything. We put on a mid-week night flight this year – it was only £4 cheaper than the day time flight, but it was the biggest seller. People will put up with a flight leaving in the middle of the night just to save a fiver.' (Quoted in *Marketing Week*, 13 August 1978).

Tour operation has only been directly regulated since the Civil Aviation Act 1971 came into force, but the airlines used by the tour operators were regulated by the predecessor of the Civil Aviation Authority, the Air Transport Licensing Board. As we have seen the

Board interpreted its function as being to protect the airlines against cut-throat bidding for capacity by tour operators by setting minimum prices for inclusive tours by air.

The early 1970s witnessed a vigorous rivalry for market share which culminated in the failure in 1974 of Clarksons (Court Line), at the time the largest operator. The survivors of the struggle have allowed the market to stabilise, and the Civil Aviation Authority has in general not sought to impose minimum prices on tour operators.

15.3.3 Cross-channel ferries

The operators of cross-Channel ferries formed a 'harmonisation conference' as early as 1962 at the suggestion of and to mitigate the effects of the then new air ferry services. Although the threat of competition from the air never materialised, the conference remained in being and by the time the Monopolies Commission had reported its findings (Monopolies Commission, 1974), all the British operators except Hoverlloyd were members. There also operated a considerable degree of pooling of both costs and revenue. The Monopolies Commission found both these features to be against the public interest. A principal object of the Conference had been the determination of fares, but with the Monopolies Commission's report, the Government delegated to the Office of Fair Trading the task of approving the ferry operators' proposed fares. In the event, the fares structure approved by the OFT has been largely designed to spread the very acute peak experienced in this market during a few weeks in July and August. The government appear to be satisfied and have indicated that they will be prepared to step aside from the regulation of cross-Channel fares.

15.3.4 The accommodation sector

From the viewpoint of an individual hotel, the degree of competition that influences it depends on local rather than national factors. An hotel experiences local competition, of a kind familiar enough in retailing. There will be a local hinterland for example from which much of its business is obtained even though by definition its tourist traffic will come from places outside that hinterland. Many traditional hotels are members of a group; Medlik (1978) lists thirty groups having at least 1000 beds each. The largest group in terms of the bed capacity it controls is Trust Houses Forte, and the two hundred or so UK establishments of the group are well-scattered throughout England, less so in Wales and Scotland. The group as a result tends to occupy the role of price leader – at least in the field of traditional full service hotels. But there is no evidence that Trust Houses Forte exercises a dominant position either nationally or locally and in very few towns does this company control as much as 25% of the capacity on offer.

15.4 PERFORMANCE

It is difficult to establish performance criteria for the tourist industry, because many of the inputs to tourism originate from organisations not wholly concerned with tourism. Thus in considering, say, the hotel sector, the published reports and accounts of large companies do not sufficiently disaggregate the figures to take account of their hotel interests alone. One is in fact trying to put together a general picture of performance from relatively small quantities of data. Much of the information needed is probably actually collected, but it has to be recast into a tourism mould.

The 1970s started with the big addition to the stock of bedrooms created under the Development of Tourism Act 1969. Most of the additional capacity was in London and other large cities. The energy crisis in 1973–4 led to some curtailment of demand and in a sense the development scheme exacerbated the situation facing the industry because the new supply appears lumpily before demand has caught up. Some check to profitability occurred at that time. Since then, however, demand has recovered; practically no new building has occurred; and there may even have been some net loss of capacity, particularly in resort areas where older buildings have proved to be beyond modernisation.

The Hotels and Catering EDC (1976) in its second view of future prospects for the industry to 1985 concludes that at current levels of demand profitability could only be maintained by annual tariff increases of 16–17%. Increases in tariffs of that order may however be counterproductive. However, an increase in demand at current price levels could transform the situation: the EDC estimates that an increase in bed occupancy of 3% per annum could increase profitability by 8 or 9%. Further, the projected increase in demand is likely to come from the lower, more price-conscious end of the market and it seems unlikely that the traditional full service hotel can meet its needs.

The performance of the tour operating sector since 1969 is shown in table 15.5. The considerable variations in profitability from year to year are noteworthy, as is the apparent lack of association of profitability with turnover. During the period however, and particularly in the early 1970s, the tour operating sector was attempting to consolidate after its very rapid growth in the 1960s. There would appear to have been excessive capacity put on the market and consequently a struggle for market share, which culminated in the collapse of two large operators. The results for 1975 illustrate the situation after these

TABLE 15.5:   Profitability of tour operators (ATOL holders)

Year	Turnover (£ million)	Net Profit (Loss) (£ million)	Net Profit (Loss) (as % of turnover)
1969	105.6	1.6	1.5
1970	140.8	(1.6)	(1.1)
1971	169.6	(8.7)	(5.1)
1972	206.0	(8.9)	(4.3)
1973	245.5	(0.4)	(0.2)
1974	226.7	(3.0)	(1.3)
1975	278.3	12.9	4.6
1976	326.1	11.7	3.6
1977	355.3	7.9	2.2
1978	530.7	34.4	6.5

Sources: Air Transport Licensing Board: 1969–71; Civil Aviation Authority: 1972 onwards.
Note: The figures for 1969 and 1970 relate to fifty-seven tour operators; for 1971 to fifty-six tour operators. From 1972 the figures relate to the thirty largest holders of air travel organisers' licences, and thus include operators of advance booking charters. The two sets of figures are thus not strictly comparable, but are sufficient to show the trend.
Losses of operators going into liquidation are not shown in the year of collapse.

failures. The larger survivors reduced the capacity they offered. But it so happened that there was a big rise in that year in real wages which fuelled the demand for holidays abroad. Further, the real price of a holiday abroad had not yet adjusted to the effects of the energy crisis and was virtually at the 1968 level. The combination of low prices, high incomes and a shortage of capacity guaranteed high load factors and buoyant profits for tour operators in 1975. Since that year, profitability has fallen partially at least because increased capacity has not been matched by higher load factors.

The airline sector is dominated by British Airways. Currently the government has set the airline a target rate of return on mean net assets of 11% (British Airways, 1978). In the ten years to 1978, the airline has exceeded that target on four occasions and has remained profitable in all but three years.

For the much smaller private sector, profitability appears to be inversely related to the number of scheduled services flown. Thus for 1973 Britannia Airways with no scheduled services and with three quarters of its revenue coming from inclusive tour charters (largely from its own sister tour operator) made an operating profit of £2.58m on a revenue of £19.09m. By contrast, British Midland with half its revenue coming from scheduled services recorded a loss of £0.70m on a revenue of £9.22m (Civil Aviation Authority, 1975). The costs of non-scheduled services are inherently less than those of scheduled operators, but the largest factor in the improved performance of the non-scheduled operator is the high load factors which are obtainable in charters; for example in 1977 the non-scheduled airlines recorded load factors of 80.1% when all the scheduled operators averaged only 60.0% (Civil Aviation Authority, 1977).

One possible overall measure of the tourist industry's performance is its position as an export trade. As shown in table 15.4, the UK's earnings from tourism (including fares paid to British carriers) in 1977 were estimated to be £2763m, thus putting tourism in sixth place in the export league. Against this must be set the expenditure by UK residents going abroad and table 15.6 summarises this balance. From

TABLE 15.6:   Overseas tourism to and from the UK, 1968–77

Year	Visits to UK from overseas	Earnings	Visits from UK by UK residents	Expenditure	Balance
	(million)	(£m)	(million)	(£m)	(£m)
1968	4.8	282	7.3	271	11
1969	5.8	359	8.1	324	35
1970	6.7	432	8.5	382	50
1971	7.0	486	9.4	439	47
1972	7.2	546	10.6	527	19
1973	7.7	681	11.5	682	−1
1974	8.0	837	10.5	683	154
1975	8.8	1123	11.6	878	245
1976	10.1	1633	11.1	1006	627
1977	11.5	2179	11.1	1102	1077

Source: International Passenger Survey (annually).
Notes: Payments of fares to British carriers are not included.
Earnings and expenditure for 1975 to 1977 include estimates for the Channel Islands.

this table, it is clear that the positive balance in recent years is as much due to the levelling off in visits abroad by UK residents in the later years as to the increase in visits by tourists from abroad. It seems reasonable to suppose that the economic pressures in the UK at that period are chiefly responsible for the reduced activity by UK residents, and that the relative cheapness of the UK resulting from the fall in the value of sterling played a part in attracting overseas visitors.

15.5 PUBLIC POLICY

It has been seen that tourism and the tourist industry are closely regulated and supervised by government. Not only are the individual sectors regulated (liquor licensing, air and road transport licensing and air travel organisers' licensing are three instances), but also the Development of Tourist Act 1969 brought a hierarchy of tourist boards. The Act gave the boards practically no powers and consequently their achievements have for the most part been the fruits of persuasion. Much of their activities has been promotional. They are financed by grant-in-aid, by contributions from the industry and by the sale of publications and similar sources. They have administered the hotel development incentive scheme and are empowered to make grants under the Act to tourism projects in development areas.

The hotel development incentive scheme triggered off the biggest wave of investment in hotels made in this country in this century. During the three-year currency of the scheme, 415 new hotels were built and 590 extensions made to existing establishments (Hotels and Catering EDC, 1976). Provided that certain conditions relating to the building itself and its methods of operation were met, the grants were of right and there was no requirement to show an economic case. Consequently, much of the new construction was in London; most catered for the business tourist and the tourist from abroad; and most was in the higher tariff ranges. Thus an opportunity was missed to encourage or direct new accommodation to underprovided areas. Further, the conditions relating to the building and its operation were conservative, ruling out the possibility of building self-catering establishments to meet the demand for lower-priced accommodation. There has been practically no new construction since the scheme ended, but provision was made in the 1978 budget for hotels to qualify for capital allowances in respect of the building.

An active role for the tourist boards is implied in the provisions of the 1969 Act for the introduction of a system of registration and classification of hotel and other accommodation. Such systems exist in Spain, Italy and several other European countries, but in the UK the assessment of standards is left to voluntary efforts, notably the motoring organisations. The Act provides for statutory registration and classification, but this provision has not been implemented. Registration may be regarded as a form of licensing, for in order to trade as an hotel, the premises would have to be registered as such. Thus a new barrier to entry would be created.

If classification into grades or classes is implemented, it may be feared that price control will follow thereafter. For while the idea of official comparability between different or like establishments is at first sight attractive, grading in this way almost inevitably involves a value-for-money judgement. A statutory body entrusted with classification would find it hard to resist indicating or controlling prices as well. There is incidentally no evidence that the public want an official scheme or are dissatisfied with the several voluntary schemes that operate today.

The tourist boards' lack of real powers is clearly seen in the lack of a co-ordinated policy for transport, public and private, a lack which remains a serious handicap for tourism. The Hotels and Catering EDC (1977) stresses the need for co-ordination.

This should also be reflected in the policies of the nationalised industries such as the airlines, railways and other carriers. Yet frequently there seems to be a conflict between the needs of tourism and policies in other areas. This is reflected in, for example, the field of transport in the consideration by British Rail of cuts and line closures in the very type of area that the statutory [tourist] Boards are being urged to promote.

In the case of air transport, the regulatory body (the Air Transport Licensing Board from 1960 to 1971, and the Civil Aviation Authority thereafter) has been charged with furthering the interests of civil aviation or some similar duty. This led in the earlier period to the ATLB imposing minimum prices on inclusive tours (via the chartering airlines): if a minimum price was fixed, the argument ran, the chartering tour operator would not need to seek excessively low charter prices from the airlines. Thus the financial health of the airlines would be ensured and the interests of civil aviation furthered.

The Civil Aviation Authority largely abandoned minimum prices, but the Civil Aviation Act 1971 did bring tour operators within the scope of the Authority's licensing. Tour operators and other air travel organisers are now required to be bonded and to hold the appropriate licence. This was in response to the earlier anxieties of government that the failure of some tour operator might leave several hundred – or even a thousand – British holidaymakers stranded on a Mediterranean beach. To be used in such an eventuality, the Air Travel Reserve Fund was established and the passenger levied to pay for it. The sensitivity of government and its statutory boards to the possible plight of holidaymakers is remarkable; and in 1978 when industrial action by French air traffic controllers disorganised many holidays abroad by British holidaymakers, it was being suggested that compensation should be forthcoming from tour operators for events that were wholly outside their control and for which they could have hardly thought to have been negligent.

15.6 CONCLUDING COMMENTS

How valid is the concept of a tourist industry? Might it not be better to use the conventional nomenclature and refer to the civil aviation industry, the hotel and catering industry and so on? For some purposes, the answer will be 'yes', but two features of tourism justify the identification of a separate tourist industry. Firstly, much of the demand for the product of the component sectors is a derived demand; for example, demand for air travel is a consequence of a desire to be elsewhere and few people travel by air for its own sake. The demand for transport thus arises from the demand for sunny beaches, well-covered ski-slopes or cultural monuments. Secondly as a consequence there is a marked degree of interdependence among the sectors. Tourists cannot reach the resorts and the hotels if there is no transport, and people cannot stay at destinations that lack accommodation.

The attitude of the principal sectors of the industry towards the regulation of tourism deserves a comment. The arguments for regulation of air transport have been discussed by Wheatcroft (1964) and against regulation by Straszheim (1969). There has however been a long tradition of transport regulation and other forms of government intervention in the UK, and regulation is accepted, if not always with pleasure, at least as inevitable. The accommodation sector has tended to be more robust in its attitudes. Despite centuries of liquor licensing experience, the sector has tended to resist regulation.

Some assessment of the performance of the four national tourist boards is perhaps overdue. Their severest critics may argue that the boards simply represent another layer of bureaucracy interposed between government and the tourist industry. The British Tourist Authority in 1977–8 spent over £7m on publicity overseas, the effect of which is very hard to estimate. Indeed, if one bears in mind the staff required to administer that expenditure and its consequences (e.g. overseas offices), the question prompts itself: would not the same effect be achieved by a very much smaller organisation than the present sum total of the existing boards? Further, it should be noted that while the English Tourist Board has established a network of regional tourist boards, the reorganisation of local government in Scotland has been accompanied by the establishment of tourism officials within the local authorities, a potentially more effective arrangement.

Can one identify structural or other features of the tourist industry which have in the past affected or which may in the future affect the industry's performance? It is hard to answer that question specifically, but the recognition of the interdependence of the individual sectors has led to increasing vertical integration between the sectors, and this trend may be expected to continue. Government intervention is also likely to continue to play an important role. However it is to be hoped that it will not increase. The effect of the various forms of regulation has been merely to delay the bringing about of a state of affairs which would have arisen sooner if market forces had been allowed full play.

NOTES TO CHAPTER 15

1. A tour operator packages a combination of transport and accommodation and sells the package to the public at a single all-inclusive price.

2. Load factor (in transport) and occupancy rate (in accommodation) both express usually in percentage terms the ratio of capacity actually occupied to capacity offered. Both may be expressed in physical terms, i.e. seats or beds, or in revenue terms.

REFERENCES

Airey, D. W. (1978) 'Tourism and the Balance of payments'. *Tourism International Research.* 3rd Quarter.

British Airways (1978) *Annual Report and Accounts 1977/78.* London.

British Tourist Authority (1977) *Annual Report.* London.

British Tourist Authority (1978) *Annual Report.* London.

Burkart, A. J. (1972) 'The Role of the large tour operator in the development and promotion of tourism' in A. J. Burkart and S. Medlik. *eds. The Management of Tourism.* London: Heinemann, 1975.

Burkart, A. J. and Medlik, S. (1974) *Tourism, Past, Present and Future.* p.v. London: Heinemann.

Civil Aviation Authority (1975) *Financial Results – UK Airlines 1968–1974* CAP 376. London: CAA.

Civil Aviation Authority (1977) *Annual Statistics 1977* CAP 415. London: CAA.

Civil Aviation Authority (1978a) *Official Record, Series 3.* London: CAA (September).

Civil Aviation Authority (1978b) press release 'One million more air holidays in 1978'. London: CAA (July).

Edwards Committee (1969) *British Air Transport in the Seventies.* Cmnd 4018. London: HMSO.

English Tourist Board (1978) *British Home Travel Survey 1977.* London.

Green, J. H. T. (1978) *UK Air Traffic Forecasting.* London: Department of Trade.

Hotels and Catering Economic Development Committee (1968) *Investment in Hotels and Catering.* London: NEDO.

Hotels and Catering Economic Development Committee (1976) *Hotel Prospects to 1985.* London: NEDO.

Hotels and Catering Economic Development Committee (1977) *Report to NEDC January 1977.* London: NEDO.

International Union of Official Travel Organisations (IUOTO) (1966) *Study on the impact of tourism on national economies and international trade.* Geneva: IUOTO (now World Tourism Organisation, Madrid).

Medlik, S. with Airey, D. W. (1978) *Profile of the Hotel and Catering Industry.* 2nd edn. London: Heinemann.

Monopolies Commission (1974) *Cross-Channel Car Ferry Services.* London: HMSO.

Sauran, A. (1978) 'Economic determinants of tourist demand'. *Tourist Review* (1) Berne.

Straszheim, M. R. (1969) *The International Airline Industry.* Washington, DC: Brookings.

Straszheim, M. R. (1978) 'Airline demand functions in the North Atlantic and their pricing implications'. *J. Transport Economics and Policy* **xii** (2), 179–195.

Wheatcroft, S. F. (1964) *Air Transport Policy.* London: Michael Joseph.

Wheatcroft, S. F. (1978) *Price Elasticity Revisited.* Address presented to the Travel Research Association, New York: 22 September 1978.

FURTHER READING

The statistics of tourist flows may be derived from the following:

International Passenger Survey: records (since 1963) flows in and out of the UK; summaries quarterly and annually are published in Business Monitor M6.

British National Travel Survey: conducted for the British Tourist Authority and its predecessor since 1951, and deals mainly with the holiday tourism of UK residents. Full analysis available only to subscribers, but key figures are available in e.g. *Digest of Tourist Statistics* (BTA).

British Home Travel Survey: principal findings relating to tourism within the UK published by the English Tourist Board on behalf of itself and the other three statutory boards.

An important critique of tourism statistics appears in Lewes, F. M. M., Parker, S. R. and Lickorish, L. J., *Leisure and Tourism (Reviews of UK Statistical Sources* **IV**), London: Heinemann, 1975. For air transport, and for tour operation, the Civil Aviation Authority Monthly and Annual Statistics bulletins give the principal operating statistics. For the accommodation sector, no single source is available.

For a general overview of tourism Burkart and Medlik (1974) may be consulted, and for the hotel sector Medlik (1978) brings together much valuable information. The report of the Edwards Committee (1969) together with the annual reports of British Airways give a good general picture of British civil aviation, and for the accommodation sector the various reports and publications of the Hotels and Catering EDC are important.

Index

Index

Abel-Smith, B., 353
Advertising,
   British industry, 7
   food manufacturing, 91
   insurance, 317, 318
   motor vehicles, 189, 197
   pharmaceuticals, 106, 113, 116, 117,
      123–4
   retailing, 296–8
   synthetic fibres, 215–16
Airey, D. N., 361, 378
Aldcroft, D. H., 17, 24, 278
Allen, G. Freeman, 279
Allen, G. R., 103, 104
Anderson, R. and Benham, L., 337, 338,
   353
Armstrong, A. G., 205
Ashby, A. W., 81, 86, 104
Association of the British Pharmaceutical
   Industry (ABPI), 107, 116, 128
Avoidable costs (in rail transport), 262
Aylen, J., 145, 152

Bacon, R. and Eltis, W. A., 18, 24
Bailey, R. M., 340, 353
Bannock, G., 10, 24
Barriers to entry,
   computers, 161
   construction, 236–7
   food manufacturing, 86–9
   insurance, 311, 315
   medical care, 339
   motor vehicles, 192–3
   pharmaceuticals, 111–12, 123, 128

   rail transport, 274
   synthetic fibres, 217, 218
   tourism, 365, 366
Barron, C., 229
Bates, R. and Fraser, N., 78
Beeching Report, 258, 259, 265
Beesley, M. E. and Gwilliam, K. M., 260,
   278
Benjamin, B., 317, 327
Benjamin, S., 327
Beresford, J. C., 340, 353
Berkovitch, I., 58, 79
Berrini, G. L., 221
Bevan, A., 86, 104
Bishop, D., 245, 246, 251
Blackaby, F., 17, 20, 24, 27
Blank, D. and Stigler, G. J., 22, 24
Bloch, E. and Galage, D., 156, 176
Bolton Committee (on small firms), 95,
   322, 327
Bonavia, M. R., 279
Bonham-Carter report, 340, 355
Bowley, M., 253
British Airways, 373, 378
British industry,
   advertising, 7
   changes in, 5–8
   competitiveness, 15–16, 18
   concentration, 9–13
   decline in manufacturing, 7
   economies of scale, 12
   employment, 5–7
   exports, 15–16
   growth, 17

import penetration, 17
industrial strategy, 20–23
innovation, 7, 15, 22
investment, 15, 18, 19
management, 19
mergers, 12, 13
output-capital ratio, 15
performance, 14–17
productivity, 7–8, 15, 17, 21
public policy, 20–22
research and development, 7, 19
services, 17
size of plant, 9–10
British National Oil Corporation, 46, 49, 50
British Rail (BR), 257, 259, 260, 262, 263, 265–78
British Railways Board, 255, 257, 258, 260, 261, 278
British Road Services (BRS), 247, 252
British Steel Corporation (BSC), 135, 136–40, 143, 144, 146, 147, 149, 150, 151, 152, 153
British Tourist Authority, 358, 361, 378, 379
British Transport Commission, 254, 256, 257
Brown, C. J. F. and Sheriff, T. D., 7, 17, 24
Brown, C. V. and Jackson, P. M., 9, 24, 27
Building Research Station, 246
Burkart, A. J., 366, 378
and Medlik, S., 357, 378, 379
Burn, D., xiii, xv
Buxton, M. J. and Klein, R. E., 346, 353
Buyer concentration, 217

Cairncross, A., 3, 24
Cairns, J. A. and Snell, M. C., 337, 354
Cambridge Economic Policy Group, 18, 19
Capel, James and Co, 84, 103
Cartels, 228
Carter, R. L., 310, 311, 315, 316, 319, 321, 324, 327, 329
and Dickinson, G. M., 325, 326, 327, 329
and Doherty, N. A., 311, 317, 327
Caves, R. A., 19, 24
Central Electricity Generating Board, 64, 65, 70, 76
Central Policy Review Staff (CPRS), 200, 205, 206

Charlesworth, G. and Gravelle, G., 77, 79
Cheshire, J. H. and Buckley, C. M., 63, 79
Civil Aviation Authority, 365, 366, 370, 371, 373, 376, 378, 379
Clayton, G., 329
and Osborn, N. T., 305, 322, 327
Clemens, E. N., 301, 302
Coal,
contraction, 67
costs, 61–3, 66
demand, 63–5, 68
economies of scale, 61–2
elasticity of demand, 63
government policy, 76–7
innovation, 74–5
investment, 66–8
labour, 75–6
methods of payment, 76
physical properties, 57
pricing, 65–6
production, 57–8, 61–3
productivity in, 70–74
quality of different types, 58–9
safety, 76
technological innovation, 72, 74–5
world output, 57
Cochrane, A. L., 353, 354
Cockerill, A., 133, 152, 153
Collusion, 241–2
Comanor, W. S., 125, 128
Committee to Review the Functioning of Financial Institutions (the Wilson Committee), 322, 324, 327, 329
Computers,
balance of payments, 171
barriers to entry, 161
compatibility, 163
concentration, 159–60
costs, 160
cross subsidisation, 164
diffusion, 158, 173
economies of scale, 160
employment, 155–6, 171, 173–5
European collaboration, 172–3
foreign competition, 157, 165–6, 168
growth, 157–8
innovation in, 158, 163
leasing, 163–4, 169
manufacture, 156–7
market structure, 158–62
mergers, 160–61
microprocessors, 174–5

multinationals, 162
net output, 156
performance, 164–8
prices and pricing, 162
productivity, 167–8
profitability, 165, 169
public policy, 168–75
research and development, 157,
    160–61, 162, 169, 170, 171, 172
servicing, 163
technical nature, 154
technological diffusion, 158, 173
Concentration,
British industry, 9–13
computers, 159–60
construction, 232–3
difficulties in measuring, 12
food manufacturing, 83–6, 92
insurance, 313
medical care, 338–9
motor vehicles, 179
North Sea oil and gas, 37–41
pharmaceuticals, 110–11
retailing, 284–5
synthetic fibres, 210–13
Conrad and Plotkin, 119, 128
Construction,
barriers to entry, 236–7
Building Research Station, 246
capital requirements, 237
collusion, 241–2
concentration, 232–3
conditions of entry, 236–8
contracts, 237, 239
costs, 240
cyclical variations, 248–9
demand, 231–2
economic significance, 231
economies of scale, 236, 237
employment, 231
E.E.C., 238
foreign competition, 238
growth of firms, 236–8
innovation, 246–8, 249
integration, 244–5
market behaviour, 239–42
market structure, 232–8
Monopolies Commission, 241
nationalisation, 251
patents, 238
performance, 240–8
prefabrication, 247
price controls, 250
pricing, 237, 241

productivity, 246
public policy, 248–51
site efficiency, 245–6
size, 231
size distribution of firms, 232
specialisation, 236
supply, 232
tendering, 240–41
Construction Industry Training Board,
    249
Consumer protection, 300–301
Cook, P. L. and Surrey, A. J., 79
Cooper, M. H., 108, 114, 129
Costs,
coal, 61–3, 66
computers, 160
construction, 240
food manufacturing, 86, 88
insurance, 310–11
medical care, 337, 339–41
motor vehicles, 182–5, 193
North Sea oil and gas, 33
pharmaceuticals, 111, 124–5
rail transport, 256, 259, 261–2
retailing, 299
steel, 133
synthetic fibres, 209, 213–15, 218
Cowling, K. and Cubbin, J., 189, 198,
    205
Cowling, K. and Waterson, M., 4, 24
Culyer, A. J., 340, 344, 345, 353, 354
    and Cullis, J. G. L., 339, 354
    and Lavers, R. J., 354
    Wiseman, J. and Walker, A., 354, 355
    and Wright, K. G., 354, 355
Cuthbert, N. and Black, W., 97, 104

Dalrymple, D. J. and Thompson, D. L.,
    302
Dam, K. W., 46, 55, 56
Davison, D. J., 59, 79
Deaton, A. S., 63, 79
Demand elasticity,
coal, 63
food manufacturing, 81
insurance, 308, 312
medical care, 337, 338–51
motor vehicles, 189, 203–204
North Sea oil and gas, 29–30
pharmaceuticals, 108, 116, 121
rail transport, 266, 270
retailing, 280, 287
steel, 143
synthetic fibres, 209–10
tourism, 363–4

Demsetz, H., 21, 24
Department of Energy, 37, 39, 48, 49, 50, 55, 56, 77, 79
Department of Industry, 35, 55, 138, 175, 203
Department of the Environment (DOE), 248, 252, 300
Department of Scientific and Industrial Research (DSIR), 237, 246, 252
Department of Trade, 312, 317, 321, 322
Development Analysts Ltd, 105
Dickinson, G. M., 322, 326, 327
Distributive Trades E.D.C., 302
Diversification,
    food manufacturing, 84–5
    retailing, 287
    synthetic fibres, 216–17
    tourism, 366
Doherty, N. A., 312, 328, 329

Economic Development Committee for Motor Manufacturing, 205
Economies of scale,
    British industry, 12
    coal, 61–2
    computers, 160
    construction, 236, 237
    food manufacturing, 86–9
    medical care, 340
    motor vehicles, 183–5, 193
    pharmaceuticals, 110, 113, 128
    retailing, 299
    steel, 137
    synthetic fibres, 213–15, 225
Economist Intelligence Unit, 317, 328
Edwards, S. L. and Bayliss, B. T., 266, 278
Edwards Committee, 364, 378, 379
E.E.C., 49, 97, 147, 153, 194, 195, 221, 223, 226–9, 238, 321
Energy,
    consumption, 30, 32
    production, 32
English Tourist Board, 358, 377, 378, 379
Erritt, M. J. and Alexander, J. C., 322, 328
European Investment Bank, 228
Excess capacity,
    steel, 132
    synthetic fibres, 221, 223
    tourism, 368–9
Externalities, 172
Ezra, D., 79

Fair Trading Act, 301
Feldstein, M. S., 340, 353, 354
Firm, concept of, 3–4
Fleming, M. C., 232, 247, 251, 252, 253
Food and Agriculture Organisation, 209, 229
Food and Drink Industries Council, 103
Food and Drink Manufacturing Economic Development Committee, 95, 103, 104, 105
Food and Drugs Act, 96
Food manufacturing,
    advertising, 91
    barriers to entry, 86–9
    competition, 92
    concentration, 83–6, 92
    costs, 86–8
    defined, 80
    diversification, 84–5
    economies of scale, 86–9
    exit, 89
    foreign competition, 96
    government controls, 83, 102
    income elasticity, 81
    labour productivity, 94–5
    links with agriculture, 81
    market behaviour, 89–92
    market performance, 92–6
    market structure, 82–9
    mergers, 85, 95
    Monopolies Commission, 86, 88, 92, 98–101
    new product development, 91, 95–6
    'own labels', 90
    price leadership, 92
    prices and incomes policies, 101–102
    profitability, 93–5
    public policy, 96–102
    research and development, 95–6
Food Standards Committee, 97
Forbes, W. S., 246, 252
    and Skoyles, E. R., 245, 252
Foreign competition,
    British industry, 15–17
    computers, 157, 165–6, 168
    construction, 238
    food manufacturing, 96
    insurance, 325–6
    motor vehicles, 186–8, 194
    steel, 134, 135–6, 143
    synthetic fibres, 211
    tourism, 367
Freeman, C., 7, 24, 95, 104, 162, 176
Friedman, M. and Savage, L. J., 311, 328

Gardner, K., 223, 229
Gardner, N. K. A., 20, 25
Gas Council (or British Gas Corporation), 31, 46, 47, 48, 49, 50
George, K. D., 11, 17, 18, 25, 27, 288, 302
Gibb, D. E. N., 313, 328
Gold, B., 133, 152
Goodenough Report, 344, 355
Government, *see* Public policy
Grabowski, H. G. and Vernon, J. M., 125, 129
Gray, A. N. H. and Topping, A., 340, 354
Green, J. H. T., 363, 378
Griffiths, B., 325, 328
Gwilliam, K. M. and Mackie, P. J., 259, 278

Hague, D. C., 218, 229
Hall, M. and Knapp, J., 298, 302
Harlow, C., 74, 79
Harris, R. and Seldon, A., 117
Hartley, K., 27
Hartwell, R. M., 349, 354
Hauser, M. M., 355
Hillebrandt, Patricia M., 240, 252, 253
Heller, R., 222, 229
Hines, C., 176
Holdren, B., 291, 302
Holton, R. H., 301, 302
Hosiery and Knitwear Economic Development Committee, 229, 210
Hotels and Catering Economic Development Committee, 360, 362, 372, 375, 376, 378

Import controls, 18
Import penetration, 16–17
Industrial Reorganisation Corporation, 141, 168, 202
Industrial Strategy, 20–23
Industry, definition of, 1–3
Innovation,
  British industry, 7, 15, 22
  coal, 74–5
  computers, 163
  construction, 246–8, 249
  food manufacturing, 91, 95–6
  insurance, 320
  medical care, 335
  motor vehicles, 196
  pharmaceuticals, 108, 113–16, 117, 123, 125

steel, 133
synthetic fibres, 208, 215
Insurance,
  advertising, 317, 318
  demand, 311–12
  Department of Trade, 312
  efficiency, 318–19
  entry, 311
  European Community, 321
  government, 311
  growth, 318
  history, 304
  income elasticity of demand, 308, 312
  innovation, 320
  intermediaries, 314–15
  international trade, 325–26
  investment, 322–24
  Lloyds, 306, 312, 313–14, 315, 317
  London market, 315
  marketing, 317–18
  market structure, 312–15
  Monopolies Commission, 317
  nationalisation, 324–5
  nature, 304–306
  overseas business, 308
  performance, 318–20
  price elasticity, 312
  pricing, 316–17, 321
  productivity, 318–19
  profitability, 319–20
  public policy, 320–26
  size of industry, 306–10
  supervision, 320–22
  supply, 310–11
International Cotton Advisory Committee, 230
International Union of Official Travel Organisations, 363, 379
International Union of Railways, 279
Investment,
  British industry, 15, 18, 19
  coal, 66–8
  insurance, 322–4
  motor vehicles, 187
  North Sea oil and gas, 34
  rail transport, 257, 258, 259, 263–5, 269, 273
  steel, 137, 147
  synthetic fibres, 220, 228
  tourism, 360, 372, 375
Iron and Steel Statistics Bureau (ISSB), 131, 152, 153

Jackson, M. P., 79

Johnson, P. S., 10, 21, 22, 24, 25
  and Cathcart, D. G., 25
  and Apps, R., 3, 25
Jones, D. T. and Prais, S. J., 23, 25, 201, 205
Jones-Lee, M. W., 353, 354
Joy, S., 279

Kaldor, N., 8, 19, 25
Kelly, P., 320, 328
Kelly, D. M. and Forsyth, D. V. C., 79
Kemp, A. G. and Crichton, D., 53, 55
Klarman, H. E., 354, 355
Kleiman, E., 338, 354
Knight, A., 217, 222, 229
Kouris, G. and Robinson, C., 29, 55
Kraushar Andrews and Eassie Ltd, 91, 104

Lafitte, F. and Squire, J. R., 345, 354
Lawrence, G. K., 82, 104
Leak, H. and Maizels, A., 82, 104
Lee Donaldson Associates, 333, 337, 354, 356
Le Grand, J., 353, 354
Livesey, F., 295, 302
Lloyds, 306, 312, 313–14, 315, 317
Lossius, T., 225, 229
Louis Harris International, 312, 328

Maddison, A., 24, 25
Manpower Research Group, 21
Market behaviour,
  computers, 162–4
  construction, 239–42
  food manufacturing, 89–92
  medical care, 341–8
  motor vehicles, 194–201
  North Sea oil and gas, 41–2
  rail transport, 268–70
  retailing, 289–94
  synthetic fibres, 217–23
  tourism, 367–72
Market structure,
  computers, 158–62
  construction, 232–8
  food manufacturing, 82–9
  insurance, 312–15
  medical care, 338–41
  motor vehicles, 180–81, 189–94
  North Sea oil and gas, 34–5, 37–41
  rail transport, 266–8
  retailing, 284–9
  steel, 134–42

synthetic fibres, 210–17
tourism, 364–7
Maunder, W. P. J., 98, 104
Maynard, A., 353, 354
  and Walker, A., 348, 353, 354
McGannon, H. E., 151, 152
Media Expenditure Analysis Ltd, 91
Medical care,
  barriers to entry, 339
  concentration, 338–9
  cost benefit analysis, 350
  costs, 337, 339–41
  demand, 337–8, 341–4
  Department of Health and Social Security, 330
  economies of scale, 340
  financing, 334
  income elasticity, 337
  innovations, 335
  inputs, 350
  manpower, 331–2, 336–7, 345–8
  market behaviour, 341–8
  market structure, 338–41
  moral hazard, 334
  National Health Service, 330f
  nature of the product, 333–4
  output, 333, 348–50, 352
  performance, 348–52
  post-war development, 330–33
  price elasticity, 337–8, 351
  pricing, 337, 339, 341–4, 351
  private sector, 333, 338
  profits, 348
  regional allocation of resources, 344–5
  research and development, 348
  supply, 334–7, 341–4
  supply elasticity, 334
  waiting lists, 341–4
Medlik, S. with Airey, D. W., 362, 366, 371, 379
Meeks, G., 12, 25
Mergers,
  British industry, 12, 13
  computers, 160–61, 162
  food manufacturing, 85, 95
  motor vehicles, 180, 191, 201
  North Sea oil and gas, 41
  tourism, 366
Mergers, effects of, 12
Merrett-Cyriax Associates, 119, 129
Meyer, J. R. and Herregat, G., 133, 152
Microprocessors, 173–5
Midgley, K., 324, 328
Minford, P., 210, 229

Ministry of Education, 246, 252
Ministry of Works, 240, 252, 253
Mitchell, J., 104
Monopolies Commission, 86, 88, 92, 98–
  101, 104, 120, 124, 129, 201–202,
  230, 241, 252, 312, 317, 318, 328,
  329, 371, 379
Moody, J. D., 55
Moore, B. and Rhodes, J., 18, 25
Moral hazard, 305, 334
Morris, D. J. (ed), 27
Motor vehicles,
  advertising, 189, 197
  barriers to entry, 192–3
  concentration, 179
  costs, 184–5, 193
  demand, 188–9
  distribution network, 197
  economic significance, 181–2
  economies of scale, 183–5, 193
  employment, 182
  foreign competition, 186–8, 194
  importance, 182
  Industrial Reorganisation Corpora-
    tion, 202
  integration, 192
  labour productivity, 200–201
  market behaviour, 194–201
  market structure, 180–81, 189–94
  mergers, 179–80, 191, 201
  Monopolies Commission, 201–202
  National Enterprise Board, 203
  nature of technology, 182–5
  organisation of labour, 185
  performance, 198–201
  post-war developments, 179–82
  pricing, 194–5, 202
  product differentiation, 191–2
  profitability, 198–9
  research and development, 196–7
  supply and demand characteristics,
    182–9
  taxes, 203
Mueller, A., 15, 25
Multiple retailing, 89

National Association of Insurance Com-
  missioners, 319, 328
National Board for Prices and Incomes
  (NBPI), 78, 79, 92, 100, 101–102
National Coal Board (NCB), 46, 49, 57,
  59, 64, 65, 67, 69–70, 75, 79
National Economic Development Office
  (NEDO), 15, 23, 25, 118, 129, 144,
  152, 170, 175, 203, 205, 240, 241,
  252
National Enterprise Board (NEB), 20,
  175, 203
National Health Service, 108, 110, 116,
  330f
National Union of Mineworkers (NUM),
  73, 78
Nationalisation, 57, 148–9, 150, 251,
  324–5
Newbould, G. D., 13, 26
Newcombe, R., 241, 252
Newhouse, J. P. and Phelps, C. E., 337,
  338, 354
Nichols, J. R., 96
Niskanan, W. A., 326, 354
North Sea oil and gas,
  concentration, 37–41
  costs, 33
  balance of payments, 33
  extraction rights, 35
  future production, 42–5
  government policy, 45–50
  history of development, 30–32
  impact on economy, 32–4
  licences, 35, 37, 38–9, 46–7, 49–50
  market behaviour, 41–2
  market structure, 34–6, 37–41
  output and export controls, 48–9
  performance, 42–5
  prices, 33, 41, 47
  production characteristics, 36–7
  profitability, 43, 45, 51
  returns, 33, 51
  taxation, 33, 45–6, 47–8, 50–55
Noyce, J., Snaith, A. H. and Trickey,
  A. J., 347, 355
Nystrom, H., 291, 302

O'Brien, D. P., xiv, 12, 26, 230
OECD, *see* Organisation for Economic
  Co-operation and Development
Oil and gas,
  development, 28–9
  elasticity of demand, 29–30
  historical development, 28–9
Oil Taxation Act, 47, 51
O'Neill, H., 212, 230
OPEC, *see* Organisation of Petroleum
  Exporting Countries
Opencast mining, 58–9
Organisation for Economic Co-operation
  and Development (OECD), 28, 55

Organisation of Petroleum Exporting
    Countries (OPEC), 32, 33, 51
Ovenden, K., 153
'Own labels', 90, 294

Paige, D. C. and Jones, K., 345, 355
Palamountain, J. C., 89, 105
Panic, M., 15, 26
Patents,
    construction, 238
    motor vehicles, 196
    pharmaceuticals, 111–12
    synthetic fibres, 207, 208, 219, 227
Pavitt, K., 15, 16, 26
Peltzman, S., 124, 129
Perfect competition, 121
Performance,
    British industry, 14–17
    computers, 164–8
    construction, 242–8
    food manufacturing, 92–6
    insurance, 318–20
    medical care, 348–52
    motor vehicles, 198–201
    North Sea oil and gas, 42–5
    pharmaceuticals, 117–20
    rail transport, 270–75
    retailing, 298–9
    steel, 142–8
    synthetic fibres, 223–6
    tourism, 372–3
Perlman, M., 349, 355
Petroleum Revenue Tax (PRT), 50–54
Pharmaceutical industry,
    advertising, 106, 113, 116–17, 123–4
    barriers to entry, 111–12, 123, 128
    concentration, 110–11
    costs, 111, 124–5
    demand, 108–109, 111, 116
    economies of scale, 110, 113, 128
    elasticity of demand, 108, 116, 121
    history, 107–108
    innovation, 113–16, 117, 118, 123, 125
    National Health Service, 108, 110, 116
    nature, 106–107
    patents, 111–12, 336
    performance, 117–20
    prices, 115, 116, 120–23, 127, 128
    price control, 120–21
    product differentiation, 113
    profits, 119, 120–23, 124, 128
    promotion, 116, 128
    research and development, 113, 115,
        118, 124–8

supply, 108–109
Phillips, A., 4, 26
Pickering, J. F., 301, 302
Plant size, 9–10
    and strikes, 12
Platt Report, 345, 355
Plymen, J., 320, 328
Posner, M., 66, 79
Prais, S., 9, 10, 23, 26, 27, 323, 328
Pratten, C., 15, 26, 105, 160, 177, 205,
    215, 230
Prest, A. R., 27
Price Commission, 65, 79, 102, 105
Prices and incomes policies, 101–102
Pricing,
    coal, 65–6
    construction, 237, 241
    food manufacturing, 92
    insurance, 316–17, 321
    medical care, 337, 339, 341–4, 351
    motor vehicles, 194–6, 202
    North Sea oil and gas, 33, 41, 47
    pharmaceuticals, 115, 116, 120–23,
        127, 128
    rail transport, 256, 268, 269–70, 274
    retailing, 289–94
    steel, 132, 143–4
    synthetic fibres, 217, 219, 220–21
    tourism, 364, 372
Product differentiation,
    motor vehicles, 191–2
    pharmaceuticals, 113
    synthetic fibres, 215–16, 219–20
Productivity,
    British industry, 7–8, 15, 17, 21
    coal, 70–74
    computers, 167–8
    construction, 246
    food manufacturing, 94–5
    insurance, 318–19
    motor vehicles, 200–201
    North Sea oil and gas, 43
    rail transport, 255, 258, 270–72, 273
    retailing, 298
    steel, 144–5
    synthetic fibres, 223–5
Profitability,
    computers, 165, 169
    food manufacturing, 93–5
    insurance, 319–20
    medical care, 348
    motor vehicles, 198–9
    North Sea oil and gas, 43, 45, 51
    pharmaceuticals, 119, 124, 128, 120–23

rail transport, 257, 261, 270
retailing, 299
steel, 132, 144, 147
synthetic fibres, 225–6
tourism, 373–4
Pryke, R. and Dodgson, J., 279
Pryor, T. L., 338, 355
Public dividend capital, 148
Public policy,
British industry, 20–23
coal, 64
computers, 168–75
construction, 248–51
food manufacturing, 96–102
insurance, 311
medical care, 348–52
motor vehicles, 201–204
North Sea oil and gas, 45–50
rail transport, 275–8
retailing, 299–301
steel, 148–51
synthetic fibres, 226–9
tourism, 374–6
Public sector, 8–9, 18

Rail transport,
Beeching era, 257–9
British Rail (BR), 257, 259, 260, 262, 263, 265–78
business objectives, 268
closure of stations, 258
competition from road, 256, 266–7
costs, 256, 259, 261–2, 268–9
decline, 255–7
demand, 265–6
demand elasticities, 266, 270
electrification, 263, 264
financial deficit, 256, 259, 261
freight traffic, 260–261, 264–5, 266, 267, 269, 277
government as purchaser, 276
government intervention, 256
High Speed Train, 264, 269
investment, 257, 258, 259, 263–5, 269, 273
labour, 262–3
market behaviour, 268–70
market structure, 266–8
modernisation plan, 257
nationalisation, 254–5
nature of the product, 260–61
output measurement, 272
passenger traffic, 261, 265, 267, 269–70, 277

performance, 270–75
prices, 256, 268, 269–70, 274
product development, 268
productivity, 255, 258, 270–72, 273
profitability, 257, 261, 270
public policy, 275–8
public service obligation, 260
Railway Policy Review, 259
safety, 275
subsidies and grants, 259–60, 274, 276
Transport Acts, 254, 256, 257
unions, 262–3
utilisation of capacity, 272–3
Railway Executive, 256
Raynes, H. E., 326, 328
Reader, W. J., 230
Redfern, P., 257, 278
Reekie, W. D., 105, 111, 121, 122, 129, 130
and Weber, 116, 129
Registrar of Restrictive Trading Agreements, 242, 252
Research and development,
British industry, 7, 19
computers, 157, 160–61, 162, 169, 170, 171, 172
food manufacturing, 95–6
medical care, 348
motor vehicles, 196–7
pharmaceuticals, 113, 115, 118, 124–7, 128
synthetic fibres, 215, 222
Resource Allocation Working Party (RAWP) Report, 345, 355
Restrictive Trade Practices Act, 83, 97, 98
Retailing,
advertising, 296–8
behaviour of firms, 288
changes in structure, 280–82
concentration, 284–5
consumer protection, 300–301
Co-operatives, 285
costs, 299
credit, 295
department stores, 286
employment, 280
location, 296
mail order, 286
market behaviour, 289–94
market performance, 298–9
market structure, 284–9
multiples, 284–6
'own labels', 294

planning decisions, 299–300
pricing, 289–94
productivity, 298
profitability, 299
public policy, 299–301
service, 294–6
small retailers, 287
stock assortment, 296
trading stamps, 295
voluntary groups, 287
wages, 282
Reynolds, D. I. N., 312, 328
Rhys, D. G., 184, 204, 205, 225, 230
Richards, K. and Colenutt, D., 314, 318, 328
Richardson, G. B., 3, 26
Robinson, C., 36, 42, 45, 47, 55
and Morgan, J., 32, 33, 36, 45, 55, 56
and Rowland, C., 33, 42, 43, 55
Robinson, J., 2, 26
Robinson, R., 230
Robinson, O. and Wallace, J., 303
Rosenberg, N., 7, 26
Rowland, C., 56

Sainsbury Report, 110, 116, 118, 119, 122, 123, 129, 130
Sale of Goods Act, 300
Salter, W. E. G., 7–8, 26
Sauran, A., 363, 379
Sawyer, M. C. and Aaronovitch, S., 4, 26
Scherer, F. M., 4, 13, 26
Schmookler, J., 7, 26
Schumpeter, J. A., 121, 129
Schwartzman, D., 108, 125, 129, 130
Select Committee on Nationalised Industries, 49, 56, 140, 151, 152, 257, 263, 271, 278
Select Committee on Science and Technology (SCSTA), 157, 159, 160, 161, 177, 178
Services, 17
Shaw, R. W. and Shaw, S. A., 219, 230
and Sutton, C., xv, 230
Shepherd, W. G., 4, 26
Sheriff, T. D., 68, 79
Silberston, A., 189, 206
Sherman, R. S., 321, 328
Small firms,
effects of Industrial Strategy, 21
finance, 322–3
Smith, A., 81, 105
Society of Motor Manufacturers and Traders (SMMT), 189, 206

Standard Industrial Classification, 2
Steel,
British Steel Corporation, 135, 136–40
closures, 139, 140
costs, 133
cyclical fluctuations, 131–2, 135, 142
demand elasticities, 143
economies of scale, 137
excess capacity, 132
foreign competition, 134, 135–6, 143
growth of demand, 138
importance, 132
independent sector in, 140–42
innovation, 133
investment, 137, 145, 147
labour productivity, 144–5
market structure, 134–42
nationalisation, 136, 148–9, 150
performance, 142–8
pricing, 132, 143–4
products, 134
profits, 132, 144, 147
public policy towards, 148–51
nationalisation, 137f
redundancies, 132
size of enterprises, 134–6
size structure of plants, 134
ten year development programme, 138
world output, 131–2
Stigler, G. J., 2, 26
Stone, P. A., 253
Stoneman, P., 156, 157, 158, 164, 173, 177
Straszheim, M. R., 363, 377, 379
Strikes, 12
Structure, conduct and performance, 4–5
Subsidies and grants (in rail transport), 259–60
Supply elasticity,
medical care, 334
motor vehicles, 182
tourism, 362
Swiss Reinsurance Company, 308, 326, 328
Synthetic fibres,
advertising, 215–16
barriers to entry, 217, 218
buyer concentration, 217
concentration, 210–13
costs, 213–15, 218
diversification, 216–17
early history, 207
economies of scale, 213–15, 225
E.E.C., 221

excess capacity, 212, 221, 223
foreign competition, 211
growth, 208–10
imports and exports, 208, 222
innovation, 208, 215
integration, 216–17, 222–3
licensing, 208
market behaviour, 217–23
market structure, 210, 217
monopoly, 218–20
oligopoly, 220–23
patents, 207, 208, 210, 219, 227
performance, 223–6
pricing, 217, 219
product differentiation, 215–16, 219–20
productivity, 223–5
profitability, 225–6
public policy, 226–9
nationalisation, 227
research and development, 215, 222

Teeling-Smith, G., 117, 124, 129
Tendering, 240–41
Textile Organon, 230
Thorpe, D., 303
Tisdell, C. A. and McDonald, P. W., 210, 230
Todd Report, 347, 355
Tourism,
accommodation sector, 360, 365–6, 371–2, 373, 375
air transport, 358, 364–5, 368–70
balance of payments, 361, 374
barriers to entry, 365, 366
Civil Aviation Authority, 365, 371, 376
cross channel ferries, 365, 371
definition, 357
demand, 362–4
demand elasticity, 363–4
diversification, 366
excess capacity, 368–9
foreign competition, 367
historical development, 358–61
IATA (International Air Transport Association), 368
inclusive tour, 360, 366–7, 370–71, 373

investment, 360, 372, 375
market behaviour, 367–72
market structure, 364–7
mergers, 366
performance, 372–3
pricing, 364, 372
profitability, 373–4
public policy, 374–6
regulation, 362, 365, 367–8, 374–5, 376, 377
supply, 361–2
supply elasticity, 362
tourist boards, 361, 375–6, 377
vertical integration, 366
Trade Descriptions Act, 300
Trafford, J., 222, 230
Transport Acts, 254, 255, 257, 259, 269
TUC, 19, 324
Tucker, K.A. and Yamey, B. S., 288, 302, 303
Tzanetis, E., 29, 56

University of Warwick, 26
Utton, M., 10, 26

Vaizey, J., 152

Walshe, G., 86, 105
Ward, T. S., 298, 302, 303
Wardell, W. M. and Lasagna, L., 126, 129
Wardle, C., 105
Watkins, B., 353, 355
Webb, M., 272, 274, 278
Weiss, L., 4, 27
Wells, J. D. and Imber, J. C., 17, 26
Wheatcroft, S. F., 363, 377, 379
White, P. R., 279
Wigley, K., 63, 79
Willink Report, 344, 355
Woodside, A. G. and Davenport, J. W., 295, 302
Wragg, R. and Robertson, J., 7, 8, 27
Wright, A. T., 91, 105

Young, S. and Hood, N., 206